Cryptocurrency for Beginners: The Newbie Friendly Guide for Making Money with Bitcoin and Altcoins in 2018 and Beyond

By Stephen Satoshi

This book contains 15 manuscripts:

Bitcoin: Beginners Bible - How You Can Profit from Trading and Investing in Bitcoin

Cryptocurrency: Beginners Bible - How You Can Make Money Trading and Investing in Cryptocurrency

Blockchain: Beginners Bible - Discover How Blockchain Could Enrich Your Life, Your Business & Your Cryptocurrency Wallet

Cryptocurrency: Insider Secrets - 12 Exclusive Coins Under $1 with Potential for Huge Profits in 2018

Cryptocurrency: Insider Secrets 2 - 10 Exciting Crypto Projects With Potential for Explosive Growth in 2018

Cryptocurrency: Mining for Beginners - How You Can Make Up To $18,500 a Year Mining Coins From Home

Cryptocurrency: What the World's Best Blockchain Investors Know - That You Don't

Ethereum: Beginners Bible - How You Can Profit from Trading & Investing in Ethereum, Even If You're a Complete Novice

Cryptocurrency: What you need to know about your taxes to save money and avoid a nasty surprise from the IRS

Marijuana Stocks: Beginners Guide To The Only Industry Producing Financial Returns as Fast as Cryptocurrency

Stock Market Investing for Beginners: The Keys to Protecting Your Wealth and Making Big Profits In a Market Crash

Cryptocurrency: The 3rd Generation - Ultra Fast, Zero Transaction Fee, Futureproof Coins that Need to Be on Your Radar

Cryptocurrency: FAQ - Answering 53 of Your Burning Questions about Bitcoin, Investing, Scams, ICOs and Trading

Cryptocurrency: The 10 Biggest Trading Mistakes Newbies Make - And How to Avoid Them

Cryptocurrency: 13 More Coins to Watch with 10X Growth Potential in 2019

Financial Disclaimer:

I am not a financial advisor, this is not financial advice. This is not an investment guide nor investment advice. I am not recommending you buy any of the coins listed here. Any form of investment or trading is liable to lose you money.

Tax Disclaimer:

I am not a tax professional. This is not tax advice. Nor is it a substitute for tax advice. Please consult a tax professional before filing your tax return.

There is no single "best" investment to be made, in cryptocurrencies or otherwise. Anyone telling you so is deceiving you.

I am not affiliated with any coin or cryptocurrency mentioned in this book.

There is no "surefire coin" - one again, anyone telling you so is deceiving you.

With many coins, especially the smaller ones, the market is liable to the spread of misinformation.

Never invest more than you are willing to lose. Cryptocurrency is not a get rich quick scheme.

Affiliate Disclaimer:

Like cryptocurrency, I too believe in transparency and openness, and so I am disclosing that I've included certain products and links to those products on in this book that I will earn an affiliate commission for any purchases you make. Please note that I have not been given any free products, services or anything else by these companies in exchange for mentioning them in this bo

Accuracy Disclaimer:

All prices and market capitalizations are correct at the time of writing. Price and market cap information is sourced from coinmarketcap.com. All information in this eBook was derived from official sources where possible. Official sources meaning literature that is publicly available, provided by the development team for each cryptocurrency or company such as a company website or GitHub page. At the time of writing, some of the information is not available in English from official sources. In this case some of the information included in this eBook was obtained from unofficially translated whitepapers. Unofficially meaning either via computer translation, or third party human translation.In this case some of the information included in this eBook was obtained from unofficially translated whitepapers. Unofficially meaning either via computer translation, or third party human translation.

Contents

Free Bonus!

As a gift to you for downloading this book I'm offering a special bonus. It's a free, exclusive special report detailing 3 microcap coins with huge growth potential in 2018. I guarantee you won't find these discussed in any mainstream cryptocurrency forums or newsletters. These 3 were picked as a result of weeks of research on microcap cryptocurrencies.

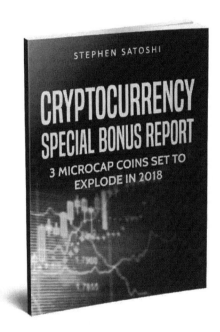

Grab the free report here!

Or go to http://bit.ly/FreeSatoshiReport

Special Offer for Audible Customers

I'm pleased to announce to my readers that I have recently entered into a partnership with Audible, and as such many of my books will be available in audio format going forward. So you can listen in the car, while working out or just while you're doing chores around the house.

Now here's the exciting part for you. If you do not currently have an Audible account, you can get any one of my books for free when you sign up (including bundles containing multiple books)

Go to https://www.audible.com/lp/freetrial to sign up and claim your free book.

And I'm going to go one step further and match this offer. So if you do sign up and select one of my books as your free book, I will give you an exclusive promo code to get another book absolutely free as well.

This applies to new sign ups only and applies to all books except my 3 book bundle *Cryptocurrency: Ultimate Beginners Guide* (although you can still choose this as your free book from Audible).

So that's 2 books entirely free! Just email me a receipt of your initial purchase at stephen@satoshibooks.com and I'll send you the promo code for your second book within 72 hours.

Thanks and happy listening,

Stephen

Bitcoin Beginners Bible: How You Can Profit from Trading and Investing in Bitcoin

Introduction

This is normally the part with the drier than the Sahara Desert explanation of "you are going to learn blah blah…" that sends you straight to sleep.

Instead, I thought I'd do something a bit different and give you a quick overview of my own experience with Bitcoin.

I first heard of Bitcoin in 2011, during the first very first bubble, when I read a news report about this "internet money" thing that was worth $30 a piece. Did I invest then? I wish - I wasn't nearly informed enough. I honestly didn't understand how the technology worked or if Bitcoin was worth anything at all. After all, if a currency isn't backed by a government, how *can* it be worth anything? Oh to be that naive once again.

By the time I finally understood Bitcoin enough to be confident in buying some, the price had risen a hell of a lot more. But, now I believe in it as more than just a commodity to be traded or invested in. I believe in the technology at its core, and the potentially game changing ramifications for society at large. In that lies the true value of Bitcoin.

I wish I had a resource like this when I started out, something that explained the core concepts of Bitcoin and blockchain technology without reading like an astrophysics phD thesis. That's precisely why I wrote this book.

Happy reading, and I hope you not only make a lot of money with Bitcoin - I hope it has a truly profound and positive effect on your life.

Finally, if you enjoyed this book - I'd appreciate you taking just 2 minutes of your busy day to leave the book a review on Amazon.

Thanks,

Stephen

Bitcoin - A Brief History

Bitcoin is the first cryptocurrency that has lasted for more than 7 years and received any sort of mass adoption, but it took some time to get to this point. Before Bitcoin, there were a number of cryptocurrencies that reached some level of popularity. It all started back in 1980 when cryptographer David Chaum first developed the idea of a currency backed by a proof-of-work computer algorithm as opposed to a central bank. Chaum later went on to found DigiCash which had a briefly successful yet ultimately failed run at becoming the world's first mass adopted cryptocurrency. US based e-gold was possibly the most notable of the Pre-Bitcoin cryptocurrencies, although technologically it was significantly different from Bitcoin due to a centralized owner and non-fixed supply.

In August 2008, Neal Kin, Vladimir Oksman and Charles Bry filed a patent application for an encryption technology. The domain name Bitcoin.org was also registered in the same month using anonymousspeech.com which allowed for anonymous domain name registrations.

The big day came on October 31st 2008, Satoshi Nakamoto (a pseudonym with the true identity still unconfirmed) published a white paper named "Bitcoin: A Peer-to-Peer Electronic Cash System". The paper outlined various uses for the coin in addition to providing information about blockchain technology and how the coin would be mined using computer algorithms. The original white paper used Bitcoin as an example of a deflationary currency and one that governments or other central lenders could not artificially increase the money supply of, therefore devaluing a certain currency. The whitepaper also outlined issues with banks as trusted lenders, and how the blockchain's irreversible transaction design could reduce risk of fraud for merchants.

From January 2009 onwards, activists began mining the coin and the first Bitcoin blocks were created. Nakamoto and other cryptography enthusiasts began exchanging the coin for services with one another and in October 2009, the first official exchange rate was established for the coin of US$1 = 1,309.03 BTC. The original exchange rate was based on how much electricity it would cost to mine 1 Bitcoin.

The first real world transaction took place in May 2010 when enthusiast Laszlo Hanyecz bought two pizzas in Jacksonville, Florida for 10,000 BTC. Today 10,000BTC is worth over $40 million. A few months later in August, the first major Bitcoin hacking incident occured, the hacker exploited a vulnerability in the Bitcoin verification system and generated 184 billion Bitcoins. This led to the first major dip in the value of Bitcoin as a currency. This then led to government investigations of potential money laundering using Bitcoin. The early scares didn't last long though and In November 2010, Bitcoin reached a market capitalization of $1 million for the first time.

In January 2011, Bitcoin received a reasonable amount of mainstream coverage for the first time. Silk Road, an underground dark net website dealing in illicit goods such as illegal drugs and stolen credit cards was launched on the back of sending and receiving payments in Bitcoin. At its peak, it was estimated that up to 50% of Bitcoin transactions were ones that occured on Silk Road. The perceived anonymity of Bitcoin made it a favorite among Silk Road users. In February, Bitcoin reaches a market price of $1 for the first time and by July the coin had jumped to a value of $31.

2012 was somewhat of an uneventful year, although real world adoption continued with hosting platform Wordpress accepting the coin in November of that year. By March 2013, the market capitalization had reached $1 billion and Bitcoin exchange Coinbase reported over $1 million of Bitcoin transactions in a single month. In June, the DEA reported 11.02 Bitcoins as an asset during a drug seizure, the first time a government agency recognized Bitcoin as having inherent value. Drugs continued to make headlines as Silk Road owner Ross William Albricht was arrested in October, the FBI seized 26,000 Bitcoins from Silk Road servers during the arrest. Brighter news came the next month when the world's first Bitcoin ATM opened in Vancouver and China arrived on the scene when Chinese market activity overtook the US for the first time. By November of 2013, the price of 1 Bitcoin reached $1,000 for the first time.

December of 2013 came with China's central bank ruling that Bitcoin was not a currency and barred financial institution from accepting Bitcoins as a form of payment. In February 2014, Japanese based exchange Mt. Gox suspended Bitcoin withdrawals, citing technical issues. Within just a few weeks, the exchange had filed for bankruptcy amid claims of poor management and lack of security protocols. Roughly $740 million worth of Bitcoin, or 7% of the overall amount in circulation was lost in the incident. This issue led to the value of Bitcoin dropping 36% over the course of the month.

In June, TeraExchange LLC received approval from the U.S.Commodity Futures Trading Commission. This marked the first time that a U.S. agency approved a Bitcoin exchange. Computer manufacturer Dell began accepting Bitcoin as a means of payment at this time, the largest company to do so up to that point. AirBaltic also became the world's first airline to accept Bitcoin payments. In December, tech giant Microsoft began accepting payments in Bitcoin.

Coinbase, now one of the largest cryptocurrency exchange platforms received $75 million in a funding round, with the New York Stock Exchange being a minor investor. Further real world scaling continued and by August 2015, over 160,000 companies were accepting Bitcoin as a means of payment. December brought news of the potential identity of the notorious Satoshi Nakamoto figure. Wired magazine claimed the Australian Craig Wright was indeed Nakamoto. This led to a series of events that eventually resulted in a confirmation that Wright was indeed NOT Nakamoto.

July 2016 marked the second "halving day" in Bitcoin's history, where the reward for mining 1 block was halved to 12.5 Bitcoins per block. This was part of Bitcoin's original design to gradually decrease the supply of new coins available. The next halving is due to occur in 2020, with the total supply available to the market around the year 2140.

At the time of writing, Bitcoin trades for around $4,000 per coin on exchanges.

Basics of Blockchain Technology

While we could spend an entire book on blockchain and the technology behind it alone, it is important to understand the fundamentals if you're planning to invest in Bitcoin, or any other cryptocurrency.

Blockchain is a decentralized ledger, meaning it is a record that is publicly accessible and can be verified by anyone. This is important for any non-tangible good as the unlike tangible goods like socks or candy, we need a record of a transaction happening in case something goes wrong. For example, we need proof that Steve paid John for the pair of socks that John sold him. The blockchain will have a record of a transaction from Steve's account to John's account, and no one else's.

Previously, we would have the use a third party, like a bank, to verify the transaction did indeed take place. The bank would then take their % of the total transaction. As the bank information is not publicly accessible, we would also have to trust that the bank did their job. By using blockchain technology, we have a 100% infallible record of the transaction taking place, and anyone can see this. There's also no need to pay a large additional fee to a middleman. The only fee involved is the cost of running the blockchain itself.

If we only use blockchain for financial purposes, this is extremely useful in countries that do not have a trustworthy banking sector. Each transaction is recorded as a block, with a date and timestamp. These blocks cannot be altered without everyone seeing. The problem this solves is known as the "double-spending problem", where digital assets (like cryptocurrency) have the potential to be spent more than once. What the blockchain allows us to do is see that Steve has already used his money to pay John, so he can't then use that same money to try and pay Sally. The blockchain creates trust among all parties, and trust is paramount when dealing with monetary transactions.

Blockchain's uses are not strictly financial. We can also use the technology to store other information that we would need in a publicly available, transparent form. This ranges from anything like voting records in an election, to a self-executing contract between two parties that fulfills when both parties have completed their obligations. Blockchain eliminates the need for a middleman, or independent auditor in these situation, as the technology itself acts both as an auditor, and as an independent. In theory, the technology has the power to replace accountants, lawyers and much of the financial services industry. Before we get ahead of ourselves though, much of the non-financial uses of blockchain technology are still strictly, in theory.

How does Bitcoin Work?

Bitcoin functions as a digital currency, by following the same three rules that traditional, or fiat currencies follow.

1. They need to be difficult to produce (cash) or find (gold or other precious metals)

2. They need have a limited supply

3. They need to be recognized by other humans as having value

When we examine Bitcoin, it ticks the boxes of all three of these characteristics:

1. Bitcoin uses complex computer algorithms in its production which take a lot of computational power and proof-of-work, so it cannot be replicated easily or at a discount

2. There are a finite supply of Bitcoins - 21 Million to be exact. As of 2015, roughly 2/3 of this number had been mined

3. There are hundreds of Bitcoin exchanges and Bitcoin is accepted as payment everywhere from Subway to OKCupid

Bitcoin miners have incentive to mine as they receive Bitcoin as a reward for their computer's endeavors. Bitcoin was designed to be a deflationary currency, so unlike fiat currencies, the supply of money is fixed. This, combined with the decentralization principle ensure that no single person or government can simply create additional coins once the supply is mined. Once all the coins are mined, the value of the currency will in theory, continue to rise.

Bitcoin transactions are recorded on a digital ledger (or record) known as the blockchain. The core concept that upholds Bitcoin's usefulness is decentralization. With decentralization, the blockchain is not owned by one single person or entity. In fact, everyone has access to it. Therefore transactions are publicly broadcasted across the network, which ensures that both parties have upheld their end of the agreement. The code is open source (like Linux or Android Operating Systems) so anyone can view it, this ensures transparency among all parties.

Decentralization allows the blockchain to be secured by multiple points of entry and backed up by multiple points of failure. This is turn prevents incidents like hacking or theft. For example, if someone offers you 1 Bitcoin, you can check the blockchain records to make sure that Bitcoin is valid and hasn't already been spent. This system means we do not need third parties to validate the transactions. The only transactions costs come from the electricity or mining power needed to run the blockchain itself.

This has tremendous real world application, from allowing cheaper international payments (since Bitcoin has no nationality) to lowering the overall price of certain goods.

Bitcoin as a Store of Wealth

Bitcoin's status as a deflationary currency makes it incredibly useful in times where fiat currency is undergoing gross levels of inflation. Like gold has been traditionally used in times of economic hardship, Bitcoin has the potential to do the same. To be used as a store of value or wealth, Bitcoin has a fulfill a few criteria.

1. It has to not be perishable

2. It has to not depreciate over time

The second criteria is somewhat debatable, as critics argue that Bitcoin could depreciate due to better technology surpassing it. However, Bitcoin has now reached a certain market point where the idea itself has an intrinsic value, like say email or Facebook. Email isn't particularly useful if you're the only one with an address to send mail to, but the more people use the technology, the easier, and more valuable it is.

Venezuela is currently undergoing the worst cash crisis of the decade. Inflation has reached a level where people's money is nigh-on worthless against the US dollar, and much of the country cannot afford basic necessities. That is, except for those who hold Bitcoins, whose value against the US dollar continues to increase.

China is doing the same thing, albeit for different reasons. Traditional investments in Chinese assets have returned less than previous years due to the government's devaluation of the Yuan. Converting money to gold and silver is heavily regulated and often incurs large transaction costs. Bitcoin does not suffer from any of these issues, and often is the only alternative for those who are looking to secure their wealth in both the short and long term.

Gold has long been the traditional backup plan, or "hedge" against uncertain financial markets. In times of war, or financial crisis, gold prices tend to rise when financial markets are falling. However, in recent times this has not been the case. At the time of writing, gold's 12 month performance is stagnant, whereas Bitcoin has risen by nearly 1000%. Growing tensions in North Korea are just one factor that has spurned Bitcoin's growth in times of uncertainty. Tensions in the region have led to increased buys from the Chinese, Japanese and South Korean markets.

8 Common Bitcoin Myths Debunked

Like all technological innovations, there are a number of points that uninformed players do not understand. As such, misinformation spreads which causes fear, uncertainty and doubt - which only hurts the technology going forward.

1. **Bitcoin is illegal**

Let's deal with the big one off the bat shall we? Just because a currency is not backed by a government, does not make it illegal. For you, the user, by operating as a virtual currency, Bitcoin is legal, so long as you are using it for legal means.

2. **Miners or developers can change the amount of Bitcoins available to benefit themselves**

The way the Bitcoin algorithm works ensures there are no shortcuts in obtaining one. If a counterfeit Bitcoin does not satisfy all the conditions required, any transactions made using it will be rejected. This is similar to how banks reject counterfeit bank notes.

3. **Bitcoin isn't worth anything because it isn't backed by a central government**

With all currencies, they are only worth what someone is willing to exchange for them. In the same way that gold or US dollars have no inherent value, Bitcoin is just a means of exchange.

4. **Bitcoin's main use is for criminals and the government will shut it down**

Yes, at one time a significant % of Bitcoin usage was used for illegal activity. Much of this activity was facilitated on the underground black market website Silk Road. However, this is no longer the case. Bitcoin is now accepted by over 160,000 merchants worldwide and adoption continues to grow. The technological uses like minimized transactions fees have far more use for large financial institutions than they do for some basement dwelling 20 year trying to buy LSD from a guy in another country. It's worth noting that fiat currencies are also used for criminal activity.

This one also relies on the myth that Bitcoin is completely anonymous. Yes, there are no named Bitcoin accounts, but each Bitcoin address is unique and every transaction is recorded on a public ledger (the blockchain). Therefore with a little legwork, it is possible to determine who is behind a Bitcoin transaction.

As far as a potential government shutdown does, that's a little trickier. Governments do have the power to make life difficult for citizens dealing strictly in Bitcoin, but this difficulty only goes as far as taxation on Bitcoin.

5. **21 Million Bitcoin is too small of a total number for effective daily use**

Where this one falls short is that it fails to compute that Bitcoin is divisible to eight decimal places. 0.00000001 BTC is actually the smallest unit available, this is also known as 1 Satoshi. There are really 2,099,999,997,690,000 (just over 2 quadrillion) maximum possible units or Satoshi in the Bitcoin system. When 1 Bitcoin becomes too large for day-to-day transactions, we will simply move on to smaller units for convenience, similar to how we use pennies now for small transactions.

6. **Hackers can simply steal all the Bitcoins**

It's important to differentiate between exchanges or websites being hacked, and the blockchain itself being hacked. Exchange hacks exploit security weaknesses of private companies, whereas the blockchain is not centralized so there is no single weakness for hackers to exploit. The same argument can be applied to the US dollar, just because a store is robbed does not mean the US dollar as a currency has been stolen from the source. That said, you should take appropriate security precautions when storing your Bitcoin such as creating a safe, offline wallet.

7. **Bitcoin is a pyramid scheme/Ponzi scheme**

My personal favorite. Pyramid schemes are a zero sum game. The founders and early adopters profit from the money put into the scheme by late adopters. With Bitcoin everyone can profit, no matter when they first made their initial investment. The other illusion here is that there is one central founder of Bitcoin. Bitcoin is decentralized and there is no "CEO" or person at the top of the pyramid.

8. **Bitcoin is dead/There is no point investing in Bitcoin now**

I have witnessed at least 20 "Bitcoin deaths" in the past 5 years alone. From hacking incidents to Silk Road Founder Ross William Albricht's arrest, detractors have used these as fuel for Bitcoin's obituary. The numbers don't lie though, and Bitcoin is in a stronger position than ever both in terms of market capitalization and real world adoption.

As early as 2012, you can find commentators saying it was "too late" to invest in Bitcoin. Yet, real world adoption continues to grow, and the price keeps on rising. Is that to say there won't be issues in the future? I'm sure there will be. However, if Bitcoin transactions keep increasing, the currency shows no signs of slowing down any time soon.

Latest Bitcoin Innovations: SegWit, Lightning Network

The number one technical issue Bitcoin faces in its lifetime is the issue of scalability. Or in real world terms, Bitcoin's ability to handle a growing number of transactions. Currently, each Block on the Bitcoin network is 1MB, representing 10 minutes per transaction, which increases during periods of heavy use. This is beneficial for banks and large financial institutions as 10 minutes is a far quicker processing time than that of say SWIFT or other payment networks. However, in terms of smaller businesses, like say a coffee shop, 10 minutes is an incredibly long and non-practical payment time.

For years, there has been a constant disagreement about the best way to upgrade Bitcoin's block sizes. The longer these arguments continue, the slower any proposed solutions are developed. There are two main camps, those who favor a hard fork, which loosens up the rules of the protocol and those who favor a soft fork, which tightens the rules of the current protocol.

Without going into advanced technical details, users who favor a soft fork are currently proposing a solution known as Segregated Witness or SegWit. The crux of SegWit is that the signature (or *witness*) of a transaction can be kept on a separate block from the transaction itself, this frees up block space for additional transactions. The witness data is encrypted and cannot be modified, so there is no ability to change the information of the payment sender. This has great real world usage in terms of lowering the ability to hack a transaction.

As with any potential change, there is a certain amount of unpredictability involved. In practical terms, SegWit activation will affect the price of Bitcoin one way or another in the short term, however at the time of writing, SegWit has only been activated for less than 72 hours, and the price has held stable thus far.

The activation of SegWit could well pave way for the lightning network, a technology that will enable instant Bitcoin transactions. Instant transactions as previously stated, will help micro and nano transactions immensely, and allow small businesses to utilize the benefits of accepting payments in Bitcoin at point of sale terminals. This will be especially useful in countries with low-value fiat currencies. One current example of this is Venezuela, where the Venezuelan Bolivar has lost around 90% of its value against the US dollar in under a year. Bitcoin transactions are helping a small, but significant portion of Venezuelan public hold value in the money they do have.

So what is Bitcoin Cash then?

Bitcoin Cash (BCH or BCC on exchanges) is a spin-off cryptocurrency that was the result of the August 1st hard fork by a small, yet significant proportion of the Bitcoin mining community. The fork involves increased block sizes and faster transaction times which in turn will lead to lower transaction fees. The blocksize has increased to 8MB, from the original 1MB that Bitcoin uses. This fork was designed to solve the scalability problems that Bitcoin currently faces.

So if Bitcoin Cash is technologically superior to Bitcoin, why don't I invest in that instead?

It's a tough question to answer because quite frankly, these are still very early days. At the time of writing the fork is only 1 month old and Bitcoin Cash has had high price fluctuations. Liquidity is much lower than Bitcoin (meaning it is difficult to sell large amounts) and real world adoption effects remain to be determined. If you're a new investor, Bitcoin Cash is certainly something to be monitored. However, the network effects of Bitcoin are still too strong to ignore, and it is still very much the number one cryptocurrency.

In terms of market price, the Bitcoin Cash split on August 1st initially led to a fall in the price of Bitcoin, before it once again rose to an all-time-high in late August. Bitcoin Cash value initially plummeted before a boom and then a reset to its current price of around $550.

If you purchased Bitcoin after August 1st, Bitcoin Cash should be treated as a completely separate currency. Any Bitcoin transaction will not be replicated in Bitcoin Cash or vice versa. If you wish to purchase Bitcoin, look for the symbol BTC on exchanges. If you purchased Bitcoin before August 1st you may well be able to receive the same amount in Bitcoin Cash - providing you held it in a wallet that was not linked to any exchange.

For miners, or those interested in mining, at the time of writing Bitcoin Cash offers greater mining rewards when compared to Bitcoin, due to a decreased difficulty in its proof-of-work algorithm.

How to Buy Bitcoin

Gone are the days when buying Bitcoin was a time consuming and somewhat uncomfortable endeavor. Nowadays buying Bitcoin is a similar process to exchanging currency when you go on vacation.

There are two ways to buy Bitcoin, the first is to use fiat currency (USD, EUR, GBP etc.) to purchase cryptocurrency via an exchange. These exchanges function the same way as regular foreign currency exchanges do. The prices fluctuate on a daily basis, and like regular currency exchange markets - they are open 24/7. These exchanges make their money from charging a small fee for each transaction.

Some charge both buyers and sellers, some only charge a fee for buying. For security reasons, most of these exchanges will require you to verify your ID before allowing you to purchase cryptocurrency.

It is also important to note the type of payments each exchange supports. Some allow for debit/credit card payments whereas other only accept PayPal or bank wire transfers. Below are the three biggest and reputable currency exchanges for purchasing Bitcoin, Ethereum and other altcoins with fiat currency like US dollars, Euros or British Pounds.

Coinbase

Currently largest currency exchange in the world, Coinbase allows users to buy, sell and store cryptocurrency. Coinbase is undoubtedly the most beginner friendly exchange for anyone looking to get involved in the cryptocurrency market. They currently allow trading of Bitcoin, as well as, Ethereum and LiteCoin using fiat currency as a base. Known for their stellar security procedures and insurance policies regarding stored currency. The exchange also has a fully functioning iPhone and Android app for buying and selling on the go, very useful if you are looking to trade.

Once you are signed up and complete the identity verification procedures you can buy Bitcoin with your credit or debit card instantly.

If you sign up for Coinbase using this link, you will receive $10 worth of free Bitcoin after your first purchase of more than $100 worth of cryptocurrency.

http://bit.ly/10dollarbtc

Kraken

Based in Canada, and currently the largest exchange in terms of volume of buys in Euros, Kraken has the advantage of more coin support (they also allow the purchase of Monero, Ethereum Classic and Dogecoin) than Coinbase. It allows margin trading, which while beyond the scope of a beginner, will be of interest to more experienced traders

For other altcoins, you will need access to an exchange that facilitates cryptocurrency to cryptocurrency trading. The best one of these is Poloniex.

Poloniex

With more than 100 different cryptocurrencies available and data analysis for advanced traders, Poloniex is the most comprehensive exchange on the market. Low trading fees are another plus, this is a great place to trade your Bitcoin into other cryptocurrencies. If you have never purchased Bitcoin before, you will no be able to do so as Poloniex does not allow fiat currency deposits. Therefore, you will have to make your initial Bitcoin purchases on Coinbase or Kraken.

Buying Locally

The second way to buy Bitcoins in exchange for fiat urrency is to locally purchase them in person. The advantage of this is that you may be able to get a marginally better price than by using an exchange. The other advantage is that users living in countries that don't have easy access to online exchanges can still buy coins in person. All transactions are protected by Escrow to prevent either party being scammed.

Website http://localbitcoins.com is the current market leader for local bitcoin transactions with sellers in over 15,000 cities around the world.

How To Safely Store Your Bitcoin

Congratulations on purchasing your first Bitcoin! Now that you've bought your Bitcoin, you'll need to keep it secure. You can do this by transferring it off the exchange and into what is known as a Bitcoin wallet. The name wallet implies that you can do all the same things you can with a regular wallet. You can see how much Bitcoin you have, and use it to spend your Bitcoin. An important distinction to make is that because Bitcoin is decentralized and stored on the Blockchain, these wallets do not "store" your Bitcoin per say.

While exchanges like Coinbase do provide you with your own wallet, unless you are day-trading, it's advisable to remove your coins from the exchange in order to prevent against issues like hacking - which unfortunately does happen

In 2011, Tokyo based Bitcoin exchange Mt. Gox suffered losses of over $27.2 million and 80,000 users lost a total of over $460 million worth of Bitcoin after the exchange was hacked. Mt. Gox wasn't some fly by night operation either, in fact at the time it was the largest cryptocurrency exchange on Earth. Yet poor security protocols and mismanagement allowed the attacks to occur. The company eventually filed for bankruptcy amid allegations of fraud, and much of the userbase's stolen coins have not been recovered to this day. This is why it's paramount that if you want to hold your coins for the long-term, you store them safely.

The understand wallets, we must first understand just how they work. Bitcoin transactions need both a private key (from the sender) and a public key (from the receiver) in order to process correctly on the blockchain.

A public key is a series of between 26 and 35 alphanumeric characters e.g. 1Co5CmEZNz35Am59EcFhKGRdNfLrzppGkJ

If you can this address to someone, they can send funds to your wallet. It is perfectly safe for you to give your public key, also known as your wallet address, to anyone, as they can only deposit into your account with this information. In 2013, a college student received 22 Bitcoins (then worth around $24,000) by holding up a sign with his public key in the form of a QR code on an edition of ESPN's College Gameday.

Your private key on the other hand should be held by you, and you alone. **Never give your private key to anyone.**

There are numerous types of wallets you can use, here is a breakdown of each one.

Desktop Wallets

A desktop wallet are a convenient medium between moving your Bitcoins off an exchange, while not having to carry around additional information like with a paper or hardware wallet. You can think of these like a Bitcoin bank account on your computer. Most desktop wallets will encrypt your private keys for you to add an extra layer of security. Here is a run-down of some of the more popular desktop Bitcoin wallets. All the wallets listed below are free, you should never pay for a desktop wallet.

Electrum - https://electrum.org

While it's design may not win any awards, Electrum does the job it's supposed to. The code is open source, which means there's a much lower possibility of the development team slipping in something malicious. Electrum allows you to store and spend your Bitcoins with relative ease. It has the advantage of storing your private keys offline, and to go online in "watching only" mode, so if your computer gets hacked during the process, hackers won't be able to spend any coins. It also has support for various hardware wallets.

Exodus - https://www.exodus.io/

Unlike Electrum, Exodus is not open source. However, Exodus does have the advantage of being capable of storing other coins like Ethereum, Litecoin and Dogecoin in addition to Bitcoin. The interface is also more user-friendly than Electrum.

It should be noted, that as desktop wallets require your computer to be connected to the internet, they can never be 100% secure.

CoPay - https://copay.io

CoPay operates on both desktop and mobile platforms, so it's great if you're looking to spend or receive Bitcoins on the go. It requires multiple signatures (ways of account verification) to spend coins, which is an added security feature. There's a multiple user option as well, which is useful for groups and families. The software's code being open source is always a plus.

Paper Wallets

Paper wallets are simply notes of your private key that are written down on paper. They will often feature QR codes so the sender can quickly scan them to send cryptocurrency.

Pros:

- Cheap

- Your private keys are not stored digitally, and are therefore not subject to cyber-attacks or hardware failures.

Cons:

- Loss of paper due to human error

- Paper is fragile and can degrade quickly in certain environments

- Not easy to spend cryptocurrency quickly if necessary - not useful for everyday transactions

You can use sites like bitaddress.org to create non-secure paper wallets online. These are known as non-secure as you have to be connected to the internet in order to use them. If the site is hacked, then hackers can access information regarding all private keys that have ever been created.

Step by Step Guide on How to Create a 100% Secure Paper Wallet

Required Material:

- **Offline download of bitaddress -** http://bit.ly/offlinebitaddress

- **Lili Live USB -** http://www.linuxliveusb.com/en/download

- **Ubuntu Operating System -** http://www.ubuntu.com/download/desktop

- **USB Flash Drive -** either a brand new or one you are willing to format the existing data from

- **A printer**

Installing Ubuntu on your flash drive

1. Download the above programs

2. Open LiLi and insert your USB flash drive into your computer

3. In Lili choose a source - select "ISO/IMG/Zip" option

4. In Lili Options - select "Format the key in FAT32"

5. Unzip the offline bitaddress file and copy it into your flash drive

Then disconnect your computer from the internet - this is so there is no way anyone can access your computer while you are creating a private key.

Booting Ubuntu from your flash drive

Reboot your computer, and press F12 before windows or OSX loads. Select USB HDD from the boot menu. Then run the Ubuntu operating system from your flash drive. After it has loaded, click on "Try Ubuntu"

Once Ubuntu has loaded, click on system settings then printers and add your printer. Print out 1 page to test it has connected.

Creating your wallet

6.   Click on the Firefox icon on Ubuntu and open the private browsing window

7.   Type in the following in the address bar: **file:///cdrom/bitaddress.org-master/**

8.   Click on "BitAddress.org.html"

9.   Move your cursor around until the timer reaches 0 (this is to ensure that you are a real person)

10. Choose Paper Wallet

11. Follow the steps to print out your paper wallet

12. Deposit BTC using the public address on the left hand side of the wallet (represented by a QR code)

Additional Recommendations

It is recommended you store your paper wallet in a sealed plastic bag to protect against water or damp conditions. Make multiple copies for extra security and if you are holding cryptocurrency for the long-term, store the paper inside a safe.

Hardware Wallets

Hardware wallets refer to physical storage items that contain your private key. The most common form of these are encrypted USB sticks. These are similar to ones you can make yourself, except someone else has already set up the security protocols for you. This is ideal for those who are non-tech savvy. Many of them also have built-in backup software in case you lose your keys.

These wallets use two factor authentication or 2FA to ensure that only the wallet owner can access the data. For example, one factor is the physical USB stick plugged into your computer, and the other would be a 4 digit pin code - much like how you use a debit card to withdraw money from an ATM.

Pros:

- Near impossible to hack - as of the time of writing, there have been ZERO instances of hacked hardware wallets

- Even if your computer is infected with a virus or malware, the wallet cannot be accessed due to 2FA

- The private key never leaves your device or transfers to a computer, so once again, malware or infected computers are not an issue

- Can be carried with you easily if you need to spend your cryptocurrency

- Transactions are easier than with paper wallets

- Can store multiple addresses on one device - good if you plan on having multiple Bitcoin accounts

- For the gadget lovers among you - they look a lot cooler than a folded piece of paper

Cons:

- More expensive than paper wallets - starting at around $60

- Susceptible to hardware damage, degradation and changes in technology

- Different wallets support different cryptocurrencies

- Trusting the provider to deliver an unused wallet. Using a second hand wallet is a big security breach. Only purchase hardware wallets from official sources.

The most popular of these are the Trezor and Ledger wallets. Both of these provide an easy to use experience in addition to being a portable and secure way to store your Bitcoin.

How to Trade Bitcoin

While you may want to hold Bitcoin for the long term, you may also wish to trade them for other cryptocurrencies or fiat currency. This is the fastest way to make money with Bitcoin, but also the riskiest. To trade for fiat currency, you can simply sell them at the current exchange rate on the same exchange you bought them at, like Coinbase or Kraken.

If you want to trade them for other cryptocurrencies however, it's best to move them to Poloniex or another large exchange like Bittrex. Once on here you will see the exchange rate between Bitcoin and other currencies. It should be noted that this may differ from the exchange rate for the cryptocurrency to fiat pairing. For example, the exchange rate for BTC to Litecoin (LTC) may differ from the rate for BTC/USD and LTC/USD. Fees are usually low for crypto-to-crypto trades, the maximum fee on Poloniex for example is 0.25%.

Another element you should examine is the liquidity for certain pairings. For example, you don't want a trade to be delayed because someone on the exchange is not selling the volume of the coin you are buying. To check liquidity of certain coin pairings go to http://coinmarketcap.com

These exchanges also along you to view the historical price charts for the various pairings as well as the liquidity (ease of making a trade) for each market.

As with any speculative market, trading Bitcoin is risky and you are liable to lose money. This is especially true if you trade on emotion, and not rationality. It is advisable to proceed with caution and do your homework before you do any trading for real. You can practice with virtual money (known as paper trading) on sites like https://www.whaleclub.co/

Needless to say though, you will make mistakes at first. You'll learn from these mistakes, but it's important that you make them with money you can afford to lose.

If you are going to trade, take intermediate profits for yourself. This way any gains you have made are in your bank account, and not just on paper. Dollar cost averaging also applies to trading in addition to investing.

What Determines the Price of Bitcoin?

If you're going to invest in Bitcoin, or any cryptocurrency for that matter, it's important to understand the market factors that drive the price one way or another. There are a number of these, which often interact with one another, but for simplicity purposes, we will examine them one by one.

China

No country has more of an effect on the price of Bitcoin than China. More fiat to Bitcoin trades from China than any other country, and some of the largest exchanges in the world are based there. Approximately 70% of the world's Bitcoin trades occur in the Chinese market.

Good news from China equals good news for the market in general. A December 2013 announcement from the People's Bank of China decreeing that Bitcoin was not a currency tanked the market by 35% in under an hour. Conversely, news of Bitcoin being adopted by Chinese business often leads to the Bitcoin price rising.

One major factor that makes China such a driving force in the Bitcoin market is the Chinese government's strict financial regulation of assets held in Chinese Yuan. Both wealthy and middle class Chinese citizens are looking for a way to secure their financial future without tying it to the value of the Yuan, which has been devalued in recent years. Bitcoin represents the perfect way for them to do this. Further Yuan devaluation will only lead to increased Bitcoin growth in the future.

Russia

Like China, Russia is also suffering from issues with its fiat currency, the ruble. The ruble has continued to fall against the US dollar year-on-year for the past 3 years. As it does so, Russians like to protect their wealth by moving their rubles into Bitcoin.

Adoption is Russia is also a major player in Bitcoin short-term price movements. An announcement in May 2017 that Ulmart, the largest online retailer in Russia, would begin accepting Bitcoin payments, took the market to a then all time high of $1800.

Government Regulation

Government support for Bitcoin will also play a part in the price of it as a commodity. Although Bitcoin is not tied to any one nation, for mass adoption to occur - it needs the support of government. The main contention for governments right now is Bitcoin's perceived "complete anonymity" and how it relates to crime, especially tax evasion. Once measures are in place to eliminate the anonymity element (regardless of your moral standpoint on this), government support will rise, and so will the price of Bitcoin.

Conversely, any time there is news of a government crackdown on Bitcoin either as a digital currency, or on a technology level - the price decreases

Technological Innovation

Advances in the Bitcoin network are vital if it is to continue increasing in value. As previously mentioned, new developments like SegWit and the lighting network, which will ease scalability issues, are important in the development of the coin on a technological front.

The coin's ability to handle micropayments (transactions of small monetary value) is one key area that was have a big effect on the future value. Currently the effectiveness of the system for micropayments is limited by the 1MB block size, which leads to minimum transaction amounts and delays in payment processing if you send too many transactions too quickly. With the implementation of lightning network, the team hopes to ease these issues and further increase Bitcoin's real world viability.

Mass Media

Despite what we'd like to believe, the vast majority of society still get their news from just 1 or 2 sources. To put it bluntly, the mainstream media doesn't understand Bitcoin one iota. Due to the lack of proper cryptocurrency or crypto asset journalists working for major outlets, they would rather give airtime to good soundbites like "Bitcoin could reach $100,000 within 5 years" or inversely "Bitcoin is the biggest bubble since the dotcom craze" than examine it at a technological level, or focus on any innovations that have been made. Positive news for Bitcoin in the media leads to new investors, and negative news leads to a decrease in price.

The other side of this is that some Bitcoin commentators have already made up their mind without even examining the technology. If you see an article in 2017 talking about Bitcoin as a front for "drug dealing" or "money laundering", then you can safely disregard it.

For your own personal news source, I recommend dedicated sites like http://coindesk.com for legitimate, non-biased or overhyped news regarding Bitcoin and cryptocurrency.

Funding for Blockchain Companies

As blockchain companies continue to receive more funding and investment, the currency receives more legitimization. Many blockchain related startups now accept investments in Bitcoin and other cryptocurrencies like Ethereum.

The Middle Class Investor

An often overlooked factor. While Bitcoin may be increasing in popularity among younger investors and some larger institutions, it is still very much off the radar of the American middle class. In other words think about Tom, aged 55, from Maryland. He's married and has a low 6 figure income from his upper management job. His portfolio currently consists mainly of blue chip stocks and low-cost index funds. He's not trying to hit any home runs, he's just trying to shore up his retirement assets. Once Bitcoin cements its reputation as a form of "digital gold" and more of a solid long-term investment rather than the speculative play thing it is seen as by some major institutions, it's value will continue to rise. In other words, we need more people like Tom as our target Bitcoin buyer for the value to continue increasing.

Technical Analysis

It should be noted that traditional technical analysis or chart analysis like one would do on stocks is tough, as the cryptocurrency market is a) only 8 years old so lacks comprehensive data and b) unlike anything we've ever seen before. However, charting does have its place in the Bitcoin universe and I would recommend you study stock technical analysis books if you are planning to trade Bitcoin on a serious level, with candlestick charting being the most useful for the cryptocurrency market.

Mass Adoption

As more merchants accept Bitcoin as a means of payment, the more it legitimizes the currency. Bitcoin's scalability issues will be the main determinant of this. Adoption shows no sign of slowing down and the total number of businesses accepting the currency continues to grow. If corporate giants such as Amazon and Apple began to accept Bitcoin payments, then the price is likely to increase once again.

Bitcoin for Business: How Your Business can Benefit from Accepting Bitcoin Payments

If you're not a small business owner, you can skip this section, but if you are, I advise you to pay close attention.

First and foremost, accepting Bitcoin payments can save you money.

While traditional credit card payment processing are around 2-3%. Using Bitcoin payment platforms such as BitPay can reduce these fees to around 1%. Even a small percentage change like this can represent big savings in the long run. If you're an internet seller tired of bank's charging you extortionate fees for currency conversions, or simply want to make your product or service accessible worldwide - Bitcoin may be your solution. Bitcoin doesn't discriminate across borders, and payments from any countries are subject to the same transaction costs.

There are millions of Bitcoin users looking for places to spend their coins, adding your business to the equation can only be good for the network as a whole. Bitcoin users are also an enthusiastic bunch, and enjoy supporting businesses that accept it. Cryptocurrency as a whole is a growing market, and making your business an early adopter is a chance to become a player in your industry via increased brand awareness.

There's also protection against chargeback fraud. As Bitcoin payments are irreversible, you, the merchant is no longer responsible for the costs of fraud.

For non-profits, Bitcoin donations have soared year-on-year since its inception. The Jamaican Bobsled team funded their trip to the 2014 Winter Olympics entirely from cryptocurrency donations. There's also the benefits of customers seeing the total donation amount and where it is spent in a sector where transparency is king.

If you're worried about the fluctuation of Bitcoin's value, then services like BitPay have you covered with daily bank transfers in your local currency.

Can I Still Make Money with Bitcoin in 2018?

Short answer: Yes

Long answer: Bitcoin continues to grow, both as a digital asset and as a currency with real world applications. Increased globalization and the need to transfer money across borders will only lead to a rise in adoption of Bitcoin. The amount of cross border money transfers continues to grow year-on-year and now represent almost 1% of the world's GDP. Bitcoin's total market cap now stands at $71 billion, more than the GDP of countries like Costa Rica and Bulgaria.

The near (but not total) anonymous element of Bitcoin is another factor that continues to drive growth. This is particularly important in countries where government's heavily regulate the fiat currency like China.

Bitcoin has now become a brand in and of itself. The currency is synonymous with a digital store of value. This is something that no other cryptocurrency can touch. Think of it like buying a property. Would you rather buy one in a "name brand" city like London or New York, where the demand for properties like yours will always be high, regardless of the general state of the market. Or one for the same price in say Oklahoma City where you may be able to buy a bigger house - but will you be able to sell during a market downturn?

Whether you want to use Bitcoin as a tool for trading, exchanging for other cryptocurrencies or as a long term store of value, there has never been a better time to invest in cryptocurrency than 2017. It's also never been easier to invest with sites like Coinbase and Kraken.

Just remember though, everyone feels like a genius or ahead of the curve when the market is going up. There will be down periods, and it's important to manage your risk correctly so that you can ride out the bad times and continue to profit during the good ones. Remember this - even the best in the business get it wrong sometimes

The Bitcoin Investing Mindset and How to Minimize Your Risk

In a market as volatile as cryptocurrency, it's important to minimize your risk as much as possible. With potential market changes of 10% on a daily basis, it's important for your portfolio, as well as, your peace of mind.

First off, never invest more than you can afford to lose. It may be tempting to try and hit a home run, but in doing so you will cause yourself sleepless nights and anxiety ridden days.

Secondly, unless you are day trading, don't check crypto price charts every few hours. Doing so will only give additional anxiety. The price is liable is swing by large percentage margins on a daily basis, that's just the way of the Bitcoin market, just remember that so far, over the long run, the price has continued to increase.

Dollar Cost Averaging

One of the best ways to minimize your risk in a volatile market is to use what is known as 'dollar cost averaging'. This simply means dividing up your total planned investment and buying Bitcoin at regular intervals instead of all at once.

With dollar cost averaging, you are simply buying less of an asset (in this case, Bitcoin) when the price is high, and more when the price is low. Your total exposure is less because you are only exposed to part of any decline in the market, as opposed to all of it with a lump sum investment. Your average cost per coin is therefore likely to be lower.

Let's use an example, both Alan and John have $1200 to invest in Bitcoin at the start of 2015. Alan decides to invest all $1200 on January 1st, John on the other hand is going to use dollar cost averaging. He will invest $100 on the 1st of each month, for a total of $1200. The prices used in this example are the actual Bitcoin trading prices as of those dates.

January 1st 2015 - $305.32

February 1st 2015 - $237.18

March 1st 2015 - $263.57

April 1st 2015 - $255.23

May 1st 2015 - $226.45

June 1st 2015 - $233.44

July 1st 2015 - $260.73

August 1st 2015 -$283.04

September 1st 2015 - $229.00

October 1st 2015 - $240.10

November 1st 2015 - $325.28

December 1st 2015 - $375.95

Alan's total investment in BTC = 3.93 (1200/305.32)

John's total investment in BTC = 4.55 (1200/269.60)

Price on January 1st 2016 - $433.57

Alan's Portfolio Value = 3.93*433.57 = $1704.02

John's Portfolio Value = 4.55*433.57 = $1974.37

Alan's ROI = 42%

John's ROI = 64.5%

So by using dollar cost averaging, John's average BTC purchase price was $269.60, whereas Alan bought a lump sum at $305.32. By having a lower average purchase price, John's ROI is higher over time. Alan bought her coins at the peak of the market before a prolonged downturn, whereas John utilized this downturn to his advantage.

Remember, time in the market beats timing the market. Generally speaking, the longer you are invested in something, the better.

FOMO & FUD

These are two terms you should become familiar with if you are going to be investing and trading in Bitcoin, or any cryptocurrency for that matter.

FOMO - Fear Of Missing Out

This is most commonly manifested when you see news reports of *<insert hot shiny new altcoin here>* increasing by ridiculous numbers like 100+% in a day. It may be tempting to trade a proportion or even all (terrible idea) your Bitcoin in for the latest cool cryptocurrency object, but it's incredibly risky. Many smaller altcoins are backed up by purely theoretical technology, and have no real world adoption for whatever product or service they are backing. Remember to do your due diligence regarding coin news. Just because the headline might read "Amazing Altcoin linked to Amazon deal", doesn't necessarily mean the deal is anywhere close, or if there even is a deal in the first place. Check your facts before investing.

It is important to understand that Bitcoin has now reached a point where there are real world uses, and it is by far the most adopted out of any cryptocurrency. Therefore, Bitcoin has greater market saturation and thus is unlikely to skyrocket in value like smaller coins. The opposite is also true though and with great rewards comes great risk. Many smaller coins can, and do lose up to 80% of their value in just a few days (for further reading check out the Chaincoin pump and dump scheme of July 2017), whereas Bitcoin continues to hold strong. If you are planning to buy and hold a single coin for the long term, Bitcoin should be your only play.

FUD - Fear, Uncertainty & Doubt

FUD is the spreading of misinformation by uninformed sources. Many of these sources have their own nefarious reasons for doing so. It may be to promote an alternative coin, or they may have shorted (bet on the price decreasing) Bitcoin. Of course, legitimate criticism of Bitcoin as a technology is fine, and should be encouraged if the technology is to advance. FUD however is mostly slander and baseless accusations about Bitcoin as a technology, the people behind it or the people invested in it.

How can you avoid FUD? Simply by obtaining your Bitcoin and other cryptocurrency news from reliable sources, who don't have a vested interest one way or another. It is important to use multiple sources to get a well rounded view of the situation.

Investing your Bitcoin - ICOs

An ICO or Initial Coin Offering, is an alternative form of crowdfunding that many blockchain startups have been utilizing as of late. Instead of donating in US Dollars in return for shares of the company, patrons can donate in Bitcoin or other cryptocurrencies in exchange for new tokens of the company.

The most famous ICO thus far was the Ethereum ICO of July 2014. Ethereum is a new blockchain based platform that allows applications and automatically executed contracts, known as "smart contracts" to be built on it. During the funding phase, Ethereum received roughly 31,500 Bitcoin, equivalent to $18.4 million at the time. In return, a total of 60 million Ethereum tokens were distributed to those who were part of the funding. The project has been extremely successful in the short term and today, 60 million Ethereum is worth approximately $24 billion.

ICOs represent a way for companies to fund their blockchain projects, in addition to providing returns for investors. Usually the offerings last for a period of a few weeks, and the company issuing the new tokens will have a goal amount that they aim to raise. ICOs have rapidly increased in popularity in the past 18 months, and 2017 is on track to be the first year that blockchain companies raise more money from ICOs than they do from traditional venture capitalists. For an investment purpose, ICOs represent a way for savvy investors to get in on the ground floor of an exciting new project.

The downside of this of course, is that with so many new ICOs popping up, some of them have far less legitimacy than others. If you are planning to invest in an ICO, do so based on the underlining usefulness of the project, and not any fancy marketing buzzwords that the company uses in their sales copy. Just because something is based on a blockchain platform, does not always mean there is a real world demand for the product or service. Another area to examine is the team of developers behind the project, and their track record of successfully developing blockchain applications.

Like any traditional startup venture, more ICOs will fail than succeed, and raising money is only part of a successful project. One such example of an ICO with problems is Bancor, an ICO based of the idea of creating a market-making (generating an automatic buy and sell price) product that provided liquidity for digital assets. The project raised a staggering $153m in just 3 hours, over 50% higher than the initial target.

However the project had problems with investor's transactions being accepted in addition to the Bancor team issuing extra token after the funding period was complete. This ultimately means a lower returns for investors. Like any investment, is important to do your due diligence before becoming involved, and never invest more than you can afford to lose. One final word, like anything in the Bitcoin or cryptocurrency space, ICOs are not a get rich quick scheme.

Lately the ICO buzz has been so intense that there are even ICOs utilizing Facebook Ads and celebrity endorsements in an attempt to gain investment. It's worth asking yourself if you would invest in a non-blockchain company based on a Facebook advertisement, and I think you already know the answer. If a company's main selling point is "amazing returns", rather than technological innovation, then it's likely to be a sub-par investment rather than a solid one.

The other area that is vital to understand, is that you ARE NOT buying stock in these companies during the ICO phase. You don't own any of the company, you simply own whatever token they denominize which will fluctuate in value due to external factors that go behind the company's own performance.

Why I Don't Recommend You Mine Bitcoin

Whenever Bitcoin's price is rising (and that's most of the time!), the mining question always pops up. Usually from those who are inexperienced or want a "free" way to get a piece of the pie.

It all starts with a variant of this question

"Why buy Bitcoin at $100/$1,000/$4,000 when you can just use your computer to mine some for free?"

Unfortunately, like everything else - there is no such thing as free Bitcoin.

As previously discussed, the way Bitcoins are created or "mined" is by using a computer to solve an of increasingly complex series of algorithms. Users are then rewarded for solving these algorithms by receiving Bitcoin. There is no man power involved, you yourself don't have to solve the algorithm, you just have to link your computer up to the Bitcoin network and the computer does the rest. There are also no shortcuts or breakthrough moments, the only way Bitcoin can be obtained quicker is with more computer power. How much computational power you supply determines the size of your reward. The more power you supply, the more Bitcoins you receive.

Now here is why mining is generally a terrible investment for the average Joe.

1. Electricity Costs - The electricity costs involved with running your computer 24/7 (which is necessary for mining) by far outweigh the amount of Bitcoins you receive for completing the task. You require access to industrial electricity rates of around $0.02 per kWh in order for the venture to be profitable on a small scale.

2. Requiring Specialist Hardware - Nowadays, the most efficient mining processes require special hardware known as Application-specific integrated circuits (ASIC). ASICs can be described as a supercomputer that can only ever perform one task. Specialist Bitcoin ASIC miners available for consumer purchase still start at around $1000 and often run around $2000-$2500.

3. Equipment maintenance - To maintain all this computing power is an additional cost. The cost of cooling alone is a large cost that has to be factored in to long term profits. Hardware running 24/7 burns out faster and replacement mining equipment will be needed in due course.

4. The increasing size of the Bitcoin network - The network pays out a fixed amount of Bitcoin, regardless of how many miners are using the network. The current rate is around 1800BTC per day, which sounds like a huge number, until you realise just how many miners there are on the network. The current mining power is equivalent to 17.6 BILLION desktop computers. Therefore the average payout for the end user running 1 desktop computer full time is around approximately $0.000107 per day. Or roughly 2 cents a year's worth of BTC. To put it lightly, you have more chance of winning the lottery than you do making a profit from mining Bitcoin your standard home computer.

Mining in 2018 is a much different proposition from mining in 2010 or even 2012. There are some opportunities which involved investing in Bitcoin farms or group purchasing processing power of ASIC at a discount. This is known as a "mining pool". Due to cheaper power costs, currently around 80% of the world's mining pools are based in China, with Iceland possessing the second largest number. Joining a mining pool requires a lower upfront investment but still requires cheap electricity rates and have debatable ROI potential.

It should also be worth noting that many of those who promote group mining or cloud mining do so under an affiliate program with whatever company that are promoting, meaning they get a commission % every time someone signs up.

However, for the average Joe without a huge amount of money to invest - I would strongly recommend buying coins instead of mining them. You are more likely to get higher returns in both the short and long run.

Is there a Bitcoin ETF or Mutual Fund I can invest in?

Exchange Traded Funds (ETFs) and mutual funds have represented some of the safest investments over the past few decades. Instead of investing in individual companies, you are buying an aggregate share of many companies. By allowing for this level of diversification, this represents a low risk use of your funds, and for many years investors have been clamoring for a Bitcoin or cryptocurrency fund like this due to the price volatility of individual cryptocurrencies.

Unfortunately attempts for a Bitcoin ETF have been thwarted by regulatory bodies thus far. In 2017, two Bitcoin ETF applications were rejected by the SEC. The reasoning from the government body was the lack of regulation and market surveillance in the cryptocurrency space.

The closest thing to a Bitcoin mutual fund today is a diversified fund offered by http://thetoken.io based out of Russia - the fund is a combination of 16 different cryptocurrency tokens, with Ethereum (22%) and Bitcoin (17%) representing the largest portions of the fund. Investments can be made with both BTC and ETH and funds are stored in Ethereum backed wallets. However, fiat currency investments are not currently supported. The fund is backed by a smart contract on the Ethereum platform to ensure the legitimacy of the tokens offered.

However, the main drawback of the site is that it is not available to those based in the US or Singapore, although this may change in the future based on the regulatory status of Bitcoin and other cryptocurrencies. Once again, like any investments you are liable to lose money in a market downturn, so only invest money you are comfortable losing.

The Ten Commandments of Bitcoin

If you get nothing else from this book, at least follow these rules and you'll be in a better position to make money than other new investors.

1. **Thou shalt believe in Bitcoin at a technological level**

2. **Thou shalt never gives one's private key to anyone else**

3. **Thou shalt always stay informed with Bitcoin news from reputable sources**

4. **Thou shalt never panic sell during a downturn**

5. **Thou shalt always take intermediate profits for oneself**

6. **Thou shalt always store cryptocurrency safely**

7. **Thou shalt not spend every hour checking cryptocurrency markets**

8. **Thou shalt never mine Bitcoin on their regular desktop computer**

9. **Thou shalt not invest more than you can afford to lose**

10. **Thou shalt always help others with less knowledge than yourself**

Conclusion

Bitcoin has changed the way we look at money and finance. Our previous reliance on banks and other financial institutions has been put into question. These long standing financial institutions now face unprecedented disruption from this groundbreaking technology. For users, cross border payments at a near-instant transaction time and far lower transactions fees are making the global economy smaller. For merchants, protecting themselves from fraud has never been easier with the rise of Bitcoin. Even non-profits can benefit hugely from Bitcoin as a payment method. Blockchain technology has an additional laundry list of benefits ranging from transparency in elections to easily accessible medical records between parties.

As a commodity, Bitcoin has produced unrivaled returns for investors over the past 7 years. No other financial asset, in the cryptocurrency space or otherwise has made more people money since its inception in 2010. For those who believe in Bitcoin, long may these returns continue.

I hope you've enjoyed this book and that you're now a little bit more informed about how Bitcoin works, and more importantly, how it can work for you. Whether you're planning on investing for the long-term, or hoping to make short-term gains by trading - I wish you the best of luck.

Remember, trade rationally and not emotionally. Never invest more than you can afford to lose, and for the love of God - don't check the charts 15 times a day.

If you're ready to make the next step and get involved in the market. I have a small gift for you.

If you're ready to take the plunge and become involved in the Bitcoin market - I have a small gift for you.

If you sign up for Coinbase using this link, you will receive $10 worth of free Bitcoin after your first purchase of more than $100 worth of cryptocurrency.

http://bit.ly/10dollarbtc

Cryptocurrency Beginners Bible - How You Can Make Money Trading and Investing in Cryptocurrency

"The ones who are crazy enough to think they can change the world are the ones who do". - Steve Jobs

"The stock market is a vehicle to transfer wealth from the impatient to the patient" - Warren Buffett

Introduction

In just 7 short years, the value of Bitcoin has increased from $0.08 to over $4000[1]

In just a single year, Ethereum's price rose from $11 to $395 and back down to $295 at the time of writing.

The current cryptocurrency market is worth around $130 billion, more than the total GDP of countries like Hungary and Kuwait.

These investment returns are completely unprecedented from any traditional stock or index fund using fiat currency - which is precisely why the cryptocurrency universe is exploding.

We have daily news articles perpetrating "Bitcoin value could reach $5000 by 2018" and yet 2 results further down on a Google search we have a contrary article with the headline "Bitcoin value has peaked says Billionaire."

In the month of July alone we saw predictions of Ethereum being at $1000 by the end of 2017, and other commentators speculating that the value would plummet to just $50 in the same time period.

It's safe to say - there's a whole lot of hype out there

This book is designed to separate fact from fiction, we want to take a step back from the hype and look at the fundamentals of some of the more prominent cryptocurrencies to examine their viability as both as technological entity and as a trading/investing vehicle. This is to give you a well rounded view on whether these coins have potential for you to make money - which many of them do

For reference purposes, I will refer mostly to Bitcoin when talking about general cryptocurrency technology and using cryptocurrency as a means of exchange. Further, in-depth explanation of Ethereum and other altcoins can be found later in the book.

---

[1] Source: Coincap.io - 2017 price as of 22/08/2017

What is Cryptocurrency?

Depending on who you ask, defining cryptocurrency will elicit answers from "the money of the future" all the way down to "the biggest bubble since the DOTCOM bubble". US senator Thomas Carper summed it up best in laymens terms.

"Virtual currencies, perhaps most notably Bitcoin, have captured the imagination of some, struck fear among others, and confused the heck out of the rest of us."

For a more accurate definition, cryptocurrencies are simply currencies that do not have a centralized lender like a country's central bank. They are created using encryption techniques that limit the amount of monetary units (or coins) created and then verify any transfer of the funds after their creation.

This creation technique is known as "mining" due to its theoretical similarity to mining gold or other precious metals. To mine cryptocurrency, one needs to solve an increasingly complex computer algorithm or puzzle. Solving these algorithms takes a lot of computer processing power, and consequently, electricity. In other words, it costs money to mine them, so we can't just create value out of thin air. Therefore these currencies and their value are secured by the laws of mathematics as opposed to any central government or bank.

As cryptocurrency adoption increases, so does the number of real world uses. Everything from physical goods, gift cards, tickets to sports games and even hotel bookings can be purchased using cryptocurrency. Certain bars and restaurants have now also started accepting it as a means of payment. A number of NGOs now accept donations in Bitcoin and other cryptocurrencies as well. There are also more illicit uses, with the cases of underground online marketplaces dealing in illegal goods, such as Silk Road and AlphaBay.

These currencies have a huge number of advantages versus the currencies that we know and use today. This is what makes them so attractive to both long term investors and short term speculators. Of course, like any investment, cryptocurrencies do indeed have some potential drawbacks to them - and we will examine these later on in this book.

An Extremely Brief History of Cryptocurrency

While the practical applications of cryptocurrencies date back a mere 7 years, the technical aspects actually date back a further 30 years to the 1980s. Cryptographer David Chaum was the first to theorize a cryptocurrency when he invented an encrypted computer algorithm that allowed secure, unalterable exchanges between two parties.

Chaum later founded DigiCash, one of the first companies to produce units of currency based of his algorithm. It's important to note that only the DigiCash company, could produce the currency, which is a model unlike Bitcoin and other cryptocurrencies where anyone can mine the currency (providing they have the necessary computing power). After running into legal problems and rejecting a partnership with Microsoft that would have seen DigiCash paired with every home Windows operating system, the company went bankrupt in the late 1990s.

Chinese software engineer Wei Dai published a white paper on "b-money", which laid the foundations for the architecture behind the cryptocurrencies that we know today. The paper included information on complex algorithms, anonymity for purchasers and decentralization. However the currency itself never came to fruition.

US based E-Gold was another failed attempt at creating a cryptocurrency in the 1990s. The Florida based company gave customers e-gold "tokens" in exchange for their jewelry, old trinkets and coins. These tokens could then be exchanged for US dollars. The website was initially successful and there were over 1 million active accounts by the mid-2000s. One E-Gold's pioneering strategies was that anyone could open an account. However, this led to a number of scams being run through the website. In addition, poor security protocols led to large hacking incidents and the company went out of business in 2009.

The modern cryptocurrencies that we know today began with Bitcoin, which was first outlined by anonymous entity (the identity has never been confirmed as a single person or group) Satoshi Nakamoto. Bitcoin was released to the public in early 2009 and a large group of enthusiasts began mining, investing in, and exchanging the currency. The first Bitcoin market was established in February 2010.

In late 2012 Hosting and website development platform Wordpress became the first major retailer to support payment in Bitcoin. This step was key as it gave the currency real world credibility and showed that large corporations had confidence in it as a currency.

Cryptocurrency vs. Traditional Currency

Currency 101: The value of any currency is determined by what someone will give you in exchange for said currency.

Currencies, crypto or otherwise need to follow three basic rules:

1. They need to be difficult to produce (cash) or find (gold or other precious metals)

2. They need have a limited supply

3. They need to be recognized by other humans as having value

Using only Bitcoin (BTC) as an example, it ticks the boxes of all three of these characteristics:

1. Bitcoin uses complex computer algorithms in its production which take a lot of computational power, so it cannot be replicated easily or at a discount

2. There are a finite supply of Bitcoins - 21 Million to be exact[2]. As of 2015, roughly 2/3 of this number had been mined

3. There are hundreds of Bitcoin exchanges and Bitcoin is accepted everywhere from Subway to online dating sites

Where cryptocurrencies differ from traditional currencies (also known as fiat currencies) is that they are not tied to any one country, nation or institution (in most cases). There are no USA bitcoins, no Japanese Litecoins or any country specific altcoin. This is known as decentralization.

---

[2] The actual supply numbers are measured in Satoshi (0.00000001BTC). There are 2,100,000,000,000,000 (2.1 quadrillion) Satoshi.

We also have to remember that fiat currencies that we know and love were not always the main players in the currency world. For centuries, Gold and other precious metals were seen as the most desirable currencies for day to day usage. It was not until governments could standardize and verify the metallic content of coins (and later paper bills) that they became the go to choice for citizens.[3]

Bitcoin was designed as a "deflationary currency" - meaning over time its value will, in theory, inherently increase. Unlike fiat currencies which are inflationary and whose value will eventually decrease. After all, in 1917, $1 was worth the equivalent of $20.17 today. So the US Dollar is worth 20 times LESS than 100 years ago. In other words, if you continue to hold $1 over the course of 100 years, you will be able to buy progressively fewer and fewer items in exchange for it, whereas with Bitcoin, in theory, the opposite will happen.

As another real world example. On 22 May 2010, Laszlo Hanyecz made the first real-world cryptocurrency transaction by buying two pizzas in Jacksonville, Florida for 10,000 BTC. Today 10,000 BTC is worth over $40 million.

Bitcoin was designed this way so that no single person (or government) could increase the supply of money, lowering the value of the money already in the market.

Legendary Economist John Maynard Keynes had this to say about inflation and inflationary currencies.

"By a continuing process of inflation, governments can confiscate, secretly and unobserved, an important part of the wealth of their citizens. By this method they not only confiscate, but they confiscate arbitrarily; and, while the process impoverishes many, it actually enriches some. The sight of this arbitrary rearrangement of riches strikes not only at security, but at confidence in the equity of the existing distribution of wealth."

While Bitcoin has an air of uncertainty about it, based on the decentralization principle - where the real potential lies is in seeing it from the opposite perspective. With no single body being responsible for the supply of money, it forces all players (government, businesses and consumers) to be transparent about

---

[3] Until rappers start rhyming about Bitcoins and Satoshis rather than Dollar Bills, Fiat will be the dominant form of currency

their processes, lowering the risk of fraud or tampering. The transparency is ensured by rewarding miners for their efforts (in the form of coin). This single dominating factor is why so many investors are confident about the long term viability of the currency.

One common argument made by Bitcoin detractors is that as there is no government backing the currency, it could totally collapse in theory. However, we have seen these happen numerous times with fiat currency under scenarios of hyperinflation where governments can no longer ensure the value of their money and as such have to create an entirely new currency. Common examples include the German Weimar Republic in the 1920s, where the currency lost so much of its value, that banknotes were used as wallpaper. Currently, the Venezuelan economy is on track to experience over 1000% inflation for the year, leaving many citizens unable to afford daily necessities like bread. Bitcoin enthusiasts see the cryptocurrency as recession-proof.

The cost of international transactions is another area where cryptocurrencies maintain a huge advantage over traditional ones. Anyone who has ever had to send money overseas will know that the cost of processing these transaction can reach ridiculous levels. There are times when these fees can top 10%. As cryptocurrencies do not view international transactions (as there are no "nations" involved) any differently from local ones, there are minimal fees for sending money to any part of the world.

The speed of transactions across borders is also much faster than regular fiat currencies, a Bitcoin transaction takes around 10 minutes to register as opposed to days for international bank transfers, and other coins process transactions even faster.

Understanding Blockchain Technology

So with no central lender like a Government backed bank, how is all this money worth anything at all? This answer is blockchain technology. If you plan to invest any money at all into cryptocurrencies, it is vital that you have at least a basic understanding of blockchain technology and its uses.

Blockchain technology allows for a permanent, incorruptible record of all transactions that have ever taken place, free from human errors or data loss. The important thing to remember is that these transactions do not always have to be financial, they can be in the form of legal contracts, auditing consumer goods and file storage.

Blockchain is essentially a giant database that is not stored in a central location. A floating database if you will. Because it is not stored in any single location, transactions recorded on the blockchain are publicly accessible and verifiable. We again go back to the idea of decentralization, and not having to rely on a single person or government to ensure our transactions will be safe.

In more practical terms, imagine all your financial information was stored on a single spreadsheet, not particularly safe right? Even if you had online and offline backups, these would be just 2 or 3 points of failure. What blockchain allows for is that spreadsheet to be shared across thousands of databases and continuously refreshed meaning that any changes would be recorded and no hacker could corrupt it at a single point of entry. As there is no single point of entry, there is now no single point of failure either.

Blockchain technology could be used to transfer everything from cryptocurrency, to tangible assets such as property without having to use a middle man such as a bank or other financial institution. This has potential to save consumers and businesses billions of dollars a year that are spent on transaction fees. While Bitcoin has gathered more mainstream press with regards to consumers, blockchain technology receives more interest from businesses.

How does Blockchain relate to Bitcoin and Cryptocurrency?

Bitcoin is not blockchain and blockchain is not Bitcoin or any other cryptocurrency. Bitcoins or other cryptocurrencies are transacted over a public network that runs on blockchain technology.

Blockchain is the underlying technology that allows bitcoin and other cryptocurrency transactions, but as previously mentioned - blockchain technology has many more potential uses. You can think of blockchain as an operating system, and Bitcoin as one of the hundreds of applications that run on that system.

Bitcoin and Cryptocurrency Drawbacks

Lack of Financial Regulation and The Ability to Fund Black Market Activity

One of the biggest strengths of cryptocurrencies is also a weakness in the system. The anonymity they provide allows them to be used to facilitate large scale black market operations and their usage for purposes of money laundering. For example, Silk Road - an underground dark net marketplace acted as a black market for illegal drugs. Payments were made in Bitcoin to protect the anonymity of buyers and sellers. The site was shut down in 2013 after amassing roughly $1.2billion in revenue. Founder Ross William Ulbricht was convicted of 8 charges and sentenced to life in prison.

Another nefarious use of cryptocurrency is in ransomware. Ransomware refers to malicious software that hackers install on a user's computer, then demand payment in Bitcoin to unscramble the software and allow the victim to access their data again. Ransomware schemes gained in popularity as using cryptocurrency as a means of payment means the people behind the attacks can seamlessly receive their ransom without revealing their identity.

Hackers

The elephant in the room regarding cryptocurrencies, with any early stage technology (which cryptocurrency very much is) there are bound to be breaches in security. Hackers have been responsible for some of the largest dips in the cryptocurrency market.

Tokyo based Bitcoin exchange Mt. Gox suffered losses of over $27.2 million and users lost over $460 million worth of Bitcoin after the exchange was hacked in 2011. At the time it was the largest cryptocurrency exchange on Earth. Amid talk of lazy management, and poor security protocols, the exchange ended up going bankrupt after the hacking incident.

Bitfinex, a Hong Kong based exchange was hacked in 2016 and its customers lost roughly $72 million worth of Bitcoin. It is important to note that any hacking incidents regarding Bitcoin or other cryptocurrencies were done at the exchange or wallet level - not at the technology level. For further information on how to safely store your cryptocurrency, visit the wallets section of this book.

Data Loss and Human Error

If properly secured, cryptocurrencies will facilitate a shift away from physical cash which can degenerate and erode over time. As the data is encrypted and stored online, there is no way anyone (bar hackers) can access your funds.

However, this theory assumes perfect accountability from the user. As you may have figured out by now, none of us are perfect. We lose things. For example, we can lose our private encryption keys if they are stored on paper, or devices can become damaged or stolen if we are using physical encrypted wallets (like USB wallets).

Speculation and Misinformation

As previously mentioned, Bitcoin, and cryptocurrencies in general are a frontier technology. As such, mainstream media outlets, many of whom do not employ experts in the field, are liable to present misinformation regarding the technology, and the market itself. Blanket statements such as "bitcoin is better at being gold, than gold" do nothing but undermine the technology in the long run - but do make good soundbites for mainstream media

In June 2017, the Ethereum market briefly crashed after unsubstantiated rumors, perpetrated by 4Chan, claimed that founder Vitalik Buterin had died in a car crash. The hoax caused the market value to drop by around $4 billion in under 24 hours. This demonstrates that the volatility of the market in general is subject to manipulation by nefarious forces.

If you are planning on trading cryptocurrencies, you must be willing to experience sharp drops and rises in the market, far larger movements than traditional stocks. This is where being a rational trader will help you tremendously.

China

China's relationship with cryptocurrency is unlike any other country. No single nation has done more for the success of cryptocurrency than the Middle Kingdom itself. Cryptocurrencies are popular among Chinese investors due to the government's strict controls on their fiat currency, the Yuan. The biggest one of these being their currency devaluations, which hurt its value for trading and investing purposes.

This has led to many private individuals, both wealthy and non-wealthy, looking for alternative ways to grow their wealth. Cryptocurrencies are viewed by many as a more stable asset when compared to traditional investments. China's large quantity of cheap energy has also made it a hotbed for the cryptocurrency mining scene, which is now financially out of reach of most regular Western European or Americans. Around 70% of the global cryptocurrency mining scene is located in China.

China is also liable for mass information manipulation. Mistranslations, rumour-mongering and coin pumps are all more susceptible in the Chinese market due to the lack of availability of foreign media - especially in the cryptocurrency space. In June 2017, the People's Bank of China (PBoC) issued a statement addressing false reports that the central bank was issuing cryptocurrency itself. The reports were thought the be part of a pyramid scheme to gain investors under the false pretense of a government backed cryptocurrency.

Survivorship Bias & Gambler's Fallacy

Contrary to what you may be seeing on internet forums & social media. There are people who have lost money in cryptocurrency. It's simply a matter of buying and selling at the wrong time.

It's the same reason casinos continue to do so well in part, the winners brag to their friends and family, while the losers stay silent.

Remember: **Never invest more than you can afford to lose**

This cartoon from XKCD sums it up perfectly.

Cryptocurrency Guide

Beyond Bitcoin, there are a vast number of currencies emerging. Some with different characteristics and advantages over Bitcoin itself.

In this section we will examine many different cryptocurrencies and the fundamentals behind them in order to give you the best possible concise information regarding each one. The prices of these coins range from <$1 to over $300 per coin so there's something for everyone here.

One additional note to remember, is that cryptocurrencies are divisible, unlike regular stocks. For example, you cannot buy less than 1 share of Apple stock (currency $159.30). However, you can buy fraction of a Bitcoin or other cryptocurrencies. Meaning that even if you only have a small amount of cash to invest initially, you can still partake in the market, even if you can't afford an entire coin.

It should be noted that as of August 1 2017, Bitcoin and Bitcoin Cash operate as 2 separate coins. A further in-depth discussion of Bitcoin cash can be found later on in this book.

For each coin I have tried to list all major exchanges that list the coin as a purchasable asset. However, exchanges continue to list additional coins all the time. For a full up to date list of exchanges that carry your coin visit http://coinmarketcap.com

Things to Consider Before Investing in Cryptocurrency

It's not essential to know all the technical details behind a cryptocurrency before investing. However, answering some basic questions will help you decide whether you should invest in a coin or not. Here are some comprehensive questions you should know the answer to before delving into a currency.

- What problem does the coin propose to solve?

- How will the coin solve this problem?

- Why is this coin's solution the best solution out there? Is it the best solution?

- Who is the team behind the coin? What is their development history? How transparent is their code? Is it open source?

- Is there a public figurehead who will take accountability for any issues with development or adoption?

- Does this coin have competitor coins? If so, what is coin A's advantage versus coin B?

Bitcoin (BTC)

Price at time of writing - $4,070.13

Available on:

Fiat: Coinbase, Poloniex, Kraken

The coin that started it all is now one of the world's premiere assets. Sitting at a market cap of over $67 billion, the coin is worth more than global companies such as PayPal. We've already discussed Bitcoin in depth previously, so this section will discuss it for investing purposes.

With the price now sitting at a staggering $4,000 per coin, many commentators have claimed that owning Bitcoin is out of reach for the regular investor, but that's a stance I disagree with.

First of all, we have to remember that cryptocurrencies are not like regular stocks, in that they are divisible. So if you wanted to invest in Bitcoin, you don't have to purchase an entire coin. You can buy fractions of the coin so even if you only have $100, you can still get started in the cryptocurrency market.

Secondly, Bitcoin's deflationary designed role as a form of "digital gold" continues to make it the world's most valuable cryptocurrency. It also makes Bitcoin ideal to hold as part of your portfolio as many other currencies price movements are linked to it.

Another reason why any portfolio should contain Bitcoin is that if you want to purchase some of the lesser known cryptocurrencies, you will have to do so via exchanging them for Bitcoin as opposed to buying them outright for fiat currency.

Bitcoin Cash (BCH/BCC)

Price at time of writing - $326.77

Exchanges:

Fiat: Bitfinex, Kraken, Bithumb (ROK) ViaBTC (CN), Bter (CN), Huobi (CN), Bitcoin Indonesia (INR)

BTC: Bittrex, Poloniex, Cryptopia (NZ)

Bitcoin cash emerged as the result of a split or "hard fork" in the Bitcoin technology on August 1st 2017. The end-goal of Bitcoin Cash is to function as a global currency.

The split occured out of problems with Bitcoin's ability to process transactions at a high speed. For example, the Visa network processes around 1,700 transactions per second whereas Bitcoin averages around 7. As the network continues to grow, so do waiting times for transactions. BCC aims to run more transactions, as well as, providing lower transactions fees.

One of the major solutions to this issue is increasing the size of each block, so that more data can be processed at once. This is in line with solving the problems of scalability that Bitcoin was facing previously. The technology itself is worked in the short-term, with the first Bitcoin Cash block registering 7,000 transactions compared with Bitcoin's 2,500.

The success of failure of Bitcoin Cash will largely depend on Bitcoin's own adoption of the SegWit technology later this year, and the ability to process transactions quicker to act truly as a currency - rather than a speculative asset. Detractors have also raised security concerns about Bitcoin Cash.

Bitcoin Cash has been widely adopted by many cryptocurrency exchanges. At the time of writing, there is only a few weeks worth of data available and thus, no one has been able to execute any long-term trends or technical analysis of BCH as a commodity. As further adoption continues, the price may well continue to rise. Early price rises for Bitcoin Cash have been largely driven by demand from South Korea, with over 50% of the total trade volume being seen on South Korean exchanges.

Miners have been quick to adopt the currency as well due to its higher mining ROI when compared to Bitcoin. The decrease in mining difficulty (leading to greater rewards for mining) will continue to see for miners move their resources from Bitcoin into Bitcoin Cash.

Ethereum (ETH)

Price at time of writing - $225.07

Available on:

Nearly every major exchange will allow buying of Ethereum for both fiat currency and exchange with BTC

If Bitcoin dominated the cryptocurrency space from 2008-2016, 2017 has undoubtedly been Ethereum's year. This relatively new cryptocurrency has made an immediate impact upon the space with some incredible technological innovations that have the potential to be groundbreaking, and game changing.

It is worth noting that Ethereum itself is not a cryptocurrency, it is a blockchain based platform. However tokens denominated as "ether" are traded on various exchanges. These tokens can be used for making payments on the Ethereum blockchain or exchanged for other cryptocurrencies or fiat currency. Many online articles will use the terms "Ethereum" and "Ether" interchangeably.

Where Ethereum shines is with a revolutionary technology known as "smart contracts". Dubbed by some as a technology that could potentially replace lawyers and accountants, these contracts are programmable contracts using blockchain technology, that can be set to execute automatically once a certain set of conditions are met. For example, an automatic deposit of 10 ether could be made into person A's wallet, once person A completes a task for person B. Person B has no way of breaking this contract once the conditions are met as the blockchain will enforce the conditions of said contract.

The potential applications for smart contracts are vast. From government, to management, to being able to set up a self-executing will, this is truly remarkable technology. A number of large international banks have already set up think tanks for technology like this, and adoption by any large institution has the potential to send Ethereum's price into the stratosphere. The Blockchain Banking Consortium project involves 43 international banks and aims to create a blockchain network that can enable large scale international fund transfer.

The platform is still in the development stage, and there are to this day, few real world examples of large scale Ethereum blockchain implementation. However, many investors have faith in the technology, which plays a big part in explaining the price rises over the course of 2017. In less than 1 month between May 18 and June 12, the price soared from $96.65 to a peak of $395.03.

Ethereum also suffered from a $4 billion single day loss in market cap after a hoax rumor regarding the death of founder Vitalik Buterin gained traction after originating on internet message board 4Chan. Let this example be another warning that cryptocurrencies are more susceptible to market manipulation than traditional assets.

Ripple (XRP)

Price at Time of Writing - $0.15

Available on:

Fiat: Bitstamp, GateHub

BTC: Poloniex, Bittrex, Kraken, Coincheck (JP), Bitso (MEX), Coinone (ROK)

The third largest cryptocurrency by market capitalization is one that flies under the radar of most investors and news sources. Launched in 2012 and acting as a payment network and protocol, Ripple aims to enable "secure, near instant and nearly free global financial transactions." Ripple transactions currently process in an average of just 4 seconds. The platform's ultimate goal is to make outdated payment platforms with slow transactions times and high fees like SWIFT or Western Union obsolete.

Many global banking institutions already use Ripple's payment infrastructure, including giants like BBVA, Bank of America and UBS. For example, using Ripple's payment platform, banks could convert currencies seamlessly, even for obscure countries and currencies such as a conversion of Albanian Lek to Vietnamese Dong. This would also negate the need for intermediary currencies such as US dollars or Euros. According to Ripple themselves, a switch to the platform can save banks an average of $3.76.

With adoption in the global banking sector, Ripple is off to a strong start. Especially if you look at it like you would a traditional startup.

Ripple also has the largest number of coin tokens (known as XRP) available out of any coin at 100 billion (39 billion available to the public), in contrast Bitcoin only has 16 million and Ethereum 94 million.

Unlike many open source cryptocurrencies, Ripple's source code is privately owned. The 100 billion coin supply was also "instamined", and in theory the owners could generate more at any given time, which would instantly devalue anyone holding coins. The central ownership is also at a clash with those who believe that cryptocurrency should be used as a force against one single owner. Researchers at Purdue University also determined that the platform had "security concerns", although as of writing, there have been no major incidents with the platform.

Dash (DASH)

Price at time of writing - $194.25

Available on:

Fiat: Bitfinex, xBTCe, Bithumb (ROK),

BTC: Poloniex, Bittrex, Kraken

Short for digital cash, Dash focuses on speed of transaction and anonymity as its 2 main selling points. Previously known as Darkcoin, it was rebranded in order to distance itself from the "dark web" of underground illegal cryptocurrency activity. Dash focuses on privacy, usability and the consumer market. Currently the coin fluctuates between the 5th and 8th largest cryptocurrency by market capitalization.

By speeding up transaction speeds from Bitcoin by using its Masternode network, payments are near instant versus the 10 minute waiting period for Bitcoin transactions. To obtain a masternode, users must deposit a total of 1,000 DASH. This had led to some debate about whether DASH is truly a decentralized currency or not.

Dash is less liquid than Bitcoin, meaning you may have a harder time executing large orders. However, the currency continues to be adopted by more exchanges every month. Dash's growth potential remains determined by its level of accessibility and adoption by the mass market. Once such example of this is BitCart, an Irish based discount gift card website which offers customers up to 20% discounts on Amazon purchases for payment in Dash.

Another interesting area in which Dash is utilized is the recent Venezuelan currency crisis. Venezuelan Cryptocurrency exchange CryptoBuyer began selling Dash as an alternative to the local Bolivar currency which was, and still is, suffering from hyperinflation. Venezuelans are seeking to protect their savings, and cryptocurrencies like Dash allow them to do this by holding value against the US dollar.

Another area to note is that the richest 10 DASH holders currently hold 10.1% of the total coin value, which is almost double that of Bitcoin and Bitcoin Cash. This could have an impact if one of these major players wanted to influence market movements.

Monero (XMR)

Price at time of writing - $43.22

Available on:

Fiat: Kraken, HitBTC, Bter (CN)

BTC: Poloniex, Bitfinex, Bittrex, Bitsquare

Monero allows users to send and receive funds WITHOUT a public transaction record available on the blockchain. All Monero transactions are private by default. If you believe in privacy first and foremost, then Monero ticks all the boxes. The currency is designed to be fully anonymous and untraceable. This goes as far as their development team, which unlike other coins has no public CEO or figurehead.

Monero also uses "ring signatures", a special type of cryptography to ensure untraceable transactions. This allows users to receive money, without being able to link the address to the sender. This could be looked at as both a positive or negative depending on your viewpoint regarding anonymity. The ring signatures also conceal the transaction amount, in addition to the identity of the buyer and seller. Unlike Dash, Monero has been open source from its inception, so anyone can view the software code for total transparency.

The anonymity of the currency has made it a favorite of the dark web. Before its shutdown, darknet market site AlphaBay had adopted Monero as well as BitCoin to process transactions. Everything from illegal drugs, weaponry and stolen credit cards were traded on the platform. Its anonymity has also made Monero a favorite among ransomware hackers.

It remains to be seen if Monero will branch out to more legitimate use, such as to conceal one's true net worth. Or if it will continue to be the favorite coin of more illicit industries, preventing it from mass adoption versus other coins. This uncertainty could be used to speculator's advantage as they seek to profit from mass adoption potential.

Litecoin (LTC)

Price at time of writing - $40.11

Fiat: Coinbase, Poloniex

BTC: Nearly all exchanges support BTC to LTC transactions

The original altcoin, Litecoin has represented unglamorous yet steady growth in a cryptocurrency scene fueled by hype and large boom/bust cycles. Because of this, many analysts have deemed it the "low risk coin". Announced in 2011 with the intention of being "silver to Bitcoin's gold" and rectifying the shortcomings that Bitcoin faced at the time. Litecoin's coin limit is 4x the amount of Bitcoin's at 84 million coins making it too, a deflationary currency, The time to create a block is 2.5 minutes, a quarter of Bitcoin's 10 minutes. Litecoin was the long standing second largest cryptocurrency by market capitalization before the rise of Ethereum in 2017.

Litecoin's ability to handle a higher volume of transactions due to its speed of block generation gives it a major advantage over Bitcoin. This means merchants can send and receive payments near instantly with zero transaction costs. Bitcoin on the other hand would take four times as long to process the same transaction at a higher cost. Litecoin also possesses one of the most active development teams in all of cryptocurrency, allowing the coin to undergo regular cutting edge upgrades such as being the first coin to adopt Segregated Witness (SegWit) technology. This also gives the coin the advantage of having the second most secure blockchain after Bitcoin itself.

Another advantage for would be investors is the uptake on major exchanges. Nearly all of the biggest cryptocurrency exchanges support Litecoin purchases in fiat currency including Coinbase in March 2017, which was great news for US and EU investors. In terms of market behavior, generally Bitcoin and Litecoin follow a similar pattern in terms of increases and decreases in the currency value. Many investors choose Litecoin as a supplementary option to Bitcoin in order to diversify their portfolio.

For those interesting in mining, Litecoin's algorithm is far simpler which makes the mining costs and barriers to entry lower. Litecoin runs on the Scrypt algorithm whereas Bitcoin runs on the SHA-256. The main significance of this in practical terms is a lower mining cost as Scrypt is less intensive on Graphic Processing Units (GPUs). In 2017, Bitcoin mining is no longer a viable option for the novice or home based miner, whereas Litecoin mining can still turn a profit, even when factoring in electricity costs in first world countries.

Litecoin's detractors have criticized the coin for being "just another Bitcoin with no innovation". The coin was also the victim of a Chinese pump and dump scheme in 2015 when investors accumulated 22% of all the coins in existence before dumping them.

Factom (FCT)

Price at time of writing - $19.71

Fiat: Coincheck (JP), Yuanbao (CN)

BTC: Poloniex, Bittrex

Like Ethereum, Factom expands on ways to use blockchain technology outside of just currency. While Ethereum is based on two way verification and ensuring contracts are unbreakable. Factom promises to do the same with large blocks of data by providing a record system that cannot be tampered with. This would allow businesses, governments to provide a track record of data without alteration or loss. The practical applications for this include legal applications, company accounts, medical records and even voting systems. Just imagine a world where it was physically impossible to rig an election, or where an accounting scandal like Enron couldn't happen again.

Like other projects utilizing blockchain, Factom cannot be altered because no single person runs the network. The network is collectively owned by millions of users, independently of each other. While data owned by one person is prone to malevolence, hacking, user error and alteration, the same is not possible with data owned by an entire network.

With regards to investing, like Ether is to Ethereum, Factoids are the "currency" of the Factom system. The more applications that are generated using Factom, the more these Factoids are worth.

Factom has already secured a deal with consulting firm iSoftStone to provide blockchain based administration software projects for cities in China. The deal includes plans for auditing and verification services.

Of the technology, Factom CEO Peter Kirby stated "We believe that this will help developers create a whole new class of accountable and tamper-proof business systems. This could be in insurance, financial services, medical records, or real estate – any system where record keeping is essential."

Like other blockchain technology, common questions surrounding Factom are ones of scalability and wider technology adoption. The other main drawback to Factom investing is whether the team can run the system at a consistent profit going forward - or whether the technology will lead to a race to the bottom in terms of price.

Neo (NEO)

Price at time of writing - $7.89

Available on:

Fiat: Yunbi (CN), Jubi (CN)

BTC: Bittrex, Binance

One of these earliest Chinese based blockchain projects, Neo, formely known as Antshares prides itself on being open source and community driven. The coin has been compared to Ethereum in the sense that it runs smart contracts instead of acting as a simple token like Bitcoin. The project is developed by a Shanghai based company called ONCHAIN.

In a June 2017 press conference held at the Microsoft China HQ in Beijing, the Antshares founder Da Hongfei announced the rebranding to Neo as well as some projects in the pipeline. These included collaborating with certificate authorities in China to map real-world assets using smart contracts.

Neo's base in China allows it unique access to the world's 2nd largest market and the largest cryptocurrency market which could be seen as a unique plus when compared to other cryptocurrencies. However current drawbacks include a limited number of wallets for the coin itself.

At the event - Srikanth Raju, GM, Developer Experience & Evangelism and Chief Evangelist, Greater China Region, Microsoft, said that ONCHAIN is "one of the top 50 startup companies in China." Support and positive press from a global powerhouse like Microsoft can only be a positive for Neo going forward.

Perhaps the biggest determining factor for NEO going forward is support from the Chinese government. While other cryptocurrencies suffer from legal battles with governments, Neo's relationship with the leadership has been low key if somewhat positive, with founder Da Hongfei attending government conferences and seminars on cryptocurrency and blockchain technology.

One thing to be wary of with Neo is once again, a Chinese factor. This time it's the language barrier, as much of the news about the coin is published in Chinese originally, there is significant potential for mistranslations in the English speaking world. For example, "partnerships" with Microsoft and Alibaba

(China's largest eCommerce company) have been overstated due to poor translations from Chinese news sources. That doesn't mean collaborations like this aren't possible in the future though.

The smart contracts running on Neo include equities, creditor claims, bills and currencies.

Update as of August 2017: NEO is currently trading at $51.99 - in just a few short weeks a price increased of over 500%

Golem (GNT)

Price at time of writing - $0.26

Available on:

Fiat: Yunbi (CN)

BTC: Poloniex, Bittrex, Liqui

Golen is a coin token, based on Ethereum blockchain technology. Described by some commentators as the "AirBNB of computing", the value of the coin is centered around the software that can be developed using it.

The founders of the Golem Project refer to it as a "supercomputer", with the ability to interconnect with other computers for various purposes. These include scientific research, data analysis and cryptocurrency mining. For example, if your computer has unused power, using the Golem network, you can rent that power (hence the AirBNB comparison) to someone else who needs it. The user who needs the extra power, has the ability to access supercomputer levels of processing power for a fraction of the cost of actually owning the processing power themselves.

The ability for users to earn money for their unused computing power is, in theory, a no-brainer, however what remains to be seen is the practical application of the technology. The Golem team's lack of marketing visibility also appears to hurt the coins value in recent times. The lack of ability to buy GNT using fiat currency (such as USD) is also a drawback for the mass market.

It should be noted that the technology is still very much in the early development stages and as of July 2017, the team are still looking for alpha testers for the project. The Golem Project has a very real possibility of petering out into nothing. On the flip side - there is tremendous potential for large future gains with the price of a coin still under $0.30.

STEEM (STEEM)

Price at time of writing - $1.10

Available on:

Fiat: OpenLedgerDEX (Eur)

BTC: Poloniex, Bittrex

Steem represents one of the more intriguing cryptocurrencies available on the market today. The currency itself is based on the social media platform Steemit. Users can publish content such as blog posts and long form articles, and this content is rewarded in the form of digital currency. Similar to how Reddit users receive upvotes, Steemit users receive Steem tokens known as Steem Dollars. The financial incentive ensures that users strive to produce quality content. The platform allows posts on a multitude of topics ranging from cryptocurrency discussion, to sports news and even poetry.

Steem dollars are worth the equivalent of $1 at the current exchange rate. They must be converted to Steem in order to exchange to fiat currency or other cryptocurrencies. The reasoning behind this is so they can be pegged to the value of the US dollar in order to decrease the risk of inflation devaluing them. Steemit goes further and actually gives users a 10% interest rate on any Steem dollars held in their account for more than a year.

The main drawback is that the success of the coin itself is based on the success of the platform. If the website reaches a plateau in traffic, so will the coin's value. Others have questioned the validity of the site itself, and whether it may be a large scale pump and dump or even a pyramid scheme. The criticism comes from the fact that many of the most upvoted posts were ones that promoted the Steemit platform itself. Concerns have also been raised with automatic posting bots stealing content in order to gain extra voters.

Creators of the site responded to the criticism by saying that there are certain safeguards in place designed to keep content fresh and give users an extra incentive to hold on to their Steem coins. Their way of doing this is with something known as Steem Power. Steem Power is a way for users to lock up their coins in the long run by directly investing them into the platform itself. By converting Steem to Steem Power, users have a greater weighting of upvotes on the platform and essentially become "power users" for lack of a better term.

One advantage Steem possesses versus other cryptocurrencies is that by design it is the easiest currency to access with zero investment. Instead of simply buying coins on an exchange, or spending money on computer hardware needed to mine coins, users can simply sign up on the website for free and begin posting content in order to gain coins. It represents the lowest barrier to entry for any asset in the cryptocurrency market. Although making significant gains may be tough initially, users have made thousands of dollars worth of Steem from just a single post.

IOTA (MIOTA)

Price at time of writing - $0.92

Available on:

Fiat: Bitfinex

BTC: Bitfinex

IOTA, or the rather uninspiringly named Internet of Things (IOT) Coin, is another coin based on blockchain technology, but with a twist.

The team behind IOTA is basing their hopes on a project known as Tangle, which is a technology currently in development that can be described as a blockchain without blocks. In theory, if Tangle does succeed, an entire network can be decentralized. This would lead to ZERO scalability problems that every other coin faces. To be frank, if the technology does indeed work - it could be a complete game changer for the cryptocurrency scene. In more practical terms, imagine a world without unnecessary middlemen, and think of the sheer cost-saving this would achieve.

The underlying theory behind the coin is near-zero transaction costs, even for transfers of minute amounts of money - something that no other coin or technology promises right now - not even giants like Bitcoin or Ethereum. By focusing on these micro, or nano payments, there are countless uses for both consumer and business based financial technology. The technology is open source, so anyone can see the code behind it, and follow along with the coin's development - if you are so inclined.

The reason for the low price of the coin as it currently stands, is that the technology is right now still firmly theoretical. Issues that plague all cryptocurrency technologies like mass adoption and security will have to be resolved before the coin can take the next step. The development team have many issues to overcome in just the construction of the technology, let alone the marketing.

Dogecoin (DOGE)

Price at time of writing - $0.0019

Available on:

Fiat: YoBit, BTC38 (CN)

BTC: HitBTC, Poloniex, Bittrex

A meme that ended up with actual monetary value. Favored by Shiba Inus worldwide, dogecoin was invented by Jackson Palmer in 2013 and became something of a fad in the cryptocurrency world.

Dogecoin's value largely comes from an internet form of "tipping". The most prominent example of this is holders donating Dogecoin to Reddit users for posts they enjoyed. Dogecoin eventually became the second most "tipped" cryptocurrency after Bitcoin and the market for Dogecoin exploded to a peak of $60million market cap in early 2014. A campaign to send the Jamaican bobsled team to the Winter Olympics was funded in part by the coin and $25,000 worth was donated to a UK service dog charity.

The coin flamed out almost as quickly as it rose after Dogecoin backed exchange Moolah filed for bankruptcy and CEO Ryan Kennedy aka Alex Green/Ryan Gentle was sentenced to 11 years in prison on sexual assault charges. Kennedy was estimated to have caused $2-4million dollars worth of losses for those who funded the project.

The coin's present day status remains that of a lighthearted, fun community based project that rewards forum posts. Dogecoin still possess one of the most active communities of any cryptocurrency and supporters hope that one day the coin will return to its position as one of the internet's most tipped coins.

Where to store your cryptocurrency - Wallets & Cold Storage

Once you've successfully bought some cryptocurrency, be it Bitcoin, Ethereum or another altcoin, you'll need somewhere to safely store it.

Your cryptocurrency wallet is akin to a regular fiat currency wallet in the sense that you can use it to store and spend money, in addition to seeing exactly how much money you have. However cryptocurrency wallets differ from fiat currency wallets because of the technology behind how the coins are generated. As a reminder, the way the technology works means your cryptocurrency isn't stored in one central location. It is stored within the blockchain. This means there is a public record of ownership for each coin, and when a transaction occurs, the record is updated.

You can store your cryptocurrency on the exchange where you bought it like Coinbase or Poloniex, it is advisable to not do this for a number of reasons.

1. Like any online entity - these exchanges are vulnerable to hacking, no matter how secure they are - or what security measures they take. This happened with the Mt. Gox exchange in June 2011

2. Your passwords to these exchanges are vulnerable to keyloggers, trojan horses and other computer virus type programs

3. You could accidentally authorize a login from a malicious service like coinbose.com (example) instead of coinbase.com

Cold storage refers to any system that takes your cryptocurrency offline. These include offline paper wallets, physical bearer items like physical bitcoin or a USB drive. We will examine the pros and cons of each one.

Cryptocurrency wallets have two keys. A public one, and a private one. These are represented by long character strings. For example, a public key could be

02a1633cafcc01ebfb6d78e39f687a1f0995c62fc95f51ead10a02ee0be551b5dc[4] - or it could be shown as a QR code. Your public key is the address you use to receive cryptocurrency from others. It is perfectly safe to give your public key to anyone. Those who have access to you public key can only deposit money in your account.

On the other hand, your private key is what enables you to send cryptocurrency to others. For every transaction, the recipient's public key, and the sender's private key are used.

It is advisable to have an offline backup of your private key in case of hardware failure, or data theft. If anyone has access to your private key, they can withdraw funds from your account, which leads us to the number one rule of cryptocurrency storage.

The number one rule of Cryptocurrency storage: Never give anyone your private key. Ever.

---

[4] This is not a real wallet address, do not send money to it

Paper Wallets:

Paper wallets are simply notes of your private key that are written down on paper. They will often feature QR codes so the sender can quickly scan them to send cryptocurrency.

Pros:

- Cheap

- Your private keys are not stored digitally, and are therefore not subject to cyber-attacks or hardware failures.

Cons:

- Loss of paper due to human error

- Paper is fragile and can degrade quickly in certain environments

- Not easy to spend cryptocurrency quickly if necessary - not useful for everyday transactions

Recommendations:

It is recommended you store your paper wallet in a sealed plastic bag to protect against water or damp conditions. If you are holding cryptocurrency for the long-term, store the paper inside a safe.

Ensure you read and understand the step-by-step instructions before printing any paper wallets.

Bitcoin:

http://bitaddress.org

http://bitcoinpaperwallet.com

Ethereum:

http://myetherwallet.com/

Litecoin: https://liteaddress.org/

Hardware Wallets

Hardware wallet refer to physical storage items that contain your private key. The most common form of these are encrypted USB sticks.

These wallets use two factor authentication or 2FA to ensure that only the wallet owner can access the data. For example, one factor is the physical USB stick plugged into your computer, and the other would be a 4 digit pin code - much like how you use a debit card to withdraw money from an ATM.

Pros:

- Near impossible to hack - as of the time of writing, there have been ZERO instances of hacked hardware wallets

- Even if your computer is infected with a virus or malware, the wallet cannot be accessed due to 2FA

- The private key never leaves your device or transfers to a computer, so once again, malware or infected computers are not an issue

- Can be carried with you easily if you need to spend your cryptocurrency

- Transactions are easier than with paper wallets

- Can store multiple addresses on one device

- For the gadget lovers among you - they look a lot cooler than a folded piece of paper

Cons:

- More expensive than paper wallets - starting at around $60

- Susceptible to hardware damage, degradation and changes in technology

- Different wallets support different cryptocurrencies

- Trusting the provider to deliver an unused wallet. Using a second hand wallet is a big security breach. Only purchase hardware wallets from official sources.

The most popular of these are the Trezor and Ledger wallets. For altcoins that are not supported by these wallet, you can create your own encrypted USB wallet by following online tutorials.

Cryptocurrency Investing Mindset

FOMO & FUD - 2 Terms to be Cautious of

In cryptocurrency terms, FOMO and FUD are two of the most potentially dangerous words in an investor's lexicon. No, they aren't the latest hotshot coins coming out of China, they are acronyms that have cost naive traders and investors money.

FOMO - Fear Of Missing Out

Fear of missing out causes people to over invest and throw money at coins without proper research or due diligence. If you spend any time on cryptocurrency forums, you will see hundreds of posts from those new to the market asking for tips on which coins to buy. It seems like every day there is a new shiny object that people are hyping up, causing less experienced investors to blindly throw their money at it. This leads to people buying coins at their peak, and then panic selling them when the coin pulls back a few days later.

The important thing to remember is this, you won't be able to win on every investment you make. You won't be able to buy every single coin at the right time, and people will make money where you cannot. The important thing is to only measure yourself against yourself, and take stock of your own profit/loss sheet. Before you invest in a coin, take a second to ask yourself why you are choosing to do so, and re-examine the fundamentals of the coin itself.

Anxiety caused by potentially missing out on huge returns is only natural, and something that nearly all of us suffer from. The best way to combat this is to understand blockchain technology, and to research each coin individually before deciding to invest. By making smart, reasoned investments, you have a much better chance of long term profits.

FUD - Fear, Uncertainty and Doubt

Fear, uncertainty and doubt is information to dissuade investors from believing in cryptocurrencies and their applications. This can be anything from spreading of misinformation (such as the fake Vitalik Buterin death rumors), to news reports discounting real world usage of cryptocurrency technology.

Certain nefarious cryptocurrency figures have used FUD to push their own agenda while attempting to harm the growth of other coins. This is where it is important to differentiate from reasonable criticism and analysis of a coin vs. FUD. The more informed you are, the easier it is for you to see the difference.

Where you are getting your news from is another factor. Social media is the king of FUD, go to any crypto group on Facebook or watch a YouTube video from one of the larger channels and you will see commentors spreading FUD on every video. Instead, focus on larger crypto news websites where FUD is less prevalent, and remember to consume your news from more than one source.

Short term gain vs. Long term investment

Billionaire hedge fund manager and cryptocurrency investor Michael Novogratz made a very good analogy when he compared the current state of the market to the third inning of a baseball game. The market is still very much developing, and there are a number of short and long term events that can effect the price of currencies.

Unlike regular stock market, the cryptocurrency market is running 24/7 365 - there are no delays between information coming to light and the market reacting, there is no dead time.

If you believe in the technology behind the currencies, then these coins absolutely make sense as a long term investment. With many coins, time in the market beats timing the market, which is where our next acronym comes from.

HODL: Hold On (For) Dear Life

A backronym that is a play on "hold" - it focuses on holding on to your coins even when the market is dropping.

A more lighthearted explanation comes from Bitcointalk forum poster "GameKyuubi" who inadvertently invented the term in 2013 while inebriated (author's note: Do not trade or purchase cryptocurrency under the influence)

"WHY AM I HOLDING? I'LL TELL YOU WHY. It's because I'm a bad trader and I KNOW I'M A BAD TRADER. I SHOULD HAVE SOLD MOMENTS BEFORE EVERY SELL AND BOUGHT MOMENTS BEFORE EVERY BUY BUT YOU KNOW WHAT NOT EVERYBODY IS AS COOL AS YOU. "

With any long term investment, you are going to see market downturns - that's simply how capitalism works. If you panic and sell every time you see a slight dip (and with cryptocurrencies, that's going to happen A LOT), then you've got a surefire way to lose money in the long run.

HODL'ing of course has its potential downsides as well, with more and more coins coming to market - it's obvious that not all of them will continue to go up in price. You can compare it to the regular stock market with blue chip stocks and penny stocks. Just because a penny stock or small market cap cryptocurrency is currently trading for $0.08, does not mean it has the right to rise indefinitely. If the company or people behind the cryptocurrency don't fulfill their promises to the market, then the coin's value will crash and it will eventually become obsolete.

Remember - hindsight is easy. Timing market movements in a market as volatile as cryptocurrencies on the other hand, is not. Approach each investment with caution, and proper research.

Paper profits vs. Actual profits

Remember, until you have sold your coins, any profit you have made is strictly on paper. With the cryptocurrency market being as volatile as it is, profit margins drastically shift and can do so on a daily, or even an hourly basis. That is why I recommend taking intermediate profits for yourself when investing, you do this by sell a proportion of your holdings at a profit.

For example, you buy 1 coin at $100, 1 month later the coin's value has risen to $150. If you trade out $75 worth of the coin at $150, then you still have 0.5 coins worth $75 on paper and an extra $75 in cold, hard cash. Taking money for yourself is a smart play, and something you should absolutely do if you are looking to make consistent profits over time.

The inverse rule of this is to not sell on the dip. If you followed rule number one of investing which was to not invest more than you could afford to lose, you have zero reason to sell at a loss. Yes, you may see scary headlines with "Ethereum drops 40%" or "Litecoin is crashing", but in the long-run, the majority of these coins return to their previous, and even higher levels. If you sell at a loss, then your money is gone forever.

The Chaincoin Pump and Dump Scheme - Why You Should Always Research a Coin Before Buying

The following is a lesson in smart investing, and who you get your information from.

Chaincoin (CHC) was a cryptocurrency that underwent a meteoric prise rise from $0.05 to over $6 in under a week. Prior to this, the coin was only available on two small cryptocurrency exchanges and had very little total trading volume. The official Github (programming community) and Twitter accounts had been dead for months prior to this, and very few technical milestones had been accomplished.

Despite this, a YouTube channel known as HighOnCoins started heavily promoting the coin. Videos titled "Buy ChainCoin $CHC" appeared on the channel. The channel also encouraged users to set up masternodes (which required 1000 CHC). The channel encouraged people to buy and hold indefinitely rather than trading out for a profit. The underlying theory behind this was that if everyone invested and held the coin, then the price would continue to increase and grow.

However Chaincoin suffered from many fundamental flaws including:

- Lack of differentiation from other coins

- Lack of innovation from developers

- Zero real world applications versus other coins

The initial surge in investing caused a stir in the cryptocurrency community. Mixed reactions ranging from confusion from investors focused on coin fundamentals, to excitement from uninformed players who believed they were about to get rich quick.

The coin reached an all time high of $6.81 on July 14th 2017, a few days later, developers returned to the coin's GitHub page and made a couple of superficial changes. Within 5 days the price of the coin crashed back to $1. HighOnCoins claimed this was as a result of hackers, although exchange activity showed a large dumping of coins from a few traders.

Chaincoin currently trades at $0.32.

GitHub blog Store of Value summarized the incident with the following statement "This was a blatant transfer of wealth from the foolish to the nefarious." Let this be a lesson, never invest in a coin based on hype. Instead, do so on fundamentals and belief in the technology.

Conclusion

I hope you have learned many things about cryptocurrency and how you can profit from investing or trading in these coins. There are various factors to consider when investing in coins and you can use these to decide on an investing or trading strategy.

You may want to read this material one or two more times, and make some choices as to what your goals are for your relationship with the cryptocurrency market.

Next, decide how you will go about reaching those goals. Decide on a cryptocurrency exchange and how you will store your assets BEFORE investing in any one or more coins.

Then plan out how much you will invest in each coin. Remember, diversity is important and you should never have all of your long-term holdings in a single coin.

If you are going to buy cryptocurrencies, do so using Dollar cost averaging – this means that you don't buy all of your coins in one trade but instead buy a fixed amount every month, week or even day throughout the year. This allows you to not be tied to a single price and instead average out your investments so they are less exposed to volatile price movements.

Trade rationally, not emotionally. If you plan on holding coins for the long-term, do not check charts every few hours, or you will drive yourself crazy. Things change quickly in this market so stay informed on cryptocurrency news and happenings, you can do this in less than 30 minutes per day. Ensure you consume information from a variety of non-biased sources.

And never invest in a coin because "some guy on the internet" told you to.

Finally, if you found this book useful, I would greatly appreciate it if you would review this book on Amazon.

Thank you for reading, I hope you make A LOT of money in the cryptocurrency market.

Blockchain Beginners Bible:

Discover How Blockchain Could Enrich Your Life, Your

Business & Your Cryptocurrency Wallet

By Stephen Satoshi

Introduction

Hi, I'm Stephen and I'm a blockchain addict.

Well, enthusiast is probably a better term - although I still definitely check my cryptocurrency portfolio far too frequently.

I've certainly come a long way from the young man who first heard about this Bitcoin thing back in the 2010s. You know, that new internet currency that people were making money from.

How could a currency be worth anything if it isn't backed by a central government? Oh, how naive I was.

This initial exposure to Bitcoin sparked an interest in blockchain technology and it's potential. I try to refrain from hyperbole but I truly believe this is mankind's greatest invention since Tim Berners-Lee invented the world wide web back in 1989.

You see, although Bitcoin and cryptocurrency in general is a large part of the blockchain movement, it goes beyond that.

There are serious political, social and economic ramifications that will come as a result of decentralization. An incorruptible permanent record, accessible by the masses, has a myriad of uses that can undoubtedly benefit society as a whole.

If you're reading this book, you're mostly likely a skeptic of big government, and you have every right to be. As recently as 2016, we witnessed a United States General Election in which both sides accused the other of vote tampering, in what is supposedly the world's leading democracy.

In short, governance as we know it has to be questioned.

Blockchain technology allows for indisputable trust on a level such as this. Banks, governments, hospitals, all the way down to small one-man-operation businesses can benefit.

That is the true future of this technology.

I hope this is just the start of your blockchain journey, and I hope it not only makes you a lot of money, I hope it enriches the quality of your life.

Chapter 1: What is Blockchain Technology?

Over the past few years, you have likely heard more and more people talking about cryptocurrency this, or blockchain that. If you don't understand these terms, don't worry, you aren't alone. It may be time to jump on the bandwagon, however, as blockchain use is rapidly approaching consumer status with IBM estimating that 15 percent of banks will already be using blockchain technology by the end of 2017.

Simply put, blockchain is the foundation that makes technologies like cryptocurrency possible. On a fundamental level, a blockchain takes data, primarily of financial nature for now, and replicates that data across a vast number of decentralized nodes that could conceivably be spread around the entire world. This process is run not by a centralized network or body, but by a peer-to-peer approach that uses cryptography and digital signatures to keep things running smoothly.

Each new block in a chain contains information regarding various transactions, and possibly what are known as smart contracts, as well as information that links it to the blocks around it. Each block is also timestamped which helps the chain determine its place in the whole thing. The transactions in individual blocks are verified by block miners, third parties who are paid for their work, and are only then added to the chain as a whole.

What miners are actually doing is solving what are known as proof-of-work systems which means they are solving complicated mathematical equations using specialized equipment designed for doing so. The equations prevent security breaches through denial of service attacks and keep things running smoothly. The amount of reward for this type of work varies based on the cryptocurrency that is being mined, as well as the number of people working to complete the block they were chosen to mine. Most cryptocurrencies also charge a small transaction fee, and a part of that fee goes to the miners as well.

Despite the fact that the database information is spread around the world with no central authority, and the fact that sections of it are inspected by third parties on a regular basis, the data that is stored in a blockchain remains incredibly secure. This level of security doesn't come from an active offense against fraud, it comes from the defensive capabilities of the way in which the blockchain is constructed.

If a specific transaction that is being transferred from a node doesn't match up with what the other nodes are saying then that block is discarded in favor of a more accurate one. Essentially, for a false block to make it past the blockchain's defenses, it would need to show up on 51 percent of all of the nodes in the system at the same time. The difficulty of such a task means that it could be done, but the costs involved would more than outweigh the potential reward for doing so.

History lesson

In order to understand the true importance of blockchain technology, it is helpful to understand a little bit about its history. In 2008, a person or a group of persons using the alias Satoshi Nakamoto put forth a whitepaper on the idea of a digital currency that would allow individuals to transfer money to one another in a largely anonymous fashion. This paper, titled, *bitcoin: A Peer-to Peer Electronic Cash System,* was soon followed by the original blockchain and bitcoin code from the same alias. The code was released in an open source fashion, and the Nakamoto name faded from sight as other developers began working on the code in earnest.

The Nakamoto alias was also the first person to distribute bitcoins and then verify the transaction, receiving 50 bitcoins for doing so. For those who are considering investing in a cryptocurrency based on blockchain technology, take note, as the first use of those bitcoins was to trade 10,000 of them for a pair of large pizzas which made each worth about $.002. If you weren't aware, they are doing a little better than that these days with each bitcoin being worth nearly $5,000 as of September 2017.

By 2014, blockchain usage was gaining some traction and a new and improved version of the original code now allowed for entire programs to be contained in blocks along with data that make it possible for a wide variety of tasks to be carried out from within the blockchain. In 2016, the Russian Federation started working on a blockchain program as a means of collecting royalties for copyrighted material, making Russia the first country to official announce a blockchain project, though since that time a number of other countries, including China and the US, have indicated they are working on blockchain projects of their own. When the project was announced, the Russian Economic Minister was quoted as saying that blockchain technology was likely the most important new technology since the invention of the internet.

Over the past few years, another blockchain based company, the Ethereum platform has been gaining a lot of support due to its wide variety of enhanced capabilities when compared to the bitcoin blockchain. The Ethereum platform has its own official cryptocurrency, ether (although the two terms are used interchanably by many commentators), and is also home to an ecosystem of other cryptocurrencies that other programmers have made to run in its framework. It is also home to a wide variety of smart contracts and apps that run on "gas", which is essentially a transaction fee the platform collects for each transaction. Ether blocks that are mind tend to be completed in a shorter timeframe than bitcoin blocks and the Ethereum chain can handle a great many more blocks at a time when compared to the bitcoin chain.

Database differences: The biggest difference between a blockchain database and a traditional database is the level of centralization that is required in order for it to run effectively. Even if a traditional server is decentralized, the core components are going to be arranged as close to one another as possible to facilitate the transfer of information. Instead, blockchains are formed of nodes that are separated by thousands of miles, each communicating with the others through a best use model that means they naturally seek out the nodes that are closest to them and the information spreads out from there.

The fact that mass collaboration and the blockchain code results in a reliable means by which funds can be transferred is a game changer. Blockchain is the first innately digital medium where value can be transferred, in much the way the internet allowed for information to be transmitted digitally.

Hashes: A hash is a mathematical function that makes up a crucial part of the blockchain security matrix. This is the function that ensures the data that is added to a blockchain remains secure regardless of who might get their hands on it. The function encrypts the data in such a way that it becomes a fixed length output, which can be thought of as a type of digital fingerprint. When it comes to blockchain security the most commonly used hash function is SHA-256. SHA-256 is used by cryptocurrencies such as Bitcoin, Omni and Zetacoin.

The hash function for every block is going to be different, which means that if that data is altered by a malevolent third party then the entire fingerprint would be rearranged in unpredictable ways. Additional hash information is added once the block is added to the chain as a whole. This process is repeated throughout the blockchain each time a new block is added so that it is always changing.

Merkle trees: Hashes are then used by a process known as the Merkle tree which is a quick and easy way for the blockchain to verify all of its data once a new block has been added. Each hash is unique and created based on the data it contains which means the Merkle tree then essentially needs to scan the hash, compare it to the root hashes which is the ultimate collection of all the hashes, and then determine if everything lines up as it should. Each time it does this, it creates a pair of roots, one where the data is correct and one where it is not, this way it keeps the core details of the blockchain intact against malicious changes.

Chapter 2: Practical Application of Blockchain Technology

As blockchain technology continues to grow in popularity, the ways in which it can be put to use are growing as well. What follows are a number of different ways blockchain technology is sure to change how business is conducted, day to day life, outside the realm of cryptocurrency and how governments and lawmakers interact with the public.

Business uses

Money transfers and payments: While blockchain technology is already synonymous with cryptocurrency payments, the fact of the matter is that more can be done in that space to facilitate the needs of businesses when it comes to utilizing blockchain to its fullest potential. The Ethereum Enterprise Alliance is a group of major corporations such as Microsoft, JP Morgan and Samsung that are working together to build a blockchain that is based on Ethereum technology but also contains the level of control that businesses would need in order to use the technology on a regular basis.

This type of service, while extremely common in some parts of the world, are extremely hard to come by in others. As such, more people in Kenya currently have a bitcoin wallet than have indoor plumbing. Connecting all these new individuals to the internet is going to have serious positive ramifications for retailers worldwide.

Notary services: Blockchain technology is constructed in such a way that it could conceivably be used to replace traditional notary services. There are already numerous different apps available that allow for notarization of a variety of different types of content.

Cloud storage: Blockchain technology is already being used as a means of connecting users with cloud storage space in an Airbnb like setup. Using this system those with spare storage space on their hard drives can rent out the extra space to those who are in need of extra storage. The estimate is that worldwide spending has reached more than $20 billion for cloud storage so this could be a profitable opportunity if this catches on.

Fraud: Blockchain technology has the potential to increase the efficacy of tracking identities online in a way that is both efficient and secure. Blockchain is uniquely situated to solve this problem because its results are sure to be properly authenticated, immutable, secure and irrefutable. This improved system will do away with complicated password or dual factor authentication systems in favor of a system that will ultimately use digital signatures and cryptography to keep everyone safe and efficiently catalogued.

Using this type of system, the transaction will be processed as normal, and the only check that will be required is if the account from which the funds are drawn, matches the account of the person who authorized the transaction. A variation of this same usage of the technology can also be used when it comes to birth certificates, passports, residency forms, account logins and physical identification. There are already apps available that utilize a blockchain to verify the identity of users from a mobile device.

Supply chain communication: If it is one thing that companies have a hard time dealing with, it is the extreme level of communication that is required in order to ensure that they have all the requirements at the ready to ensure they are ready to do whatever it is they do. Blockchain technology allows for companies to easily track products from door to door, with the internet of things (the ability for everyday objects to send and receive data) connecting shipping containers to accounts that get a steady stream of details about the product in question as it crosses various thresholds and ultimately automatically pays for the goods once they have reached their final location. SkuChain and Provenance are two companies that are working to create these types of systems.

Gift cards: Gift cards are a good idea in theory that ultimately falls apart in practice when it comes time for the customer to actually hold onto the card in question. Blockchain technology has the potential to change all that by connecting customer loyalty products directly to a blockchain which can then verify and update relevant information as needed. Gyft Block is a company that already has a digital gift card up and running on the bitcoin blockchain that can be traded just like a cryptocurrency.

Internet of things: Samsung and IBM are currently working together on a concept referred to as the Autonomous Decentralized Peer-to-Peer Telemetry or ADEPT, which uses blockchain as a means of creating a system that mixes proof of stake and proof of work systems to better secure transactions. Essentially, what they are trying to do is to create a blockchain that would act like a public ledger for a wide number of devices. This public ledger would then serve as a hub which can create a bridge between devices for a very low cost. These devices could then communicate with one another in a practically autonomous fashion, making it easy to save energy, sort out bugs and issue updates.

Insurance contracts: Smart contracts have the possibility to reinvent insurance in a big way. Rather than deal with insurance agents who have to determine liability in case of a business-related injury, a blockchain would be able to make use of a smart contract that issues payments if a specific interconnected item registers a faulty signal. Blockchain would then allow for a more streamlined claim process that would improve the customer experience and ultimately save the company money.

Funding: 4G Capital is a company that provides access to credit for small businesses in Africa through the use of a decentralized app that is running off of the Ethereum blockchain. Donors are able to use the app to spend their cryptocurrency funds directly to the recipient of their choice. The money is then converted to the currency of the applicant and dispersed using a proprietary transaction system. In addition to providing 100 percent unsecured loans to those who often would not be able to get them otherwise, it also provides business training and consulting services. While currently operating in a limited capacity, if it proves successful more operations offering this type of funding are sure to appear.

Microblogging: Businesses are always looking for new ways to interact with their target audience and blockchain may be the next new frontier. Projects like Eth-Tweet offer decentralized microblogging services through the Ethereum blockchain. The service operates much like Twitter, except that as a truly decentralized entity there is no one who can pressure users to take content down and no one can remove messages after they have been added to the chain.

Day to Day Life

Healthcare: Real world tests are already being done that link individuals to their healthcare status as they are going through a hospital. Early studies from the MIT Media Lab show that this practice can decrease errors by up to 30 percent in nonemergency situations. This is a huge step forward for hospitals that are often not designed for the volume and range of data that is being created these days. Patient data can even continue to be gathered on an outpatient basis or if the individual has agreed to be part of a test group. Payment for these tests could then be issued automatically once the required data has been successfully gathered.

Internet decentralization: With the rise of Google, the internet is a much more centralized place than it once was. A startup by the name of Blockstack is working to change all of that. It is on track to release prototype software in the second half of 2017 which will make it possible for anyone to utilize blockchain technology to access a version of the internet where you have much more control over your personal data. This decentralized internet will act the same way the traditional internet does, except that instead of creating a different account for every website, the process will reverse and you will create a primary account, then give certain sites access to it.

If you are then finished using a specific site you can then completely revoke its access to your data at any time. While this might seem like a small step, it is actually a giant leap for a new and improved internet. Blockstack makes use of a digital ledger to track usernames and various levels of encryption, with the end result being a greater degree of privacy control for the individual user. The blockchain will also keep track of domain names as well, potentially making ICANN, the web domain oversight body, obsolete. Microsoft is already in talks with Blockstack to make use of its technology.

While the way it handles web functions might seem extreme, it is actually the low-level features of the internet as a whole that have led to the dominance of corporations who essentially have free reign to treat user data as they see fit. The new platform will still offer companies ways to make money while providing services, the balance of power is just going to favor the consumer more than it does now.

Improved property rights: Both tangible and intangible property from cars and houses on one hand to company shares and patents on the other, can all be connected via smart contract and blockchain technology to make determining the rights to these items much less complicated than it currently is. These details could be stored in a type of decentralized ledger along with related contractual details regarding the true ownership of the property in question. The technology could even extend to smart keys which could then give specific users access to specific property.

The ledger would keep track of the finer details and activate specific keys as needed. In this case the decentralized ledger is also a system for managing and recording property rights and also creating duplicates if smart keys are lost. Implementing smart property protocols will help to decrease the average property owner's risk of fraud, questionable business deals and mediation fees.

New types of money lenders: With blockchain technology making it easier and easier to transfer funds between individuals, new types of hard money lenders are already popping up to take advantage of the fact. Hard money lenders are more likely to offer terms to individuals who already have subpar credit, unfortunately the terms are often quite high and often property is listed as collateral. This, in turn, causes many debtors to default on loans, and leaves them in a worse position than they were in initially. Lending via blockchain technology has the potential to change all of that as the binding nature of the transaction means that less collateral will be required and smart contracts can take care of the transactions themselves so costs will be decreased as well.

Smarter smartphones: Smartphones already operate on a type of cryptography in that they require either your fingerprint, a scan of your face, or a password in order to activate them. This is already a form of smart property, just in its nascent stages. This facet of personal technology will be enhanced via blockchain technology in that, rather than having these details tied to your physical SIM card, they will be stored in the blockchain where you can easily access them no matter where you are. While issues concerning security would typically arise in these sorts of situations, the fact that each transaction needs to be verified in order to add it to the chain ensures security remains tight.

Passports: Blockchains have been helping people manage their passports since at least 2014 by making it easier for users to identify themselves regardless if they are online or offline. This system works by taking a picture of the user and encoding it with a private key as well as a public one. The passport is then stored in a public ledger which can be accessed via a blockchain address by the person who has the key.

Important documents: It doesn't matter if it is a wedding certificate, birth certificate or death certificate, all of these documents confer various rights or privileges. This would be less of an issue if it weren't for the fact that the physical systems that keep track of these details are prone to mistakes. In fact, according to UNICEF, as many as 30 percent of all children who are below the age of five do not have a birth certificate. Implementing a public blockchain to streamline this process would not only make keeping track of these services more manageable, it will make these documents easier to obtain as well.

Identification: Currently you have to carry your driver's license, your work identification card, your social security card, the list goes on and on. With the right blockchain, however, all of this could be a thing of the past. Eventually everyone is going to have a digital ID that goes with them everywhere. It will be connected to a worldwide protected ledger and it will contain all the basic details you now need to carry around with you.

Improve digital interactions: With a wider and wider variety of interactions being initiated online, it is often difficult to know whom you can trust. Blockchain can alleviate that problem by storing a version of your identity in a blockchain that is available for everyone to see. It would automatically pull in things like review scores and rankings from a wide variety of sites so you always have at least a general idea of what you are in for before taking an online interaction into the real world. Unlike with more traditional types of social media, users would not have the ability to remove their information and start fresh, once it is in the blockchain it would be there forever.

Change the way you fuel your vehicle: Modern electric vehicles have already made great strides when it comes to the fueling process. Another important stride is on the horizon and it has to do with blockchain. Soon blockchain technology will be able to track the electricity that a given owner uses and automatically deduct the funds from the relevant account. All the owner would need to do is pull up to the charging station, the blockchain will take care of the rest.

Beyond Cryptocurrency

Fund HIV research: The UBS bank recently donated a platform to Finclusion systems that will launch a smart contract called HealBond which will seek out efficient trades on the bonds market so that the funds that it makes can ultimately be put to use for HIV research. Analysts are confident that with the right level of passive strategy it could start making money right away. If this proves successful then it will give those with the resources to do so even more ways to help out their favorite causes.

Data security: The company Factom is turning its focus to properly securing data. Currently it is working with the country of Honduras to more accurately register land and also with a number of cities in China on what are known as Smart Cities. Blockchain technology is looking to an integral tool in getting all the various different systems communicating with one another on the same level. This includes things like data notarization services as well as information management with a much higher level of integrity than what is currently available to the public. Factom has also already received funding from the US Department of Homeland Security, specifically the Technology and Science Directorate to work on the Blockchain Software to Prove Integrity of Captured Data project.

Decentralize the power grid: Rather than requiring a centralized power provider that is in charge of sending energy to workplaces and homes, a decentralized blockchain could be built to allow people to generate power through solar and other means and then sell what they don't need on an open market. All of these transactions would then be visible on the blockchain, keeping fraud to a minimum. As more and more individuals are purchasing high-capacity batteries along with solar panels for their rooftops, this type of scenario is fast becoming a realistic possibility.

Track things that are difficult to track: The fact that a blockchain can show up at any time and cannot be altered makes it uniquely qualified to track the types of items that always seem to go missing. For example, the company Everledger is currently working on a way to identify specific objects and then determine whether or not they are legitimate. So far, they have created a distributed ledger that follows various diamond transaction verifications including law enforcement agencies, claimants, insurance companies and owners to put together a mine to store view of each diamond. The system is useful in that it keeps the supply chain honest and also makes it easier for individual buyers to determine if a given diamond is right for them. Furthermore, smart contracts make it possible for the diamond transactions to clearly be paid for while also tracking them, guaranteeing to consumers that they are not purchasing blood diamonds.

Getting artists what they deserve: Rather than having to worry about making sure their music isn't used without generating compensation, with blockchain, musicians will soon be able to determine who used each song and for what, with each individual transaction being carried out via smart contracts through a blockchain platform. What's more, rather than having to wait for funds to hit a specific level, or for someone, somewhere, to cut a check, these funds would be distributed in relatively real time. This same process can be applied to music licensing as a whole which means it will eventually be possible to cut out middlemen from the equation entirely. This, in turn, means a decrease in costs to the consumer and an increase in profit for the musicians as it means people are more likely to pay for content again.

Improved communication: Currently if your vehicle receives a safety recall then the maker of the vehicle sends out a notice to all of its licensed sales outlets and each of these outlets then reaches out to its customers who have purchased the vehicle in question. This information then may or may not reach you, allowing you to then make an informed decision based on the details you have available to you. The recall could be for something major, or something inconsequential, but regardless you are certainly going to want to know about it. Placing all of this information onto a blockchain would dramatically simplify the process as after the defect was found, the chain could automatically notify the owners in question.

Clarifying asset lifecycles: It doesn't matter who you are or what you do, you have certain tools that make your life possible. Blockchain technology has the ability to make sure you know as much about them as you need to when combined with the internet of things. Asset lifecycle is important for everyone from home business owners to multinational corporations, and the information provided by this type of blockchain could literally save lives. For example, think about an airplane which is likely to have several different owners during its time in the air. This type of blockchain would make it possible for every owner to understand every part on their airplane more completely and to ensure that proper maintenance has been completed throughout its lifetime.

Tracking the food chain: An increase in the ready availability of blockchain technology means that slowly but surely concerns about the quality of the food that you consume on a regular basis will be put to rest. Regardless of the final state of the product when you purchase it, you should be able to see the entire route it took to get to your table. Not just the completed product either, everything that went into the construction of the completed whole. This is particularly useful as there may be more to the traditional food chain than you might first realize. For example, a farm could produce vegetables that head to a processing facility before ending up in a distribution center before being purchased and run through another processing facility, all to end up in a can of tomato soup.

Change the value of ownership: The company Slock.it is based on the Ethereum platform and runs a blockchain for what is known as the Universal Share Network, this network is an opensource marketplace where anyone can go to list their unused asset, regardless if it is machinery, shipping containers, office space and more. It is a sort of automated AirBnB that works for anything and everything, not just temporary living arrangements. The fundamentals of blockchain technology are then passed on to tangible, real world assets.

Transportation: A variation in the trend towards the crowdsourcing of ridesharing applications, La'Zooz is a decentralized transportation platform that is owned by its users who use blockchain technology to organize and optimize a variety of smart transportation solutions.

Government and lawmakers

Everywhere around the world, government organizations are rapidly exploring the many possibilities provided by blockchain and distributed ledger technology. The ability to suddenly be able to record and distribute ledger information easily and securely has created a market for a variety of new governmental approaches when it comes to establishing trust, preventing fraud and improving transparency.

From a recent survey from the Economic Intelligence Unit as well as IBM, it is clear that the interest in blockchain technology from various worldwide governments is quite high. In fact, as many as 9 out of 10 government agencies are already planning on investing in blockchain based contract management, asset management, regulatory compliance and transaction management by 2018. Meanwhile 7 of the 10 predict blockchain is going to significantly change the way that contract management is handled. Finally, nearly 20 percent say that they expect to have a blockchain plan up and running before the end of 2017.

Voting: As recently as the 2016 United States general election, both Republicans and Democrats could be heard questioning the security of the existing voting system. Likewise, the 2000 presidential election proved that the way that votes are tallied is remarkably out of date. While concerns about hacking have limited the acceptance of electronic means of voting so far, blockchain technology could easily put those fears to rest. A decentralized public ledger would naturally be encrypted but specific individuals could still confirm their votes were counted accurately. This system would not only be more efficient, but it would be more cost effective, and clearly more secure as well.

Responsive, open data: The blockchain ledger would also create a platform for what is known as responsive, open data. Studies show that this type of freely accessible data is likely to bring in nearly $3 trillion worldwide within the first year. Startups will be able to utilize this data to help get ahead of fraudulent activity, parents would be able to access details about the medications their children are receiving, the list is literally endless. Currently, this type of data is only available via limited, government approved windows which are not designed to put citizens first. As a blockchain is a type of public ledger, citizens would be able to access its data at any time and place.

Self-management: Blockchain provides the opportunity for governmental agencies to self-manage more easily as the exchange of information on a global scale would be greatly improved overall. There would be a great deal more trust as well because the information in the blockchain would be public for everyone to see.

Reducing administration costs: If property records were recorded to a blockchain then prospective buyers could more easily, quickly and cost effectively verify ownership information. This process is currently still done manually which means government agencies spend hundreds of thousands of dollars per year paying individuals who do this type of job. Manually verifying such things can also lead to an increased number of errors which helps to further increase potential costs.

It would also greatly decrease the amount of manual effort which would be required on the banks' end as they would have to do much less work when it comes to title insurance. Title insurance is required by lenders as a means to protect their interests. This, in turn, would decrease prices for homebuyers who are refinancing or buying for the first time because they would have to pay less throughout the entire process as the amount of labor would be reduced significantly.

Decrease money laundering: If identity data was readily store on a blockchain, the government agencies could more easily keep track of those who are moving large amounts of money from one place to another. Financial organizations could scan the details of every new client and that information could then be passed along to appropriate agencies if a need presented itself. Furthermore, storing payment and account information in a blockchain would go a long way to standardize the type of information required for an account. This, in turn, will help to improve the quality of the data that is gathered and reduce the number of legitimate transactions that are falsely listed as fraudulent. Finally, having a record that was known to be tamper-proof would make it easier for these organizations to comply with AML regulations.

Ensuring taxpayers are paying up: The Federal Government is likely already working on its own form of cryptocurrency, so there is no reason to assume they are not already working on a means of linking a blockchain to the current IRS system. This blockchain would not only record the amount of money each citizen earned in a year but also any incentives, subsidies, grants and loans that individual might have been provided with as well as there original source. While this will likely lead to more individuals having to pay more in taxes than they are currently, it will also keep the government accountable for every dime that they bring in. It will be much more difficult for money to disappear into the folds of bureaucratic pockets when a blockchain that anyone can see is keeping track of the tab.

Keeping track of incorporated company details: The state of Delaware marks the first state in the nation offer incorporated businesses the ability to keep track of their shareholder rights as well as their equity via blockchain. As it is common for many companies to incorporate in Delaware to take advantage of friendly taxation privileges, this has the potential to be a change that has wide-ranging results. The state is also moving its archival records onto a distributed ledger, so that more people can view it, for free, at less cost to taxpayers.

Digital proof of residency: In Estonia, long known for its forward-thinking practices, it is now possible to digitally apply for residency in the country through the use of a governmental blockchain. New residents then receive a digital key card that corresponds to a cryptographic key that can be used to sign secure documents, taking the place of any signatures on official paperwork. Virtual residents are then free to open up bank accounts in Estonia's online banking system, which also utilizes blockchain, as well as incorporate a company or access other e-services. Estonia is proud to be pushing the boundaries of digital transactions and seeing a variety of new monetary streams in the process.

Welfare: In the United Kingdom, blockchain has already been turned into a service that is available to purchase through the Digital Marketplace run by the government. Through this service, various governmental agencies freely experiment, deploy and build digital services based on blockchain and technology based on distributed ledgers. Last year they ran a trial through the Department for Work and Pension that allowed users to take advantage of a mobile app that let them access their monthly benefit payments along with transferring details to a separate distributed ledger as a means of helping them with managing their finances, with their consent of course.

Global Blockchain Council: The Global Blockchain Council has been set up in Dubai and represents more than 50 public and private organizations that have already launched proof-of-concept blockchain projects across the shipping, tourism, digital wills, business registration, title transfer, healthcare records and diamond trading sectors. IBM has also partnered with the organization in hopes of using its blockchain for a logistics and trade solution. The government of Dubai has also announced plans for an initiative to transfer all of their government documents onto an interconnected blockchain by 2020. The estimated cost reduction from this program is anticipated to be at 25.1 million-man hours per year.

The future of blockchain

While blockchain technology is still in a nascent enough stage that virtually anything can happen, there are a number of things that are being worked on at a governmental level that should be consider in the context of your future usage.

More control: As previously mentioned, one of the biggest benefits of a blockchain is its ability to function completely autonomously. However, due to the fact that bitcoin then allowed for near-anonymous transactions, it made it very easy for those with an interest in avoiding the law to do so. As cryptocurrency becomes more well-known, regulatory and governmental agencies including the Securities and Exchange Commission, Department of Homeland Security, FBI, and the Financial Crimes Enforcement Network, just in the US, have all started becoming more interested in its potential for unlawful activities.

Scrutiny began to increase during 2013 when the Financial Crimes Enforcement Network decided that cryptocurrency exchanges represented a form of an existing money service business. This meant that they would then fall under government regulations. DHS quickly took advantage of this fact to freeze the accounts of Mt. Gox, the biggest bitcoin exchange in the world at this time based on accusations of money laundering.

This was then followed up with a more recent SEC ruling to deny bitcoin the ability to open an official cryptocurrency exchange trade fund. This move led to a decrease in the price of bitcoin, though that decrease was then countered by an even stronger increase. The denial of this application was still pending review as of September 2017. This then places cryptocurrencies into a bit of an odd situation as their increasing levels of scrutiny makes it harder for them to follow through on their purpose, despite being more popular than ever.

If cryptocurrency is every going to reach a truly mainstream level, and be absorbed into existing financial systems then it needs to find a way to remain true to its initial purpose while also becoming complex enough to hold off the security threats it is sure to face in the future. What's more, it will also need to become simple enough that the average person can use it without issue. Finally, it would need to remain decentralized enough to still be recognizable, while also including various checks and balances to prevent misuse when it comes to things like money laundering or tax evasion. Taken together, this makes it likely that the successful blockchain of the future is going to be some sort of amalgamation of the current form and a more traditional currency.

United States: The United States government is currently working hard to crack down on those who are using blockchain as a means to launder money. They aren't going to be content with that level of control for long, it seems, as signs point to the fact that they are currently working on their own blockchain based cryptocurrency known as Fedcoin. The idea here is that the Federal Reserve could generate a unique cryptocurrency quite easily. The only difference between the blockchain they create and any other is the fact that it would allow for the Federal Reserve to retain the power to go in an remove transactions that they don't approve of.

The rollout of the Fedcoin would occur after the genesis block were created and the rate of Fedcoins being set to 1 to 1 with the dollar. Over time, it would become more and more difficult to come across regular dollars until they were phased out entirely. This would then ultimately lead to a type of cryptocurrency that is both decentralized for its individual transactions, and centralized when it comes to things like limiting available supply and keeping an eye on all types of transactions.

The Federal Reserve is already on its way towards making this plan a reality, so much so that they hosted a closed-door meeting with bitcoin authorities in the fall of 2016. The Chair of the Federal Reserve sat in on the meeting in person, along with representatives from the Bank for International Settlements, World Bank and the International Monetary Fund. During this meeting, one of the talks was literally titled Why Central Banks Will Issue Digital Currencies.

Russia: Russia issued a dramatic shift in its cryptocurrency polices in 2017. Prior to this point anyone caught using cryptocurrency could face jail time, now however the country is embracing digital currency wholeheartedly. The reason for this is related to the extreme level of corruption that Russia has seen in its banking sector over the past several years. More than one hundred banks have been closed in the past three years, and a rash of money laundering schemes still can't be stopped.

To better track where its money is going, the Russian government is currently working on several blockchain based technical applications that will make it easier for them to monitor real time transactions. This makes it appear as though they are less interested in creating a new digital currency and are instead more interested in the distributed ledger portion of the blockchain technology. There is currently no word yet on if Russia plans to create a new blockchain or utilize an existing blockchain for its own ends.

China: China is currently a major supporter in the blockchain space. In June of 2017, the People's Bank of China released and official news report regarding the creation of its own type of digital currency with the ability to scale dramatically depending on the number of transactions that are seen per day. While all of the details have not yet been released, various sources seem to indicate that the bank could release the currency to the world alongside its renminbi project. While no firm release date is forthcoming, the currency is already well underway in the development process and has already seeing testing amongst many of the country's commercial banks and the People's Bank. This testing is a huge step forward for officially sanctioned cryptocurrencies and blockchains of all types. It also proves how committed China is to the idea of thoroughly exploring the digital currency space.

The digital currency they are creating is likely to cause major gains for their economy overall. This is due to the fact that it is back by the People's Bank which means it is functionally the same as a bank note with far fewer associated fees. It would also do a good deal when it comes to bringing banking in China to the modern age as many of its citizens do not have access to traditional banking services.

Chapter 3: Cryptocurrency and Blockchain Interactions

While blockchain is poised to do a great many different things in the near future, for now the most important thing you are going to want to keep in mind is that blockchains make cryptocurrency possible, and bitcoin jumped in price more than $2,000 during the summer of 2017. While this price has pushed it out of the league of many amateur investors, there are more than 1,000 different cryptocurrencies on the market these days so there are plenty of opportunities out there for those who are interested in a potentially profitable investment. This is not to say that there isn't risk involved as well, however, so it is important to keep the risks of cryptocurrency investment in mind as well before making any investments in the space.

Pros

Lowers risk of identity theft: As cryptocurrencies are purely digital, they are naturally susceptible to far less risk than traditional types of currency. They cannot be forged or counterfeited and the transaction cannot be manipulated so that it never happened do to the underlying blockchain. Additionally, once you have bought into a cryptocurrency you can move it about freely without have to worry about transactions with specious companies or individuals putting your details in places they would rather not be. Instead, with most exchanges if you already own cryptocurrency there is no type of verification whatsoever. With most exchanges, without cryptocurrency in hand, you need to generate a new debit or credit transaction with each round of funding.

Easy access: There are roughly 3.5 billion people who have some type of internet access and also do not have any reliable form of banking. This is a niche that the cryptocurrency market is looking to take advantage of to the fullest, and is expected to cause significant growth in the industry as it becomes more commonplace. Assuming this type of banking catches on, then those who invest in cryptocurrency early are going to see more than just a profit, they could potentially see profit on a significant scale.

Low cost: While every cryptocurrency interaction involves a transaction fee, the fees for making this type of exchange is still generally lower than making an exchange on a traditional broker website.

Cons

New technology: While bitcoin has been a quality investment for the past few years, the cryptocurrency market as a whole is still extremely untested overall which means that many of its risks are still very poorly defined, especially when compared to more traditional markets. This naturally makes the highs in the market more dramatic than similar markets, but it also makes the lowers much more dramatic as well. There are no guarantees when one is going to become the other, trends can come and go in completely unpredictable patterns that no one has seen before. What it all comes down to is that there just is not enough information available to be able to accurately predict where the market is going to be in a year, much less five. Until the market stabilizes somewhat, there is no way of telling if every dollar you invest is going to be worth $2, one year from now or if it is going to be worth $.02.

Extreme volatility: Bitcoin, the most stable of all of the cryptocurrencies, is still five time more volatile than gold and has nearly seven times more volatility than if you were to invest that money into the S&P 500. While volatility means a greater chance at profit, it also means the chance at a loss is going to be much higher than it would otherwise be. It is also important to understand that most of the purchases of cryptocurrency that are made, are done for speculative purposes. This means that the currency is being purchased by investors, not people who are actually planning to use it on a day-to-day basis. This, in turn means that prices are likely to rise higher than a true supply and demand market would indicate. This early adopter phenomenon means those who buy in early are going to experience a nice price increase, but the upward movement ultimately won't last. This isn't a question of if, it is a question of when.

Lack of physicality: While the fact that cryptocurrency is a digital means of payment is one of its leading characteristics, the fact remains that this concept does present some challenges. Specifically, consider the fact that if the server holding your cryptocurrency goes down, and there is no backup, then your investment is gone forever. You can take a variety of methods to put the control of your cryptocurrency in your hands, but the fact remains that a real coin is always going to be easier to hold onto than a digital one.

The vast potential for profit when it comes to hacking into a blockchain also means that hackers are never going to stop trying to do just that. What this also means, is that they are occasionally going to be successful. For example, the Ethereum platform has seen a variety of different attacks throughout its lifetime, one of which was so successful that it necessitated a hard fork that saw the Ethereum blockchain divided into those that saw a profit from the attack and those who lost out because of it. A split in the value of the dollar is never going to occur, no matter how many are stolen in a bank robbery which just proves how unpredictable investing in a new opportunity can be.

Trading cryptocurrency

Regardless of how familiar you are with trading traditional securities, trading in the cryptocurrency market can prove to be extremely profitable, as long as you have come to terms with the potential for risk. Don't forget, it is important to never invest any money that you can't afford to lose. There is very little barrier to entry, as previously mentioned, if you already have cryptocurrency then you won't even need to worry about verifying your account.

Another useful thing about trading in this market is the fact that there are no centralized exchanges which means it is every exchange for itself. This then leads to a market that is very fragmented, which means it naturally produces spreads that are much wider than you are likely to see anywhere else. This lack of regulation also means it is often quite easy to find a very large margin which means that small investments have the potential to become large returns faster than with virtually all other types of investment, though the same can be said about losses as well. Finally, depending on the cryptocurrency you are trading in, you will likely be able to find it for different rates on different exchanges which means you might be able to make a profit simply by purchasing them in one place and selling them somewhere else.

The most common way to trade cryptocurrencies through a trading company is with a contract for differences. This type of contract binds the buyer and seller together for the length of the contract, once it ends, the buyer will pay the seller the difference between the price of the asset at the end of the contract and what it was at the start. If the price moves the other way then the seller has to pay the buyer the difference. When it comes to securing leverage, you will likely be able to find rates in excess of 20 to 1, though it is not recommended that you seek them out until you are very familiar with what it is like to trade in this market.

Global currency: When it comes to standard currency, the number of things that can influence the price is naturally going to be fairly limited. The opposite is true for cryptocurrencies, however, and it is difficult to tell what is going to set investors off before it happens. Any currency news anywhere has the potential to set prices shifting dramatically, in fact, several of bitcoin's most significant moves have come about due to the introduction to controls for capital in Greece and when China devalued the Yuan.

Market always ready: While the forex market is traditionally thought of as the most robust market as it is open 120 hours each week, the cryptocurrency market is open 168 hours each week, and trades are always happening regardless of what part of the world is currently active. Currently there are about 100 major cryptocurrency exchanges in the world who all offer various levels of trading along with differing rates based on their level of service. As such, it should not take more than a little research to find the one that is right for you.

This can also be seen as a negative, depending on your tolerance for risk as these factors can be enough to generate large swings on a daily basis. In fact, price shifts of more than 5 percent are common on most days for the larger cryptocurrencies and the smaller ones aren't surprised if they see 15 percent movement or more.

Finding your exchange

When it comes to committing to a specific exchange, it is important to always do the relevant research that you need in order to feel comfortable about your choice. Moving forward without doing enough research can cause you to end up in a situation where you exchange suddenly disappears with your money or you find out that it doesn't have the funds to cover all of its obligations and there is a run on it as everyone tries to get their money back at once. If this sort of thing were to happen, it is important to keep in mind that you are going to have very little recourse, especially if you choose an exchange that is not based in your country. This is why the initial choice you make has the potential to be so impactful.

Prioritize transparent exchanges: As a general rule, the more transparent the exchange you choose is willing to be, the more on the level it is going to be. This means you are going to want to be able to take a look at their order book, which is just a version of their distributed ledger and shows how much of everything is being bought or sold on a regular basis. You should also be able to request details regarding where their funds are held and their system for verifying their appropriate level of reserve currency. If you have a hard time getting answers to these very basic questions then the exchange might simply not have the means to make that information public. On the other hand, it could mean that they are a fractional exchange and can't cover their debts. When it comes to choosing the right cryptocurrency exchange it is always better to be safe than sorry.

Available security: It is very important to always choose an exchange with a healthy level of security, after all, as previously mentioned your cryptocurrency profits won't exist outside this exchange without your help which means security is of the upmost importance. You will only want to use exchanges that have an HTTPS in front of their URL as this indicates they are operating off of a secure protocol which means they are actively working to keep your account details from being stolen. You will also want to ensure that the exchange is utilizing a type of two-factor authentication in addition to standard secure login practices. If your exchange isn't at least this well protected then you are flirting with theft of both your identity and your investments.

Fees add up: Almost every type of cryptocurrency has an associated fee that is paid, part of which goes to the blockchain platform holder and part goes to the miner or miners who verify your transaction. While these fees are certainly voluntary, in most cases, not paying them removes much of the incentive for your transaction to be verified which means the entire process might end up taking longer than it otherwise would. Unless you choose an exchange in China, you will then also have to pay a transaction fee to the exchange as well. With so many fees flying around, they can add up quickly which means you are always going to have a trading plan in place before you make your first trade to prevent yourself from losing a sizeable portion of your trading capital to fees.

Try for something local: Despite the fact that there are cryptocurrency exchanges worldwide, you should aim for one that operates in your home country if possible. This is advantageous in multiple ways, the first of which is that you will naturally be able to take advantage of periods of higher volume simply because you will be on the same general time zone as your exchange. Choosing a local option will also make it easier should you ever need to contact support, and your deposits will go through more quickly as well. Even better, depending on your country and its laws, there might even be some type of oversight regarding cryptocurrency exchanges which means getting your money back after some funny business might not be completely out of the question.

When choosing a local exchange, make sure to verify they offer the cryptocurrency pairs that you are looking for. Exchanges vary dramatically from one to the next so there are no guarantees you will even be able to trade in your local currency, even if you pick an exchange that is close to home.

Understand transaction times: As all cryptocurrency transaction need to be verified and added to the blockchain before they can clear, exchanges often work on a bit of a lead time to let this process breathe. It is important that you choose an exchange whose transaction time is reasonable, for the best results. Likewise, you are going to want to ensure that the price you buy at is the price that is locked in regardless of how long the transaction takes. If this is not the case then you risk making a trade that looks promising, only to have the price change and ruin everything before it actually goes through.

Well-known exchanges

Kraken: This is a European exchange that handles the highest volume of euro trades each day. They are also within the top 15 when it comes to USD exchanges as well.

Coinbase: This is the elder statesman of the cryptocurrency exchanges in the US and has the honor of being the oldest continuously active USD exchange. It is known for being strictly regulated and is still one of the top five when it comes to pure volume traded per day.

OKCoin: This is primarily a USD exchange that is based in Japan which means it is subject to far fewer regulations than most of the other exchanges in this list. If you are looking for higher margins and few fees, and are comfortable with the extra risk, then this is the exchange for you.

Bitstamp: This exchange has been running continuously since 2011 and the second most commonly used USD exchange with a volume greater than 10,000 units a day.

Bitfinex: This exchange does the greatest amount of USD trading by volume of all the exchanges, worldwide, clearing more than 200,000 units of cryptocurrency every single week. If you are interested in going with this option, be aware that if you already own cryptocurrency then you can get started without submitting to any type of verification.

Initial coin offerings (ICOs)

In 2017, a blockchain based company managed to raise more than $150 million in less than 24 hours and another, Status.im managed half that amount. These outpourings of investor generosity are known as initial coin offerings and, like everything having to do with cryptocurrency, they offer a heavy risk in exchange for a potentially lucrative reward. As of summer, 2017, the process had already raised nearly $500,000,000.

Despite being a play on the term initial public offering, the initial coin offering is actually a very different beast in almost every way. An initial coin offering is really just another crowdfunding strategy where a blockchain company offers its new cryptocurrency at a very investor-friendly rate and then investors buy it up in hopes of seeing the price rise even as little as 50 cents. The company then, in theory at least, will have the money to complete its project and come to market, where its products or services will be so widely adopted that the price of its cryptocurrency will rise based on increased demand. The Ethereum platform has quickly proven itself the most popular home for companies who are looking to offer an initial coin offering.

A majority of this money currently comes from China, though investors from around the world have been known to open their checkbooks if the price is right. While investing on what is more or less an unknown quantity always comes with certain risks, initial coin offerings are even riskier still. This is due to the fact that they are not currently under the SEC regulatory umbrella which means their business plans are not put through the same testing that those who apply for an initial public offering are. There is also some concern that the success that the first few initial coin offerings garnered is actually due to another bubble which means it is unlikely to last.

While they do have issues, initial coin offerings also have the potential to generate serious profits for investors who make the right decisions at the right times. Nevertheless, if you are considering this type of investment then you need to understand that if you choose to invest in an initial coin offering, then you are making one of the riskiest investments possible.

To counteract the potential danger as much as possible, you will need to approach all initial coin offerings with a quizzical mindset and the first thing you will want to do is look through any information the company has made available including, hopefully, a business plan. This will make it easier for you to determine if a specific project makes sense on a financial level and to ensure that is business proposition checks out in the long-term. You will also need to know that the market is going to actually want the product or service the company is hoping to provide. Furthermore, you will want to double check and see what the role of the cryptocurrency that you are buying into will be when the product or service is up and running.

You will also need to keep in mind that buying into an initial coin offering is going to be quite different than buying into an initial public offering. When buying into the latter, you come away with ownership shares that essentially mean you own a small portion of the company in question. Initial coin offerings grant you no such rights, just a pile of digital currency that may or may not eventually be worth something. Additionally, initial public offerings have stricter requirements placed on them including accreditation obligations and fiduciary requirements that the company must meet before it can have its offering, none of which is required for initial coin offerings.

In reality, you are likely never going to see more than a whitepaper, business plan and website from an initial coin offering company, and sometimes not even all of these. They are more than likely not going to have a product or prototype to show off either which means you are going to be taking a lot of what is being told to you on faith. You also need to be aware that just because an initial coin offering sees a good amount of response early on, doesn't mean this goodwill will last until its launch day, much less beyond it. Also noteworthy is the fact that many analysts believe that giving new companies too much money too soon actually limits their potential as the owner's feel the need to spend all the money available to them while feeling less inclined to actually complete a usable product.

While the list of poor ICOs ranges from those with overly optimistic ideas to downright scams with the sole goal of taking your hard earned cash. There are an increasing number of ICOs out there with nothing more than a flashy website filled with a ton of buzzwords and a high valuation based on nothing more than their own opinion. The single biggest factor you should examine before investing is the real world viability of the project. What solution to a current problem does the company promise to solve? Even more so, is there even a problem in the first place that requires blockchain technology? It's important to examine the team behind the project, and more importantly their previous track record with projects like it. Another main determinant should be whether the token they are offering has actual utility for the project, or are investors just going to dump it for a quick profit as soon as it hits the open market? You should also watch out for any huge bonuses offered for early investors. It's not uncommon for a pre-sale bonus to be offered, but if these bonuses top 100%, you can and should question what the incentive is for non-early adopters, and if the team are just trying to generate as much cash as quickly as possible. One advantage the Ethereum platform does have is the ability for smart contracts to be coded into the ICO, such as funds held in a service similar to escrow, to ensure they are returned to investors if the project founders do not uphold their end of the agreement.

Last but not least, it is worth noting that a majority of the currently successful initial coin offerings have been based on the Ethereum blockchain platform which means the basis of these companies is still essentially an untested technology. While the Ethereum blockchain platform has a better chance of making it than making it than most, the fact of the matter is that it is still untested technology so there is still downside potential as well as upside. Overall, it might be the best choice to instead wait and see how the first round of initial coin offering companies pan out before getting too involved with these types of investments directly.

Tips for investing successfully

While starting to invest in cryptocurrency is as easy as finding an exchange and putting some money into the cryptocurrency machine, doing so and turning an investment profit is something else completely. What's next is a list of things you will want to keep in mind in order to invest successfully in the long-term.

It's a commodity: The first thing you are going to need to do is to think about cryptocurrency in the same way you would any other commodity. Just like any other commodity, cryptocurrency is used for practical as well as investment purposes, just as precious metals have commercial uses and base metals have industrial ones. Additionally, they are all trade through exchanges that more or less all follow the same rules. This means that in order to choose a cryptocurrency that is likely to increase in value, you are going to want to pick the one that is likely to provide the most real-world value or has the greatest number of probable uses beyond just P2P transactions.

Increasing usage: When gathered together as a whole, all the currently existing cryptocurrencies have a market cap of about $160 billion. This puts them in the same league as companies like Tesla and Microsoft in terms of pure numbers. What makes this number particularly interesting is that real world usage and increasing market cap have gone hand in hand so far, and reports show that blockchain and cryptocurrency usage is only likely to increase for at least the next five years.

This is when market saturation is expected to occur and is likely when many of the existing bubbles break for the first time. Nevertheless, while the market is still extremely volatile in the short-term, cryptocurrency as a long-term investment should be relatively reliable. When this number is looked at through the lens of the current market cap then the potential for growth is truly staggering. Essentially the price of cryptocurrency across the board has nowhere to go but up. Even better, once the number of users eventually stabilizes, investor won't have to worry about the bubble effect nearly as much because prices will likely stop decreasing dramatically at that point as well.

Point in the cycle: The market cycle is a type of investment pattern that every investment goes through sooner or later. On the positive side, it starts with optimism before moving up to thrill, and then peaking with euphoria. It then decreases through anxiety, denial, fear, depression and finally, panic. After it bottoms out it then rises back up through depression, hope and relief before once again reaching optimism.

While bitcoin has already been through the cycle more than once, most recently bottoming out during the 2014 crash, the vast majority of all cryptocurrencies are still very much in the optimism stage so there is still plenty of time to get in while the getting is good. As long as you do your research correctly in the first place there is no reason you couldn't realistically see five reliable years of growth on your investment before it hits the euphoria stage.

While this is decidedly good news, it is also important to keep in mind the fact that the cryptocurrency market today, is very much the same as the dotcom boom of the 90s. What this means, is that roughly 80 percent of all the cryptocurrencies on the market today are going to fail before or during the period when the market hits its saturation point. This is due to the fact that there will only be so many options in a limited marketplace that only a handful will be able to survive the buildup. Many investors will end up throwing their money at a company without having any idea what that company actually does and the market will crumble because of it, though if you know what's coming you will be able to avoid the worst of it.

Solving problems is key: It doesn't matter what the potential for profit on a given cryptocurrency turns out to be, buying into it and then sitting back to wait for the magic to happen will never be the most effective money-making strategy. Instead, you will be better served putting time into finding those cryptocurrencies that solve problems for individual markets or, even better, the world at large. The bigger the problem being solved, the more likely it will turn into something that is worth investing in for the long-term. It is especially important to consider solutions when it comes to the banking services that some parts of the world take for granted. Cryptocurrencies that focus on solutions when it comes to making payments and wiring money are going to be good bets in the near future.

Long-term view: Given the amount of movement you can expect to see on a regular basis, the ideal cryptocurrency portfolio is going to be one that focuses solely on the long-term. You are also going to want to make a point of picking several different cryptocurrencies to invest in, between three or five, so that you will never be too negatively affected by serious drops in one place or another. More than anything else it is going to be important that you control your emotions as thoroughly as possible and strive to avoid rash decisions when investments are on the line. When you are first getting started it is a good idea to not watch your investments too closely, as they are likely going to be all over the place. Don't forget, the goal to long-term investing is a steady overall upward trend which means a little back and forth is to be expected.

It is also important to remember that cryptocurrencies do not come with the lock-in risk that many other long-term investments do. If you feel that a certain cryptocurrency's time has come, you can quickly and easily exchange it with any other currency you choose, instead of having to go through the hassle of trading in a more traditional fashion during a down market. As such, you may want to think about investing in cryptocurrency as just keeping money in a savings account, but one that has a much higher potential for return on your primary investment.

Conclusion

Thank you for reading, let's the book was informative and able to provide you with all of the tools you need to achieve your goals, whatever it is that they may be. Just because you've finished this book doesn't mean there is nothing left to learn on the topic, expanding your horizons is the only way to find the mastery you seek.

This is especially true for the blockchain market as it is a new enough technology as to literally be always changing. Only by making it a habit to become a lifelong learner will you ever truly get a grasp on it that you will be able to use for your advantage. Whatever you do, always keep in mind that the market is heading towards an inevitable saturation point which means however you decide to interact with blockchain technology you need to ensure you end up on the right side of it.

It is extremely likely that you will not see another technology this disruptive in your lifetime, and with so many technology variations and cryptocurrencies all vying for the market at once, all you need to do is be aware of the possibility of success to be able to seek it out and reap all the related rewards. It also means that there are plenty of ways to fail, however, so you are going to really need to do your homework and ensure that you never make a move without taking all of your options into consideration fist. Remember, investing in blockchain technology is investing in the long-term, slow and steady wins the race.

Finally, if you found this book useful in anyway, a review on Amazon is always appreciated!

Cryptocurrency: Insider Secrets - 12 Exclusive Coins Under $1 with Potential for Huge Profits in 2018

By Stephen Satoshi

Factors to Consider Before Investing

While larger cryptocurrencies like Bitcoin, Ethereum and Litecoin have long track records and multiple real world functions, some of the coins mentioned in this book do not - hence their lower price.

There are a number of different variables to investigate before you undertake any investment, and cryptocurrency has its own set.

Proof of Concept (PoC)
In other words, does the technology have a working model, or is it still in a theoretical stage. Obviously more mature coins will have a higher value, with the more theoretical coins being a bigger risk. As the different coins here are in different stages of their life cycle, that is up for you to decide.

The development team
Who are the developers and what is their track record. Particularly within the cryptocurrency and blockchain space? Another thing to consider is their record within the particular industry they are targeting.

The utility Of the coin
Ideas are great, but if the coin token itself doesn't have usage, then the true potential of the project must be questioned. This is especially true in the case of certain coins where the theory and market potential checks out, but the question of "why can I just use Bitcoin/Litecoin to do the same thing" is often raised.

The roadmap
Roadmaps are important for short-term gains because they set out development targets for the coin. If these goals are reached and the products/platforms move from alpha to beta to a fully launched product, then that only means positive things for the coin and its value.

Which exchanges the coin is listed on
Many of these coins are still only available on smaller exchanges. Once the coin is listed on larger exchanges (for example Bittrex), the coin has greater visibility and this leads to a rise in value.

Mining Algorithm - Proof of Work vs. Proof of Stake
You'll notice later on when discussing individual coins that I talk about which mining algorithms are used. The two most popular are Proof of Work (PoW), used by Bitcoin and Proof of Stake (PoS), which will be used by Ethereum from Q4 2017 and beyond, and is currently used by a number of Ethereum based tokens.

In my previous book *Bitcoin: Beginners Bible* I discussed why I don't recommend mining as an effective method for obtaining cryptocurrency, for the regular user. That still holds true for the majority of the coins listed in this book, but it's important to understand why the difference in mining algorithm matters.

Why do we need mining?

We need mining to ensure a transaction (or block) is correctly validated, in other words, we need to ensure the same transaction doesn't occur twice - known as the double spending problem. As a reward for validating this transaction, miners are rewarded with a tiny percentage of it (known as the network fee).

To put it bluntly, Proof of Work takes a lot more energy than Proof of Stake. A 2015 study showed that one Bitcoin transaction takes the equivalent daily energy of 1.57 US homes. Proof of Stake is also a fairer, more energy efficient system, which is a huge advantage for community based coins.

Minimizing Your Risk with Dollar Cost Averaging

One of the best ways to minimize your risk in a volatile market is to use what is known as 'dollar cost averaging'. This simply means dividing up your total planned investment and buying cryptocurrencies at regular intervals instead of all at once.

With dollar cost averaging, you are simply buying less of an asset (for this example, I will use Bitcoin) when the price is high, and more when the price is low. Your total exposure is less because you are only exposed to part of any decline in the market, as opposed to all of it with a lump sum investment. Your average cost per coin is therefore likely to be lower.

Let's use an example, both Jamal and Rachel have $1200 to invest in Bitcoin at the start of 2015. Jamal decides to invest all $1200 on January 1st, Rachel on the other hand is going to use dollar cost averaging. She will invest $100 on the 1st of each month, for a total of $1200. The prices used in this example are the actual Bitcoin trading prices as of those dates.

January 1st 2015 - $305.32
February 1st 2015 - $237.18
March 1st 2015 - $263.57
April 1st 2015 - $255.23
May 1st 2015 - $226.45
June 1st 2015 - $233.44
July 1st 2015 - $260.73
August 1st 2015 -$283.04
September 1st 2015 - $229.00
October 1st 2015 - $240.10
November 1st 2015 - $325.28
December 1st 2015 - $375.95

Jamal's total investment in BTC = 3.93 (1200/305.32)
Rachel's total investment in BTC = 4.55 (1200/269.60)

Price on January 1st 2016 - $433.57

Jamal's Portfolio Value = 3.93*433.57 = $1704.02
Rachel's Portfolio Value = 4.55*433.57 = $1974.37

Jamal's ROI = 42%
Rachel's ROI = 64.5%

So by using dollar cost averaging, Rachel's average BTC purchase price was $269.60, whereas Jamal bought a lump sum at $305.32. By having a lower average purchase price, Rachel's ROI is higher over time. Jamal bought his coins at the peak of the market before a prolonged downturn, whereas Rachel utilized this downturn to her advantage.

Remember, time in the market beats timing the market. Generally speaking, the longer you are invested in something, the better.

Why you shouldn't touch a coin in the initial Post-ICO period

I made a conscious decision not to include any cryptocurrencies that were within 1 month of the end of their ICO. For those who are unware, an ICO is an initial coin offering, and a common method for companies behind cryptocurrencies to gain investment. Like IPOs in the stock world, a total portion of the company is sold to the public. Investors donate Bitcoin or Ethereum, and in return they are given a number of cryptocurrency tokens from the ICO. For example, in the case of Neblio, those donating were rewarded with 20,000 NEBL for every 1 Bitcoin donated. Though it should be noted that unlike IPOs, with an ICO, you do not own a % of the company, merely the tokens associated with it.

The post ICO period is extremely volatile price wise, and not a good period for anyone to enter the market, especially if you are an inexperienced cryptocurrency investor.

The reason for this volatility is often linked to ICOs offering a pre-sale bonus for early investors, who then sell their bonus in the post-ICO period for a quick profit, which ends up causing the price to fall. Usually, once the month after the ICO has ended, the price tends to become more stable.

All of the coins discussed in this book have been out of the ICO period for at least 1 month (many for years). Investing during the ICO period is a different matter, if you choose to do so for future coins, I advise you to read any instructions carefully so you don't send any coins to the incorrect wallet address.

7 Giant Mistakes Guaranteed to Cost You Money

1. Not double checking all links (including the ones in this book)
Unfortunately, phishing scams are rife in the cryptocurrency space. Just this week, I saw 3 new ones either via email, paid search traffic (Google ads) or from reading about them on cryptocurrency message boards. Remember to check any link you click that is asking for you username, password or any other personal details.

2. Storing your cryptocurrency on an exchange
While rare, exchange attacks do happen, and cryptocurrency does get stolen. If you move your cryptocurrency off an exchange and into a private wallet, hackers cannot touch it (provided that wallet follows proper security measures). For each of the coins mentioned, I have included the appropriate wallet information for them.

3. Giving your private key to anyone
Your private key is what you need to send cryptocurrency from your wallet. You should never give this to anyone, for any reason. Keep it secure, preferably written on a piece of paper that is stored inside a physical safe. Never keep your private key on a server, and never enter it on a public Wi-Fi network.

4. Panic selling during a dip in the market
Unless you need the money to feed your family, there is ZERO reason to sell your cryptocurrency at a loss during a dip in the market. Remember, this investment should represent a small percentage of your overall investing portfolio, in other words - you can afford to take a small loss on paper. More often than not in the cryptocurrency market, waiting it out, and long term holding, is the best investment strategy.

5. Not using dollar cost averaging when buying
Time in the market beats timing the market. You can minimize your risk by using dollar cost averaging and spreading your investment out over time. This prevents getting burned by buying at the top of the market.

6. Not doing your research/due diligence
This book is designed to be a comprehensive introduction to these cryptocurrencies, but it is certainly not the only resource available. I encourage you to do your own research in addition to what I've provided in this book. The best source for information will come from the coin's own website and white paper (although at times white papers can read more like a press release than a technical document, this alone is a good indicator).

7. Borrowing money to invest in cryptocurrencies
This really should be obvious, but I've personally witnessed it too many times that I feel it needs to be reiterated. You should NEVER borrow money to invest in anything, let alone a market as volatile as cryptocurrency. Losing your own money is one thing, losing someone else's money is another. So, next time you're considering borrowing money from a bank, or using your student loan to invest - don't. Trust me, it's not worth it.

Bonus tip/mistake 7.5 - Checking the price of your investment on a daily basis

Just leave it alone - trust me

How to Buy Bitcoin

Gone are the days when buying Bitcoin was a time consuming and somewhat uncomfortable endeavor. Nowadays buying Bitcoin is a similar process to exchanging currency when you go on vacation.

There are two ways to buy Bitcoin, the first is to use fiat currency (USD, EUR, GBP etc.) to purchase cryptocurrency via an exchange. These exchanges function the same way as regular foreign currency exchanges do. The prices fluctuate on a daily basis, and like regular currency exchange markets - they are open 24/7. These exchanges make their money from charging a small fee for each transaction.

Some charge both buyers and sellers, some only charge a fee for buying. For security reasons, most of these exchanges will require you to verify your ID before allowing you to purchase cryptocurrency.

It is also important to note the type of payments each exchange supports. Some allow for debit/credit card payments whereas other only accept PayPal or bank wire transfers. Below are the three biggest and reputable currency exchanges for purchasing Bitcoin, Ethereum and other altcoins with fiat currency like US dollars, Euros or British Pounds.

Coinbase

Currently largest currency exchange in the world, Coinbase allows users to buy, sell and store cryptocurrency. Coinbase is undoubtedly the most beginner friendly exchange for anyone looking to get involved in the cryptocurrency market. They currently allow trading of Bitcoin, as well as, Ethereum and LiteCoin using fiat currency as a base. Known for their stellar security procedures and insurance policies regarding stored currency. The exchange also has a fully functioning iPhone and Android app for buying and selling on the go, very useful if you are looking to trade.

Once you are signed up and complete the identity verification procedures you can buy Bitcoin with your credit or debit card instantly.

Coinbase also recently launched the Coinbase Vault, which is a secure way of storing your cryptocurrency while still having it accessible to trade. The vault uses double email address + phone verification in order to access your funds. If you're planning on holding long-term, I still recommend offline storage - but as an intermediary option, the Vault is a step in the right direction.

If you sign up for Coinbase using this link, you will receive $10 worth of free Bitcoin after your first purchase of more than $100 worth of cryptocurrency.

http://bit.ly/10dollarbtc

Note, if you're going to be trading Bitcoin, I recommend doing so on Coinbase's partner platform GDax, which has lower fees.

Bittrex

Based and regulated in the USA, Bittrex is a great exchange to buy altcoins for Bitcoin or Ethereum. With over 190 different cryptocurrencies, it is the most comprehensive in terms of altcoin support.

Their support isn't as good as Coinbase's, and you'll have to transfer the coins to a wallet if you want to securely store them long-term, but for trading altcoins - you can't go wrong with Bittrex.

Poloniex

With more than 100 different cryptocurrencies available and data analysis for advanced traders, Poloniex is the most comprehensive exchange on the market. Low trading fees are another plus, this is a great place to trade your Bitcoin into other cryptocurrencies. If you have never purchased Bitcoin before, you will no be able to do so as Poloniex does not allow fiat currency deposits. Therefore, you will have to make your initial Bitcoin purchases on Coinbase or Kraken.

Buying Locally

The second way to buy Bitcoins in exchange for fiat currency is to locally purchase them in person. The advantage of this is that you may be able to get a marginally better price than by using an exchange. The other advantage is that users living in countries that don't have easy access to online exchanges can still buy coins in person. All transactions are protected by Escrow to prevent either party being scammed.

Website http://localbitcoins.com is the current market leader for local bitcoin transactions with sellers in over 15,000 cities around the world.

Transferring your newly purchased Bitcoin to your exchange of choice.

Once you have bought your Bitcoin from Coinbase/Kraken, you'll need to then transfer it over the Binance, Bittrex or whichever exchange your coin of choice is listed on. To do this, simply go to the exchange you need to transfer the coins to (e.g. Bittrex) and click on "deposit", choose BTC (remember to double check you've clicked the correct coin). This will generate an address that looks like this 1F1tAaz5x1HUXrCNLbtMDqcw6o5GNn4xqX

From there, go to your Coinbase/Kraken BTC wallet and select "send", then in the "recipient" section copy the BTC address of the new exchange. Double check the amount of BTC you are sending, then click send and the transfer will initiate. Most of the time transfers take around 10 minutes, however some exchanges take longer to process. Once your transfer is complete you can then exchange your BTC for any of the altcoins listed below.

Storing Your Coins - How to set up MyEtherWallet

Many of these coins are based on the Ethereum blockchain, and therefore use ERC20 tokens. Therefore, these tokens can be stored in Ethereum wallets. Wallets can be daunting to set up at first, so I recommend you use something simple to get started, the most convenient of these is MyEtherWallet.

Step-by-Step guide to setting up MyEtherWallet

1. Go to https://www.myetherwallet.com/
2. Enter a strong but easy to remember password. Do not forget it.
3. This encrypts (protects) your private key. It does not generate your private key. This password alone will not be enough to access your coins.
4. Click the "Generate Wallet" button.
5. Download your Keystore/UTC file & save this file to a USB drive.
6. This is the encrypted version of your private key. You need your password to access it. It is safer than your unencrypted private key but you must have your password to access it in the future.
7. Read the warning. If you understand it, click the "I understand. Continue" button.
8. Print your paper wallet backup and/or carefully hand-write the private key on a piece of paper.
9. If you are writing it, I recommend you write it 2 or 3 times. This decreases the chance your messy handwriting will prevent you from accessing your wallet later.
10. Copy & paste your address into a text document somewhere.
11. Search your address on https://etherscan.io/ Bookmark this page as this is how you can view your balance at any time
12. Send a small amount of any coin from your previous wallet or exchange to your new wallet - just to ensure you have everything correct

Hardware Wallets

Another safe, offline solution is to use a hardware wallet. The most popular of these being Trezor and Nano S. Both of these cost around $100, but represent a convenient, yet safe way to store your cryptocurrency. Further explanation of hardware wallets is in my first book *Cryptocurrency: Beginners Bible*.

12 Exclusive Coins Under $1 with Potential for Huge Profits

District0x (DNT)
Price at Time of Writing - $0.039
Market Cap at Time of Writing - $23,255,100

Available on:
BTC: Binance, Bittrex, Liqui

Where to store:
District0x is currently an ERC20 token and can be stored on My Ether Wallet. You can view how to add DNT as a custom token on https://etherscan.io/token/district0x

District0x has the goal of breaking the internet down into smaller, more manageable pieces. If you've ever seen the movie The Hunger Games, you'll remember each district was focused on a single task: District 7 was the lumber district, District 8 focused on textile production, District 9 with grain etc.

District0x plans to do the same thing with the blockchain technology and Decentralized Autonomous Organizations (DAO). Each district will have its own payment and invoicing system, along with complete self governance. The venture will use the Ethereum blockchain to run smart contracts.

What District0x has done to make to the process user friendly, is combine different necessary (like smart contracts and payment processing) elements into a package, so it's not essential for users to completely understand the technology behind the platform. You can think of this as similar to how Wordpress works for web development. At the core of every district is the ability to operate a market or a bulletin board application.

Currently, there are over 100 district ideas in play. Theoretically, it would allow an individual such as you or me to implement their own version of AirBNB, Craigslist or Uber, without having to go through a middleman like the current system has to. This in turn reduces transaction fees and makes the overall cost lower for all parties involved. There are no fees to create districts, which makes them available to everyone. Currently, refundable deposits are required to put forward a district proposal, once the district passes quality control checks (ensuring the district is not there for malicious intent), the deposit is refunded to the district creator.

One such idea already running is Ethlance, an online freelancing platform similar to Upwork or Fiverr, but without the large transaction fees. Interestingly enough, the District0x team has actually hired developers via Ethlance to help them execute the project.

Another promising proposal is ShipIt, which focuses on the multi-billion dollar shipping industry. The idea is to create a decentralized maritime logistics platform. The sheer number of transactions in this industry alone (trucking, forwarding, warehousing etc.) make this a perfect foil for a blockchain solution.

The framework is in place, however the team needs to do more to gather traction, plus a larger user base to utilize their own districts. The current team is small, with just 10 members, plus an additional advisor, but there will certainly be additions in the future as the project continues to grow. Progress reports are frequent and developments are regular posted on GitHub.

One interesting approach the District0x team are employing is creating a free "education portal" to inform the wider public about the platform, and the real world functionality of districts. They are doing this are they believe the current limiting factor is a general ignorance of the potential of the platform. The portal is scheduled for rollout in Q4 2017.

District0x tokens (DNT) can be used to fund project and stake voting rights in different districts, the more tokens one has, the greater of a say they have. The one issue here is a possible abuse of a "pay to play" system.

The decentralized element of District0x means there is no single point of failure, for example there is no single server that all of the individual districts run from. This ensures that targeted hacking attacks cannot take down the entire network.

Supply wise, there are 600 million DNT available, with a total projected supply of 1 billion. It should be noted that in the white paper, the District0x team does reserve the right to add additional coins to the total supply, however this is contingent on the exchange rate between ETH/USD. For example, if ETH's value declines significantly vs. USD, the team can add additional coins to account for this fluctuation. This isn't necessarily something to be concerned about (financial hedging occurs all the time in fiat markets), but it's definitely something worth nothing.

Listing on larger exchanges will help spike the price in the short term. The team are in ongoing discussions with large exchange Bittrex, and a listing on there could easily see price rises of 100%. Long term prices will be largely determined by the number of popular districts that are set up using the platform. The next two planned district launches are Name Bazaar and Meme Factory.

Neblio (NEBL)

Price at Time of Writing - $0.984
Market Cap at Time of Writing - $12,220,794

Available on:
BTC: Cryptopia

Where to store?
Wallets can be downloaded from https://nebl.io/wallets/

Based out of the USA, Neblio aims to provide a simple blockchain solution to the business sector. The project was born out of a need to simplify currently complex blockchain tools in order to achieve wider adoption within the business sector.

Taking into account blockchain solutions for transparent data, plus reliability and security owing to a lack of central server - the technology has a huge advantage for businesses over traditional methods. However, cost of maintenance, and difficulty of integration have made uptake in the business world somewhat slower than blockchain enthusiasts would like. Certain industries are waiting for more mature blockchain solutions to appear, rather than take a risk on technology that is unproven in their particularly sector. The Neblio team plan to streamline this process and make blockchain solutions more accessible for businesses as a whole.

A real world example of this would be a doctor's office needing to access patient records. Rather than use a traditional central database, that is liable to server downtime, or cyber attacks - they could use a blockchain solution which provides the same data, but without the risks. This same system could be used for any business that needs to utilize frequent audits, as the data would be unalterable with a record of who altered it and when.

Neblio plans to support current popular programming languages give it a great advantage in this area. Developers in languages such as Python, Java, Javascript and PHP won't be forced to learn a new programming language to develop applications on the Neblio blockchain. This is an area that is vital if the platform wants to attract developers to Neblio versus other platforms. This also makes Neblio applications compatible with mobile devices running iOS or Android.

In terms of competitor coins, the space is extremely competitive with giants such as Ethereum and Neo already occupying some of the real estate. Stratis is another big one, however, Stratis has had a year headstart and in terms of development, yet Neblio is already neck-and-neck in terms of having a working product.

The beta version of the Neblio network is currently scheduled for a launch in Q3 2018, with a larger scale marketing campaign due in Q2 of the same year. The team has been extremely active in developments, and recently both an iOS and Android wallet were both launched ahead of schedule.

Supply wise, there are approximately 12.5 million NEBL tokens in circulation currently, with a total supply of 13 million. NEBL tokens can be used as a means of exchange on the Neblio network

There is certainly a gap in the market for this type of blockchain solution. However, Neblio's future may lie with working within a specific industry, as the goal of solely providing broad "enterprise solution" is one that is susceptible to a large amount of competition, particularly from vast entities like Ethereum and Neo.

Bytom (BTM)

Price at Time of Writing - $0.069
Market Cap at Time of Writing - $80,324,168

Available on:
Fiat: Cryptopia (NZ)
BTC: Cryptopia, BTER (CN), Bit9 (CN)

Where to store?:
Bytom is currently an ERC20 token and can be stored on My Ether Wallet. You can view how to add Bytom as a custom token on Ethplorer via http://bit.ly/bytomwallet

Bytom is a true sleeper coin. Coming out of China, it's only natural that the coin has received initial comparisons to NEO (formerly Antshares), one of the most talked about cryptocurrencies of 2017.

Although their official Whitepaper is currently only available in Chinese, the roughly translated opening reads as "Bytom will not be another Bitcoin, or an Ethereum 2.0. Bytom is an intermediary connecting generalized blockchains with specialized blockchains." The whitepaper then goes on to discuss the idea of connecting physical and digital assets while resolving issues like compliance and trustworthiness.

In laymen's terms, Bytom has the potential for offline assets to be registered on the blockchain. In their own words, "bridging the online world and the atomic world". This bridging allows users to seamlessly swap between digital assets (like cryptocurrencies), and physical ones. This is something that no other cryptocurrency in development promises to utilize.

Real world applications for the technology include the management of income assets and dividend distribution for investors.

A very strong development team is headed up by Chiang Jia, who previously founded 8BTC - one of China's largest resources for cryptocurrency news and insights. Anyone who has been involved in the cryptocurrency market will understand just how important news from China is in affecting the price of Bitcoin and other crypto assets. The CEO was invited to speak at the 2017 Global Blockchain Summit.

Another determinant of the price is the viability of mining. Bytom has embraced the popular AI ASIC friendly mining algorithm. China is currently the world's largest base for cryptocurrency mining, with 70% of the entire mining work done in the Middle Kingdom. Part of Bytom's plan is to reward miners at a technological level as well as a financial one. CEO Jia stated in a June interview with 8BTC that "As for the mining industry, the outdated mining farm could be transformed into data center that provides AI hardware acceleration service." Chinese miners tend to support their own currencies, which is part of the reason for NEO's success in 2017. If Bytom can replicate this at even a fraction of the uptake, it will only mean good things going forward.

One particular thing to note about Bytom, is the team's dedication to continued, if somewhat slow progress. However, you can look at this in a positive light. Rather than succumbing to spending their entire budget on marketing like other coins, Bytom's roadmap is well laid out with realistic goals. You don't need to expect life changing developments within the next 6 months for example. But a solid alpha product in Q1 2018 could certainly lead to decent short term gains. Right now, the scheduled release of v1.0 of the Bytom blockchain is due in Q2 2018.

Other notable figures include Long Yu, a former Senior System Engineer at Alipay, a huge Chinese POS payment system (similar to Apple Pay or Samsung Pay).

In early September the Bytom team took home 2nd prize in a field of over 100 competitors in the 2017 Cosmos Hackathon, a blockchain network designed to solve problems like scalability and interoperability. 2nd Place is currently the best achievement from a Chinese team at the competition.

The roadmap shows that by early 2018, many of Bytom's most exciting features will be put to market, in beta form. A large press conference for the release of their alpha product is scheduled for Q1 2018.

Currently Bytom is in a unique place where there are no strict competitor coins.

The have been some blips in the development stages already, with Bytom removing the coin from Binance in mid August. However the coin is now listed on Cryptopia, which while being a small exchange compared to giants like Bittrex and Poloniex, does make it accessible to the US and western market. The Chinese market has easy access with direct BTN/CNY trades available on the BTC9 exchange. Those holding ETH can exchange it for Bytom at the BTER exchange.

Bytom's value comes from the fee each user will have to pay to use the Bytom blockchain. Holding Bytom coins essentially represents shares in the blockchain itself. Bytom believes strongly in this community based ownership model, and their concept of "distributed autonomy" is one that they hold dearly to the project. The aim is structure the management system for a balance between efficiency and fairness.

Circulating supply is high at 664 million BTN currently available, with a projected total supply of 2.1 billion BTN. Of this total supply, 7% is reserved for private equity groups and angel investors, whose funds will be used in the technology's initial development stages.

Overall, Bytom might not make any major price movements in the next 2 months, but as soon as 2018 rolls around, the coin has potential to make a big impact in the blockchain space.

Note: On some cryptocurrency exchanges, Bitmark will be listed as BTM, these two currencies are not related. Double check before executing a trade.

Golem (GNT)

Price at time of writing - $0.267
Market Cap at time of writing - $222,516,176

Available on:
Fiat: Yunbi (CN)
BTC: Poloniex, Bittrex, Liqui

Where to store?
Golem is an ERC20 token so can be stored in MyEtherWallet

Golen is a coin token, based on Ethereum blockchain technology. With nearly 10 months since the original ICO, Golem is somewhat of a granddad in the cryptocurrency world. Described by some commentators as the "AirBNB of computing", the value of the coin is centered around the tasks that can be accomplished using it.

The founders of the Golem Project refer to it as a "supercomputer", with the ability to interconnect with other computers for various purposes. These include scientific research, data analysis and cryptocurrency mining. For example, if your computer has unused, or idle power, using the Golem network, you can rent that power (hence the AirBNB comparison) to someone else who needs it. The user who needs the extra power, has the ability to access supercomputer levels of processing power for a fraction of the cost of actually owning the processing power themselves. Like other Ethereum based projects, the decentralized element provides an additional layer of security as there is no single point of failure on the network. The first use case of the network's alpha release was using shared processing power to produce a 3D CGI rendering.

One fantastic potential usage for this power is the ability for a company to prevent downtime during a urge of users. There are many examples of websites being down during periods of unusually high demand, such as waiting for a livestream of a popular event to start. One notable example of this is Rockstar's website crashing during the release of the Grand Theft Auto 4 trailer. Using idle power from other computers on the Golem network, has the potential to prevent issues like this from occurring in the future.

The growth of such services is currently in demand in the non-crypto space, with cloud computing services accounting for roughly $175 billion global turnover in 2015. For example, Amazon's Amazon Web Services (AWS) business is an increasing part of the online giant's overall holdings.

If you look at Golem vs. Traditional cryptocurrency mining, Golem is definitely a step ahead. Because it only utilizes idle power, there is no wasted energy, which traditional mining suffers from a lot of. Even for a casual user, the ability to offset some of their electricity costs is a big positive.

The ability for users to earn money for their unused computing power is, in theory, a no-brainer, however what remains to be seen is the practical application of the technology. The Golem team's lack of marketing visibility also appears to hurt the coins value in recent times. The lack of ability to buy GNT using fiat currency (such as USD) is also a drawback for the mass market, however for small cap coins, that is somewhat of a given at this stage of the overall cryptocurrency lifecycle.

Supply wise, 1 billion GNT tokens were generated during the ICO, and that is the sum total that will be available for the lifetime of the project. Tokens will be used as a transfer of value on the Golem network.

It should be noted that the technology is still very much in the early development stages and as of August 2017, the team are still looking for alpha testers for the project. The Golem Project has a very real possibility of petering out into nothing. On the flip side - there is tremendous potential for large future gains with the price of a coin still under $0.30.

Tron (TRX)

Price at time of writing - $0.0018
Market Cap at time of writing - $125,420,800

Available on:
BTC: Liqui
ETH: Liqui, EtherDelta

Even in small and medium cap cryptocurrencies, Tron is a true wildcard. Lead by Justin Sun, known in China as "The next Jack Ma", and part of Forbes Asia 30 Under 30 - the project is one with wide reaching implications for the in-app currency movement.

You can think of Tron as both a facilitator for in-game or in-app transactions (also known as microtransactions) and as a way of increasing the value of your own content.

The biggest trend in video games for the past 5 years has been the rise in in-game microtransactions, also known as the pay-to-win model. This frustrates gamers as any assets they have built up in game 1, are not transferable to game 2. For example, take the popular mobile game Clash of Clans. The game features a huge amount of microtransactions, and players have spent hundreds of dollars building up their in-game assets. Currently there are only very limited ways for him to sell those assets in exchange for money. Plus, if a new game comes out and the gamer wants to try it out, they'd have to start from the bottom and work their way up again. Tron would allow said gamer to transfer his Clash of Clans assets over to the new game in exchange for a small transaction fee.

Content creators can also use Tron as a payment system for their content. Similar to how YouTube users use Patreon donations as a method of making additional income from their content.

The development team continues to grow, and the recent announcement of one of Alibaba's (the Amazon of China) chief engineers joining the project is another coup for the Tron team.

The future of Tron will depends of two things. The first is adoption, which games will support TRX as a middleman for cross-game transactions? Secondly would these games choose TRX over the coins currently available like BTC or LTC. Like many of the coins mentioned in the book, they idea in theory is a multi-billion dollar one, but does the token have enough utility to warrant it?

Supply wise, Tron is huge. With over 40 billion TRX coins currently in circulation, with a projected total of 100 billion. However, as the coin is designed to facilitate microtransactions (fractions of a cent), a large supply is needed.

In a show of good faith, in early October 2017, the Tron team air dropped 500 TRX coins into the wallet of everyone with an account on the exchange liqui.io. Air drops like this have useful community building and general awareness effects.

Aeon (AEON)

Price at time of writing - $0.84
Market Cap at time of writing - $12,359,745

Available on:
BTC: Bittrex

If you've read my first book *Cryptocurrency: Beginners Bible*, you'll remember I talked about Monero (the price has risen 3x since the release of said book) being the only truly private cryptocurrency currently on the planet. Well, that's no longer the case. You can think of Aeon as Monero's little brother. In a market of overhyped, overbought ICOs and heavily marketed copycat projects, Aeon brings lightweight innovation - the coin is a mobile-friendly, decentralized digital currency.

The team behind Aeon feature some of the core Monero developers - in the words of Aeon's founders "everybody's main internet device continues to be their cellphone, a device with a low-powered CPU and limited available storage. Aeon is about enabling this era, enabling an age where all people everywhere have the freedom to privately send and receive money with whatever gadget they already own."

By focusing on smaller transactions like this, Aeon aims to take a firm hold on the daily consumer market, all while offering a completely private service. So why the need for privacy? Frankly, many of us are sick and tired of our data being stored on central servers, privy to anyone that wants to take a look. Aeon uses cryptography to completely encrypt the information of both the sender and receiver in a transaction. Therefore, the identifying information of each user is not available on the blockchain itself. This is compounded with what is known as "ring signatures", which means the funds are untraceable.

Aeon will often be compared to Monero, however the faster blockchain verifications (thanks to their lighter weight Proof of Work algorithm) allow transaction to process faster, making it more useful for day-to-day use. You could look at the relationship similar to Litecoin's relationship with Bitcoin.

The lightweight features of Aeon allow users to run a full node on their mobile, this speeds up transactions due to no longer needing a third party app running a public node. Another addition area where Aeon shines is by using a limited amount of storage space on a given device, this reduces the likelihood of any age-based attacks on your mobile or laptop.

One area that could be seen as a drawback for Aeon is the lack of a publicly released roadmap. This is due to an extremely small development team, of officially just 1 person at the time of writing. However, Aeon's open source code is publicly available, and everyone is welcome to contribute to the project, in a similar vein to Monero - which benefited greatly from a enthusiastic community. A community generated development fund currently stands at over $400,000 - which is far higher than other coins with much larger market caps. This fund will be used to attract elite developers to the project in the short and medium term.

Supply wise, Aeon has a relatively small number of coins released at around 14.5 million. For those into mining, Aeon currently offers some of the better rewards in the cryptocurrency mining space, plus in theory their lightweight nodes could allow for efficient mobile mining (albeit for significantly reduced rewards).

Where Aeon's future growth may lie is a release their mobile wallet in the short term and wider adoption of private cryptocurrencies in the long term. This is one coin that certainly has gamechanging potential.

RISE (RISE)

Price at Time of Writing - $0.401
Market Cap at Time of Writing - $45,404,571

Available on:
Fiat: Litebit.eu (EUR)
BTC: Bittrex, YoBit

Where to store?
You can download RISE wallets for desktop (Windows, Mac and Linux) from the Rise website
http://rise.vision

RISE is an ecosystem for developers, businesses, tech startups, investors and device users. The platform offers decentralized applications and the creation of smart contracts. The platform aims to increase adoption of RISE versus competitor platforms by providing Software Development Kits (SDKs), so that RISE applications can be run on Windows, Mac and Linux. The platform also supports popular programming languages like Javascript, Python and Ruby. There's also a RISE investment platform where RISE holders can pool resources together to invest in projects.

Where RISE really shines is their "blockchain incubator" service for startup Decentralized Apps (DApps). These developers can use the RISE platform to develop their companies/coins, and RISE holders will be entitled to 20% of these coins when the product successfully launches. While RISE isn't the first cryptocurrency to offer a form of passive income like this, a 20% reward is far higher than competing coins.

The two current projects built using the RISE platform are Interlet and Chipz. Interlet is an Ethereum based person-to-person vacation platform that aims to compete with AirBNB, by charging a much lower fee to operate. Anyone who has used AirBNB in the past will know about often ridiculous fees (up to 20% of the vacation price) that AirBNB takes as a middleman, and Interlet plans to use this is a basis for providing competition.

The second project is Chipz, an online casino platform due for launch in Q1 2018. Those who hold RISE will be given a % of Chipz tokens based on how much RISE they hold at the time of launch. Chipz plans to integrate with the Waves platform so that holders of the token can directly exchange their Chipz for fiat currency, which in theory will make the casino a lot more accessible. A successful launch of Chipz will certainly mean good things for the price of RISE in the short term.

Competition wise, RISE can be compared to Ark and Lisk in broad terms. However, RISE offers token holders a much bigger share of DApp coins launched on the platform at 20% when compared to Ark's 5%.

The roadmap is an area where RISE is lacking when compared to other coins mentioned in this book. Projects are in the pipeline, including the release of Interlet, as well as a mobile friendly version of RISE. However, a lack of dates for these releases is something that the RISE team needs to address to inspire investor confidence.

That being said, the RISE team is a strong one, with 10 developers, many of which have a long and successful history in the blockchain and cryptocurrency space. One area I particularly like is the weekly release of a RISE newsletter, these 4 page posts give updates on the RISE ecosystem, as well as announcing team members, and any new projects in development. Easily digestible new bites like this are useful if you don't come from a tech or development background, or are more interested in the business side of things.

The RISE community continues to grow rapidly, and often times community driven initiatives can help maintain and increase the coin's value over time.

Supply wise, RISE currently has 114 million tokens in circulation. The utility of these tokens has already been discussed, and there are strong use cases both as voting tools and as a currency to be traded. The trading volume is very high for a coin of RISE's size, and this bodes well for it as an investment tool as it is less susceptible to price manipulation than coins with lower trading volumes.

Funfair (FUN)

Price at Time of Writing - $0.026
Market Cap at Time of Writing - $100,375,472

Where to store?
FUN tokens are ERC 20 tokens, so you can add them to MyEtherWallet by using the following information:
Address: 0xbbb1bd2d741f05e144e6c4517676a15554fd4b8d
Token symbol: FUN
Decimal places: 8

Funfair is a decentralized gaming platform powered by Ethereum smart contracts, based out of London and Singapore. Powering the creation of "smart casinos", the platform is attempting to capitalize on the potential $40 billion a year online gambling industry, an industry which has increased by 50% since 2010 and in projected to increase by another 50% by 2020.

The platform's main aims are to facilitate the building of online casinos with 3D games that can be built with current technology (namely HTML5) for both desktop and mobile platforms. In terms of gas costs (Ethereum transactions fees), these will be up to 10x cheaper than current online casino platforms.

As the games are executed with the use of Ethereum smart contracts, their fairness is not in question. The random number generated is transparent on the blockchain so anyone can see the results are truly randomized, and not artificially in favor of the house. This ensures that no one is being cheated by the casino operator.

Cryptocurrency gaming in itself is not a new phenomenon, in fact Bitcoin casinos have been running for years. However, the fluctuations in the currency itself, along with notoriously slow payouts and lack of regulation, has yet to see mainstream adoption.

The development team is built largely of members with previous experience in game creation. Founder and Angel Investor Jez San has a storied history in the gaming sector and helped play a part in the creation of multi-million dollar selling video games like Star Fox, while recently his experience lies in the online gaming space at leading online poker website PKR.com, before leaving the site to focus on Funfair. These connections could play a vital role in the adoption of Funfair within the gaming space, which is undoubtedly the number one challenge it faces going forward.

There are already complete 3D games built using the platform, which means the technology is now firmly beyond the theoretical stage, and into the execution stage. The Funfair launch suite itself already has 6 games under construction, which will be used as playable prototypes at industry events.

It is important to note that Funfair's value will not just come from the operation of 1 casino. Licensing the software itself will potentially create thousands of online casinos, which in turn will be in significantly more revenue than a centralized model. However, the challenge of getting that initial casino to decide to use the platform is a large one.

The main problem that has previously plagued this sector the transaction fees that occur with every new game or spin. This has led to other blockchain casinos suffering from slow playing times and costly fees to play. After all, nobody wants to have to wait 30 seconds between blackjack hands or between dice rolls for roulette. There's also a limit with the number of players that can play at one time. Current technology has a general rule of about 10 players per table, whereas with blockchain technology, the number, in theory, is unlimited.

The transactions costs are estimated to be at a ridiculous $1 per hand for blockchain based blackjack games and $0.75 per bet on dice games. With typical bet sizes, this represents around 10% per hand. Transactions costs have a further effect, because of the house edge of casino games. Even with higher bets minimizing the cost per hand, the house edge + transaction costs are simply too large for the player to even have a chance of profiting in the long term. Funfair's aim to reduce these will lead to a much higher uptake from players. One of Funfair's key goals is to reduce player transaction costs to a much more manageable 0.1% per hand.

Supply wise, over 3 billion FUN tokens were generated in the ICO - with no further token due to be generated during Funfair's life cycle . The sounds like a large number, however it is important to note that many of this are designed to be "burned" as transaction fees for the games themselves.The FUN token value itself will be utilized in a number of ways. Including for playing the games themselves, paying affiliates (which is a significant part of the online casino industry), and paying the game creators themselves.

Mothership (MSP)

Price at Time of Writing - $0.167
Market Cap at Time of Writing - $23,389,520

Where to store?
MSP token are ERC20 tokens so can be stored on MyEtherWallet

Mothership is one of the most intriguing cryptocurrencies on the market today. Built on the Ethereum platform, the coin's aim is to make cryptocurrency markets accessible for EU companies and Estonian e-Residents.

To truly understand Mothership, it's important to first understand Estonian e-residency, and how that process works.

E-residency takes place in the form of an Estonian government issued "digital ID card", which is combined with an authorized digital signature. The signature is legally binding and allows anyone in the world to register an EU company online. This gives unprecedented access to the European market. In a time where previously repressed parts of the world are looking for ways to attract new business and investment, Estonia is certainly at the forefront of this movement.

Where Mothership comes in, is that for blockchain businesses, it allows incorporation in Estonia, with 100% remote online access. A bank account will be provided, which is then linked with the built-in cryptocurrency exchange. Estonia also offers 0% corporation tax for companies inside the e-residency scheme. This is an extremely attractive proposition for blockchain companies that were previously forced to operate in countries with less friendly regulation, both in terms of the legality of cryptocurrency based firms, and general business tax laws.

The project entails three parts. A cryptocurrency exchange with 24/7 access to the markets, which combined with automatic identification (linked to your e-residency) makes the transactions from cryptocurrency to fiat currency near instant. Anyone who has signed up to a cryptocurrency exchange will know the pains of having to wait days (or even sometimes months) for identity verification.

The built-in cryptocurrency wallet is connected to your e-residency, which provides an automatic digital signature, which in turn protects your funds from fraudulent activity.

The e-residency program continues to grow, and Estonia estimates more than 10 million e-residents by 2025. Government support is one area that many crypto-based assets lack, whereas Mothership has been truly embraced by the Estonian government.

The project's timeline is publicly available to view on Trello. The short-term goals include launching the beta version of the MSP token market whereas the actual exchange itself is planned for a launch between Q1 and Q2 2018. This is also the time period where the team plans to launch the e-residence wallet.

Supply wise, there will are currently 140 million MSP tokens, with an additional 60 million planned in the future.

The inherent risk to the Mothership project is that they are not specifically offering anything *new* to the market. There are already hundreds of cryptocurrency exchanges. However, the tie-in with the e-residency scheme, and the instantaneous swapping between cryptocurrency and fiat makes the project an attractive one in the short-to-medium term at the very least.

OKCash (OK)

Price at Time of Writing - $0.317
Market Cap at Time of Writing - $23,143,613

Where to store?
You can download the official OKCash wallet (available for both desktop and Android) from https://okcash.org/

Available on:
Fiat: Litebit.eu (EUR)
BTC: Bittrex, Cryptopia

Dubbing itself "the future of cash", OKCash plans to operate a worldwide payment system for microtransactions. With no cross-border payments and near instant confirmation times, the platform plans to target those in countries where bank account usage is not widespread. In other words, people have the ability to make payments to one another without needing a bank account.

The low-fee system allows OKCash to be useful for small donations or even online tipping. These tips can be made public and donations can be made over social networks for greater visibility. This could even be used in the case of emergencies to transfer funds fast to those affected.

While other cryptocurrencies promise similar things with regard to microtransactions and quick payments, where OKCash shines is the extremely low payment fee. There is no fee to receive a payment and the current fee to send OK coins is just 0.0001 OK, or $0.00003

One cool feature of the OKCash wallet is a built-in encrypted messaging system to protect users privacy.

OKCash has seen some strong initial adoption, with over 136,000 OKCash wallets being created already, and more than 19,000 addresses holding at least 1000 OK coins.

The proof-of-stake mining algorithm ensures minimal wasted energy when compared to a traditional proof-of-work algorithm (used by Bitcoin). The decentralized model also allows anyone to contribute to the OKCash network.

The team's marketing efforts have been unique and quite successful so far. A focus on video games has led to OKCash being a prize in both Minecraft and FIFA tournaments so far, with more projects like this to come in the near future.

The development team, and their lack of public visibility is an area that OK is lacking in. Although their site lists more than 40 team members, all of them currently go by pseudonyms, which is not helpful if the coin wants to achieve wider adoption.

Supply wise, there are roughly 72 million OK in existence currently. This number is deliberately larger than some other currencies in order to facilitate micro payments.

Note: OKCash is not to be confused with the Chinese Bitcoin exchange OKCoin.cn - double check any news regarding OKCash

Status (SNT)

Price at Time of Writing - $0.022
Market Cap at Time of Writing - $76,414,847

Available on:
Fiat: BTC9 (CN), b8wang (CN)
BTC: Bittrex, Liqui

Where to store?
Status users ERC20 tokens so can be stored using MyEtherWallet.

Status is an intriguing project that focuses on the mobile space. Based out of Switzerland, it's a free, open source mobile client targeting Android and iOS. The platform itself is built on Ethereum technology. Currently the platform supported 30 languages including Chinese, Korean and Russian. The main focus of the Status project in terms of high level goals is providing a fully private platform, with focus on a lack of censorship and economic transparency.

Co-Founder Jarrad Hope stated "One way to think about Status is that it'll eventually serve as a sort of onramp or gateway so that everyday people can benefit from decentralized applications built on Ethereum, whilst simultaneously helping DApp developers to reach new users."

Status users can search and discover decentralized apps (DApps). Similar to how one would do so on the Apple Store or the Google Play Store on their smartphone now. Examples of these apps include the freelancing platform Ethlance and Ujo, which is a decentralized music licensing and distribution platform. Status definitely have first mover advantage when it comes to a platform like this.

The other main usage here would be a decentralized peer to peer trading market. Similar to how localbitcoins.com currently operates. If Status can provide this for Ethereum based tokens, it could potentially be a game changer for the platform as a whole.

The aim of all this is to provide a digital hub where users only need one identity, as opposed to various usernames, passwords and apps that are common in the current system.

Status also features a built-in messenger with encrypted messaging and the ability to send Ethereum payments between parties, as well as smart contracts. The team chose to focus on messaging first and foremost, as they believed that this was the best and most efficient way to achieve mass market potential. Instant messaging software also has the highest install, and lowest uninstall rate of any mobile software.

The community element is a strong core belief of the platform. Status tokens (SNT) can also be used to ask questions to prominent community members, similar to how one would ask questions on the website Quora. Users can set a minimum number of SNT required to send them a message. This could lead to the rise in "celebrity users" with high levels of SNT required to contact them.

The team also offers rewards for those who can uncover bugs in their code. So far, the team has developed a fully functioning alpha product, with the help of over 6,000 testers.

In terms of competitors, you can think of Whatsapp as being the application with broad similarities to Status. The growth and true potential of Status will depend on the adoption of DApps as a whole, because it's unlikely that it's true calling will be purely as a mass-adopted chat app like Whatsapp or WeChat. If the team can facilitate a DApp store, then there is indeed a lot of room for growth in the coming years. In terms of cryptocurrency based competitors, kik is the one that is likely to be competition to Status in the short term.

One thing to factor with Status, is that first time movers often do not have a long-term advantage. The growth of Status will depend solely on their ability to stay ahead of the market, which is tough when competitors could come in and exploit Status' weaknesses as a platform.

Unlike other cryptocurrency projects, Status was self-funded for the first two years of its life. Supply wise, Status has a total supply of 6 billion, with 41% of this being funds contributed by the public during their July ICO. Interestingly enough, their ICO was designed so that large investments could not dominate the holdings. The Status team actually refunded more ETH than they took in during the ICO period.

The team are very active on their Slack channel (which currently has over 15,000 members), which is something that can't be said for some of the other coins mentioned in this book. Like any complex project, transparency is always a good thing, especially in times when there may not be much to report on the development front.

In terms of roadmap, Status is aiming for a public release towards the end of 2018, or beginning of 2019 - making this a good opportunity to get involved before then. A beta release in the middle of 2018 would give a clearly indication of the long term potential of Status, both as a platform, and as a messaging system.

Tierion (TNT)

Price at Time of Writing - $0.081
Market Cap at Time of Writing - $34,638,811

Available on:
BTC: Liqui, HitBTC (CN),
ETH: EtherDelta

Tierion aims to use blockchain technology as a data verification platform. Using their open source timestamping proof Chainpoint - Tierion has the ability to verify the integrity of a file, record, or process - without having to rely on a third party.

The practical applications for this are widespread. The ability to issue digital receipts for purchases, insurance claims or stock trades, which act as an immutable proof of purchase is a great asset in fighting fraudulent chargebacks and fraudulent transaction claims.

For auditors, the ability to timestamp data with a proof of record will drastically lower the chances for people to go back into a database an alter it. For example, a situation like Enron would not be allowed to happen with data stored on the blockchain. Going one step further, the auditing industry as a whole faces a huge threat from blockchain solution such as Tierion

Medical records, legal records are other areas where blockchain's verification process could have great benefits for society at large in the future.

Many of the above examples are ones that don't just apply to Tierion, but blockchain technology as a whole. That being said - why Tierion?

The answer is simple, speed. Tierion's API lets developers add up to 100 records per second, this is far quicker than previous blockchain solutions. An additional big advantage is their usage of current technology to make the process user friendly. It is much easier to create data stores using HTML forms which are both desktop and mobile compatible, than it is to learn an entire new programming language just for this purpose. This bridge between generations of technology, has great usage potential in the blockchain space for the near future.

Another cool thing about Tierion is its integration with widely used applications such as Salesforce, Gmail, Google Docs, and Mailchimp.

Unlike many of the blockchain based firms in this book, Tierion also has a full functioning product, which you can actually sign up to use for free today. The free version is limited to 15,000 data records per month, which should be more than enough for the average home user. Obviously, from a business standpoint, the money will be made with the Enterprise versions of the software.

The project already has links with some larger multinational companies. An invitation to join Dutch electrical giant Phillips' Blockchain Lab, a thinktank dedicated to see how blockchain technology can be used in healthcare. January 2017 bought an announcement of a working agreement with Microsoft to use blockchain technology to prove data existence and validity.

The big question with Tierion, is the utility of the TNT token itself. Will TNT be adopted as part of the Tierion ecosystem, or will users still prefer to carry that their transactions using a different cryptocurrency.

First Blood (1ST)

Price at Time of Writing - $0.517
Market Cap at Time of Writing - $44,310,766

Available on:
BTC: Bittrex, Liqui

Built on the Ethereum platform and based out of Boston with heavy ties to China, First Blood focuses on the ever growing esports space. First Blood aims to build a blockchain support esports platform that will allow gamers from around the world to compete against one another for prizes.

The use of smart contracts will ensure all results are fair and just, and that no cheating can occur. For those not in the know, the esports world has been plagued by cheating scandals ever since cash prizes were first introduced.

Their marketing efforts have been solid to say the least, and their "from the ground up" marketing strategy includes offering sponsorships to video game live streamers.

In terms of game themselves, First Blood's main focus for now is on the extremely popular Multiplayer Online Battle Arena game DOTA2 - with other game support planned for the future

An already established relationship with blockchain video game developer MOLD was compounded by a huge announcement on October 2nd 2017.

"We are proud to announce we will be working with the Chinese Government and Chinese esports companies to organize esports tournaments!"

More specifically, they're going to be used by the General Administration of Sport of China., the government agency responsible for sports in China. In a statement on their website the team announced

"First Blood will be a partner for hosting the Chinese University Esports League (CUEL). CUEL is a huge competition in China and each year hundreds of thousands of students participate. The partnership with First Blood was put into place as CUEL aimed to reduce their overheard."

The full version of the platform isn't out yet, but previous developer updates have mentioned banning cheaters from the beta platform, which shows that the technology is working at a basic level at least.

Future plans for the coin include support for additional popular games such as League of Legends and Counter Strike: Global Offensive - making this coin one to watch as we move into 2018

2Give (2GIVE)

Price at Time of Writing - $0.0053
Market Cap at Time of Writing - $2,786,042

Available on:
BTC: YoBit, Bittrex

Where to store?
The 2Give team currently has desktop wallets for Windows and Mac available on their website. A Linux wallet is coming soon.

2Give (or GiveCoin 2.0) is a comparatively tiny project when compared to some of the larger ones discussed here like Bytom and Status. With a market cap of just under $3 million dollars, it's safe to say that this one is a long shot indeed, but it's one with a good cause at heart, which is why it made the cut for this book.

From the official website "2GIVE makes it easy to support your favorite non-profit or pro-social cause and can be used for "repaying it forward" through social tipping!" The coin is supported by the Strength in Numbers Foundation, a non-profit digital trust. The idea is that user can donate to their charity of choice, without giving a significant portion of the funds to a payment process, while simultaneously revealing their online identity.

As previously mentioned, 2Give is the newer version of what was known as GiveCoin. The reason for the switch is that GiveCoin suffered from "pool hoppers", miners who switched between mining chains because it was financially advantageous to do so. This led to a system where the top 2% of GiveCoin miners took home most of the mining profits. 2Give's switch to a Proof of Stake model allows fairness to be restored among the mining community.

2Give attracts miners with a social conscience with their reward system, which offers a 5% to miners and stakeholders who help keep the platform operational. Miners then get an additional 1% as a transaction fee for processing payments on the 2Give network.

Many online rumors are flying around regarding 2Give's partnership with a number of large companies, including online streaming service Twitch and even UNICEF. It should be noted that with a market cap as small as this, these rumors can and do have a significant effect on the price.

2Give has received some early adoption, including a partnership with the Japanese Bitcoin ATM network coinoutlet. Coinoutlet ATM users can now buy 2Give at any of the ATM's around the country.

Future plans for the coin include mobile wallets for both iOS and Android, as well as a real world "air drop" in which gift cards will be left in various location to spread awareness of 2Give. The growth of 2Give will be determined largely by the adoption of the idea from non-profits around the world. If larger ones do get involved, then 2Give tokens will therefore have more utility and increase in price accordingly.

Conclusion

Well there we have it. 12 altcoins under $1 that have HUGE potential for gains in the next 12-18 months.

I hope this information has been beneficial to you and has given you a foundation to invest some of the more unknown cryptocurrencies. There has never been a more exciting time for cryptocurrencies than right now, so there's no better time to get involved.

I encourage you to do additional research before investing in any of these, particularly by checking out the white papers on the individual coin websites, which will give you a much more in-depth look at the technology behind them.

Remember to invest wisely (with your own money), don't check your investments on a daily basis, and don't panic sell if you see a dip in the market.

I wish you the best of luck in the cryptocurrency market, and I hope you make a lot of money.

Finally, if this book has proved useful to you, I'd appreciate it if you took 2 minutes to leave it a review on Amazon.

Thanks,
Stephen

Cryptocurrency: Insider Secrets 2 - 10 Exciting Crypto Projects With Potential for Explosive Growth in 2018

By Stephen Satoshi

Factors to Consider Before Investing

While larger cryptocurrencies like Bitcoin, Ethereum and Litecoin have long track records and multiple real world functions, some of the coins mentioned in this book do not - hence their lower price.

There are a number of different variables to investigate before you undertake any investment, and cryptocurrency has its own set.

Proof of Concept (PoC)

In other words, does the technology have a working model, or is it still in a theoretical stage. Obviously more mature coins will have a higher value, with the more theoretical coins being a bigger risk. As the different coins here are in different stages of their life cycle, that is up for you to decide.

The development team

Who are the developers and what is their track record? Particularly within the cryptocurrency and blockchain space. Another thing to consider is their record within the particular industry they are targeting.

The whitepaper

A good whitepaper discusses the technical aspects of the coin, in a way that the average investor can understand. Many low quality crypto projects take shortcuts in their whitepaper and tend to fill it with hypey language rather than actual technological information. If a whitepaper doesn't discuss exactly how the project works, then that is a huge red flag.

The utility of the token

Ideas are great, but if the coin token itself doesn't have usage, then the true potential of the project must be questioned. This is especially true in the case of certain coins where the theory and market potential checks out, but the question of "why can we just use Bitcoin/Litecoin to do the same thing" is often raised.

The roadmap

Roadmaps are important for short-term gains because they set out development targets for the coin. If these goals are reached and the products/platforms move from alpha to beta to a fully launched product, then that only means positive things for the coin and its value. If a team consistently meets targets on or before a deadline, then we can look at that as a positive sign.

Which exchanges the coin is listed on

Many of these coins are still only available on smaller exchanges. Once the coin is listed on larger exchanges (for example Binance), the coin has greater visibility and this leads to a rise in value.

Mining Algorithms - Proof of Work vs. Proof of Stake vs. Others

You'll notice later on when discussing individual coins that I sometimes talk about which mining algorithms are used. The two most popular are Proof of Work (PoW), used by Bitcoin and Proof of Stake (PoS), used by coins like Neo, Stellar Lumens, Ark and a number of Ethereum based tokens. Ethereum plans to move to Proof of Stake in 2018.

In my previous book *Bitcoin: Beginners Bible* I discussed why I don't recommend mining as an effective method for obtaining cryptocurrency, for the regular user. That still holds true for the majority of the coins listed in this book, but it's important to understand why the difference in mining algorithm matters.

Why do we need mining?

We need mining to ensure a transaction (or block) is correctly validated, in other words, we need to ensure the same transaction doesn't occur twice - known as the double spending problem. As a reward for validating this transaction, miners are rewarded with a tiny percentage of it (known as the network fee).

To put it bluntly, Proof of Work takes a lot more energy than Proof of Stake. A 2015 study showed that one Bitcoin transaction takes the equivalent daily energy of 1.57 US homes. Proof of Stake is also a fairer, more energy efficient system, which is a huge advantage for community based coins.

Other systems include Delegated Proof of Stake (DPoS), which is a more community based initiative. DPoS is where stakeholders vote for delegates to make decisions for them, allowing both parties to profit from those decisions.

How to Buy Bitcoin, Ethereum & Litecoin in Under 15 Minutes

Gone are the days when buying Bitcoin was a time consuming and somewhat uncomfortable endeavor. Nowadays buying Bitcoin is a similar process to exchanging currency when you go on vacation.

There are two ways to buy Bitcoin, the first is to use fiat currency (USD, Euros, GBP etc.) to purchase cryptocurrency via an exchange. These exchanges function the same way as regular foreign currency exchanges do. The prices fluctuate on a daily basis, and like regular currency exchange markets - they are open 24/7. These exchanges make their money from charging a small fee for each transaction.

Some charge both buyers and sellers, some only charge a fee for buying. For security reasons, most of these exchanges will require you to verify your ID before allowing you to purchase cryptocurrency.

It is also important to note the type of payments each exchange supports. Some allow for debit/credit card payments whereas other only accept PayPal or bank wire transfers. Below are the three biggest and reputable currency exchanges for purchasing Bitcoin, Ethereum and other altcoins with fiat currency like US dollars, Euros or British Pounds.

Coinbase

Currently largest currency exchange in the world, Coinbase allows users to buy, sell and store cryptocurrency. Coinbase is undoubtedly the most beginner friendly exchange for anyone looking to get involved in the cryptocurrency market. They currently allow trading of Bitcoin, as well as, Ethereum and LiteCoin using fiat currency as a base. As of January 1st 2018, you can now buy Bitcoin Cash on Coinbase as well. Known for their stellar security procedures and insurance policies regarding stored currency. The exchange also has a fully functioning iPhone and Android app for buying and selling on the go, very useful if you are looking to trade.

Once you are signed up and complete the identity verification procedures you can buy Bitcoin with your credit or debit card instantly.

Coinbase also recently launched the Coinbase Vault, which is a secure way of storing your cryptocurrency while still having it accessible to trade. The vault uses double email address + phone verification in order to access your funds. If you're planning on holding long-term, I still recommend offline storage - but as an intermediary option, the Vault is a step in the right direction.

If you sign up for Coinbase using this link, you will receive $10 worth of free Bitcoin after your first purchase of more than $100 worth of cryptocurrency.

http://bit.ly/10dollarbtc

Note, if you're going to be trading Bitcoin, I recommend doing so on Coinbase's partner platform GDax, which has lower fees.

How to buy Altcoins

The vat majority of cryptocurrency projects cannot be bought directly for fiat currency. They require you to buy Bitcoin or Ethereum first and then exchanging that into these altcoins.

Binance

My personal favorite altcoin exchange, and the one with the most liquidity on a number of coins. Binance has over 100 cryptocurrencies available, and nearly all of them now have both BTC and ETH trade pairings.

Their support is top notch, and probably the best of any exchange. You'll have to transfer the coins to a wallet if you want to securely store them long-term, but for buying and trading altcoins - you can't go wrong with Binance.

Poloniex

With more than 100 different cryptocurrencies available and data analysis for advanced traders, Poloniex is the most comprehensive exchange on the market. Low trading fees are another plus, this is a great place to trade your Bitcoin into other cryptocurrencies. If you have never purchased Bitcoin before, you will no be able to do so as Poloniex does not allow fiat currency deposits. Therefore, you will have to make your initial Bitcoin purchases on Coinbase or Kraken.

Other sites I have personally used to purchase cryptocurrency include Liqui and Cryptopia. Please do your due diligence when selecting which exchange to buy and store coins on, and ensure you are always typing the correct web address to avoid phishing sites.

Transferring your newly purchased Bitcoin to your exchange of choice.

Once you have bought your Bitcoin from Coinbase/Kraken, you'll need to then transfer it over to Binance, Bittrex or whichever exchange your coin of choice is listed on. To do this, simply go to the exchange you need to transfer the coins to (e.g. Bittrex) and click on "deposit", choose BTC (remember to double check you've clicked the correct coin). This will generate an address that looks like this 1F1tAaz5x1HUXrCNLbtMDqcw6o5GNn4xqX

From there, go to your Coinbase/Kraken BTC wallet and select "send", then in the "recipient" section copy the BTC address of the new exchange. Double check the amount of BTC you are sending, then click send and the transfer will initiate. Most of the time transfers take around 10 minutes, however, some exchanges take longer to process. Once your transfer is complete you can then exchange your BTC for any of the altcoins listed below.

Storing Your Coins - How to set up MyEtherWallet

Many of these coins are based on the Ethereum blockchain, and therefore use ERC20 tokens. Therefore, these tokens can be stored in Ethereum wallets. Wallets can be daunting to set up at first, so I recommend you use something simple to get started, the most convenient of these is MyEtherWallet.

Step-by-Step guide to setting up MyEtherWallet

13. Go to https://www.myetherwallet.com/
14. Enter a strong but easy to remember password. Do not forget it.
15. This encrypts (protects) your private key. It does not generate your private key. This password alone will not be enough to access your coins.
16. Click the "Generate Wallet" button.
17. Download your Keystore/UTC file & save this file to a USB drive.
18. This is the encrypted version of your private key. You need your password to access it. It is safer than your unencrypted private key but you must have your password to access it in the future.
19. Read the warning. If you understand it, click the "I understand. Continue" button.
20. Print your paper wallet backup and/or carefully hand-write the private key on a piece of paper.
21. If you are writing it, I recommend you write it 2 or 3 times. This decreases the chance your messy handwriting will prevent you from accessing your wallet later.
22. Copy & paste your address into a text document somewhere.
23. Search your address on https://etherscan.io/ Bookmark this page as this is how you can view your balance at any time
24. Send a small amount of any coin from your previous wallet or exchange to your new wallet - just to ensure you have everything correct

Hardware Wallets

Another safe, offline solution is to use a hardware wallet. The most popular of these being Trezor and Nano S. Both of these cost around $100, but represent a convenient, yet safe way to store your cryptocurrency. Further explanation of hardware wallets is in my first book *Cryptocurrency: Beginners Bible*.

10 High Potential Coins Under $1

Ambrosus (AMB)

Price at Time of Writing - $0.55
Market Cap at Time of Writing - $80,288,043

Available on:
BTC: Binance, Kucoin, Livecoin
ETH: Binance, Kucoin, RightBTC

Where to store:
AMB tokens are ERC20 tokens so you can store them in MyEtherWallet or other Ethereum wallets.

Ambrosus is another supply chain cryptocurrency project. This time based out of Switzerland and focused on two main market sectors, namely food and medicine. One of the core technology partners for the Ambrosus project is Parity Technologies.

By using real time sensors, linked to a blockchain, the project promises to monitor the distribution and food and medicine across the entire supply chain network. This will allow for anti-tampering monitoring as well as the enforcement of smart contracts to ensure the product reaches its end destination and an automatic payment is released based on the fulfillment of certain conditions.

For example, if you have a certain food that requires specific temperature, humidity and PH conditions to be met during transportation, a tracking device with a sensor that monitors these would be implemented in the container used to transport the goods. If all conditions are met when it reaches its end destination, then payment would automatically be released. If any of the conditions fail, the recipient would be notified in real time, and thus action could be taken accordingly.

There is also the issue of data storage, a blockchain solution means the data is publicly viewable so there are no issues regarding fraud, data hacking or manipulation.

Ambrosus' main asset at this time is the team behind its development. I would go as far as saying this is the best crypto development for a low market cap coin that I've seen in a long time. Headed up by CEO Angel Versetti, who has a wide industry background including time spent working at the United Nations, where he was the youngest project leader in UN history, and the World Resources Forum. He also has a corporate background with both financial firm Bloomberg and technology giant Google. CTO Dr. Stefan Meyer has a vast supply chain and food industry background having previously led R&D projects at Swiss food giant Nestle. The rest of the team is made up of equal parts storied corporate history and successful blockchain developers. They are backed up with some world class advisors including Oliver Bussman, previously named CTO of The Year by the Wall Street Journal. As well as Prof. Malcolm J W Povey, one of Britain's leading experts in food sensor technology. In a world of fake bio pictures, and develop aliases, a team as open and transparent with a history like this is frankly unprecedented in any but the biggest cryptocurrency projects.

Like many cryptocurrency projects, the Ambrosus project is built using the Ethereum blockchain.

So how is the token valuable? One of the biggest reasons for the low price right now is that the token economics have not yet been finalized. The main usage for AMB will be to facilitate transactions in the Ambrosus network, like how ETH is used for Ethereum and Gas is used for Neo. There are talks of masternodes being available, so users could stake their AMB tokens to help run the network and receive dividends in return. There are current debates about whether there would be larger funds needed to run a node or smaller funds with a legal contract. The alternative for this would be a two tier system with masternodes running alongside peer nodes.

In terms of competitors, there are a number of companies and crypto projects in the supply chain space. Two of the bigger ones out of China are VeChain and WaltonChain. WaltonChain is an RFID centered project, so the two may not be directly comparable. RFID is a limited technology that is pretty much limited to one (albeit important) function. However, with sensor technology, Ambrosus has a much larger usage scope. For example, the ability to monitor temperature and humidity. The project could be compared to Modum in this respect.

Where Ambrosus may be able to win though is the Swiss factor. It is much easier for European companies to do business with a fellow European company than it is for them to deal with Chinese ones. There is also the legitimacy issue. Will a company needing specialized supply chain solutions opt for a partnership with a Swiss company, in a country that has a long standing history of quality and impartiality. Or a Chinese company with a previous history of manipulation, in the case of WaltonChain's fake social media giveaway scandal. Getting first mover advantage and partnerships with large companies is going to be huge in which one of these supply chain projects has the highest ceiling, but Ambrosus certainly has a geographical advantage over its competitors in this respect.

Overall, this is certainly a long-term project with potential industry leading ramifications. As such, I wouldn't expect any giant price movements in the coming months. But as we move forward into 2019, there could well be big things for the Ambrosus project.

Jibrel Network (JNT)

Price at Time of Writing - $0.47
Market Cap at Time of Writing - $71,386,200

Available on:
BTC: Bibox, HitBTC, Gate.io
ETH: Bibox, HitBTC, Gate.io

Where to store:
JNT tokens are ERC20 tokens and thus can be stored using MyEtherWallet or by using a Ledger Nano S.

An interesting project based out of Switzerland that aims to bridge the gap between cryptocurrency and traditional markets. Jibrel focuses on government backed cryptocurrencies, so cryptocurrencies issued by central banks, but that still are backed by blockchain technology. You can think of Jibrel as a "decentral bank" in this respect.

The reason for the project is that while blockchain technology is an incredibly useful innovation, it is still limited in real world implementation due to the lack of widespread adoption for cryptocurrency. Co-Founder Yazan Barghuti summed this up well by saying "People pay their bills, their loans, and their mortgages in dollars, Euros, and pounds. They don't pay them in ETH or BTC."

So by bridging the gap, and implementing smart contracts with non-cryptocurrency based currencies, it will allow optimized real world transactions. For example, if a smart contract had been implemented on sub-prime loans and ratings before the 2008 financial crisis, we could have seen adjustments made prior to the market crash based on the actual performance and makeup of these assets, rather than outside pressure which forced ratings agencies to keep these bonds at a AAA rating. This is just one of the wide ranging theoretical applications of the Jibrel Network project.

Barghuti argues that the end user doesn't necessarily need to know their money is backed by cryptocurrency. They would want to use it the same way they always have. Similar to how online banking doesn't change the currency you are using, it's just backed by a computer instead of a bank book.

How Jibrel plans to do this is by using what it calls CryptoDepository Receipts or CryDRs. This will allow traditional financial assets to be backed by the Jibrel Network's cryptography. So if you held $100 in silver, for example, a USD CryDR would back this up with $100 worth of JNT tokens. These CryDRs could also be used for trading.

As far as the user side of things goes, Jibrel aims to make things simple and this is where the jWallet and jCash make their mark. jWallet will function as a regular cryptocurrency wallet, but aims to bring greater security to the equation. You can also use the wallet to exchange cryptocurrency for fiat currency the same way you would do so on an exchange. This can help protect your assets if you are worried about cryptocurrency volatility.

Initially, the project will run using the Ethereum network. It is interesting to note that all jWallet's will run using Jibrel's own Ethereum nodes, so the end user doesn't have to connect themselves. While some may argue that this is a centralized model, one which cryptocurrency purists often fight against - there are practical implications for this. Barghuti argues that this approach is one that favors scalability more than anything else, stating "'Yeah, but the whole point about Bitcoin is it's off-grid, etc.' Okay you can stay off-grid, and that's a $500 billion market. But if you go on-grid, you can start tackling the issues with the $34 trillion global economy."

Initially, Jibrel will support 6 fiat currencies and 2 further money market instruments, with plans to roll out further currencies in the future. Ultimately it would seem that support for 20 or 30 currencies at the same time would be completely possible.

In terms of the team behind it. Co-Founders Yazan Burghati and Talal Tabbaa both have a strong financial services background, both having previously worked for the Big 4 firms. The technical chops come from Victor Mezrin, who previously ran one of the largest altcoin mining operations in the world.

Going forward, we have the release of the Jibrel institutional level banking platform scheduled for Q3 2018. This will be a big determinant of whether the project is successful or not. There are very few cryptocurrency projects this close to launching such a significant venture, and if it is successful in the early stages, I doubt that Jibrel will stay at its current price. The only competitor coin I can think of who are targeting financial institutions on this scale would be QASH, based out of Japan, who I covered in a previous book.

Then in Q4, the team has planned the full scale launch of the decentralized Jibrel Network. By this time we will have a solid grasp of whether the project is going to be a smash hit, or if it will fall by the wayside. Like any project that deals with banks, licensing is going to be a tricky hurdle to overcome. Different countries have different licensing procedures which take different lengths of time to pass - and we've seen how this can delay projects in the past in the case of debit card projects like Monaco.

Either way, Jibrel Network is an extremely exciting project which huge ramifications if it is successful. A breath of fresh air in the sense that it addresses the current limitations of blockchain technology and aims to give real world application without needing to reinvent the wheel. I wouldn't expect too much price movement in the next quarter, but by the end of the year, we will have a better idea of just how successful the project can be.

LoMoCoin (LMC)

Price at Time of Writing - $0.07
Market Cap at Time of Writing - $18,033,963

Available on:
BTC: Bittrex, CoinExchange

Where to store:
The native LoMo app has a built in cryptocurrency wallet

LoMoCoin, also known as LoMoStar is an intriguing project out of China that focuses on the incentivized shopping space.

First and foremost to truly understand the potential of the coin, you must understand the market it is targeting. Incentivized shopping, in other words, shopping via the use of digital coupons, is a huge deal in China and across Asia. Many businesses have social media accounts, for example on WeChat, China's biggest smartphone social media platform, in which they distribute coupons directly to customers. In other words, if you want to go to Dunkin Donuts, for example, you can follow their WeChat account and you will receive a coupon for doing so. As businesses compete for foot traffic, coupon based shopping is becoming more popular than ever.

The concept centers around the Chinese tradition of "red envelopes". Traditionally these are given out on special occasions like Chinese New Year and contain money. With LoMo, these envelopes would be in the form of discount codes for local stores.

For example, you are out shopping with friends, when suddenly you get a notification on your phone notifying you of a flash sale in a nearby store. This store might even be one of your favorites, and thus you've just scored a huge discount. From the store's perspective, performing airdrops like these builds brand loyalty, and gives them a chance to win new business that they would not previously have had access to.

LoMoStar is the app itself that the currency is distributed through. The app promises to be an all-in-one shopping and social platform where users can not only claim rewards and spend their cryptocurrency, but also perform their own airdrops with their friends. The app also has a built in cryptocurrency exchange, which while not revolutionary, will be convenience once increased adoption continues.

This kind of native advertising brings disruption to the traditional model of sponsored ads like Google AdWords and Facebook Ads. Year by year these are representing lower returns for those using them, as ad price increases and customers get more and more "overmarketed". In other words, they make a lot of money for Google and Facebook, but often represent poor ROI for the businesses running the ads.
The main driving force behind LoMo is the number of users downloading the app itself. As the user base becomes bigger, more businesses have incentives to do airdrops, and thus we can see somewhat of a snowball effect. Having a low barrier to entry "on-ramp" so to speak is a great way to attract those who are new to the cryptocurrency space. We have seen this in the past with coins like Ripple that became "accessible" due to their low price, despite their high market cap and limited room for growth going

forward. Being able to take your first step into the crypto world just by downloading a smartphone app is a very simple solution for many users. Especially in target areas like Shanghai as well as other large Asian cities like Tokyo and Seoul.

Many users have reported earning over $100 USD worth of coins within the first few months of having the app on their phones. Which isn't bad seeing as you don't really have to do anything to get them. You can then transfer these tokens to more established cryptocurrencies like Bitcoin and Ethereum if you wish. Once again, this just reiterates the low barrier to entry effect and how this could be a huge bonus going forward.

The big question with this project is the same question we have with any project based in China. There is a certain risk involved with Chinese companies due to the cultural and regulatory differences when compared to the West. This is then compounded by the Chinese government's reactionary stance on cryptocurrency and often sweeping change in the law. For example, one of the biggest events in 2017 was when the government decided that Chinese citizens could not participate in ICOs, which led to a big downturn in the market. What further compounded this drop is that many media outlets in the West reported this event as "China bans cryptocurrency."

In terms of the team, I have to say I was very impressed. There are over 70 employees, many of whom have a solid blockchain background. CEO Xiong LiJian was previously involved in Litecoin mining development on both the hardware and software side.

Then we have to examine the potential for the project outside of China. Although the app currently has airdrops in multiple countries, it remains to be seen just how widespread adoption will be outside of the Middle Kingdom. That said, even if the idea is *only* successful within China, there will still be significant growth from the current price.

Overall, I like the idea of LoMo and their app. The social element could play a big part in bringing new users into the cryptocurrency space, which is vital if the technology is going to grow as we move forward. Low barriers to entry combined with incentivized rewards for using it, mean we could see industry changing ramifications. These are still early days, but if you are interested and want to see for yourself just how the project works, I recommend downloading the app on your iPhone or Android and check it out. After all, if you aren't yet invested in crypto, this could be your first chance to own coins of your very own, without having to invest a single penny.

WePower (WPR)

Price at Time of Writing - $0.17
Market Cap at Time of Writing - $60,534,439

Available on:
BTC: Huobi, Liqui
ETH: Huobi, Liqui

Where to store:
WePower is an ERC20 token and can by stored in MyEtherWallet

An eco-friendly blockchain solution that focuses on the renewable energy sector. By creating a platform that allows green energy producers to interact with energy investors and green energy consumers, they have an incentive to keep creating renewable energy sources. For consumers, they would be able to purchase energy directly at a rate below the market price due to the lack of need for a middleman such as a government body. The project has already been listed as one of the Top 10 innovative energy initiatives in Europe by Fast Company magazine. The size of the renewable energy sector is growing every year with an estimated $200 billion of new investment annually. The team estimates the token market potential to be approximately $1.2 trillion per year.

By using blockchain technology and smart contract implementation, the project solves compliance issues such as a green energy owner selling energy that isn't theirs for example.

The tokens themselves will be tied to energy prices, and thus will naturally be more stable than other cryptocurrencies. This is important when we ask the question of "why can't the project just use BTC or ETH for transactions". By running the platform like this, it gives an inherent need for the WPR token and thus the WPR token itself has an intrinsic value, which is a big part of any cryptocurrency project.

The platform will use an auction model, in which producers put their tokens up for sale and buyers have 48 hours to bid on them. After these 48 hours have expired, non-token holders have the opportunity to buy them as well. This unique approach to trading green energy gives WePower a huge first mover advantage when it comes to the energy trading sector, particularly in the eco-friendly part of it.

The project's initial focus will be on the European market because EU member states all share a common energy agreement with regards to regulations. This agreement makes cross border energy trading relatively seamless. The project is currently in talks with the Lithuanian government about a joint venture with nationalized energy companies. Pilot projects are also underway in Estonia.

The renewable energy sector is one that continues to receive a lot of government support, for both blockchain and non-blockchain ventures. This support could be huge for WePower when we compare it to other cryptocurrencies projects that often run into red tape and bureaucracy. Having backing from a government, rather than having to fight it, will be vital if the project is to succeed.

In terms of the team behind the project, Co-Founder Nikolaj Martyniuk has over 10 years experience in the green energy sector. He is backed up by team members with FinTech backgrounds, energy consultants and blockchain experts.

Progress has been solid so far and a demo platform is already available on the WePower website for users to test out.

A big step for the project came in late February 2018 when it was announced that Binance included WePower in the latest round of voting for inclusion on the platform. This is a community poll where Binance members can vote on coins they want to see included on the platform. If the coin wins the poll then it will be included on Binance for trading. Early results indicate that the coin has been doing well in the polls and at the time of writing ranked number 2 behind Dentacoin.

Going forward, there are a number of near future dates on the roadmap that you need to be aware of. April 2018 will see a full scale testing of the project in Estonia, if this is successful then it will no doubt mean big things for the project. Especially in a space where many crypto projects are still firmly in the theoretical stage. Later testing is scheduled for Q4 2018 in Spain and Australia. The first actual distributed energy will be in December 2018. Then there are further expansion plans for 2019.

Overall, I like the approach of the project with the token system being particularly appealing. The idea of a green energy trading platform without middlemen is a fantastic application of blockchain technology. The need for the WPR token is another huge plus that just can't be overlooked. Listing on a larger exchange will be key in the short term, but the real challenge will be seeing if the testing phases in Estonia, Spain and Australia are successful. If they are, then this coin won't stay this low for long.

TheKey (TKY)

Price at Time of Writing - $0.0187
Market Cap at Time of Writing - Currently unknown due to lack of concrete information about circulating market supply. Based on estimated supply of 3.63 billion, we can make an approximate market cap estimation of around $65,000,000.

Available on:
BTC: Kucoin
ETH: Kucoin
NEO: Kucoin

Where to store:
TheKey uses the Neo protocol (NEP5) and thus you can store it in a Neo wallet. You can download one from the official Neo website https://neo.org/download - desktop, mobile and web wallets are available

Another project coming out of China, TheKey aims to use blockchain technology to create a decentralized national identification system.

This has many different uses in practical terms. One of the main ones being in healthcare. For example, individual citizens could apply for a smart identification card which would be linked to their cellphone. They could then use this to book doctor's appointments online. When they arrive at the hospital, the doctor could have automatic access to their medical records, and their insurance details. The ID could also be linked to a payment method, which could automatically pay for any medical bills required.

This then has anti-fraud ramifications, which could be useful for things like automatically ordering medication. For example, elderly patients could have medicine delivered to their home, so they wouldn't have to leave the house in order to get necessary medicines. Currently, there is no system in place which allows them to do this, because of concerns about people stealing identities to order medicine in order to resell it on the black market.

One of the first ICOs to use the Neo platform rather than Ethereum. ONCHAIN, the company behind Neo is also listed as a strategic partner for the project. The ICO itself was not without problems, as it went live at 2AM CET, which was immediately followed by a website crash and the donation amounts being filled without any chance for European investors to take part.

The coin boasts a number of big partnerships with Chinese companies, namely AliPay (AliBaba's payment platform). There are also plans to trial the technology in two pilot cities, with Jiaxing being the first one.

15 different patents have already been awarded by the Chinese State Intellectual Property Office (SIPO) which is promising to see and shows that the project clearly aims to have a larger scope than others.

The project is headed up by Catherine Li, who boasts an incredibly strong track record of entrepreneurship within China. In 2017 she was awarded Most Outstanding Women Entrepreneurs in China by the All-China Women's Federation. She previously worked at IMS Health, which provides big data solutions in the healthcare space. She is backed up by blockchain lead Ken Huang who worked at phone manufacturer Huawei as a Chief Blockchain Developer.

In terms of competition, the biggest project would be Civic. However, TheKey's focus on China is what makes it stand out. Chinese governments tend to favor internal projects rather than international ones. And if TheKey can garner some early adoption within China, this will make any nationwide or international rollout much easier. This is what sets it apart from the other identity verification blockchain projects. The other factor to remember, especially for a project like this, is that there doesn't only have to be "one winner", many competing projects can and will co-exist side by side, and take up a decent market share.

In terms of roadmap, the project mainnet is scheduled for release in December of 2018.

Right now the low price can be attributed to overall market conditions and lack of listing on a larger exchange. Kucoin is fairly solid and reliable but there just isn't the volume of a Binance or a Bittrex to support higher prices. A March announcement that the coin would be listed on Chinese exchange LBank, which is currently the 16th largest exchange in the world by volume, so this could have some additional growth effects in the short term.

The other drawback is the lack of literature available about the project in English. After studying the official website for some time, I still had a number of unanswered questions that I had to go to unofficial sources within the community to find the answers to. Once greater clarification is made in English on the official website, I have no doubt that more investors will be attracted to the project.

Out of all the projects I've discussed in this book, I'd say this is no doubt one of the more high-risk, high-reward type projects. The Chinese factor, and lack of English communication does mean we could all be mislead into believing the project is further along than it is. However, if you are willing to accept this, this could well be one of the biggest gainers of 2018 and beyond. From a blockchain enthusiast standpoint, it's interesting to see how scalable a NEP5 token will be when compared to one running on the Ethereum network. If TheKey fits your risk/reward profile then it is definitely a project worth checking out.

Note: The project is not to be confused with KeyCoin or SelfKey, which both use the (KEY) symbol. SelfKey in particular focuses on the same space so please ensure you are buying the correct token.

Oyster Pearl (PRL)

Price at Time of Writing - $0.97
Market Cap at Time of Writing - $72,546,189

Available on:
BTC: Kucoin, Cryptopia
ETH: Kucoin, CoinExchange, IDEX
NEO: Kucoin

Where to store:
PRL Tokens can be stored in MyEtherWallet. To create a custom token take the following steps.

Contract Address: 0x1844b21593262668B7248d0f57a220CaaBA46ab9
Symbol: PRL
Decimals: 18

Oyster Pearl addresses the issue of advertising on websites and provides a solution that satisfies both business owners and consumers who are browsing the websites. In their own words "Goodbye banner ads. Hello Oyster." The project combines decentralized storage and payment for content creators.

Currently, it is estimated that 50% of web users have some sort of ad blocking software installed on their computer or on their browser. Much of the other 50% have become somewhat immune to ads due to their frequency.

How it works is by using web visitors' excess computing power (CPU and GPU power) to store files on a decentralized ledger. This excess power provides Proof of Work which maintains the storage network. Site owners are then paid by the storage users, and in turn, web visitors get an ad-free browser experience.

The files themselves are stored on the IOTA tangle and uses Ethereum smart contracts in order to verify correct storage data. Because of all the data is encrypted and decentralized, fragments of files are stored rather than complete ones, this makes the files more secure than if they were stored on a centralized server like Dropbox for example. This model is open source, so the community can monitor it and ensure there is no nefarious action occurring at any time.

The project makes it extremely simple for businesses to adopt. In fact, all you need to do is add a single line of HTML code to your existing website. So any website that can run Javascript, can run the Oyster protocol. In theory, this should also provide little to no browser slow down or impacted computer performance on the user end either. This simplicity is quite remarkable in a space where many blockchain projects require developers to learn entirely new programming languages just to take advantage of a particular project.

There are a number of blockchain cloud storage projects, with a chief competitor being Storj, which is built entirely on the Ethereum blockchain. However, the main difference between the two is that Storj is strictly focused on storage, without the advertising incentives given to website owners. Siacoin is another competitor, although that project has run into numerous difficulties since their ICO last year. Oyster also has no plans to charge fees for downloading any stored files, whereas Sia does charge per download.

The team is headed up by anonymous developer Bruno Block. This person's anonymity is a cause for concern for some investors, while others are less worried about it. I should say that developers wishing to remain anonymous, while strange, is not uncommon in the crypto space. Much of the other team has come forward with their identities, and maintain public LinkedIn profiles. CTO Alex Firmani has a solid background in the cloud storage space, so industry experience is there. Many of the engineers on the project also have active GitHub profiles which is promising to see.

The main areas to monitor going forward are adoption. Will websites actually use the Oyster protocol versus the traditional advertising models like Google AdSense? Another area of caution would be whether the code added to the HTML will flag a site a malicious by certain anti-virus and anti-malware software.

A more technical concern would be the scalability of IOTA's Tangle network, which at this point has yet to be tested. The Oyster team have already said they will move to their own blockchain solution if the Tangle cannot live up to their needs. This is fine in theory, however, in practice, any switch will have a significant impact on the project.

In terms of roadmap, the team are currently in the Testnet A stage of thins, with Testnet B scheduled for later this year. Testnet B will be a public testnet. Mainnet is currently scheduled for April 2018 which is when Oyster will be fully up and running, and tweaks can be made if necessary.

Oyster Pearl tokens (PRL) are ERC20 tokens. After the latest coin burn there are around 98 million tokens in circulation. The token will be used to pay website owners who install the Oyster code on their site.

If you can overlook an anonymous figure heading the project up, Oyster Pearl is an ambitious project with great potential. Seeing a project running on IOTA's tangle is great to see from an adoption standpoint, and this is certainly a coin to look at closely.

ChainLink (LINK)

Price at Time of Writing - $0.51
Market Cap at Time of Writing - $179,183,250

Available on:
BTC: Binance, Huobi, OKEx
ETH: Binance, Huobi, OKEx

Where to store:
LINK tokens are ERC 20 tokens and can by stored on MyEtherWallet or other Ethereum wallets.

Based out of the US, ChainLink is one of the more ambitious projects out there and aims to create a platform where users can attach smart contracts to existing apps and data. This acts as a bridge between non-blockchain resources like bank accounts and data services and a public smart contract ledger. This would allow users to create contracts that perform the same function as real world binding agreements, but without the expensive middleman.

The entire theory behind the project is that current smart contract platform does not function with off-chain resources. Therefore a bridge is needed and that's where ChainLink comes into play. By acting as a bridge, the contract can be verified on the blockchain, without the data feeds needing to be on that blockchain as well.

In terms of use cases, there are many. For example, say you own a large warehouse that stores valuable goods. These goods are stolen one night, and you need to make an insurance claim. However, the insurance company is pushing back by claiming that the magnetic doors to the warehouse may not have been locked and thus this represents user error. By using ChainLink to connect the monitoring data for the doors, with your insurance contract - you would have an undisputed answer to the question. The same goes for an issue like a payment for a delayed flight, using ChainLink you have publicly verifiable data about how late the flight arrived and for what reason.

Maybe the biggest real world use case is in financial reporting. This could be anything from bond rates, interest rates and other derivatives. ChainLink would allow users to connect to external networks (like Bloomberg) in order to verify the correct data and thus the contract would pay out accordingly.

One of the bigger factors ChainLink has going for it is the ability to let users settle contracts in both fiat currency and LINK tokens. This will no doubt help real world adoption of the technology. The team even discusses this on their website and states that the current limitation of other smart contract platforms to mimic real-world financial agreements. As we saw int he case of the Jibrel Network, in the short to medium term, we will need some sort of bridging between traditional finance and cryptocurrency before we see widespread adoption of cryptocurrency only platforms.

The platform currently has partnerships in place with a number of other smart contract firms including zeppelin_os which powers over $1.5 billion worth of smart contracts. Another agreement is in place with Cornell University's Town Crier initiative - a patent pending system which verifies the security and trustworthiness of data.

An agreement is also in place with the payment network SWIFT. This came after the team won the Innotribe Industry Challenge in 2016. They are now working with SWIFT to develop a Proof of Concept - this will be centered around LINK smart contracts verified interest rates across data sources in order to generate a LIBOR average rate. The smart contract will then be used to generate secure payments based on this rate.

The main things holding back the project right now are the small development team. For the first 3 years of the project, there were only two developers, although CEO Sergey Nazarov confirmed at the end of 2017 that they had hired more members. Lack of updates from the team has been an issue, and a lack of public roadmap is also a cause for concern. For a project as mature as this one, greater public visibility is needed in the short term to reassure investors that everything is moving forward as they would have hoped.

In terms of the token itself. There are 1 billion LINK tokens in circulation, of which 350 million are in the current circulating supply. The team holds 30% with the other 70% split between Node Operators (needed to upkeep the network) and the general public. One interesting thing to note is that unlike other projects, there is no minimum staking requirement to become a node operator. Therefore this allows any users to participate in the network and earns passive income for doing so. Although the payout structure is yet to be finalized, this is certainly something to be aware of if you are interested in staking coins but don't have a huge amount of them.

Overall, ChainLink is a solid project that has proven real world application already. The partnerships in place are impressive, and the only thing holding it back is lack of transparency from the team. I would like to see them hire a full time press officer and marketing manager in order to better communicate the progress going forward. However, the technology alone makes this project well worth looking into.

SONM (SNM)

Price at Time of Writing - $0.15
Market Cap at Time of Writing - $54,959,826

Available on:
BTC: Binance, Tidex, Liqui
ETH: Binance, Liqui, Kucoin

Where to store:
SNM tokens are ERC 20 tokens and can by stored on MyEtherWallet or other Ethereum wallets.

SONM is a fascinating supercomputer project powered by the Ethereum blockchain, powered by miners using their idle computer resources. The project has already received some decent mainstream media attention and was voted #6 on the Top 10 Blockchain Projects To Watch Out For in 2018 by EntreprenEuros Magazine.

This has tremendous application including everything from web hosting to mobile and web applications, machine learning, scientific research, servers for hosting video games and video streaming.

This represents advantages to those needing to use these services when compared to the standard centralized solutions that we see today. Because the rental time on the supercomputer is completely flexible with no minimum amounts or minimum contract lengths - buyers only pay for the exact amount they need to use. If the task then takes fewer resources than the buyer anticipated, they will be refunded for the resources they did not need.

Miners have an incentive for powering the network as they will be paid in SNM tokens. You don't have to have a super powerful computer either, you can use your regular desktop or laptop. You can even use other devices with internet capabilities like your XBox and even your cellphone. Originally there were plans for SNM token holders to be rewarded with the network fees from the project, although this was dismissed due to potential regulatory issues (as the token would then be deemed a "security" by the SEC). There are still plans to reward token holders, but the economics have yet to be finalized. This isn't a major issue at this early stage, but it would be nice to see some additional information about this from the team within the next 6 months.

The project can be looked at as similar to Golem (GNT) which I discussed in the first edition of Cryptocurrency: Insider Secrets. Both aim to use idle computer resources to power supercomputers and thus we can view them as direct competitors. The one advantage SONM does have is that it plans to use the supercomputer for a wider variety of applications than just GPU rendering like the Golem project. In terms of development, SONM also has the advantage being further ahead on its roadmap. Once again, we should restate that there's no reason these two projects can co-exist with equal market shares.

Both projects share the same growing pains, namely, can the Ethereum network handle the sheer volume of transactions required to run a supercomputer like this. SONM's solution is to build their own sidechain (essentially an additional blockchain) which will process some of the transactions and lower the overall load on the Ethereum network. This sidechain will reduce all internal transaction costs to zero.

SONM has already announced a partnership with fellow Ethereum project Storj (discussed in Ethereum: Beginners Bible), the decentralized cloud storage platform. This will allow users to share files on the SONM platform. This additional step towards fully decentralized cloud computing is certainly an achievement going forward. Plus, it is always good to see blockchain project working together in order to gain mainstream adoption.

March brought news of another partnership, this time with blockchain AI platform DBrain. DBrain will be utilizing SONM's supercomputer to convert raw data into real world AI solutions for businesses around the world. SONM CEO Alexei Antonov stated, "Collaboration with Dbrain is an excellent way of demonstrating the possibilities of our project."

One thing SONM does extremely well is hitting their roadmap deadlines. From my research, I found they consistently hit project advancements on or before they were scheduled to. This demonstrates consistency from the team, and adds an extra layer of trustworthiness that other cryptocurrency projects simply do not have. Trust is vital in a space where the early years were dominated by news of theft, hackings and criminal activity.

As previously mentioned, users can buying resources using the SNM token, and those donating their idle computing power will be paid using the token as well. This already gives the token an intrinsic value, and use case - which is always one thing to look for when examining cryptocurrency projects.

In terms of roadmap, an MVP was released in late 2017 and a successful bug bounty round (rewarding users for finding bugs or errors in the code) occurred after that. A Windows client was also launched around this time. The first fee payouts are scheduled for Q2 2018. Followed by a full network release along with the full version of the SONM wallet on the Ethereum network - which is scheduled for July-August 2018.

In the short term, continued announcements of collaborations with other companies will be key to driving price action. In terms of growth potential, Golem currently has a market cap 6X higher than SONM's, and while the project is more mature, it seems that the SONM team are moving forward at a faster rate. This is one of the projects in the book that could have significant price action on both a short and long term basis.

OriginTrail (TRAC)

Price at Time of Writing - $0.18
Market Cap at Time of Writing - $48,535,364

Available on:
ETH: IDEx, HitBTC, ForkDelta

Where to store:
TRAC tokens are ERC 20 tokens and can by stored in MyEtherWallet and other Ethereum wallets.

OriginTrail is a blockchain project that focuses on the supply chain sector. The project was developed in order to combat the scalability problems that other decentralized supply chain projects are facing. The project has already won a number of plaudits in the industry including Walmart China's Food Safety Innovation and the Food + City People's Choice Award.

Supply chain data is often fragmented, as it comes from multiple different sources. This makes it difficult to track and monitor. OriginTrail aims to make this data more manageable without slowing down the process. You could potentially use this to track foos deliveries and authenticity of products when looking at their labels among other things. For example, a 2017 study showed to 70% of wine sold in China was fake. Meaning that it's origins were not what was stated on the bottle and was instead a mix of cheaper wine and water. This fake wine is then sold at a huge markup, which is often over 1000%. There have also been stories of rice contamination across the country. Another investigation, this time by the Wall Street Journal indicated that over one third of the fish sold in the United States was mislabeled. Needless to say, the current solutions are not offering the level of transparency that consumers require.

One very important thing to note is that the OriginTrail network can function across different blockchain protocols. This is known in the industry as being "blockchain agnostic". So it can be used in conjunction with projects built on Ethereum, Neo and IOTA for example, rather than just being limited to one of these at a time. This cross-operability is a huge step in any blockchain project, let alone one that has a lot of potential adoption like the supply chain sector. This would also allow large institutions (like Walmart for example) to build their own blockchain solutions and OriginTrail would be compatible with these. This could also potentially lead to partnerships with some of the biggest players in the industry.

This has many different applications across the sector including product authentication, supply chain management and food journey visibility. As well as backend functions like inventory management and production alert systems.

This is not a new initiative, and the core team has been performing supply chain tracing since 2013. However, they only began implementing blockchain technology in 2016.

The coin is backed up by a solid development team, each with a visible public profile on LinkedIn and extensive industry experience. Co-Founders Tomaz Levak and Ziga Drev both having backgrounds in supply chain management and tracing supply chains in Eurosope and the Middle East.

In terms of token use, TRAC tokens are a necessity for the network to function. The tokens are used to create nodes that hold up the network and process data transactions. Those who run nodes will be rewarded in the form of TRAC tokens. It is not yet confirmed if the project will use masternodes, and if so, how much these will be. Nor has any potential reward amount been confirmed yet. If you do have enough TRAC tokens to run a masternode, this would represent a fantastic passive income opportunity.

In terms of roadmap, the beta version of the testnet is currently scheduled for June. This will be the iron out any kinks and test OriginTrail's applications in various environments. After this, the mainnet is planned for Q3 2018 release.

Lack of a big exchange is the big thing holding back the price as of now. Not only are they not on the bigger exchanges like Binance or Bittrex, there aren't even any coin pairings on an exchange I would consider "mid-level" at this point.

OriginTrail is one of those cryptocurrency projects with industry changing ramifications IF they can achieve widespread adoption. It's a big if, as supply chain management is arguably the most competitive of the cryptocurrency project niches. However, their blockchain agnostic design may well be the "killer application" of this particular project. The ability to work with both open source and private blockchains is simply too be to be ignored, and thus this makes OriginTrail a project well worth looking into.

Note: BTC/TRAC trading is available on CoinFalcon (not to be confused with scam crypto lending platform Falcon Coin) - but the volume available is so low (<$1000 daily) I have not formally included it

Mercury Protocol (GMT)

Price at Time of Writing - $0.02
Market Cap at Time of Writing - $4,420,198

Available on:
ETH: ForkDelta

Where to store:
GMT tokens are ERC 20 tokens and can be stored in MyEtherWallet and other Ethereum wallets

By far the smallest crypto project discussed in this book, with a market cap of just under $4.5 million, Mercury Protocol is a decentralized communication platform. The project itself has been around for over 4 years, with blockchain implementation starting in 2016. On the website, Mercury Protocol lists famed billionaire Mark Cuban as an advisor. Cuban is an investor in Radical App LLC, the parent company behind the project.

The reasoning behind the project is that the current messaging model is centralized and relies on selling user data to advertisers for profit.

The platform offers demographic targeting as well, so advertisers can focus in on their audience, without wasting money by sending announcements to those who are not interested in what they are selling.

The main question you may be asking yourself at this point is - why would someone use Mercury Protocol built apps over other messaging apps that have their own internal economy such as WeChat? The answer to this is that GMT tokens are transferable across different Mercury Protocol apps. The theory behind this is that by allowing use across multiple platforms, it will create a network effect that will expand the user base and encourage widespread adoption. To give an example, imagine if there was a single token you could use on Facebook, Instagram, Whatsapp and Slack - this would be rather handy for both advertisers and users alike.

There are plans to make the entire platform open source in future released, so developers may then be able to make modifications and find any code bugs. There are concerns that this would lead to the rise of "clone platforms" - however, any clone platforms would need a large user base themselves to benefit from this.

GMT or Global Messaging Tokens can be used by network providers to make announcements on the network. The wider audience you want to make an announcement to, the more tokens it will cost. Users could be rewarded with tokens for watching adverts as well, which encourages them to use the platform in the first place. The team also believes that these tokens can incentivize good behavior on the platform and be used to eliminate trolling and online bullying. For example, users will be deducted tokens for harassment. The use of GMT versus BTC or ETH was done to minimize volatility from external factors. For example, if you buy a premium message with 1 ETH, then the price of ETH rises because of unrelated news, then you have just lost out. By using GMT, the price is generally only affected by activity within the Mercury Protocol network.

The token supply is fixed, so there is no mining involved. Users can earn more tokens by participating in the apps themselves.

In terms of roadmap, the mainnet release of the Dust app, the first built on the protocol, is scheduled for Q1 2018. You can download the beta version right now from the App Store or Google Play Store if you want to check it out for yourself. A second app known as Broadcast is currently in development.

The primary concern right now is the complete lack of any marketing effort from the core team. I understand they are working hard on the platform itself, but personally I believe that a coin should always be marketing itself, at least in order to stay relevant in a space that sees multiple projects pop up every day. Even a small weekly update on development progress would be a start. Once we move further into 2018, then talks of partnerships can be discussed and moved along.

In summary, this is no doubt a high risk project because of the small size and need for mass adoption to be successful. I think that it may see more success in niche markets rather than a full on social media 2.0 vision that some share. Even with niche market success though, there's no doubt the current token price and market cap would rise. They have a working product out which is a plus as well. All in all, for the low barrier to entry, it's a solid project with a lot of room to grow and should be looked at closely.

How to Buy Coins on Coinbase With Zero Transaction Fees

Please note: This method only works for countries eligible for Revolut bank accounts which include the USA, Canada and the UK.

If you haven't heard of Revolut, it's a digital bank based in the UK. There have free currency transfers among 26 currencies - which is how we can use this to our benefit. You can even open an account in less than 30 seconds by using the Revolut app.

This is beneficial for Coinbase users because you can save up to 4% on each transaction by doing this, so if you're heavily involved in crypto you can potentially save hundreds of dollars per year.

Now, onto how Revolut can help you save money on cryptocurrency transactions.

Step 1: Send your native currency like GBP or USD, to your Revolut account via debit card. This step is easy and Revolut walks you through it when you set up an account. This transfer should be near instant.

Step 2: Exchange your native fiat currency to Euros on Revolut. Revolut has no transaction fees for this, so you get the market rate.

Step 3: Bank transfer your Euros from Revolut to Coinbase. This is the only step which is not instant, it takes 1 business day, so if you do it before 3PM EST you should get your coins before 9AM the next morning.

Step 4: Once your Euros are in your Coinbase account, transfer them to your GDAX wallet from Coinbase. If you're not familiar with GDax, it is Coinbase's sister platform designed for traders. Transfer between Coinbase and GDax are instant and free.

Step 5: Buy your coins on GDAX using Euro pairings, making sure to use Limit orders instead of Market orders, as these are free. If you use market orders, you will pay a 0.25% transaction fee.

Step 6: Transfer your newly purchased coins from GDAX to a personal wallet, or another exchange like Binance.

A Brand New Way to Buy Cryptocurrency Which Could Have Huge Market Ramifications

March brought news of an exciting development for those of you who want to get involved in cryptocurrency, but don't want to go through the process of buying and storing coins yourself.

I should note at the outset, this method is not viable for those of you only looking to buy a small amount of coins. This is strictly reserved for this with a lot of cash to spend.

US exchange Coinbase announced that they would be beginning the Coinbase Index Fund, aimed at becoming the "Dow of Cryptocurrencies". The fund will automatically diversify your cryptocurrency portfolio and rebalance it on a monthly basis. In the beginning, the fund will feature Bitcoin, Ethereum, Litecoin and Bitcoin Cash, any new coins added to Coinbase will automatically be added to the fund.

In the beginning stages, the fund will be offered to accredited US investors with assets of more than $1 million. Eventually, the threshold will be lowered in stages until the minimum investment is $10,000. There are also plans to roll the fund out across other geographical markets. The fund will charge a 3% management fee, which on the surface seems high. However, if you are looking for a truly passive crypto asset, this may well tick all your boxes.

How does this benefit the rest of the market? Any kind of institutional adoption is a positive sign. Last year we had 2 different Bitcoin ETFs rejected by the SEC on volatility grounds, so this is the next best option in the interim.

Things You Need to Be Aware of With Certain Cryptocurrency Channels on YouTube

For those of your planning to do extra research before buying coins, which is something I always recommend - YouTube is a great place to start. Many content creators do an in-depth analysis of coins in a similar fashion to what I do here. However, there are certain red flags you should look out for when determining how reliable the information on a certain channel is.

The creator has been paid to advertise coins in the past

Many of these channels, especially the ones with larger followings, are paid by the cryptocurrency teams to advertise the coin on their channel. There is no inherent problem with this, after all, it is just a form of advertising. The problem lies where the creator does not disclose they received payment to discuss the coin. And instead disguises this analysis in the form of a supposedly unbiased review.

The creator uses high pressure sales tactics or fake scarcity

Language such as "this coin will go up any day now" or "get in fast before you miss out", designed to spark a fear of missing out among the viewer, are rife in the crypto space. If a channel discusses a coin's price moreso than the project or team behind it, then you must be skeptical. If you find a channel that does this, then you have to take their "advice" with a pinch of salt.

The creator does not disclose their current holdings

There's nothing wrong with cryptocurrency personalities having their own portfolio, however, they should disclose whether they own a coin or not before discussing it in a public space.

The big one: They make promises of guaranteed returns

This one is the biggest red flag. There is a huge difference between discussing projects with potential and promising guaranteed returns if you invest in a certain project. This often is associated with coin lending platforms, such as BitConnect and Davor Coin, both of which exit scammed and caused anyone invested in them to lost 95% of their money. Remember this moreso than anything else. **There is no such thing as guaranteed returns in any investment - cryptocurrency or otherwise.**

Note: While writing this book, another lending platform Falcon Coin performed an exit scam, leaving investors with 98% losses on their initial investment.

Conclusion

And that's it - 10 more exciting altcoins under $1 that have fantastic potential for gains in the next 12 months and beyond.

I hope this information has been beneficial to you and has given you a foundation to invest some of the more unknown cryptocurrencies. Even with the rocky start to the year, there has never been a more exciting time for cryptocurrencies than right now. Even if you missed the boat with coins like Neo and Stellar, it's not too late.

As always, I encourage you to do additional research before investing in any of these, particularly by checking out the white papers on the individual coin websites, which will give you a much more in-depth look at the technology behind them.

Remember to invest wisely, and always with your own money. Never borrow money to invest in cryptocurrency or anything else. For your own sanity, don't check your investments on a daily basis. This is a volatile market, and you have to be willing to accept that if you are to make long term profits. Perhaps most importantly, don't panic sell if you see a dip in the market. From a personal standpoint, if I had sold during the crash caused by the famous Mt. Gox incident, in which Bitcoin lost over 60% of its value - I would be a much poorer man than I am today.

I wish you the best of luck in the cryptocurrency market, and I hope you make a lot of money.

Finally, if this book has proved useful to you, I'd appreciate it if you took 2 minutes to leave it a review on Amazon.

Thanks,
Stephen

Cryptocurrency: Mining for Beginners - How You Can Make Up To $18,500 a Year Mining Coins From Home

By Stephen Satoshi

Introduction

Welcome to the exciting world of cryptocurrency mining. First things first, congratulations on buying this book and thank you for doing so.

The following chapters will discuss in detail what exactly cryptocurrency mining is, how it works, and most importantly, different ways you can make a profit from mining cryptocurrency.

You'll learn about various mining techniques such as staking, pool mining, and rig mining. You'll also discover "outside the box" ways to profit from mining coins, some of which don't even require you to do any mining yourself. Of course, as is the case with all my books, we'll also be highlighting any cryptocurrency scams or schemes which I feel you should avoid as well.

These are truly exciting ways of earning coins without having to buy at the exchanges.

Finally, this book assumes you have little to no knowledge of cryptocurrency mining and how it all works, so the language is designed to be as easy to understand as possible.

I hope you enjoy the content of this book, and I wish you the best of your cryptocurrency journey.

Thanks,
Stephen

Basic Overview of Mining Cryptocurrencies

By now you probably already know a decent amount about cryptocurrencies. They are digital assets that function as a medium of exchange and use cryptography to secure transactions and to create additional units. Cryptocurrencies are mined into existence through a process known as mining. This process of mining new cryptocurrencies involves two functions. These are adding transactions to the blockchain and releasing new currency to the system.

Mining Cryptocurrencies

In order to mine cryptocurrencies, you need access to a powerful computer and special software. There are new, sophisticated computers in the market that have been developed specifically for cryptocurrency mining.

A miner is basically anyone who invests his or her time confirming cryptocurrency transactions and adding new currencies to its network. Mining cryptocurrency requires plenty of resources. The computers needed for this process are costly and operating costs are very high. This is because the mining process consumes a lot of electricity.

Miners generally spend most of their time trying to confirm a block containing data using hash functions. To understand better how the mining process works, it is important to first understand the basic aspects of blockchain technology.

Mining and the Blockchain

Cryptocurrencies use publicly distributed and decentralized ledgers known as blockchain. Blockchains are secure networks and this is in part due to the mining process. Mining is, therefore, an essential component of the blockchain and is integral to its stability. It provides an additional level of security because the process validates each transaction that takes place on the blockchain.

In fact, the validity of each cryptocurrency coin is secured by the blockchain. Each block contains what is known as a hash pointer. The blockchain is decentralized with no central server to log in all transactions. However, without sufficient computing power, the blockchain ledger cannot operate. Cryptocurrencies rely on the combined power of numerous mining computers spread out across the world.

These computers are operated by miners who lend their computers for a common cause. In return for their input, they receive an incentive or reward. Miners receive payment when they solve a challenging mathematical puzzle and validate transactions before others do.

Each block in the blockchain contains transaction data, a timestamp, and a hash pointer.

Hash Function

The hash function in cryptocurrency is an algorithm that maps data of varying or arbitrary size to a hash and is by design a one-way function. A hash pointer is present in all block and always points to the previous block. It acts as a pointer, making it easy to track transactions.

Proof of Work

Most of the blockchains in use today use a concept known as Proof of Work. Proof of Work protocol or system is simply an economic measure that requires some work from the requesters to be done. This work is often processing time by a computer. This helps prevent service abuse.

Proof of Work scheme is the first timestamping scheme that was invented for the blockchain. The most popular proof-of-work schemes are based on scrypt and SHA-256. Scrypt is the most widely used among cryptocurrencies. Others include SHA-3, Crypto-Night and Blake.

CPU versus GPU Mining

There are several options available when it comes to cryptocurrency mining. At the onset of cryptocurrencies, you could effectively run the mining algorithms on your computer as an individual miner. The regular computer at your home or office operates on a CPU or central processing unit which was powerful enough to handle mining functions.

Mining at the onset simply meant downloading or compiling the correct mining software and the wallet for a preferred coin. A miner would then configure the mining software to join their preferred cryptocurrency network then dedicate your computer to the task of mining cryptocurrencies.

In recent months and years, miners turned from CPU computers to GPU-based PCs. The GPU is the graphics processing unit that processes video systems on your computer. Basically, a GPU is like a CPU but a lot more powerful and designed to execute specific tasks. It is this specialization that makes the GPU suited for tasks such as cryptocurrency mining.

Compare CPU vs. GPU Capacity

A CPU core can execute only 4 or 32-bit instructions per clock while a GPU can execute 32—32-bit instructions in the same period of time. This simply means a GPU processor executes 800 times more instructions per clock.

Even though the latest, most modern CPUs have even 12 cores and much higher frequency clocks, still one GPU, like the HD5970, is more than 5 times faster than 4 modern CPUs combined. Therefore, GPU mining can result in faster transaction times and you can gain more coins in the same time frame.

Functions of the GPU versus the CPU

The CPU is the executive arm of the computer. The central processing unit is essentially a decision maker that is directed by the software in use. CPUs do all sorts of mathematical computations. On the other hand, a GPU is more of a laborer than an executive. GPUs contain large numbers of ALUs, or arithmetic and logic units. This makes them capable of executing large quantities of bulky mathematical labor in a greater quantity than CPUs.

What you need to be concerned with is the fact that the advent of GPU mining has made CPU mining almost obsolete. This is because the hash rate of most cryptocurrency networks increased exponentially. CPU mining is hardly profitable on some cryptocurrency networks but is thriving on others. It has largely been affected by the increased hash rate.

GPU mining is significantly faster in comparison and hence profitable on all cryptocurrency systems. Today, cryptocurrency mining heavily relies on GPU-based mining rigs. A mining rig is a computer system or arrangement that is used for mining coins. Most rigs are dedicated to accomplishing only one task, which in this case, is crypto mining.

Buying GPUs

When it comes to considering specific graphics cards for your mining rig, the first choice for many miners is the NVIDIA GeForce 1080 Ti which provides the greatest overall hashing power of any GPU on the market, though it is also known to consume more power when under a full mining load than any other GPU as well.

The more midrange option is currently the GTX 1070 or the AMD Radeon RX 480 for a more balanced mix of performance and power consumption. In fact, with the proper modifications, the GTX 1070 can generate performance that is nearly on par with the 1080 Ti while still consuming significantly less power overall.

While the popularity of cryptocurrency mining means that the market for GPUs is occasionally hit with artificial market scarcity as miners buy up the whole supply as soon as it is released, you should typically be able to find a GTX 1070 for under $500. When they are hard to find, however, you can easily see the price skyrocket to $700 or more. If you find that the prices you are seeing are in this upper range, then you will likely want to keep a close eye on Amazon for when a new shipment hits the market as you will then be more likely to find it at the traditional MSRP.

With the GTX 1070 in hand, you can then make use of a program known as MSI Afterburner to increase the memory interface clock to 650 MHz and reduce the power target to 66 percent to decrease heat output and board power consumption as much as possible. This, in turn, will ensure that GPU temperatures remain around a reasonable 66 degrees Celsius which is nearly 15 degrees cooler than what it would be running at without the tweaks. This, in turn, raises the average hash rate from 27.24 MH/s to 31.77 MH/s. With this hashing power, combined with an average power consumption of 177 and a cost per kilowatt hour at 10 cents, you are looking at a profit of about $140 per month.

Proof of Work vs. Proof of Stake

Proof of Work was designed as a protocol to achieve consensus and deter or prevent cyber attacks, especially distributed denial-of-service or DDoS. Such attacks have the sole purpose of diminishing or even exhausting the resources of computer systems through repeated sending of fake requests.

Proof of Work concept has been around for many years, way before cryptocurrencies. Today, it is adopted by different cryptocurrency systems such as Ethereum, Bitcoin, and Litecoin because it allows distributed consensus across systems. It is used mainly to create decentralized agreements about adding blocks to the network between different computers or nodes within the network.

HashCash is an example of Proof of Work function used by Bitcoin. Bitcoin miners spend a lot of time mining the currency. For a block to be added to the network, HashCash needs to produce very specific data that will verify the amount of work that goes into producing the currency.

Proof of Work is Integral to Crypto Mining

Being the traditional mining method many of the older cryptocurrencies use, Proof of Work has become an essential requirement when mining cryptocurrencies. When cryptos are mined, miners verify transactions on blocks are legitimate. In order for the verification to happen, miners have to solve a complex mathematical problem. This problem is also known as the proof-of-work problem.

One thing to note is that as the network increases in size and the coins gain in value, the problems become increasingly harder to solve. Therefore more computational power is required as we move forward, I discuss this in greater depth in the chapter "Why I don't recommend you mine Bitcoin".

Proof of Stake

Another aspect that is commonplace with crypto mining is Proof of Stake. Proof of stake is another different method of validating crypto transactions. It is an algorithm that produces the same result as Proof of Work but using a different process. Proof of Stake came much later and was first used in 2012.

While Proof of Work algorithm compensates miners who solve mathematical problems, Proof of Stake identifies miners using a different approach. On the Proof of Stake protocol, there is no block reward. This is because digital currencies using this system are pre-mined and their number does not change. Since there is no block reward, miners are paid a transaction fee and are referred to as forgers instead.

Benefits of Proof of Stake over Proof of Work

- Validators do not have to use any computing power.
- It saves validators a lot of money in energy costs.
- Proof of Stake ensures a safer network.
- It makes attacks very costly because those doing the attacking must own a significant proportion of the coins themselves. Therefore they are essentially attacking their own coins. It would be like robbers deciding to rob a bank they owned 51% of.

Why I Don't Recommend You Mine Bitcoin

Whenever Bitcoin's price is rising (and that's most of the time!), the mining question always pops up. Usually from those who are inexperienced or want a "free" way to get a piece of the pie.

It all starts with a variant of this question.

"Why buy Bitcoin at $100/$1,000/$4,000 when you can just use your computer to mine some for free?"

Unfortunately, like everything else - there is no such thing as free Bitcoin.

As previously discussed, the way Bitcoins are created or "mined" is by using a computer to solve an of increasingly complex series of algorithms. Users are then rewarded for solving these algorithms by receiving Bitcoin. There is no man power involved, you yourself don't have to solve the algorithm, you just have to link your computer up to the Bitcoin network and the computer does the rest. There are also no shortcuts or breakthrough moments, the only way Bitcoin can be obtained quicker is with more computer power. How much computational power you supply determines the size of your reward. The more power you supply, the more Bitcoins you receive.

Now here is why mining is generally a terrible investment for the average Joe.

5. Electricity Costs - The electricity costs involved with running your computer 24/7 (which is necessary for mining) by far outweigh the amount of Bitcoins you receive for completing the task. You require access to industrial electricity rates of around $0.02 per kWh in order for the venture to be profitable on a small scale. The vast majority of people cannot access these rates without some sort of special connection.

6. Requiring Specialist Hardware - Nowadays, the most efficient mining processes require special hardware known as Application-specific integrated circuits (ASIC). ASICs can be described as a supercomputer that can only ever perform one task. Specialist Bitcoin ASIC miners available for consumer purchase still start at around $1000 and often run around $2000-$2500.

7. Equipment maintenance - To maintain all this computing power is an additional cost. The cost of cooling alone is a large cost that has to be factored into long term profits. Hardware running 24/7 burns out faster and replacement mining equipment will be needed in due course.

8. The increasing size of the Bitcoin network - The network pays out a fixed amount of Bitcoin, regardless of how many miners are using the network. The current rate is around 1800BTC per day, which sounds like a huge number until you realize just how many miners there are on the network. The current mining power is equivalent to 17.6 BILLION desktop computers. Therefore the average payout for the end user running 1 desktop computer, with a standard, not designed for mining GPU, full time is approximately $0.000107 per day. Or roughly 2 cents a year's worth of BTC. To put it lightly, you have more chance of winning the lottery than you do making a profit from mining Bitcoin your standard home computer.

Mining in 2017 is a much different proposition from mining in 2010 or even 2012. There are some opportunities which involved investing in Bitcoin farms or group purchasing processing power of ASIC at a discount. This is known as a "mining pool". Due to cheaper power costs currently around 80% of the world's mining pools are based in China, with Iceland possessing the second largest number. Joining a mining pool requires a lower upfront investment but still requires cheap electricity rates and have debatable ROI potential.

It should also be worth noting that many of those who promote group mining or cloud mining do so under an affiliate program with whatever company that is promoting, meaning they get a commission % every time someone signs up.

However, for the average Joe without a huge amount of money to invest - I would strongly recommend buying coins instead of mining them. You are more likely to get higher returns in both the short and long run.

Ethereum Mining & Switch to Proof of Stake

Ethereum is one of the most popular cryptocurrencies on the market today and is second only to Bitcoin in terms of popularity and market capitalization. Ethereum mining is the process of mining Ether, the token used on this cryptocurrency system. Ether provides the only pathway of using this powerful network.

Ether mining does not just increase ether volumes but also helps secure the network. When ether is mined, it creates, verifies, propagates, and publishes blocks on the blockchain. We can conclude, therefore, that mining ether also secures the network and ensures transactions are verified.

There are major organizations and developers running smart contracts on Ethereum network. In fact, ether is looked at as an incentive to motivate developers who wish to create powerful applications.

Essentially, a developer has to mine ether which will be used on the network or sold to interested buyers later. Executing transactions on Ethereum network is a much cheaper method of using the network compared to buying ether directly.

How Ethereum Mining Works

Ethereum mining is very similar to Bitcoin mining. For each block of transactions, miners have to repeatedly compute and come up with a solution to a complex mathematical puzzle. In other words, Ethereum miners have to run a block's unique metadata through a hash function. The metadata includes software version and timestamp.

The hash then returns a scrambled, fixed length string of letters and numbers. Only the nonce value changes which in turn affects the resulting hash value. When a miner finds the hash that matches the current target, he or she will be rewarded with ether and the entire blockchain will be updated with this information.

If you are mining a particular block but another miner finds its hash, then you will have to cease work on that block and begin working on the next block. It is almost impossible for anyone to cheat at crypto mining. You cannot fake the work and then emerge with the correct solution to the puzzle. This is why they use Proof of Work protocol to secure the network. However, verifying transactions takes almost no time.

Miners find a block approximately every 12 to 15 seconds. Should this speed get faster or slow down, then the Ethereum algorithm will automatically reset the difficulty level of the mathematical puzzle. The readjustments of the difficulty level are meant to maintain the solution time at 12 – 15 seconds.

Mining profitability depends a lot on luck and the amount of computing power devoted to the mining process.

Ether mostly uses a Proof of Work algorithm known as Ethash. Ethash demands more memory so that it is difficult to mine using these costly ASIC computers which are specialized computers with advanced processors that are largely used to mine Bitcoin. This is probably why there are no ASICs specifically designed for mining ether.

Even then, Ethereum mining will not go on forever. The network is transitioning from Proof of Work to Proof of Stake. Proof of Work essentially protects the network from tampering and determines which transactions are valid. On the other hand, proof of stake is where stakeholders secure the network through their own tokens.

How to Start Mining Ethereum

The process of mining is considered as the glue that holds the entire Ethereum network together. It achieves this by engaging in consensus on any changes that take place on the applications running on the network.

As a miner, you need to add your computer to a node in the network to join others trying to solve complex mathematical puzzles. You need to try a large number of mathematical problems until one of them gets solved and releases new ether.

Joining the Network

In theory, anyone with a computer can join the Ethereum network and begin mining coins. However, as more and more miners join, the blockchain requires more and more power so that joining now requires a very powerful computer. To be successful, you will need a high-powered computer with the appropriate mining software.

Find Appropriate Mining Hardware

As you already know by now, to mine ether, you require specialized computer hardware that will be dedicated to full-time computer mining. Ideally, you can choose between CPU or GPU mining hardware. However, as of today, CPUs have become almost a novelty and only GPU hardware is available, especially for Ethereum mining.

There are plenty of GPU computers in the market and setting up one is not a simple task. First find out which particular models are the most profitable based on parameters such as power consumption, hash rate performance and cost. It is advisable to set up a mining rig. A mining rig is simply a system of GPU computers assembled together. Such a rig might take you up to a week to set up.

You should work out your profitability, so you know how much profit you will be making. There are mining calculators available that can help you compute your expected profitability. The most accurate one right now can be found at CryptoCompare.com/mining

The results will let you know how much ether you will earn at a particular hash rate.

Ethereum's Switch from Proof of Work to Proof of Stake Protocols

Ethereum is expected to make its biggest upgrade ever. According to its inventor, Vitalik Buterin, Ethereum will move from use of Proof of Concept to Proof of Stake. The switch and adoption is expected to end in about one year's time.

Ethereum is expected to achieve this move by implementing the software known as Casper. Casper v1 is a hybrid of Proof of Work and Proof of Sale concepts. This software is going to decrease and finally end the use of Proof of Concept. This essentially means that Ethereum mining will no longer be profitable.

What is Casper?

Casper is a Proof of Stake algorithm that will start running on the Ethereum network this year (2018). The first version of the software is a hybrid of both Proof of Concept and Proof of Stake. However, it is expected that Proof of Concept consensus will eventually be eliminated so a lot of the power that miners currently have will be removed. Also, Proof of Stake algorithm uses far less energy to operate the network. It offers additional protection such as reduced centralization and preventing 51% attacks.

The Ethereum community believes that this switch will help address the problem of scalability that the network is currently facing. Casper will allow the network to scale more efficiently and also enable new blocks to be created faster and added to the network. Scalability will be managed through a process known as sharding. Sharding is the process of partitioning a large database horizontally into smaller and easily managed parts.

Benefits of Shift from PoW to PoS

The Network will not consume as much power as is currently the case. It is estimated that both Ethereum and Bitcoin consume $1 million worth of energy and hardware per day just to keep the networks up and running.

The network will not need to issue as many coins as it currently does in order to motivate participants to keep operating within the network. PoS will discourage the formation of centralized cartels that may cause harm to the network. The 51% attacks will be minimized as economic penalties can be used to make the attacks very costly.

Will Miners be Affected by this Shift?

The profitability of mining on the Ethereum network will definitely be affected. Miners will not earn as much as they currently do. The complete shift to PoS is expected to take between one and two years so there is no immediate effect on current miners.

The Ethereum community has agreed to this shift so it will happen. Starting 2018, the reward from a single block will decrease from 5 ether to 3 ether. Miners can start mining other coins such as Ethereum Classic or Monero.

To understand why this change could be so huge for Ethereum, it is important to understand just how it differs from the proof of work model. With a proof of stake verification system, instead of having the miner solve the equation in order to verify the block, a validator, who is confirmed reliable by the stake they have in the system, will commit to its accuracy, knowing that if they lie they will lose their own ether as well. The Alliance is currently testing the new system through a limited use verification process to make sure it is ready for a wider launch soon.

This will ultimately serve to make mining more egalitarian as a whole as it will no longer be based around who has the best mining machine, thus leveling the playing field as all the mining will be done on the blockchain itself. It will also serve to make 51 percent attacks more difficult to pull off as it requires direct contact with other miners as opposed to just having enough hardware to brute force the blockchain successfully.

Mining Versus Buying Cryptocurrencies

At this point, you're probably wondering if it is more profitable to buy coins than to mine them. Answering this question is not easy as there are many factors which affect the final outcome. However, it is possible to examine the two and come up with a reasonable conclusion. The question is if you had $10,000, would it be better to invest it in a mining operation or just buy coins?

Cloud Mining for Cryptocurrencies

Let us first try and understand different mining operations. Cloud mining has become rather popular in the recent past because it enables small investors to pool resources and participate in crypto mining. There are a number of companies that provide credible cloud mining services.

Cloud mining is a service that offers you an opportunity to invest a small amount of money and participate in the mining of a given cryptocurrency. What you are doing by joining such an operation is essentially to rent crypto mining hardware and receive a share of the mined coins in return.

As a participant in a cloud mining operation, you will be paying for a given hash rate for a set period of time. For instances, you can rent 10 THS for a 3-year period to mine Ethereum. Sometimes your contractual obligations may require that you pay for some expenses such as electricity and maintenance. These are often charged on a daily basis but billed weekly or monthly.

Pros and Cons of Cloud Mining

Pros

- As an investor, you do not need to invest in actual equipment. Crypto mining equipment can be quite expensive, especially high-end hardware.

- Setting up mining equipment can be tricky and time consuming. It can take up to one week just setting up a series of powerful crypto mining hardware. Fortunately, cloud mining members do not have to worry about equipment setup or even monitoring and maintenance.

- There is no need to worry about electricity things such as the noise and heat generated by the mining operation.

- You are also able to invest a relatively small amount of money in such a major operation and earn handsome returns. If done well, crypto mining can be a source of additional revenue and sometimes even your main source of income.

Cons

- As an investor in a cloud mining operation, you do not own any of the hardware or other equipment used in the operation. As such, you are left with no hardware at the end of your contract even though any money you paid upfront will not be returned.

- Sometimes it costs a lot more to join a cloud mining operation especially if you want a higher hash rate for a higher return on investment.

- You are not guaranteed that the cloud mining company will be there at the end of your contract. There is a certain level of risk involved here.

Crypto Buying versus Mining

To find out which one, between mining and buying, is more profitable, we need to find out how much we can make using either process by investing $10,000. At today's rate of 1BTC=$8,240 (as of Feb 7th, 2017), our $10,000 will fetch about 1.21 BTC. You can check the latest rates at sites such as www.CoinLlama.com.

Now we need to see if we can make more money than this through mining. It is never an easy thing working out profitability because of the many factors at play. Some of the variables involved include increasing mining difficulty and energy costs.

Find the Best Crypto Mining Equipment

Now since most of the $10,000 will be spent buying equipment, it is advisable to find the best in the market. The main issue you are likely to face is that most credible mining products are often out of stock and so you may have to create a pre-order. However, if you search harder, you are likely to find excellent products. You can check out companies like Butterfly Labs or Bit-Main.

Calculate the Number of Bitcoins You Can Mine with $10,000

You can easily find a Bitcoin mining calculator online which you can use for this purpose. Even then, there are some variables that still remain unknown and you will have to work with estimates. One of these variables is the rate at which the mining difficulty will increase while the other is the exchange rate of Bitcoin with time.

The equipment you need might cost something like $8000. This is the cost of about 7 Antminer S4-B2 miners. You do not have to host the computers at home or in your office. Instead, you can have them hosted in China where hosting and energy costs are quite low. These machines are also quite noisy and generate plenty of heat. The rest of the costs including shipping, daily hosting, and electricity amount to a little over 9,200. The balance can pay for electricity and hosting costs for a period of about three months. Daily expenses are roughly around $7.2.

Now, most calculators show that you are likely to make just about the same amount of crypto initially invested. This means that, in some instances, buying and mining coins add up to almost the same amount.

Ethereum Mining versus Buying

Ethereum mining seems to be a lot more profitable than buying. Take the example of tech researchers who invested 1500 Euros in a mining operation and another 1500 Euros buying ether. They mining rig was mining Ethereum at 147 MH/s. This was a real experiment that was conducted starting June 2016.

Outcomes

The 1500 Euros bought 136 ETH or ether tokens. However, after 6 months, the mining rig had generated almost 105 ETH. By the end of March 2016, the researchers had mined over 140 ETH. By June of 2017, the mining operation had earned about 152 ETH compared to the 136 initially purchased.

In both operations, it seems like mining has an edge over buying. This is true because you can continue mining coins for a long time, recover your initial investment, and continue making money.

The only downside is that machines do break down with time, hash rates change, and conditions in the crypto mining sector hardly remain the same. There are always policy changes and so on.

In conclusion, if you want to make instant money, then invest in cryptocurrencies, subject to performance in the market. However, for long term investment, then mining may well be the better of the two options.

Pros of Crypto Mining

- You can work out how much you will expect to earn on a weekly, daily, or monthly basis
- It provides an additional source of income
- Once you set up the mining rig, you can set it and forget it. It doesn't need constant monitoring or tinkering.
- You can continue mining for a long time to come
- You get to keep any equipment that you buy and then resell it if you decide to no longer mine yourself

Cons of Crypto Mining

- The equipment needed is very expensive
- Mining generates a lot of noise and heat
- The equipment can break down from time to time
- You have to learn how to set it up, which can be daunting for some.
- Crypto mining computers consume a huge amount of energy daily

Pros of Buying Crypto

- You can purchase cryptocurrencies at any time at market rates
- There is no need to invest in any equipment
- You receive your investment's worth instantly
- Transaction fees are negligible

Cons of Buying Crypto

- Price fluctuations may affect your investment
- Exchanges often charge buyers high fees

How to Setup your Own Mining Rig

Building your own cryptocurrency mining rig is more like growing your own money tree. You will create wealth in the form of cryptocurrencies even as you go about your daily business.

What is a mining rig? A mining rig refers to a system of computers that are set up together for purposes of mining cryptocurrencies such as Ethereum or Bitcoin. Mining is the process of extracting crypto tokens from a blockchain network.

A mining rig can be dedicated, which means it has been constructed and set up specifically to mine cryptocurrencies. The rig can also be a system of computers that have the capacity to mine crypto coins.

Setting up a Rig

Setting up a mining rig is a two-step process. First, you will have to identify the equipment that you need. Choosing and sourcing the right equipment for your preferred mining operation. The second step involves putting the equipment together. Putting the rig together is a technical process that is similar but more complex to building your own computer.

Mining rigs consist of similar components found in most desktop computers. However, there are a couple of differences. For instance, in your regular desktop computer, there is a general balance between components such as HD, GPU, RAM, and CPU. With mining rigs, you want a very basic HD, bare minimum RAM memory, the lowest clocked CPU and 5 – 7 GPUs. It is not possible to fit this kind of equipment in a normal computer case, so you will most likely need a custom-made case that will hold all your equipment.

How to Pick the Correct Mining Rig Parts

GPU Mining Cards

GPU stands for graphics processing units. When it comes to GPUs, you want to select the very best in the market. Basically, search for GPUs with low power usage, low cost, and a high hash rate. It's easier to start with just one GPU then scale up to 5 or 6. Anything beyond 7 will be difficult to stabilize. You should aim to find a balance between a GPU with low power consumption and the highest hash rate. The hash rate denotes the speed at which it can mine cryptocurrencies. There is quite a variety of GPUs to choose from, depending on the currency that you intend to mine. Make sure you do not buy your GPUs or any other components off a street corner because they often have problems that you won't notice until you get home and plug in the card. However, you can find good quality, second hand processors at reputable outlets.

Mining Rig Case

As already noted above, crypto mining rigs cannot fit in regular computer cases. You will need to either buy a custom-made case or build your own. You can easily build your own case at home. Most miners do so using either plastic storage crates or a milk case. They both function really well even though they may not look that great. You can even choose to create a wooden case if you wish. It's really all up to you, aesthetics are not our main focus here.

Power Supply

The standard desktop computer uses a standard power supply ranging from 300W – 500W. When it comes to a mining rig, you will require a lot more power. If you create a mining rig with 6 to 7 GPUs, you need to ensure that you have access to sufficient power. You should have access to at least 1,200W. The supply efficiency should be certified at Gold or better. Make sure that the power supply is modular so that you configure your cables individually. This will turn out to be extremely important when building your rig.

A Motherboard

A motherboard is essential the brain of your computer and forms the base of your mining rig. It is on the motherboard that you build everything. When searching for one, you will be looking to find one with sufficient GPU slots because these will determine the number of GPUs or graphics card that can be accommodated. The number of GPUs will also determine, in the end, your total hash power. Most GPUs work on a PCI express so find a motherboard with at least 3 PCI Express slots. You can fit 3 GPUs on this motherboard each with a hash rate of 20 MH/s so that in total you have 60 MH/s. You can also opt for CPU-Motherboard combinations which are readily available. For purposes of coin mining, you will have to maximize the number of GPUs that your motherboard can support. Find one that can accommodate between 6 and 7 GPUs. Such motherboards are hard to find in stores, so you may want to search for them online. Great examples include the ASUS Prime Z270-P Motherboard or the Intel Celeron G3930.

Powered Riser Cables

Also crucial for your mining rig are powered riser cables. You will need these to extend PCI-e connections from the motherboard. This way, you will be able to mount the GPUs within your crate, or case. You should find as many PCI cables as you can and ensure that they match up with the total number of GPUs that you have.

Hard Drive

You will require a suitable hard drive where you will store your mining software and operating system. A good, solid state drive will do just fine. SSD hard drives are so called because they do not have any moving parts which can break or give in. the size will basically depend on what things you will do when mining so take that into consideration. For instance, if you need to download the entire blockchain, then you will need a sizeable hard drive to store the blockchain. However, if you have no such intentions, then a standard, 120 GB SSD will do.

The Operating System

Linux has some of the most powerful operating systems capable of mining multiple coins such as Monero, Z-cash, and Ethereum. There are also Window's based mining operating systems. Some are specific such as the Eth OS which is the operating system that mines Ethereum on Linux. There are a couple of others to choose from so ensure that you choose the correct one for whichever coin you are focusing on.

Accessories and Other Essential Components

You will also require additional components for your mining rig. These include RAM memory, a basic monitor and mouse, and a couple of box fans. Get a single fan for each separate rig. For the RAM, you will need a single 4GB 1600MHz and nothing more.

Put the Mining Rig Together

Now that you have all the components with you, you need to put it all together. If you have experience building a PC, then this will not be much different. You will probably find it easy. However, anyone can learn how to assemble a mining rig.

Crypto Wallet

First things first, you will need a cryptocurrency wallet. The wallet will store the coins you mine. You will want to get a reliable hardware wallet such as the Ledger Nano S. This wallet is immune to viral and malware attacks and just cannot be hacked.

The monitor will provide you with additional security because it displays crucial wallet details. You can use the Ledger Nano S to store Bitcoins, Litecoin, Z-cash, Dash, DodgeCoin, and Ethereum.

How to Put it All Together

First, confirm that your power supply unit is able to handle the GPU cards in your system. Also, ensure that your riser cables can reach your additional GPUs within your rig. The GPUs should be safely located and secured. So, set up the GPUs and ensure they are well distributed. Remember that GPUs do get quite hot and they generate plenty of heat. Place the GPUs in a well-ventilated room. Also, ensure that your rig is mining once it is set up.

First install the operating system, followed by the mining software onto your PC. You can choose either Ubuntu from Linux or Windows from Microsoft. Windows is preferable because it has automated the installation of drivers. This enables all components within your computer to communicate and interact easily. However, Ubuntu is free and offers you more options.

Once the GPUs have been set up and attached to the motherboard, you will need to check that everything else is in place. For instance, are the fans available to cool the GPUs? Once everything is setup, you can test the equipment and then proceed to mine your preferred cryptocurrency. If you want to mine Ethereum, then you can download EthOs. This is an APP specifically designed for mining Ethereum. While it is advisable to have this APP, it is not essential and you can do without it.

Beginning Mining

Now that your equipment is all set up, you can then begin the mining process. There are two different approaches that you can use. These are solo mining and pool mining.

Solo mining: As a solo miner, you will be working against the other miners because you will be competing to mine ether. If you rig is able to generate the correct hash, then you earn the block reward. If you have a rig of 60 MH/s against the network's 1.2 GH, you will not earn ether as often as you would want. You may also have to download the entire blockchain. You will need sufficient memory space for this.

Pool mining: This is a crypto mining process where you join other miners and team up in order to minimize the volatility of your earnings. This way, you will be able to earn ether every day due to increased hash power. The reward you get on a regular basis will be equivalent to the amount of work your system puts in. You will also not have to download the entire blockchain onto your computer.

You can choose to join programs such as Miner Gate for more efficient pool mining. Miner Gate allows its members to mine coins via options. You can also mine two different currencies at the same time and without losing any hash rate that is geared towards your main currency. However, Miner Gate is not the only option you have, and you can still join other less sophisticated mining pools.

Equipment Cost

Mining equipment is not cheap especially the latest models which are specifically designed for crypto mining. It should be noted, all these ROI figures are just an estimate based on the prices at the time of writing. Actual returns figures will vary.

L3+ Antminer ASIC: This mining equipment costs about $1580 on average. It has a hash rate of 504 MH/s and can bring in a return of about $5.15 per day. You can expect a payback on your investment in 305 days.

Bitmain Antminer S9: One of the best pieces of mining equipment is the Antminer S9. It is designed to mine Bitcoin and is a very costly piece of equipment. It costs $6,600 at Amazon and has an impressive hash rate of 14 TH/s.

Bitmain Antminer S7: The Antminer S7 from Bitmain costs $1,400. It comes with a hard disk of 512 MB, SD-RAM memory and operates on a Linux platform.

Antminer Power Supply: The power supply for the Antminer costs $170. Second hand versions are much cheaper, costing about $130.

What is Cloud Mining?

Cloud mining can be described as the process of mining cryptos via a remote data center where mining power is shared among members. Such arrangements enable interested members to join the cloud and participate in coin mining operations without the need to buy or manage the hardware.

In cloud mining operations, mining rigs are located and maintained within a facility owned or rented by a mining company. Members simply need to register and purchase shares or mining contracts in return for a share of the mining rewards. However, there are weekly or monthly costs such as overheads, rent, and electricity costs that have to be paid. This amount is normally deducted from the earnings of the cloud members.

Therefore, if you want to invest in coin mining operations without the trouble of buying and managing your own hardware, there is an alternative in cloud mining. By joining a could mining operation, you get to share processing power with other remote miners. All you need to join a cloud is your own computer for communication purposes, a wallet to receive your pay and payment required for sign up.

Different Types of Hosting

Companies providing cloud mining services can either lease a virtual private server or a physical mining server then install mining software. Sometimes these companies opt for hashing power hosted at a data center instead of leasing dedicated servers. Hashing power is normally denominated in GH/s or GigaHash per second. The contracts signed often indicate the period for the contract and desired hashing power.

Pros of Cloud Mining

- Mining operations are outside your premises. This means a quiet, cool home.
- No additional energy costs.
- You will not be stuck with costly equipment should miner stop being profitable.
- You will not experience any ventilation problem.
- There is very little chance of being let down by equipment suppliers.

The Cons of Cloud Mining

Cloud mining can sometimes be a risky option. Some of these risks are described below;

- Mining operations are opaque in nature and lack transparency.
- There is a risk of fraud.
- Reduced earnings as profits are split and costs have to be paid.
- There is a general lack of control and flexibility.

Avoiding Cloud Mining Scams

Investments in cryptocurrencies have grown immensely in the last one year. Plenty of small term investors earn a recurring income through cloud mining. Here are a couple of things to watch out for.

1. Must have ASIC Miner vendor support: Ideally, any legit miner will voluntarily and willingly let you know about their provider and IT support firm they are dealing with. If a company does not have such support, then it probably is suspicious.

2. Data Center and mining equipment photos: A genuine cloud mining operation should have photos of its data center and mining equipment on its website. Any firm that cannot show you photos of its operations is honestly not worth investing in. Some companies even show proof of electricity bills, so you should not take any excuses from companies that do not provide photos.

3. Check for presence of mining address: Any legitimate cloud mining company is likely to display its public mining address. Many of the legitimate ones actually do, like Genesis Mining. If the firm is unable to provide one, then it most likely is not genuine.

4. Take a look at the company's registration: Genuine cloud mining companies often have every clear registration with proper domains and are open. They should never be anonymous as they are supposed to be very open with members or investors. Full contact details, for instance, are absolutely essential. When these are missing, such as an official address, phone number, and so on, then it is probably a scam so avoid such a firm.

5. Watch out for referrals: Cloud mining sector makes thin profits because there are many members who have to be paid as well as certain costs such as electricity, rentals and so on. As such, they cannot afford to have referral programs that pay 5% or 10%. Any cloud mining firm offering to pay such high fees to affiliates is probably not genuine so take your money and run.

6. *Be cautious when they offer guaranteed profits:* In cloud mining operations, profits or income are never guaranteed. However, a scammer will try all ways and means to lure you into their scam. Also, some companies provide no option to withdraw your earnings. This is actually absurd. You should be allowed to withdraw your earnings whenever you want. Firms with opaque payment systems and those with unclear withdrawal processes should be avoided like the plaque. Please keep off such websites to avoid losing your money.

Basically, there are plenty of red lights to watch out for. You need to be comfortable with a company's profile and image. If you have any doubts or feel like something just does not add up, then your instincts are probably right. Make sure you find only genuine companies, check the reputation and reviews online and if you feel confident enough, you are probably right.

Guaranteed Returns in Cloud Mining Operations

If you join a cloud mining firm, you will enjoy certain benefits. While you are likely to get a return on investment in a couple of months, it is not possible to give a certain guarantee of return on investment. The reason is that cryptocurrency mining relies on a couple of factors, one of these being luck with regards to market prices for your chosen coin.

Since luck is a factor in mining, getting a return on investment is not always guaranteed. It is possible to earn a good return every day over a long period of time. It is also possible to finally recover your initial investment. However, no cloud company should give you a guaranteed return as it is not in control of the entire process. If you join a reputable crypto mining company, then you are likely to make your money back and keep earning a residual income for some time. Not all companies are able to provide you with the kind of return you would want.

List of Noted Mining Scams to Avoid

There are a number of cloud mining programs that are Ponzi schemes masquerading as legitimate mining operations, or have already been proven to be Ponzi schemes. Many of since shut down, but unfortunately, some are still running to this day. Below is a list of some of the schemes you can avoid.

1hashmining.com - Ponzi scheme pretending to be a mining operation. Update: The website has now been shut down by authorities

50BTC.com - A mining pool that stopped paying out. The host's whereabouts are currently unknown.

7cly.com - A mining scam that promises returns of 2% per day. You should know by now that this just isn't realistic in any market.

Minerjet.com - Another one with guaranteed returns promised. Stay well away.

Mininghub.io - Another cloud mining operation. This one has a made up UK limited company behind it. Avoid like the plague.

Store4mining.com - A website claiming to sell mining hardware. They don't, only use trusted sources to purchase mining equipment.

Bc-prime.com - This one was actually running Google Ads for a while so even the world's biggest search engine thought they were legit. Fake mining platform which will steal your cryptocurrency.

Bitcoin-mining.group - This and all subdomains (which are focused on other coins like XRP) are fraudulent.

Bitminer.world - This one makes you send in more Bitcoin if you want to withdraw your earnings. Absolute sham high yield Ponzi scheme, and an utter disgrace to the mining world.

An Introduction to Mobile Mining

It is possible to mine cryptocurrencies using your mobile phone. There are apps in the market available for android smartphones that can mine cryptocurrencies. However, it is a challenging prospect as mining operations require a lot of power and consume huge quantities of energy.

Bitcoin and Ethereum mining operations require mining rigs. They consume huge quantities of energy, so such operations can hardly be performed on your smartphone. The only possibility of mining these major coins is to get one of the latest and most powerful smartphones in the industry then connect it to a mining pool. Therefore, mining the way we know it using a mining rig is not possible via smartphones.

Mobile Mining Apps

There are certain apps that you can download that will mine cryptos for you. These are mostly android apps so if you have a powerful smartphone, think about downloading one of these apps and begin mining immediately.

1. DroidMiner BTC/LTC Miner: This is a bitcoin mining app that lets you mine cryptocurrencies if you connect to a pool. It connects to the Get-Work pool. It is only through the pooling of resources that smartphones can actually mine altcoins such as Ethereum. Droid Miner is an Android based tool that was developed by ThatGuy. The architecture of the DroidMiner is based on Pooler's CPuminer and AndLTC Miner software.

Apart from Bitcoin, you can also mine Litecoin and Dodger Coin. In fact, it can mine all coins that use SHA-256 or scrypt. There are currently just under 500 users mining with this app and they give it an average rating of 3.5 out of 5.

2. Easy Miner: The Easy Miner is yet another pool mining application program. This app is easy to use, comes with an improved user interface, and displays crypto charts showing the latest prices. It also displays the network's hashing rates, so you are always aware of the mining situation.

3. LTC Miner: This is yet another android app that can be used to mine cryptocurrencies. It is specifically designed to mine within the Litecoin pool. You can easily join the pool and earn Litecoins on a regular basis.

While these apps are great for pool mining, they are still not suitable for actual mining using your phone's hardware mining just yet. Not until android develops much faster hardware will you be able to profitably mine on your phone.

MinerGate Mobile Miner

MinerGate is a mobile mining app for android phones. With this app, you can turn your smartphone into a portable mining rig. This was developed by an ordinary crypto miner who submitted it for a contest. It was such an impressive app that it was immediately adapted for use.

You first need to download the app onto your smartphone and then set it up. Once it is set up and ready to use, simply open an account with your details then log in. Now all you need to next is choose your preferred cryptocurrency. Simply find the coin you want to start mining and click on it.

Once you identify your preferred currency, simply start mining and earning. Ensure that you have a mobile wallet attached so that your earnings are storied in there. You can always check the balance any time you want. You can also see which currencies you are currently mining because, apparently, you can mine more than just one crypto.

Even as you mine, you are given plenty of options. For instance, you can choose to mine only when your smartphone is charging, or request mining to stop when the battery is low. You can choose to mine on the go so that you connect to the pool and mine coins as you go about your day.

Top Crypto-Mining Apps for Android

People all over the world are mining cryptos on their phones. They are mining Dogecoin, Bitcoin, Litecoin, and Ethereum among many others. If you want to start mining coins on your smartphone, then you can consider one of these apps. They are considered among the top android apps for coin mining.

1. BTC Safari
2. Bitcoin Farm
3. Easy Miner

However, before choosing an app to use, it is advisable to do your due diligence, learn more about the app before investing in one. Like previously stated, Bitcoin mining is not as profitable on your cellphone, so I'd recommend against any Bitcoin mining apps. You are better off mining smaller altcoins on your smartphone rather than Bitcoin.

How to Make Money Staking Coins

You can earn cryptocurrencies through a process known as staking. Many cryptocurrency investors are now looking at alternative investment streams and staking is certainly one of them.

What is staking? Staking is also referred to as Proof of Stake.

Proof of Stake is a concept where you buy coins and store them in your wallet for a given period of time, say, three months. It compares well with putting money in a fixed deposit account. You can save money in a fixed deposit account for a couple of months or weeks and then earn a decent return at the expiry of the said period.

Basically, Proof of Stake has so many technical benefits to any network. However, apart from these, investors also enjoy some economic benefits. They get to earn dividends by staking their coins in a particular wallet. Essentially you can make money by simply holding many POS (Proof of Stake) coins in the right wallet. This wallet is referred to as the staking wallet.

The system appreciates PoS because it helps secure the network and keep it stable. It also creates additional opportunities for network users to earn dividends based on their coins.

Understanding Basic Staking Terms

Distributed consensus: The term distributed consensus refers to a large group of investors who live in vastly different regions of the world but have a unifying agreement. In the world of cryptocurrencies, the agreement is mostly on the blocks or transactions that are valid and should be added to the network.

Proof of Stake: This is a specific algorithm that is used by some cryptocurrencies to manage their distributed consensus. It compares to Proof of Work and is considered a better alternative for achieving the same consensus.

Most Profitable Proof of Stake Cryptocurrencies

1. DASH: This cryptocurrency is also known as digital cash and is a very popular coin. It is among the first to introduce Proof of Stake and is built on Bitcoin's core but with better security and added privacy features. Dash does have a higher barrier to entry at 300 DASH to run a masternode, which gives 7.5% annual interest.

2. OKCash: This is yet another cryptocurrency that makes use of Proof of Stake. All you need to do is buy some of this currency and store in a stake-able wallet. OKCash currently has a 10% annual return for

staking, with no minimum amount required, which makes it advantageous when compared to Dash for example.

3. NAV Coin: NAV Coin is among the first cryptocurrencies to operate on a dual blockchain. It's been in operation since 2014 and uses Proof of Stake for block verification and stability. You can use POS stake rewarding on this coin to earn extra cash regularly. This also enables you to earn even as you sleep, with an annual return rate of around 5%.

4. ReddCoin: ReddCoin is very popular on social media networks. You can use this POS based cryptocurrency to leverage content on social media to get handsome returns.

5. Stratis: This is another POS coin that you can use to stake and earn rewards. STRAT is the token that operates on the Stratis platform. You will, therefore, need a Stratis wallet to stake your tokens. While profits are not quite as high as with other coins, with time, this is expected to get better.

6. Neo: My personal favourite staking opportunity. Neo is similar to Ethereum in that it uses what is known as Gas (similar to Ether) to keep the network running. Unlike other Proof of Stake currencies, Neo doesn't require you to keep your wallet open at all times for staking.

Currently you require around 20 Neo to return 1 Gas, which represents an annual dividend of just less than 6%. The bonus with Neo is that as more applications run on the Neo network, the more Gas is needed, and thus your Gas is worth more. So you actually get a 1-2 punch of higher Neo values plus higher Gas values. This is what makes Neo my personal favourite of the staking coins.

Examples of Initial Investment vs. Expected Return on Investment

Remember that Proof of Stake operates in an almost similar manner to fixed deposit accounts. For fixed deposit accounts, you are paid an interest after maturity of the deposit. However, for Proof of Stake, the rewards you receive are crypto tokens.

1. The longer your coins are held in the staking wallet, the higher the rate of return. For instance, you receive 20% return after 3 months, 50% after 6 months, and 100% after a year. Thus the rate of return will depend on the maturity period.

2. The rate of return is sometimes calculated as simple or compounded interest.

Let us say you invest 100 ETH in a staking wallet for 3 months. At the end of 3 months, you will expect to earn 20% more ETH. This means you will own 120 ETH in that period of time.

(100 * 20/100) + 100 = 120 ETH

Please note that you can only stake with altcoins and not Bitcoin. Bitcoin rewards miners through the algorithm known as Proof of Work.

Advantages of Staking Crypto

The benefit of staking crypto is that you will not need to invest in expensive mining equipment. All you need to do is buy the coins you need then save them in a staking wallet. Then just sit back and watch your investment grow. It is a pretty decent, safe, and lucrative way to make money.

Another advantage of staking is that you get to have a predictable, secure, and guaranteed income. This is because the value of the coin increases predictably and its value at maturity can easily be determined. Staking does guarantee you will get your investment back.

Mining based stocks - An often overlooked opportunity

What if you could profit from cryptocurrency mining, without having to mine yourself? It's true, it's completely possible.

Two of the biggest cryptocurrency winners in the past few years, haven't been cryptocurrencies themselves, but ones that are affected by the boom in cryptocurrency mining.

You see, mining cryptocurrency requires a huge amount of computing power, in the form of Central Processing Units (CPUs) and Graphics Processing Units (GPUs). Manufacturers of these parts have seen their stock prices skyrocket since the beginning of 2016 when cryptocurrency mining really took off.

AMD ($AMD) and NVIDIA ($NVDA) are the two biggest winners thus far, in fact, in Q3 2017, NVIDIA's revenue from mining soared to $220 million for the quarter. Now, nearly 5% of the company's bottom line is attributable to cryptocurrency mining. AMD, on the other hand, sees roughly 10% of its overall revenue being from cryptocurrency mining sources.

The companies themselves have different approaches to how cryptocurrencies will affect their profits going forward. AMD CEO Lisa Su stated that they were expecting a "cryptocurrency cooling off period" in 2018, and the company doesn't consider demand for GPUs as a part of its long term gameplan.

NVIDIA, on the other hand, is more bullish and has openly admitted that it considers cryptocurrency mining a big part of future business plans.

So if you're into traditional investing as well as cryptocurrencies, it may be well worth checking out both of these stocks and seeing if they have a place in your portfolio.

Another Cryptocurrency Lending Scheme to Be Wary Of

In my previous books I have warned readers about BitConnect and DavorCoin, both of which are lending platforms that promised users guaranteed returns on investment. Like the regular financial world, you should be extremely skeptical of any platform that promises guaranteed returns. Since those books were published, both of these platforms have performed exit scams and taken thousands of dollars (millions in the case of BitConnect) from users. BitConnect and those who promoted it is currently in the process of a lawsuit for fraudulently acquiring assets. The same fate may well happen to DavorCoin.

In the meantime, however, there is a third lending platform that has been making waves recently in the shape of FalconCoin. According to their website, users will receive daily interest on coins with the monthly interest rate being 46%. That figure alone should have your alarm bells ringing because 46% interest in a month is a frankly absurd figure. The other big red flag is that investments must be locked up within the platform for a minimum of 180 days before users can withdraw them. They also claim you'll be able to "earn 180% by staking Falcon Coins".

Like these other lending platforms, FalconCoin, of course, has a referral program and is aiming to use social media to spread the word. This is what caused BitConnect to get extremely popular as larger YouTube channels (such as CryptoNick and Craig Grant who are both named in the BitConnect lawsuit) were advertising the project to their followers, who would sign up under their referral links. Referral programs don't necessarily mean a project is bad, however, if that ends up being the main source of income, as we see with many MLM/pyramid schemes, then we indeed have a problem. Through a few minutes of research, I already found multiple YouTube channels that were promoting FalconCoin and encouraging their viewers to sign up under their particular referral code.

Overall, FalconCoin displays the exact same red flags as BitConnect and DavorCoin before. Guaranteed returns and promises of ridiculously high interest rates are just too big to ignore, and as such, I would advise anyone to stay well away from the project.

Conclusion

Thank you for reading, and I hope what you read was informative and able to provide you with all of the tools you need to achieve your cryptocurrency mining goals, whatever they may be.

I encourage you to do additional research on top of what you've read here. Especially with regards to mining specific cryptocurrencies, as the procedure will be different for each one.

The next step is to find the best website where you can apply all the wonderful knowledge obtained through this book. Mining cryptocurrencies is a lucrative way of earning an extra stream of income, and many people just like you are making a decent secondary income from doing so. While this might not be your golden ticket to early retirement, who can say no to an extra few thousand dollars a year?

Remember, stay away from mining and lending platform scams. And with any investment you do make, only invest what you can afford to lose.

Finally, if you found this book useful in any way, a review on Amazon is always appreciated!

Thanks,
Stephen

P.S. If you want to buy cryptocurrency, and haven't done so yet. I recommend Coinbase as the easiest way to do so.

If you sign up for Coinbase using this link, you will receive $10 worth of free Bitcoin after your first purchase of more than $100 worth of cryptocurrency.

http://bit.ly/10dollarbtc

Cryptocurrency: What the World's Best Blockchain

Investors Know - That You Don't

By Stephen Satoshi

Cryptocurrency Market Cap 2017

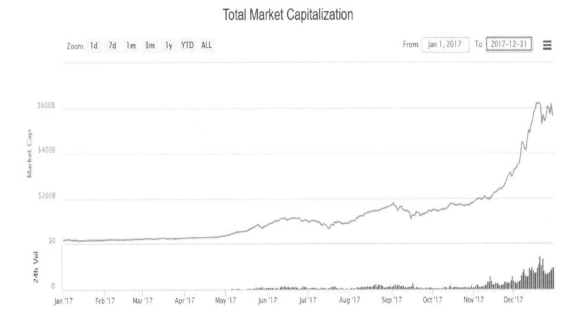

Introduction - The current cryptocurrency playing field

Today the market cap of the cryptocurrency market stands at $560 billion. For the record that's up around 3000% from January 1st 2017.

We saw Bitcoin, the original cryptocurrency, hit highs of $20,000.

Then came the rise of Ethereum, the revolutionary smart contract and decentralized application platform, went from $9 to over $1000.

And then there were lesser reported success stories, like that of Neo, formerly known as Antshares, the Chinese smart contract token that rose from less than $1 to over $100 in the space of 7 months. Then there was that of Dogecoin, a microtransaction platform and tipping coin, which was started as a fun inside joke reached a market cap of over $800 million.

We even saw bizarre stories such as that of a Turkish amateur soccer team buying a player from a rival for 0.0524 Bitcoin, which was around $520 at the time the transfer occurred.

It doesn't take a genius to see that 2017 was a big year for cryptocurrencies. This was the year that finally hammered home that they are here to stay.

So now the chaos is temporarily over, let's take a step back, and examine where the market is going heading forward.

You see this influx of money is not just limited to cryptocurrency, we have to consider the blockchain technology behind it, and it's wide reaching ramifications for not only financial markets but also society as a whole.

Major firms like IBM, Walmart and Samsung are spending billions of dollars in blockchain research, or in developing their own blockchain solutions. A video played at the Davos World Economic Forum, attended by some of the world's most powerful figures, including US President Donald Trump, was titled "Blockchain is Coming and It Could Save Lives"

What's even more exciting is that we're still very much in the initial stages of the blockchain boom. For comparison, the global stock market cap for comparison is $80 **trillion,** this alone demonstrates that we are still in the extremely early stages of adoption. For further comparison, the cryptocurrency market is still smaller than the stock exchanges of countries like Taiwan and Spain. Needless to say, we've still got a long way to go, and in terms of an investment standpoint, there's a lot more money to be made.

That doesn't mean there won't be periods of turbulence, 2018 is off to a rocky start, and we're likely to see a significant pullback that could last as long as the first 3-6 months of the year. That's OK if you're a long term believer in the technology, but if you're looking for a get rich quick scheme, you probably aren't going to be too happy.

Even so, there are still huge gains to be made in the cryptocurrency market, you just have to know where to look.

If all else fails, remember the timeless phrase "bulls make money, bears make money, pigs get slaughtered."

What this book is not

This book is designed as a guide to help you become more informed in how the boom in Bitcoin, other cryptocurrencies and blockchain technology is affecting to wider financial market as a whole. How it affects different sectors of the market, and the correlation between cryptocurrency and blockchain.

This is not a blind recommendation to buy all stocks, ETFs or managed funds with "blockchain" in their name. Doing so would be a great way to lose money very quickly.

As with all my books, I am not a financial advisor, and I am not advising you to buy any of the stocks, or cryptocurrencies listed in this book.

As with any investment, never invest more than you can afford to lose.

Separating cryptocurrency from blockchain technology

So if you have a basic understanding of blockchain technology, you'll be fully aware that without it, there is no basis for cryptocurrency to exist. Blockchain gives us the ability to create indisputable, public ledgers, which everyone can see, but no single person can control. These ledgers can verify financial transactions, and this is what gives cryptocurrency the ability to have inherent value, and allows people to have trust in the system, without having to rely on third party institutions like banks.

This has led to some calling blockchain "The Backbone of Finance's Entire Future". And a survey by the World Economic Future estimates that 10% of the world's GDP will be stored on a blockchain ledger by 2025 - that's roughly $10 trillion if we use 2018 numbers.

However, blockchain technology has far wider reaching ramifications than merely a cryptocurrency facilitator. From smart contract platforms, all the way to having the ability to verify federal election results. The ramifications stretch across hundreds of different industries and have the ability to change society for the better. This is precisely why giant corporations like Microsoft, Tesla and Walmart are spending billions of dollars on blockchain research and blockchain protocols of their own.

The key takeaway from blockchain technology is that of trust. Due to the fact that information recorded on a blockchain cannot be altered, there is an indisputable record of all transactions that have taken place. These transactions don't have to be strictly financial in nature. They can be used to verify who owns certain assets, to optimize supply chain processes (more on that later) and to identify tampering and fraud.

By being able to identify exactly which industries and companies are becoming early adopters of blockchain, we can begin to see just exactly where growth areas will begin to emerge.

Why are so many "experts" predicting Bitcoin's downfall?

For as long as cryptocurrency has existed, we've been inundated with news articles professing the "death" of Bitcoin. What these experts neglect to tell you is that they've already predicted the so-called "death" of Bitcoin over 200 times in the past 5 years.

The first mainstream media article of this type was back in January 2011 when Forbes published an article "So that's the death of Bitcoin then". The Huffington post called Bitcoin a "hoax" during this time.

In fact, there are now so many Bitcoin obituaries, that there's even a website dedicated to them. https://99bitcoins.com/obituary-stats/ generously lists 245 different predictions of the death of Bitcoin. There were even predictions as far back as 2010, needless to say, those naysayers have been proven wrong time and time again.

Bitcoin has overcome a number of hurdles up to this point. From a 68% drop in value in mid 2011, to the Mt. Gox exchange hacks of 2014 and the misinterpreted rumors of China banning cryptocurrency in 2017.

Mainstream adoption for Bitcoin and other cryptocurrencies continues to grow year-on-year, in fact at the beginning of 2018 there were less than 10 countries worldwide that do not recognize Bitcoin as having value (note, this differs from Bitcoin transactions being legal in said country).

So why do so many different news outlets predict the downfall of Bitcoin? Simply put, the vast majority of mainstream news outlets have ZERO experience with cryptocurrency. Even their financial reporters are outsiders when it comes to blockchain technology and its implications. Yes, that includes traditional stock market analysts, many of whom are no more clued in than the average investor when it comes to this new asset class.

One of the major reasons for this is that at its core, Bitcoin is a decentralized financial model, which of course disrupts the traditional banking system. Therefore the voices of this system, a system that has made them more money than they could ever know what to do with, have often spoken out against anything that they perceive as a threat to their status quo.

Arguably the biggest critic of Bitcoin has been Jamie Dimon, the CEO of JP Morgan Chase. Previously calling Bitcoin a "fraud" and "worse than tulip bulbs". Dimon also threatened to fire any staff member who traded bitcoins.

It is only now, from around mid 2017 onwards that we've started seeing some level of institutional adoption of cryptocurrency. This is because banks and other large financial institutions have worked out a way that they can profit from cryptocurrencies themselves. However as we saw in early 2018, banks would prefer to do this at a lower price point, which has been a major factor in the depressed cryptocurrency prices we've seen at the beginning of 2018.

I'll be explaining this more in depth later on in the book, but I believe that we'll be seeing less and less "death of Bitcoin" predictions as we move forward.

How will blockchain technology affect banks?

While there are some who predict that blockchain technology will lead to the downfall of the entire banking system as we know it, it's unlikely that this will be the case.

It's true that in the original Bitcoin whitepaper, there was revolutionary language talking about doing away with the need for financial institutions. Many cryptocurrency enthusiasts fervently discuss "the original Bitcoin vision" when debating about the use of traditional banks. This has also led to many people on the ideological side of cryptocurrency dismissing coins like Ripple (XRP) which help facilitate payments in the banking sector.

However, banks themselves have now begun to integrate blockchain into their own business model. First, there is the Ethereum Enterprise Alliance, a group of 200 organizations who are testing Ethereum blockchain solutions in a wide variety of industries. This group includes some mega banking corporations such as Credit Suisse and JP Morgan Chase.

Mega banks are developing their own blockchain solutions. Goldman Sachs for example now has a page dedicated to blockchain on its website, aimed at educating customers about the potential uses of the technology.

There's also the question of how central banks will utilize blockchain technology, and even if they will create their cryptocurrencies. More on that subject later on in the book.

It should be noted that there is a specific sub-sector of cryptocurrency that banks do not favor, namely privacy based coins like Monero, ZCash and Aeon. These coins do represent a real threat to banking by offering completely anonymous transactions and essentially allowing users to be their own bank. This has led to some calling Monero, the most widespread and highest market cap privacy coin, "Swiss bank 2.0"

How similar is this to the DOTCOM boom?

Detractors of blockchain technology are eerily similar to those who said the same thing about the internet in the early to mid 90s. As AOL CEO Steve Case said "The conventional wisdom was that the internet would always be limited to hackers and hobbyists"

Then there is the famous 1995 Newsweek article written by Clifford Stoll entitled "Why the Web won't be Nirvana" with now laughable claims such as "The truth is no online database will replace your daily newspaper." Stoll, a widely respected astronomer also went on to called the idea of ecommerce "baloney". Needless to say, he missed the mark by just a little bit.

The point of re-visiting these claims is that we are still in the very early stages of cryptocurrency and blockchain technology. Even experts in other technological fields have very little idea of how it works, and the wider ramifications for society at large. Therefore we are liable to misinformation, hot takes and all round confusion.

These similarities also go the other way though. Just like many companies saw their stocks rise by putting ".com" at the end of their name. We are seeing the same effect with blockchain.

For example, in October 2017, On-Line PLC renamed itself to On-Line Blockchain PLC, and saw its shares jump 394% in less than 24 hours.

Another example was seen In December 2017, when a microcap company called Long Island Iced Tea Corp simply changed its name to Long Blockchain and saw its stock rise 289% in just over a week. The company, which sells non-alcoholic beverages and at the time of writing has no blockchain agreements in place.

Examples like these go to show, that there may be a "bubble-like" effect. Not all of these projects will succeed. In fact, over 90% of ICOs will fail, and I would estimate the same figure would be true for "blockchain startups" that trade on stock exchanges. There will, without doubt, be future Amazon's and Google's coming out of this cryptocurrency and blockchain boom. However, it's a pretty safe bet that for every one of these future tech giants, there will be at least 5 pets.com type busts.

An additional lesson we can learn from the DOTCOM boom, and one that may well help your own investing, is our tendency as investors to overestimate the speed of adoption of new technology. We've ever seen this as recently as 2 years ago with the 3D printing industry. Hundreds of millions of dollars flooded into the 3D printing space and share prices of 3D printing companies soared. They've since come crashing down, but are still above the level they were 5 years ago.

So don't go heaping all your money into blockchain stocks just yet. There are a number of exciting blockchain projects, and alternative ways to profit from this current market, and I'll be discussing those in greater depth later on in this book.

What everyone needs to know about ICOs

For the uninitiated, Initial Coin Offerings (ICOs) are the process of where a cryptocurrency startup offers its own tokens to the general public, in exchange for funding in the form of other cryptocurrency tokens. The funding tokens are usually Bitcoin or Ethereum, with the vast majority of ICOs being built on Ethereum. However, we are now also seeing ICOs using Neo and Stellar Lumens as a funding source. The exchange rate of BTC or ETH to the new token is pre-determined before the ICO. For example, during gambling platform Funfair's (FUN) ICO used an exchange rate of 1 ETH = 32500 FUN.

For example, in 2014 Ethereum's ICO raised 31,500 Bitcoin with a market value of approximately $18.4 million at the time). Since then we have seen ICOs raise hundreds of millions of dollars worth of Bitcoin or Ethereum. Decentralized storage platform Filecoin currently holds the record for largest ICO at around $257 million.

We have seen ICO investment funds pop up such as Pantera Capital and FinShi Capital. However, due to their relative accessibility, we are seeing more and more consumer investors moving towards ICOs in an attempt to get their slice of the cryptocurrency pie.

Skeptics will say that an ICO is merely a way for a company to raise capital without giving up any equity. This statement has some merit. If you invest in an ICO, you do not own shares of the company, you merely own their token. The token value is tied to company performance for some ICOs, but for others, the tokens may not have any inherent value of their own.

We've seen ICOs revolving around bananas, and a female-centric coin that threatens to "disrupt the patriarchy". We even saw an ICO by the name of "Useless Ethereum Token", whose whitepaper pleaded with people not to invest, raise over $100,000. It goes without saying that as the numbers of ICOs increase, the number of bad ones increases as well. This, combined with a number of ICO whitepapers focusing more on revolutionary language, and large bonuses for early investors to spark a "fear of missing out", has led to some very questionable cryptocurrencies receiving funding. I'm now going to explain a few very basic warning signs that you should look at for before you invest in an ICO.

Fundamental usage of blockchain technologies

Remember how we discussed companies putting "blockchain" in their name then seeing large price increases? We can apply that to ICOs as well. The first major question you should ask yourself is, does this company have an actual need for blockchain technology in their business model?

This goes further, does the token have an actual, or even theoretical use case? The general rule is, the more specific the use case, the better the chances of it being a legitimate operation. If the answer is unclear from the whitepaper, then you should stay well away.

That use case has to go beyond "a store and transfer of value" as well, we already have Bitcoin and then some smaller coins that focus on speed and low transaction fees.

Be careful our promises of token utility within the cryptocurrency's own ecosystem as well. For example, the ability to execute your own smart contracts and pay people via your fingerprint may sound good in theory, but if the ecosystem doesn't exist, then your tokens still have no actual value as of yet.

Percentage of tokens held by founders

Generally speaking, less than 10% of the overall tokens available should go to the founders. There are however ICOs with more than 50% of the tokens reserved for the project founders. ICOs like these are more than likely just a cash grab from a few developers.

Plagiarism in whitepapers

Whitepapers are technical documents outlining how exactly the company's blockchain solution will work, and which industries it will benefit. These documents are lengthy, and often will be over 30 pages long. However, with the rise in ICOs, there is now a rise in less than reputable companies plagiarizing the whitepapers of legitimate ICOs.

There is the case of TRON, which at the time had a market cap of $14 billion, and was accused of copying pages from the Filecoin whitepaper. Founder Justin Sun came out and said the English translation of the whitepaper was done by volunteers who did not understand the scope of the project. TRON has since seen a decline in value of nearly 60% since these allegations were revealed.

The biggest case of this was DADI. The project was called out for plagiarizing large portions of SONM's whitepaper. Significant parts were directly copied and pasted, including citations. It is worrying that a company with a multi-million dollar operation would be careless at worst. The DADI team claims the SONM whitepaper "inspired" them and apologized for the event. I should note that DADI has since revised its whitepaper and now it does not contain any of the same content as SONM's.

Wall Street's Influence on Bitcoin

2017 was the year when Wall Street first starting making big moves into the cryptocurrency space, after dismissing it as merely a fad for so long. This isn't unprecedented by any means, It should be noted that Wall Street is *always* sceptical of new asset classes. We saw it with junk bonds in the 80s, and then internet stocks in the 90s.

In December 2017, a landmark event occurred as Bitcoin futures were launched by the Chicago Mercantile Exchange (CME). This was the first time any cryptocurrency was openly traded on a US regulated trading floor and shortly following the launch we witnessed a 400% increase in Bitcoin prices within less than 6 weeks. Let's make one thing clear, full scale institutional adoption and cryptocurrency trading floors would see colossal price increases in Bitcoin.

What you may not know is that there are now over 100 Bitcoin and blockchain hedge funds in existence, with more new ones starting up every single month.

Early adopters

One area that some early adopters have profited massively is in cryptocurrency arbitrage, the practice of using price disparity on different exchanges to their advantage. This practice is nothing new and has been around in the securities market for centuries, but there are less and less opportunities now with the computerization of everything.

However, cryptocurrency still has massive arbitrage opportunities, with price disparities between exchanges sometimes being as high as 10%. The most notable of these is what is known as the "kimchi premium", as cryptocurrencies on South Korean exchanges tend to trade up to 10, or as much as 15% higher than on US based ones. This phenomenon was so widespread, that the cryptocurrency ticket website coinmarketcap.com had to remove Korean exchanges from their price listings because of said discrepancies.

One such fund taking advantage of this is Virgil Capital, which monitors the price differences on 40 different exchanges around the world. Despite Bitcoin's 28% price drop in January, the fund was up by over 12% after fees. Wall Street's high frequency trading firms such as DRW Holdings are also getting in on the action.

JP Morgan

Jamie Dimon, one of Bitcoin's loudest detractors recently stated he "regrets" calling cryptocurrency a fraud. He also went on to say he believes in blockchain technology. What went unnoticed is that 3 months before this statements, when Dimon was still positioning himself as Mr. Anti-Bitcoin, his own bank launched a blockchain based system. The system aims to lower transaction fees and times for cross-border payments.

The real takeaway from this is that even if Wall Street leaders are openly opposing cryptocurrency, the behind the scenes story is very different indeed. Especially when it comes to implementing blockchain solution that could lead to increased profits for their own business.

Over 60% of Apple shares are held by institutions, others large companies have even higher percentages.

Diversification

Wall Street has taken a liking to cryptocurrencies in recent months because they do not move in line with the stock market. This is known in the finance world as a "non-correlated asset", and represents a great diversification proposition for the customers of these banks. As such, more and more large investment funds are starting to use cryptocurrency as a financial instrument of their own, rather than mocking it as they had done previously.

Diversification in this sense doesn't mean investing in little known altcoins though, institutional money is still attracted to the safer side of things. This is precisely why we saw large increases in both Bitcoin and Ethereum towards the end of 2017.

Correlations between Bitcoin and other cryptocurrencies

As discussed in a previous book, there is a significant correlation between Bitcoin and altcoins. Part of this is a key reason why the small number of investors who are praying for the death of Bitcoin are misguided in their wishes. For now, Bitcoin is still the King of the cryptocurrency space, and the cryptocurrency market as a whole is still very much relying on Bitcoin to continue to grow.

When new money flows into the cryptocurrency market, it always goes into Bitcoin first. This is money both from consumer investors, and institutional ones. This leads to a rise in Bitcoin, but also a dip in altcoin values as money is transferred from altcoins into Bitcoin as holders try to make extra profits.

Conversely, when Bitcoin falls in value - this signals that money is leaving the cryptocurrency space as a whole, and altcoin values decrease as well. This lack of confidence leads to a shrinking of the overall cryptocurrency market cap.

Traditionally, altcoins have performed best when Bitcoin is stable, and not moving significantly in either direction. This is when cryptocurrency investors have sought new opportunities, and what leads them directly to altcoins.

Will Bitcoin eventually be usurped from the top spot by another cryptocurrency? - It's possible. But for now, we should hope that Bitcoin continues to perform well.

One of the big things keeping Bitcoin at the top of the pile is it still maintains its position as the biggest exchange pairing for smaller cryptocurrencies. For those are you who have not yet invested in cryptocurrencies, what this means is that there are only a few cryptocurrencies you can buy directly for fiat currency (like US Dollars or British pounds), for the rest of them you need to buy Bitcoin first, and then exchange Bitcoin into a different cryptocurrency.

However, due to the rise in Bitcoin transaction fees, more and more exchanges are listed Ethereum as the preferred exchange pair. Ethereum possesses faster and lower fee transactions than Bitcoin, and thus at the current time, makes it an ideal exchange pairing. This is one factor that could affect Bitcoin' growth going forward, although it is working on solutions in the form of the upcoming Lightning Network.

Are Bitcoin and Ethereum finally separating?

In the month of January, Bitcoin's market dominance, in other words, Bitcoin's percentage of the total cryptocurrency market cap, halved from 66% to 33%, it's lowest, mark ever and down from a peak of 80% in June 2017.

Traditionally, prices of Ethereum, the number 2 cryptocurrency, have long been tied to Bitcoin's price, and trends have moved in similar directions. However, we are now seeing Ethereum somewhat move towards independence from the incumbent King of Cryptocurrency. There are a number of reasons for this.

In terms of the total number of transactions, Ethereum now accounts for roughly 50% of them, compared to 33% for Bitcoin. At its peak in December 2017, Ethereum was processing over 1 million transactions a day. Then there's the Ethereum ecosystem, 80 out of the top 100 coins on coinmarketcap.com at the time of writing were built on the Ethereum blockchain. The vast majority of ICOs launched in 2017 were Ethereum based ones, and that trend is predicted to continue in 2018 and beyond.

Ethereum trading pairs are now increasing in popularity on major exchanges. Where before users had to use a Bitcoin pairing with another coin, they can now use Ethereum for the same coin. This is preferable to many traders and investors as Ethereum transaction fees are roughly 90% less than those of Bitcoin. In terms of the very largest exchanges, Binance now has 101 out of 103 coins available for trading against Ethereum and BitFinex now accepts all coins traded against Ethereum. This also has ramifications for new entrants to the market, who previously had to buy Bitcoin in order to buy any cryptocurrency. So the new money flowing into the market is now flowing into Ethereum rather than just Bitcoin.

The key ratio to look out for in Ethereum to Bitcoin prices is 0.13, this has traditionally been the level that Ethereum has struggled to break through. If we see a move to even 0.15, this demonstrates that there is inherent confidence in Ethereum as being able to take over the number one spot in the cryptocurrency ecosystem. Due to the higher supply of Ethereum, at the time of writing, a price increase to $1350 would see it overtake Bitcoin and become the number one cryptocurrency in terms of market cap, this is, of course, assuming Bitcoin's price remains stable.

Should you invest in a Bitcoin ETF or Investment Trust?

There are a number of Bitcoin investment trusts and "Bitcoin ETFs" appearing now, on the surface these appear to be a low-risk way to invest in Bitcoin.

One such example of this is the Bitcoin Investment Trust run by Grayscale . The fund owns a fixed amount of Bitcoin on behalf of its investors. In January 2018, the fund decided to perform a 91-for-1 stock split. In other words, for every share owned up to that point would receive an additional 91 shares. Conversely, those shares would be worth 1/91th of the value of the initial share. Under the new pricing structure, each share is worth the equivalent of 0.00101 Bitcoin. The reason for doing this is to lower the base level price and make the fund more accessible to the everyday investor. Share prices fell from $1,970 to a much more consumer friendly $21.65. The aim of this fund is to make owning cryptocurrency as accessible as possible for people.

There are two major problems with this though. Number one, the fund trades at a significant premium when compared to Bitcoin's actual value. A slight premium would be acceptable based on the work involved, however, at current market prices, investors are paying over a 50% premium for Bitcoin under this structure. There's also an additional annual 2% management fee when all the "management" required is holding Bitcoin in a wallet. Taking all this into account, you're better off just buying Bitcoin yourself, with the two easiest methods for a first time investor being Coinbase or Robinhood (if available).

Bitcoin ETFs

There are no pure Bitcoin ETFs available at the time of writing. A public statement by the SEC in January 2018 stated that "significant investor protection issues" needed to be examined before firms could start offering one. There were attempts prior to this to register a Bitcoin ETF, the most notable of which was by the Winklevoss Twins. The twins collectively known as the world's first Bitcoin billionaires after investing much of the money they were paid as part of their successful lawsuit against Facebook's Mark Zuckerberg in Bitcoin back in 2011, had their ETF rejected by the SEC in May 2017.

The solution

There are a number of blockchain ETFs currently available for consumer investors, including the Reality Shares Nasdaq NexGen Economy ETF ($BLCN) and Amplify Transformational Data Sharing ETF (BLOK). Both of these funds track stocks which are either pure blockchain companies or have significant portions of their business dedicated to blockchain.

HLBK

In February 2018, Canadian regulators approved the country's first blockchain based ETF under the ticker HLBK, this ETF is the first North American ETF that actually tracks cryptocurrencies themselves as opposed to just blockchain stocks.

The correlation between Bitcoin and gold

Bitcoin has long been dubbed "digital gold", and Bitcoin billionaire Cameron Winklevoss described at as "gold 2.0" but just how similar are the two assets? Gold, which at the time of writing trades at around $1250 per ounce, has always been "safe haven" asset, the one investors believe will always have intrinsic value, even in the case of a complete stock market collapse. We already discussed how Wall Street has traditionally used gold as a hedge against the stock market and is starting to do the same with cryptocurrencies.

However, that's largely where the similarities end, in fact, it seems that Bitcoin is eating into gold's market share. RJO Futures' Philip Streible stated that "Bitcoin has stolen a large market share of gold". It should be noted that this was before the launch of the Bitcoin futures contract on the CME and CBoE. If Bitcoin took a 5% share of the global gold market, we would be looking at prices of around $50,000 per Bitcoin.

At this point, there is a well documented inversely correlated relationship between Bitcoin and gold. This is when Bitcoin goes up, gold goes down and vice versa. This may well help us predict the future price movements of both assets, as we see in which direction institutional money is moving. A January report

One interesting thing to note in the large downturn of January 2018, was that gold sales rose significantly during the month. On January 16, the first day of the crash, gold sales spiked by a factor of 5. In the same interview s previously quoted, Streibel stated: "If all of a sudden we see Bitcoin futures go into a free fall and collapse, [gold will benefit]."

It should also be noted that silver prices have been in freefall since the rise of Bitcoin and the cryptocurrency market at the beginning of 2017.

9 different expert's Bitcoin price predictions

Everyone loves to predict the future, especially when it could get their name features on a news report on CNBC or Fox. So we're seeing a lot of Bitcoin price predictions for 2018.

For example, a price of $60,000 would see a market cap of $1 trillion. Gold's current market cap is around $9.7 trillion. For reference, the entire cryptocurrency market cap was still below $200 billion in July.

A Monte Carlo simulation, which is based on past investor behaviour run by data scientist Xoel L Barata showed that with an 80% confidence level, the year end price for Bitcoin would be between $13,200 and $271,277. With an equal chance of both possibilities. At the 50th percentile, in other words, the most likely price, the price estimate was around $58,000. According to the simulation, which was run 100,000 times, there is a 9% chance that Bitcoin would end the year at a lower price than it began ($12,951).

Here are a number of other predictions from those on Wall Street and others involved in the cryptocurrency space.

"I wouldn't be surprised if over the next year it's down to $1,000 to $3,000," - Peter Blockvar, CEO, Bleakley Advisory Group

"A lot more money is going to come into Bitcoin, Bitcoin will go up to $30,000-35,000 this year" - Imran Wasim, financial analyst, AMSYS Group

"Even on a risk-adjusted basis, I think bitcoin is going to easily outperform the S&P." "[we can expect] a return to $20,000" - Tom Lee, Fundstrat Global Advisors

"As high as an overvalued $115,000, based on previous behaviour cycles" - Trace Meyer, Blockchain evangelist and early adopter

"Between $50,000 and $100,000 in 2018." - Kay Van Peterson, analyst, Saxo Bank

"all the way down to zero" - Nouriel "Dr. Doom" Roubini, professor of economics, New York University

"[$20,000 based on] An argument can be made that the good news is still not fully reflected in the current price." - Ronnie Moas, founder, Standpoint Research Inc.

"Bitcoin could be $40,000 at the end of this year" - Michael Novogratz, Bitcoin millionaire and Hedge Fund Manager

...plus 1 more from the infamous John McAfee, who promised to eat his own penis on TV if he was incorrect.

"$1 million by 2020"

OK John, we'll see about that one.

The growth of the Internet of Things market

The Internet of Things and blockchain go hand in hand. The IoT industry is estimated to grow around 300% in over the next 5 years and will reach $1.4 trillion by 2021.

Blockchain technology will play a huge part in this. The sheer number of data transactions, between multiple devices on multiple networks, means monitoring all these transactions is incredibly complicated, especially in terms of accountability. Where blockchain comes in is by providing a permanent, transparent and irrefutable record of transfers of both physical goods and data. If there is an error, or something goes wrong, blockchain can see where the error was made, and even rectify said error if possible.

In terms of cryptocurrency, IOTA is the largest one with a strong IoT focus. The coin has already received plaudits as well as investments from major companies such as Bosch. Focusing on just the pharmaceutical sector, Modum (MOD) is one example of the interaction between blockchain and the IoT. This specific use case has massive social benefits in the forms of lowering the circulation of counterfeit drugs and reduce the amount the industry spends on shipping logistics.

IBM is another company that has heavily focused on the IoT and blockchain interactions. The tech giant's biggest move thus far has been to invest over $200 million in it's Watson IoT headquarters, with much of this money going towards integrating blockchain solutions within the company. IBM also recently partnered with shipping giant Maersk to launch a new venture aimed at utilizing blockchain solutions for the shipping industry. Another IBM backed project is Hyperledger, an open source project in collaboration with JP Morgan among other companies that aims to demonstrate to customers how they can use blockchain in their own business.

A smaller company, that may not be on your radar is Filament. The Nevada based blockchain firm produces microchips that can be integrated into products and automatically create their own smart contracts and verify their own transactions. These are all stored on a decentralized server, so there is no risk of tampering. This is a useful alternative to centralized cloud based systems.

The only place where you can trade cryptocurrency and stocks at the same time

Yes, it's true, the development consumer investors have been crying out for is finally here. Stock-trading app Robinhood, known for its zero commission policy, is planning to integrate cryptocurrency trading. This move is sparked by the growing interest in cryptocurrency from younger investors, and those who don't yet have any investments of their own.

After all, 78 percent of Robinhood's customer base is 18-35 year olds, and the app has taken a significant market share in that demographic from traditional leaders like TD Ameritrade. The initial currency pairings will be Bitcoin and Ethereum, both traded against the US Dollar.

This will be the first of its kind, stock trading and cryptocurrency in the same place. It should be noted that this is actual cryptocurrency you are trading, not futures contracts denominated in USD. The initial rollout will be in 5 states (California, Massachusetts, Missouri, New Hampshire and Montana), with purchases limited to below $1,000. Even with these caveats, more than 1 million wannabe investors signed up for the chance to be given early access to the platform. For comparison, the last move of this kind by Robinhood was the announcement of commission free options trading, which garnered just 150,000 sign ups.

It's also worth noting that the new crypto venture will allow users to set price alerts for 14 additional cryptocurrencies. It will be interesting see if these currencies are also adopted by the platform at a later date. Although many of the currencies don't have fiat pairings themselves so that could prove to be troublesome. Robinhood CEO Baiju Bhatt stated that there are future plans to support all of these currencies, which include lesser known ones such as QTUM and Stellar. It remains to be seen if this will be via fiat to crypto pairings or a more traditional model like crypto to crypto pairings. The cryptocurrency move will not include ICOs either, which is in line with Robinhood's current model of not offering OTC stocks within the app.

The interesting development will be seeing if Robinhood can disrupt Coinbase's hold on the consumer cryptocurrency market. Coinbase has revenue of over $1 billion and briefly was the number one downloaded app on the Apple store, yet has its fair share of growing pains. Coinbase has suffered from long support ticket times during the last few months due to the sheer number of new users. Robinhood's initial 5 state rollout plan will be beneficial for them as it will help them test their internal support team's capabilities.

There is also the debate of where Robinhood will store user's coins, and whether investors will be covered in the case of hacks. According to their website, they will be using a mixture of online and offline storage for coins, and have "cutting-edge security measures that are both processes and technologically driven to secure your coins." There are no more specifics than this at the current time, so we will have to wait and see an exact plan for investors going forward.

What will the emergence of the Bitcoin futures market mean for cryptocurrency?

In December 2017, the Chicago Board of Exchange (CBoE) launched the first Bitcoin futures market, the first of its kind in the US. A week later, the Chicago Mercantile Exchange (CME) offered the same contract. This allows traders to buy and sell Bitcoin based on a predicted future price. The initial length of the futures contract was 1 month, with the original asking price being set at $15,000 for 1 Bitcoin. It should be noted that with futures contracts, the Bitcoin tokens themselves do not change hands between traders, and all trades are executed in US dollars only. In the run up to the launch of the CBoE futures, Bitcoin broke $20,000 for the first time based on speculated demand from Wall Street.

Futures contracts being offered have a number of ramifications. The first of which is more liquidity in the market. More money flows in from Wall Street and as more brokers, especially at a consumer level begin to offer their customer this option, could lead to a short term price rise.

There's also the matter of the futures contracts leading to an expanded investor base. Investment banks can now offer futures contracts to their clients as an asset.

The third is overall confidence. The CBoE and CME are both regulated exchanges, which signifies Wall Street's confidence in Bitcoin as a legitimate financial asset. If this confidence spreads to other cryptocurrencies like Ethereum and Ripple, it will only mean good things for the space as a whole.

The long term effects are debatable. If you look at gold as an example, in the first 5 years after gold futures were launched in 1974, there was very little correlation between the futures contracts and the price of gold, which was more influenced by geopolitical events such as the 1979 Soviet invasion of Afghanistan. The same analysis holds true for silver, which was also largely unaffected int he long term by futures contracts.

Some speculators have debated whether the launch of a futures market for a volatile asset could lead to a 2008 style crash based on bankers not being able to pay their debts. However, this is largely based on questionable "what-if" scenarios than anything to do with cryptocurrencies themselves.

It should also be noted that initial uptake of futures contracts on the CBoE was slow compared to other futures markets like gold or forex. On the first day of trading there were approximately 3,500 trades made compared to 400,000 daily for the gold futures market.

What every potential investor needs to know about Ripple (XRP)

Cryptocurrency investors have long been aware of Ripple, the payment platform that focuses on partnerships with large, already established, financial institutions. Ripple and its token XRP entered the mainstream media in December 2017 after a meteoric rise saw the coin's value soar from $0.25 to a peak of more than $3. If we look at the year as a whole, Ripple was the highest returning cryptocurrency with gains of over 37,000%, making creator Chris Larson one of the world's richest men based on his XRP holdings.

Today Ripple can boast of partnerships with mega banks like Santander, credit card provider American Express and international transfer service MoneyGram. The later is perhaps the most important, as it saves MoneyGram users huge amounts in transaction fees.

How does Ripple work? Simply put, transfers are made from one currency (like the US dollar) into XRP (Ripple's token), then the XRP is converted into a second currency (like Yen). The base level transaction cost for this is just 0.00001 XRP which is just a fraction of a cent, and much lower than traditional cross border payment systems like SWIFT.

This all sounds extremely promising, and Ripple is probably the most well developed cryptocurrency outside of Bitcoin and Ethereum, in terms of real world adoption and partnerships. However, there are a number of things to note about holding Ripple.

Ripple vs. XRP

By buying XRP, you are not buying shares in Ripple Labs. The major underlying point here is that XRP is not required for the Ripple network to function (other currencies can be used), nor are banks required to use XRP in order to partner up with Ripple. It should be noted therefore that banks do not directly buy XRP like they do with Bitcoin. There is no large scale institutional level investment in XRP.

Where the confusion lies is that if a private investor invests in Ripple company, the incorrect assumption is made that the value of XRP should also increase. However, XRP token's valuation and Ripple company's financial situation are irrelevant.

Competition

Ripple currently has the capability to process around 1,500 transactions per second which is roughly 200 times that of the Bitcoin network. However, there are other cryptocurrencies emerging that are potentially even faster. RaiBlocks (XRB) for example has processed over 7,000 transactions per second on its test network, and a little known cryptocurrency XtraBytes (XBY) has outlined the steps needed to process over 10,000 transactions per second.

XRP Supply issues

A third thing to note about XRP, is that only 40% of the tokens are currently in circulation. A further 20% of the tokens are held by the founders themselves. Ripple Labs controls the supply of XRP issued, so unlike a decentralized approach like that of Bitcoin or Ethereum, they can release XRP as they wish. This means they could release large amounts of XRP to the market, which would lead to significant inflation and a decrease in value of the current XRP token. It should be noted that you cannot mine XRP, and must rely on Ripple Labs for the supply of the token.

Banks creating their own solution

Due to Ripple's targeting of large financial institutions, this leaves them vulnerable to competition from the banks themselves. Many banks including Barclays and HSBC are working to develop their own blockchain solution for cross border payments. One area banks have to their advantage is that it is much easier to sell a blockchain solution internally to upper management than it is for an outside company to pitch one. In terms of development speed, this is another area where banks have an advantage as they have much deeper pockets than Ripple Labs.

An analysis of Blockchain based stocks and stocks which utilize blockchain technology

If cryptocurrencies are still overwhelming, confusing or too risky for you - that's OK.

You can still very much profit from blockchain technology in the regular stock market. Below are some companies that are utilizing blockchain technology in their own unique way.

Once again, I should note that I am not recommending or advising you buy any of the stocks listed here.

Alphabet Inc. ($GOOG)
Price at time of writing: $1,175.58

We start with one you've probably all heard of, unless you've not only been living under a rock but an entire mountain! Google is actually the second largest blockchain investor over the past 5 years through its investment arm, Google Ventures.

One of their most recent investments was that of Storj (discussed in depth in one of my previous books - *Ethereum: Beginners Bible).* Storj offers consumer and enterprise level blockchain solutions for decentralized online storage. Storj will act as a competitor to traditional cloud solutions like Amazon Web Services and AliBaba's Cloud service. Other notable investments from Google Ventures include cross-border payment processor Veem.

Overstock ($OSTK)
Price at time of writing: $86.90

Overstock.com is a fairly under the radar boomer from the past few months. Like the company's name suggests, they deal in excess manufactured goods and sell them at a deep discount. This is everything from furniture, to sporting goods to jewelry - but nothing revolutionary right?

However, Overstock was the first major retailer to accept Bitcoin as a payment method, way back in 2014, which sparked the first wave of cryptocurrency adoption on main street. The company also owns a subsidiary called Medici Ventures, which is focused solely on investing in, and developing blockchain technology. Medici holdings has invested heavily in a number of blockchain products, most notably the cryptocurrency Factom. Investments like have seen Overstock's price rise over 400% in less than 6 months. More importantly, these are exactly the kinds of patterns we want to look out for when examining how we use blockchain technology to profit from traditional stocks.

SBI Holdings (NASDAQ:SBHGF)
Price at time of writing: $25.30

Based out of Japan, but also listed on the NASDAQ, SBI Holdings which is part of the SBI Group. The firm gained notoriety after investing heavily in the Japanese Bitcoin exchange BitFlyer and in a move that garnered more mainstream attention, the cryptocurrency Ripple. SBIs investment in Ripple included using the platform to test cross-border payments between Japan and South Korea. The investment in Ripple was one of the key catalysts that not only saw Ripple's price increase, but also those that adopted its technology.

SBI continued their cryptocurrency charge in October by making a move into mining. The company released a statement outlining the motivations for their move saying.

"The SBI Group will endeavor to acquire cryptocurrencies, for the further development of products and services, and to secure market liquidity. This includes the mining of [bitcoin and bitcoin cash], and investments into U.S. Ripple"

IBM ($IBM)
Price at time of writing: $166.80

It should come as no surprise that a company that's always been on the forefront of the tech industry is betting on blockchain. In October the tech giant announced a partnership with then little known cryptocurrency Stellar, aimed at utilizing Stellar's payment platform for banking focused on 12 countries in the South Pacific region, including Australia and New Zealnd. IBM has a huge overseas customer base and thus is always looking for ways to save money on cross-border transfers.

This seal of approval if you will from the financial sector, leads us to the next step in blockchain technology, going from strictly theoretical, to being used mainly in cryptocurrency, to the next step which represents true widespread adoption.

This caused not only a positive bump in IBM stock but also a whopping 127% overnight growth in the price of Stellar Lumens (XLM) itself. This goes to show that adoption works both ways. Traditional companies benefit from blockchain solutions, and the cryptocurrencies themselves benefit from adoption by these companies. It's pretty safe to say that going into 2018 and beyond, we'll only be seeing more of these types of partnerships.

Mining based stocks - An often overlooked opportunity

Two of the biggest cryptocurrency winners in the past few years, haven't been cryptocurrencies themselves, but ones that are affected by the boom in cryptocurrency mining.

You see, mining cryptocurrency requires a huge amount of computing power, in the form of Central Processing Units (CPUs) and Graphics Processing Units (GPUs). Manufacturers of these parts have seen their stock prices skyrocket since the beginning of 2016 when cryptocurrency mining really took off.

AMD ($AMD) and NVIDIA ($NVDA) are the two biggest winners thus far, in fact, in Q3 2017, NVIDIA's revenue from mining soared to $220 million for the quarter. Now, nearly 5% of the company's bottom line is attributable to cryptocurrency mining. AMD, on the other hand, sees roughly 10% of its overall revenue being from cryptocurrency mining sources.

So is it time to go long on AMD & NVDA - not so fast. There are a number of factors at play which will have a large effect on prices.

What if mining decreases in popularity?

It could be argued that due to the nature of cryptocurrencies, miner payouts will continue to decrease (like in the case of Bitcoin and Ethereum). There have also been suggestions that as cryptocurrencies develop, there may not be a need for GPU mining at all.

There's also the wildcard of Ethereum switching to Proof of Stake mining which will make GPU mining for Ethereum obsolete. This switch was originally scheduled for 2017 but was delayed at least a year, and there are rumors swirling that the switch may not happen before 2019 now. For the time being though, miners are currently earning around $1.76 profit per GPU per day from mining Ethereum, which may seem low on the surface, but you have mining farms with thousands of GPUs, these profits add up fast.

Either way, the companies themselves have different approaches to how cryptocurrencies will affect their profits going forward. AMD CEO Lisa Su stated that they were expecting a "cryptocurrency cooling off period" in 2018, and the company doesn't consider demand for GPUs as a part of its long term gameplan.

NVIDIA, on the other hand, is more bullish and has openly admitted that it considers cryptocurrency mining a big part of future business plans.

What if China bans mining?

70% of the world's cryptocurrency mining operations are in China, however, China is volatile when it comes to cryptocurrency, to say the least. We've already seen the government ban Chinese citizens from investing in ICOs outside of China, which had a significant detrimental effect on the market. So naturally, there is some concern that a mining ban or cutback or any kind could immediately send any mining based stock into free fall.

However, Bitmain Technologies, the owner of one of the world's largest mining operations is looking to expand it's operations to Canada and Switzerland to mitigate some of this risk. Canada is on its radar due to the generous tax incentives offered by Manitoba and Saskatchewan provinces.

Additional mining resources

There are two more ETFs that specialize in semiconductor companies that make the computer chips required for mining. These being the iShares PHLX Semiconductor ETF (SOXX) and VanEck Vectors Semiconductor ETF (SMH). Both of these funds have seen significant growth as a result of the mining movement, and their future success will be heavily determined by the continued uptake of cryptocurrency mining.

Will Central Banks issue cryptocurrencies of their own?

This is a central (pardon the pun) question that we should all be asking going forward. Will central banks launch their own cryptocurrencies in 2018? This question a tricky one for financial, technological and ideological reasons.

We'll address the ideological reason first as they are the most simple. Part of the identity of cryptocurrency as a whole comes from being a solution to centralized institutions having control of our money.

What we need to note though is one extremely important distinction. Central banks have significantly different financial goals from the consumer investor. The consumer investor wants to maximize their returns in the shortest possible time, and with cryptocurrencies, we've seen this more than ever. Central banks on the other have an obligation to provide financial stability for the citizens of that particular country.

It's for this reason that we're unlikely to see central banks holding large amounts of any cryptocurrency, whose volatility makes it a less than ideal asset in their eyes. However, banks still want to embrace blockchain technology, which leads us to the natural solution to this, central banks launching their own cryptocurrencies.

These currencies would be available for the citizens of each country to buy, but unlike regular cryptocurrencies these would likely be pegged to that country's base currency. The question is however, is they are pegged to the base currency, what incentive is there for consumers to hold a central bank owned cryptocurrency? It takes away the consumer's main motivation of short-term profits because it functions the same as holding your money in a bank account, except on a blockchain. You could argue that holding any money on a blockchain is more secure than storing it with a private bank. However in first world countries, bank deposits are all automatically insured up to a certain amount anyway, so in practical terms, the two would function the same.

So the second way in which banks could use their own cryptocurrencies is in a way similar to Ripple, as an intermediary payment processor. The question there, is if they could reasonably develop a system better than a privately owned on (like XRP) or decentralized cryptocurrency (like XRB). This is likely to be low down on a bank's list of priorities, so it's unlikely that we'll be seeing a central bank cryptocurrency in the near future. That doesn't mean they won't be looking to profit from blockchain technology, so it'd be wise to monitor blockchain solutions for partnerships with central banks.

The next best alternative to a cryptocurrency ETF

For those of you familiar with traditional investments, then you'll likely to be aware of Exchange Traded Funds or ETFs. For those unfamiliar, an ETF is a security that trades like a regular stock, but instead of buying shares in one company, you are buying an aggregate of many companies. ETFs have an inherent advantage over single stocks in that by diversifying your risk over many companies, you are less likely to see sudden drops in price.

Based out of Slovenia, and active since November 2016, Fintech start-up Iconomi is currently running a blockchain based digital asset management platform using Ethereum technology. Known as Digital Asset Arrays (DAA), these are similar to ETFs and Index funds, as you are buying an aggregate of multiple cryptocurrencies instead of just one or two. Initial investments can be made with ETH or BTC, although there are plans to support fiat deposits in the coming months.

Their BLX blockchain index is the first passively managed array of digital assets, compromising of over 20 different cryptocurrencies, with the highest weight being in Bitcoin and Ethereum. The portfolio is re-balanced on a monthly basis, and different cryptocurrencies are added and removed based on performance. What's more is the BLX has currently outperformed both Ethereum and Litecoin over the past 6 months. There is also a more conservative fund which is composed of 60% Bitcoin, 20% Ethereum as well as 4 other ERC20 tokens. All Iconomi funds have a 2-3% annual management fee, plus a 0.5% exit fee.

This could well be a good option if you're looking to invest in a multitude of cryptocurrencies, but don't want to deal with the hassle of signing up for multiple exchanges, and keeping track of various wallets. Iconomi currently offers 15 different DAAs, ranging from conservative, heavily Bitcoin based ones, to more risky ones featuring a multitude of smaller cap cryptocurrencies. Of course, like any investment, there are inherent risks involved, but if you're a more risk averse investor, who still wants to be a part of the cryptocurrency market, Iconomi is worth checking out.

How to buy your first cryptocurrency - even if you're a technophobe

Gone are the days when buying Bitcoin was a time consuming and somewhat uncomfortable endeavor. Nowadays buying Bitcoin is a similar process to exchanging currency when you go on vacation. While I previously discussed Robinhood as an option, until the nationwide rollout occurs, and limits are increased, Coinbase still represents the best option for the majority of people.

There are two ways to buy Bitcoin, the first is to use fiat currency (USD, EUR, GBP etc.) to purchase cryptocurrency via an exchange. These exchanges function the same way as regular foreign currency exchanges do. The prices fluctuate on a daily basis, and like regular currency exchange markets - they are open 24/7. These exchanges make their money from charging a small fee for each transaction.

Some charge both buyers and sellers, some only charge a fee for buying. For security reasons, most of these exchanges will require you to verify your ID before allowing you to purchase cryptocurrency.

It is also important to note the type of payments each exchange supports. Some allow for debit/credit card payments whereas other only accept PayPal or bank wire transfers. Below are the three biggest and reputable currency exchanges for purchasing Bitcoin, Ethereum and other altcoins with fiat currency like US dollars, Euros or British Pounds.

Coinbase

Currently largest currency exchange in the world, Coinbase allows users to buy, sell and store cryptocurrency. Coinbase is undoubtedly the most beginner friendly exchange for anyone looking to get involved in the cryptocurrency market. They currently allow trading of Bitcoin, as well as, Ethereum and LiteCoin using fiat currency as a base. Known for their stellar security procedures and insurance policies regarding stored currency. The exchange also has a fully functioning iPhone and Android app for buying and selling on the go, very useful if you are looking to trade.

Once you are signed up and complete the identity verification procedures you can buy Bitcoin with your credit or debit card instantly.

Coinbase also recently launched the Coinbase Vault, which is a secure way of storing your cryptocurrency while still having it accessible to trade. The vault uses double email address + phone verification in order to access your funds. If you're planning on holding long-term, I still recommend offline storage - but as an intermediary option, the Vault is a step in the right direction.

If you sign up for Coinbase using this link, you will receive $10 worth of free Bitcoin after your first purchase of more than $100 worth of cryptocurrency.

http://bit.ly/10dollarbtc

Note, if you're going to be trading Bitcoin, I recommend doing so on Coinbase's partner platform GDax, which has lower fees.

Where to buy altcoins?

Binance and Bittrex are the two largest altcoins trading platform, and both of these now feature Ethereum as well as Bitcoin pairings for nearly all of the coins available. It's on platforms like these where you can purchase popular altcoins such as Neo (NEO), Cardano (ADA), VeChain (VEN) and Stellar Lumens (XLM). Personally I prefer the Binance interface more, but in reality, the two sites are very similar in function.

I should note that I no longer recommend Bitfinex after they stopped serving US customers completely in November 2017. Customers from other countries can still use Bitfinex and it is a perfectly fine platform for those outside the United States. Apart from these, Cryptopia is another good exchange for a number of smaller cap cryptocurrencies such as Bytom and Xtrabytes. Liqui.io also comes recommended as does EtherDelta. All recommendations are based on my personal experience with the platforms and I do not recommend any platforms that I haven't personally used.

Conclusion

So there we have it, a look into how Wall Street and some of the world's top financial institutions are playing this cryptocurrency mania we've been seeing of the past 12 months.

We've covered both the cryptocurrencies themselves, and also how this market affects traditional securities, as well as gold. Hopefully this has given you a greater understanding of the relationships between these 3, and some additional knowledge that you can apply to your own investment strategies.

Just how cryptocurrency will play out in 2018, not even the best and brightest minds in the financial world could tell us, but one thing is for certain, it's going to be a wild ride either way. We need to take a step back and think about the potential applications of blockchain technology beyond just finance, and appreciate just how exciting this technology is. It's rare that we see truly life changing advancements in fields like financial monitoring, supply chain management and even healthcare, but blockchain has the ability to provide all of these.

I encourage you to do your own research on top of what you have read in this book and to not rely on one single source for your cryptocurrency news. If you would like to do some further reading, in my opinion the two best resources for unbiased news on cryptocurrency and blockchain developments are coindesk.com and cointelegraph.com.

As with any investment, never invest more than you can afford to lose. This is a volatile market the likes of which we have never seen before, and as such should be looked at as a high risk investment. For those over the age of 30, I recommend cryptocurrency be no more than 15% of your overall portfolio holdings. For those under 30, this can be increased to 25% due to your greater future earning potential.

I hope you've enjoyed this book, and if you have, I'd appreciate if you went ahead and left it a review on Amazon.

I wish you the best of luck in your own cryptocurrency journey, and if you are invested, or decide to invest in the future, I hope you make a lot of money.

Thanks for reading,
Stephen

P.S. Don't forget - if you're a cryptocurrency first timer, you can get $10 worth of Bitcoin for free after spending $100 or more on any cryptocurrency at Coinbase using this link http://bit.ly/10dollarbtc

Ethereum: Beginners Bible - How You Can Profit from Trading & Investing in Ethereum, Even If You're a Complete Novice

By Stephen Satoshi

Introduction

Wow, what a year it's been for Ethereum, and the cryptocurrency market as a whole. We've seen a 5000% price rise, passed 500,000 daily transactions, survived a Vitalik Buterin death rumor, and witnessed Ethereum truly arrive on the stage of the general public and cement itself as the number two cryptocurrency on the planet.

After opening the year sitting at a modest $7.98, with the market cap at a now unthinkably low $698 million, Ethereum continued to steadily rise and then saw its price explode by nearly 400% in just a 3 week period between May and June. After a few months of steady fluctuation between $250-$350, another breakout occured in mid-November and all time highs of over $500 were reached. At the time of writing, Ethereum's price sits at a cool $453, with a market cap of $45 billion. The Ethereum network now processes more than twice the amount of daily transactions as the Bitcoin network, despite Bitcoin's much higher notoriety.

It hasn't all been smooth sailing though, a June rumor, believed to have been started on the anonymous internet forum 4chan, claimed that Ethereum's founder Vitalik Buterin had been killed in a car crash. This led to an almost instant drop in market value of over $4 billion, which was recovered within a few short days.

So that begs the question, are we in a bubble? Only time will tell, but as I'll explain later on in this book, Ethereum is arguably the must bubbleproof cryptocurrency on the market itself for a variety of reasons. The main one being the sheer number of developments and potential use cases for the platform beyond just a means of exchanging value. The fundamental infrastructure of Ethereum has the potential to revolutionize the internet, plus how financial audits, and business transactions are conducted. That alone is enough for it to continue strong gains in the short and long term on the road to mass adoption. That's without discussing the other billion dollar industries it could potentially disrupt

It should also noted, that the cryptocurrency market as a whole is still only 20% as big as the tech market during the Dotcom crash ($300 billion vs. $1.75 trillion).

Finally, thank you for purchasing this book. If you enjoy reading it, I'd appreciate it if you left it a review on Amazon.

Thanks,
Stephen

What is Ethereum?

Ethereum was born in 2013 from a core team of 3 individuals: Vitalik Buterin, a Russian-Canadian programmer, Dr. Gavin Wood a British economist and game theory enthusiast, and Canadian entrepreneur Joseph Lubin. The fundamental idea behind Ethereum is that blockchain technology can be useful for things outside of just cryptocurrency. These included asset issuance, crowdfunding, domain registration, gambling, voting and prediction markets among innumerable other uses.

The main issue with blockchain platforms up to this point is that they were only designed to do one specific action, like Bitcoin for example, which only processes and verifies monetary transactions between two parties.

You can think of Ethereum as more like a smartphone. Smartphones are able to handle a variety of different types of application, with just one operating platform. Likewise for developers, if someone creates a smartphone application, then all they have to do is upload it to the app store, and users can download it without needing to buy additional hardware. Applications that run on Ethereum are known as Decentralized Apps (DApps).

What is a smart contract?

One of the fundamental ideas behind Ethereum is the use of self-executing smart contracts. We can think of a smart contract like a digital vending machine. A vending machine is a very basic way to ensure a financial agreement is upheld by two parties. Party a) the user and party b) the machine itself. Using a vending machine that dispenses Coke cans as an example. Let's say the cans cost $1.

- If we put it $1, and a coke comes out - successful transaction, and enforcement of the contract
- If we don't put in $1, and no coke comes out - successful enforcement of the contract
- If we don't put in $1, and a coke comes out - something has gone wrong, the contract hasn't been enforced correctly

In the case of a smart contract, the machine in question is a computer algorithm.

To use another example, you could set up a contract where the title deed of a home is transferred from a seller to a buyer, as soon as the buyer's money is sent to the seller. This transaction would usually require a third party to verify it (and thus incur an extra cost), but using smart contracts, the transaction executes automatically once both sides have upheld their part of the agreement, so a third party is not necessary. The lack of a third party, such as a bank or auditor, has the potential for huge cost savings across a wide variety of industries.

Is Ethereum the same as Bitcoin?

Not really. They are both distributed public blockchain networks, that much is true - but that's pretty much where the similarities end. As previously mentioned, Bitcoin only has a singular function which is a peer-to-peer electronic cash system to handle payments online between two parties. Bitcoin's blockchain is only used to track these payments and determine who owns how many coins.

Ethereum on the other hand is used as a platform for running many different kinds of decentralized applications. Unlike Bitcoin, Ethereum has multiple functions, beyond just functioning as an alternative method for payments. Ethereum tokens (known as Ether, although the terms are often used interchangeably) are used to process the running of the applications, essentially to "pay" for space on the Ethereum platform. A kind of fuel that is used to run the requested operations of the specific application and the execution of smart contracts.

To use an example of a smart contract versus just a transaction. We can compare Bitcoin to Ethereum.

Bitcoin can process a transaction of 1 Bitcoin (BTC) from Steve to Sarah. We can see how much Steve sent, and how much Sarah received.

What Ethereum can do is set up a contract where Steve will send Sarah 1BTC on a set date in the future, but only on the condition that Sarah has less than 10BTC in her Bitcoin wallet on that date. So if Sarah has more than 10BTC on that date, the contract knows it is should not execute, and transaction will not take place.

Another way you could look at Bitcoin vs. Ethereum is that Bitcoin is version 1.0 of a blockchain use case whereas Ethereum is version 2.0. Others like to use a Netscape vs. Google Chrome analogy.

So is Ethereum a programming language like Javascript or Ruby on Rails?

Again, not really. Ethereum is just a blockchain platform that applications can be built on. You can think of it more like an operating system like Windows or iOS. The apps and smart contracts themselves are programmed in a variety of languages such as Solidity.

How does Ethereum have value?

So if Ethereum isn't purely a cryptocurrency, how does it have value? The answer is that Ethereum tokens (ETH or ether) have value as long as the Ethereum network is up and running. The more programs that are running on the network, the more ETH are needed to keep the network running, and therefore the higher the value of ETH. You can think of this like the total amount of gas needed to run all the cars in the world. By buying Ethereum, you are showing faith in the network and the applications that are running on it.

Who is Vitalik Buterin?

While the identity of Bitcoin's "figurehead" Satoshi Nakamoto has never truly been revealed, and may not even be a single person - Ethereum followers can look firmly towards Vitalik Buterin as the leader for the project.

An unassuming looking 23 year old born in Russian, raised in Canada, with a love of unicorn t-shirts, mismatched socks and decentralization principles, Buterin's first entry to the cryptocurrency world was hearing about Bitcoin from his Father at the tender age of 17. He claims he dismissed the idea of cryptocurrency at first, believing there was no intrinsic value, but after quitting his World of Warcraft obsession, he sought something else to sink his time into.

Naturally, being a teenager and having somewhat of an "us versus them" mentality against large centralized institutions, he reexamined cryptocurrency and eventually began writing for a Bitcoin blog, in which he was paid 5BTC (then worth around $50) for each article. Buterin then went on to co-found Bitcoin Magazine, while studying at the University of Waterloo.

Buterin co-founded Ethereum at the tender age of 19 - with the aim of creating a network that could deliver multiple digital services without the need for a middle man by using smart contracts. This in turn would help regulate and govern the "double spending problem" that cryptocurrencies face.

In Buterin's own words, Ethereum was created to be a "general purpose blockchain", a move that some commentators called "impossibly ambitious", although many in the cryptocurrency space saw the move as revolutionary. A 2014 crowdsale raised 31,000 Bitcoins, which was trading at around $650 during the time, but crashed a few weeks later, leaving Buterin and his team with a much lower dollar value than they had previously anticipated. This didn't deter them and by spring of the following year, the early stages of the Ethereum project were online. Within just a few short years, his vision has already begun to take shape. After co-founders Wood and Lubin left the project, Buterin continued as the sole figurehead of the Ethereum foundation.

On June 25th 2017, Buterin was the subject of a hoax regarding his death, believed to be started on 4chan. The rumor stated that Buterin had died in a fatal car crash and this caused $4 billion to be wiped from Ethereum's value as a number of parties panic sold their ETH. Within 12 hours, Buterin himself responded and proved that he was, in fact, alive.

Today, Buterin continues to be part-programmer, part-figurehead for the Ethereum project, albeit with a much larger team behind him. Dealing with the political and social consequences of running a giant blockchain project, as well as, working behind the scenes to improve the technology at the heart of it.

Challenges Ethereum faces going forward

Ethereum, like Bitcoin is now experiencing more and more of a network effect, and has cemented itself as the number 2 cryptocurrency going forward. It's addition onto popular newbie friendly exchange Coinbase has served as a positive for the mass market looking to get involved with cryptocurrencies. However, there a still a number of challenges Ethereum faces going forward on its path towards mass adoption.

Hacking Incidents

The 2016 DAO hacking incident

"The DAO" was a cryptocurrency that had an ICO in April of 2016, with the intention of providing the market with "smart locks" that essentially let people rent out their assets including cars and housing. Sort of a decentralized AirBNB model.

In the first 15 days of its ICO, The DAO raised over $100 million, and reached over $150 by the end of the funding period, which at the time was the largest amount raised by any ICO to date, and represented roughly 14% of all the ETH tokens on the open market. Although during the sale period, several commentators noted that the code was vulnerable to an attack.

On June 18th, a hacker moved 3.6 million ETH (then worth around $50 million) into a clone of the network. 2 days later, in a controversial move, the Ethereum community voted to hard fork the blockchain and restore the funds. This led to the creation of Ethereum Classic (traded as ETC), which maintains itself on the original blockchain.

The incident caused a 33% drop in Ethereum's value overnight. A year later, the thief's identity has still not been brought to light, although Ethereum itself has recovered.

The 2017 Parity wallet deletion incident

One of the stranger Ethereum events of 2017 was the freezing of roughly $200m dollars worth of Ethereum in the digital currency wallet Parity in November. A user managed to trigger an error during a wallet update which led to thousands of ETH being frozen. This error was caused by the user making himself the "owner" of one of Parity's smart contracts and deactivating the contract, which in turn froze the assets inside it.

Due to the way cryptocurrencies work, the only way these funds would be recoverable is to do a "hard fork" of the Ethereum blockchain when a certain fraction of miners refuse to update their ledgers, which would result in new ones being created. Hard forks themselves are risky, and usually have short term damaging affects on consumer confidence.

It should be noted that this was a problem with Parity's smart contracts, and not the Ethereum blockchain itself. There was a small dip in price (<3%) which showed that the market understood that this was a third party error. However, it does serve as a warning to keeping your crypto assets in a centrally controlled third party wallet.

As of the time of writing, total losses from the parity incident are unconfirmed, with most estimates ranging from $150 million to $300m dollars worth of ETH.

Motherboard news summed up the incident with a great analogy *"[The User] was jiggling door handles and when one door opened, they tried to close it and the whole house exploded."*

With both of these hacking incidents it should be reiterated that the Ethereum network itself was not hacked. All networked systems are vulnerable to various kinds of attacks. The Ethereum network, which supports (depending on the price) around $1bn worth of ether, has not been hacked and is continuously executing many other smart contracts.

Vitalik as a Central Figurehead

Vitalik Buterin himself is another point where Ethereum could face issues going forward. Any central figurehead is going to be largely scrutinized and Buterin is no different. A comparison can be made to Litecoin, with founder Charlie Lee coming under continued pressure for comments he has made about various cryptocurrencies and the cryptocurrency space in general.

However, Buterin continues to take on the role of developer first and foremost rather than a traditional "frontman" so to speak. The argument could also be made that as the project is still very much in the early stages, a central figurehead is needed. It is likely that once Ethereum reaches more a "finalized" version, Buterin would be expected to move away from a public position.

Scalability

The problem with most larger cryptocurrencies is the problem of scalability. Can their networks handle a huge volume of transactions, without incurring high fees. For example, the average Bitcoin transaction now costs around $4 in network fees. Ethereum on the hand has lower amounts, but will need to keep these low, will still trying to handle a large volume of transactions. Vitalik Buterin outlined a plan at the BeyondBlock conference, for Ethereum to reach "Visa levels" of scalability, without compromising core values such as safety, security and decentralization. To give an example of how ambitious that is, Ethereum processes 15 transactions per second, compared to Visa's 45,000 per second.

Ethereum's solution to the scaling problem in the short term is the launch of the Raiden network. Raiden aims to shift the majority of transactions off of the main Ethereum blockchain by using a technique known as "sharding". This essentially breaks the transaction down into tiny pieces, allowing the pieces to run on different networks, and because the networks are all interlinked - the transaction can process the same way as it were on a single network.

While no specific time frame has been discussed for reaching this so-called "Visa level" - the launch of Raiden and continued updates to the Ethereum network could see much of Ethereum's scalability issues solved within the next 5 years.

Advice on investing in Ethereum and cryptocurrency

Beyond my usual advice of never invest more than you can afford to lose. There are a number of areas your should consider before you invest in Ethereum or any other cryptocurrency.

1.   Market Volatility

Cryptocurrency as a market is extremely volatile when compared to other financial markets such as derivatives and foreign exchange. Swings of 10% either way in a day are not uncommon, and smaller currencies can see their price double in a matter of hours (or in the case of Ethereum, rise 400% in just under 3 weeks). If you are a cautious investor, then cryptocurrency may not be for you, because with the potential for large gains comes an inherently larger risk. One additional note should be that the cryptocurrency market is open 24/7, and price moves can often happen while US or European citizens are asleep, thanks to the large volume of trading that occurs in China and South Korea. That said, Ethereum is one of the more stable cryptocurrencies.

2.   Dollar Cost Averaging

Before investing in cryptocurrency, it's wise to do some basic risk management. Traditional investing advice dictates that you should only invest 10% of your overall portfolio in high risk investments, and cryptocurrency definitely checks the box as a high risk investment.

Secondly, to remove your exposure to market volatility, you should employ what is known as dollar cost averaging when investing. That means, instead of investing a large lump sum at once, you divide that sum up and invest a little bit at equal time periods.

For example, instead of investing $12,000 all at once, break that $12,000 up and invest $1,000 every month over the course of the year.

The reason for this is that if the price suddenly dips 20% the day after your initial investment, your loss in terms of $ is lower if your use dollar cost averaging. You can then benefit from buying more at this new lower price the next month. So over the course of the year, your average purchase price is usually lower. I would strongly advise you utilize dollar cost averaging when you invest in cryptocurrency, or any financial market.

3.   Diversification

If you do decide to invest in cryptocurrency, then Ethereum should by no means be your only holding. It should make up a large chunk of your portfolio, but diversifying is never a bad idea. Bitcoin of course is well worth looking into, as are the other smaller cap coins I discuss later on in this book. Once again, do you own research, and buy on fundamentals rather than hype.

4.   Misinformation, fake news and FUD

Because the cryptocurrency market is still in its infancy, there are still very few reliable news sources, and unfortunately a larger number of unreliable ones. There's no bigger proof of this than looking back to the rumors of Vitalik Buterin's death in June 2017, which caused Ethereum's value to drop by $4 billion in just a few short hours.

The flipside of this is that mainstream major outlets do not employ cryptocurrency experts, and often will have traditional stock market analysts try to analyze the cryptocurrency market, which works in a completely different way. As such, there are often misleading headlines, poorly researched news stories, and downright incorrect technical information.

There are also those who intentionally spread misinformation about that cryptocurrency market, which causes Fear, Uncertainty & Doubt, known in the space as "FUD". FUD is different from pointing out legitimate flaws or challenges in cryptocurrency, as the sole intentional is to cause negative price movements, rather than spark actual discussion about the technology.

You should certainly stay informed with the latest Ethereum news, but there are better sources than others. Below are 4 websites that in my opinion offer the best, unbiased cryptocurrency news, without any of the hype or spin that you'll find on other websites.

http://coindesk.com
http://cointelegraph.com
https://coincenter.org - Focuses on cryptocurrency legislation
http://cryptopanic.org - A cryptocurrency news aggregator platform

I would also be wary of paid newsletters or websites that offer cryptocurrency investment advice. While many of these predictions and "tips" have grown in value in 2017, it should be noted that this is one of the biggest bull markets ever seen, so there are a disproportionately high number of winners this year alone. I advise you to do your own research first and foremost, before blindly putting your faith in one of these services.

5. Your reasons for investing

You should ask yourself if you believe in Ethereum, and blockchain technology as a whole, at a technological level before you invest. Blockchain is transforming the landscape of computing, finance and governance as we know it, but that doesn't necessarily mean all of these companies have functional or even useful products that the mass market will gladly adopt.

If you truly believe (as many do, including myself), that Ethereum and blockchain technology is here to stay, and that will correspond in higher prices, then by all means invest your money. However, if your motivations for investing are purely down to the fear of missing out, and the expectation of indefinite continuous price rises, then you may be better off keeping your money elsewhere.

6. Don't day trade unless you know what you're doing, and have previous day trading experience

While day trading may seem like the quickest way to make a lot of money, it's also the quickest way to lose a lot of money if you don't know what you're doing. If you've never day traded before, I would *not* recommend you start with something as volatile as cryptocurrency. Remember, the vast majority of day traders lose money.

Is Mining Ethereum worth it?

In one of my other books, *Bitcoin: Beginners Bible*, I outlined why I believed mining Bitcoins was a bad idea for the average person. I believe the same general advice is true for Ethereum, but for slightly different reasons.

While ASICs (powerful computer that are only built to perform one task, in this case cryptocurrency mining) are not available for Ethereum, which makes the network rewards higher for smaller miners, the electricity costs of mining in the Western world now offset these rewards. The Ethereum block reward was recently decreased from 5ETH per block to 3ETH per block. So once again, you will need a dedicated mining machine to make any sort of significant mining gains.

These dedicated machines require large capital investment, for example, the NVidia GTX1070, currently considered the best mining GPU available, costs $500, and for an efficient mining rig you'll need 6 of these. That's not even considering the other computer parts you'll require.

As a rough estimate for a US citizen mining at home, it would take 2 years for you to recoup your investment, and that is assuming mining rewards stay the same throughout those two years.

The opportunity cost of your investment is also money you could have just invested in Ethereum itself. For example, if you'd spent $5,000 on a mining rig at the start of the year, you'd have recouped roughly half of your initial investment by November. Whereas if you had invested that $5,000 in Ethereum tokens, your returns would be roughly $280,000.

There are other cryptocurrencies that are still profitable to mine at home, Monero being the main one as of November 2017, but as for Ethereum, you are better off putting your resources into direct investments.

How to buy Ethereum in less than 15 minutes

Okay, so you've done your reading and you're ready to jump into the world of cryptocurrency and buy some Ethereum of your very own. First of all, congratulations and welcome to the club. Now, let's get you some Ethereum.

Coinbase

Coinbase represents the most simple way to buy Ethereum for those living in the US, Canada, the UK and Australia, in exchange for your local fiat currency. Based out of the US and regulated by the SEC, Coinbase is undoubtedly the most trustworthy cryptocurrency exchange out there today. Rates are competitive with the other major cryptocurrency exchanges, and the verification requirements are solid without being a hassle.

Currently Coinbase supports both wire transfers and purchases by debit and credit card. Once you signup for a Coinbase account and verify your ID, you can buy Ethereum, along with Bitcoin and Litecoin, instantly with your debit or credit card.

You can also store your cryptocurrency in Coinbase's vault system. If you do this, you will have to pass 2 factor authentication in order to spend it. This is one step more secure than simply leaving it on the exchange, but still is not as secure as offline storage option such as MyEtherWallet.

Another advantage of Coinbase is that they have a fully functional mobile app that allows the buying and selling of cryptocurrency on the go.

Now, as a special bonus to you - if you sign up for Coinbase using this link, you will receive $10 worth of free Bitcoin after your first purchase of more than $100 worth of Bitcoin, Ethereum or Litecoin.

http://bit.ly/10dollarbtc

Once you have purchased your Ethereum, there are a number of other exchanges I recommend if you want to trade Ethereum, many smaller cap cryptocurrencies do not allow for direct exchanges with fiat currency like USD, so you'll have to buy Bitcoin or Ethereum from Coinbase first, then exchange that for the other cryptocurrencies.

Poloniex

With more than 100 different cryptocurrencies available and data analysis for advanced traders, Poloniex is arguably the most comprehensive exchange on the market. Low trading fees (between 0.1 and 0.25%) are another plus, which makes this is a great place to trade your Bitcoin or Ethereum into other cryptocurrencies. The big drawback of Poloniex is that it does not allow fiat currency deposits, so you will have to make your initial Bitcoin or Ethereum purchases on Coinbase.

EtherDelta

EtherDelta is especially useful for buying and selling ERC20 in exchange for Ethereum. While not the most aesthetically pleasing website to look at, EtherDelta employs Ethereum smart contracts to function as a decentralized Ethereum exchange. Currently there are over 100 different token available for purchase.

Exchanges I do not recommend

Kraken

I used to recommend Kraken as a solid Coinbase alternative, however their decreasing levels of customer support and increased downtime over the past 6 months has led me stop recommend them.

BitStamp

Questionable customer service decisions. One user reported a termination on an account with more than 60,000 EUR worth of ETH and XRP inside, but did not receive the funds back from Bitstamp, either in cryptocurrency or in fiat. While this issue, and others like it, are still ongoing, I cannot recommend the exchange.

Where to store your Ethereum - setting up your Ethereum wallet

It is advisable that you do not keep any Ethereum (or any cryptocurrency for that matter), on a centralized exchange. The reason for this is that any cryptocurrency you store on an exchange is that directly controlled by you. This makes it vulnerable to attacks from third parties, and hacking incidents like the Mt. Gox hack of 2014.

Setting up Mist Wallet

Mist wallet is a simple way to store your Ethereum on your own personal computer rather than on a centralized exchange. This is more secure than an exchange, but for maximum security online storage (such as MyEtherWallet or a hardware wallet) is still recommended.

1. Go to https://github.com/ethereum/mist/releases and download the latest version for either PC, Mac or Linux
2. Install the wallet on your computer
3. Once installed click on "USE THE TEST NETWORK" and set your password. Use a unique password that you DO NOT use for any other website
4. Now you'll be able to see the wallets page and you balance should read 0.00ETH
5. Click on "Main account" - you will see your unique wallet address here, this will be 40 characters longer and will start start with 0x. If you share this address with someone, they will be able to send you Ether.
6. You can also send ETH from your account to any other ETH wallet address using Mist. You'll need your password to do so. When you do this you will see a confirmation number, you can check the transaction has processed correctly by copying this to http://testnet.etherscan.io/

How to set up an offline wallet with MyEtherWallet

All the coins in this book are based on the Ethereum blockchain, and therefore use ERC20 tokens. Therefore, these tokens can be stored in Ethereum wallets like regular ETH. Wallets can be daunting to set up at first, so I recommend you use something simple to get started, the most convenient of these is MyEtherWallet.

Step-by-Step guide to setting up MyEtherWallet

25. Go to https://www.myetherwallet.com/
26. Enter a strong but easy to remember password. Do not forget it.
27. This encrypts (protects) your private key. It does not generate your private key. This password alone will not be enough to access your coins.
28. Click the "Generate Wallet" button.
29. Download your Keystore/UTC file & save this file to a USB drive.
30. This is the encrypted version of your private key. You need your password to access it. It is safer than your unencrypted private key but you must have your password to access it in the future.
31. Read the warning. If you understand it, click the "I understand. Continue" button.
32. Print your paper wallet backup and/or carefully hand-write the private key on a piece of paper.
33. If you are writing it, I recommend you write it 2 or 3 times. This decreases the chance your messy handwriting will prevent you from accessing your wallet later.
34. Copy & paste your address into a text document somewhere.
35. Search your address on https://etherscan.io/ Bookmark this page as this is how you can view your balance at any time
36. Send a small amount of any coin from your previous wallet or exchange to your new wallet - just to ensure you have everything correct

Hardware Wallets

- Another safe, offline solution is to use a hardware wallet. The most popular of these being Trezor and Nano S. Both of these cost around $100, but represent a convenient, yet safe way to store your cryptocurrency.

Cryptocurrencies built using Ethereum blockchain technology

It' not just Ethereum that relies on Ethereum technology. There are many other cryptocurrencies that use the same blockchain for specific use cases.

It may surprise you to know that there are currently **over 5000 ERC20 tokens.** One of the many positives of Ethereum technology is that it has made token creation extremely accessible, and as such the number of new tokens on the market has increased exponentially in the past 18 months.

Now obviously some are better than others, and in this section we'll examine a few of the more interesting ones and their potential use cases moving forward. Alongside each currency I've included its price and market cap at the time of writing, as well as, which cryptocurrency exchanges you can purchase it from.

Augur (REP)

Price at Time of Writing - $20.19
Market Cap at Time of Writing - $219,749,200

Available on:
Fiat: Kraken
BTC: Poloniex, Bittrex, Liqui

Where to Store: Augur is an ERC20 token so can be stored in MyEtherWallet

Augur is a prediction market platform that uses Ethereum smart contracts to ensure correct payouts for correct predictions. Users can user it to predict real world events, and are rewarded if they are correct.

For example, you can predict the outcome of a Presidential election, a sporting event like the NBA finals or the winners of an Oscar award. Where Augur differs from a traditional gambling platform, is that instead of laying down a flat fee on an outcome at certain betting odds - you actually buy shares in an event.

For example, if you think Hillary Election would be elected President, and the market gives that a 50% chance, you essentially buy 50% of the shares of that outcome. If the market then moves, the odds become better than even, say 60%, your 50% share is now worth more than when you originally bought so you can sell it for a profit, before the event outcome is known.

Prediction markets like this have been proven to be more accurate over time than individuals. This phenomenon is known as "the wisdom of the crowd", or that a group of people is better on average at predicting events than any one person inside that group. This is especially true when those predicting are laying real money down on an event outcome.

Where Augur really shines though is that anyone can create their own prediction market. A small fee is required (to provide initial funding), and in return the creator of the market receives a percentage of all trading fees from that particular market. This decentralized approach is one that allows much lower fees than traditional, non-blockchain based prediction platforms.

This decentralization also adds an additional element of security, as the market cannot be subject of the manipulation of an individual, or small group of individuals like centralized markets. For example, someone has to actually report whether the event occured or not e.g. whether Clinton or Trump became President. With a centralized market, this can be subject to lies or outright corruption. With Augur, because each market has hundreds or even thousands of reporters, and the reports are publicly available for every to see, the correct result is always ensured. The Ethereum smart contracts also ensure regular, on-time payments for the correct amount - free from human error

Currently, a beta version of the platform is in development. This beta version will use virtual money only. This is done to test the coding of the smart contracts, and in case anything does go wrong in the beta stages, no one's funds are lost. The beta version of the AUGUR is also currently limited to markets with binary or "yes/no" outcomes, although there are plans to expand on this in the final version of the platform. The release date is currently scheduled for Q1 2018, although no formal release date has been announced yet.

Augur's tokens are known as reputation tokens or REP. 11 million were denominated during the ICO period, and this supply is designed to be fixed, so none can be mined. Those holding REP, and with a status set to "active" on the platform, will be expected to participate in the markets. If reporters do not report accurate results, they will be docked REP, which again ensures the legitimacy of the platform.

The team currently provides bi-weekly updates on their blog, part of these updates include offering REP in return for beta testers solving bugs in the code. Garnering community involvement like this has been hugely beneficial for other cryptocurrencies in the past.

Augur's price in the short term is likely to depend on how successful the launch of their beta platform is. Longer term, mass adoption versus traditional prediction markets is the main factor - will the masses see a blockchain solution as necessary in this particular use case?

TenX (PAY)

Price at Time of Writing - $2.26
Market Cap at Time of Writing - $209,278,662

Available on:
Fiat: Kraken
BTC: Bit-Z, Bittrex, Liqui
ETH: Bittrex, Liqui, EtherDelta

Where to store: Augur is an ERC20 token so can be stored in MyEtherWallet

Based out of Singapore, summarizing TenX can be best done with this quote from Inc. Magazine about the project

"TenX has figured out how to solve one of the biggest problems for people that are involved in cryptocurrency – actually spending the currency."

To elaborate, the TenX project is a platform that allows blockchain assets to be spent by individual users in the real world. One of the main issues with the growth of the cryptocurrency market as a whole, is with the constant additions of new token, how do uses actually spend them - without having to convert them back to Bitcoin or Ethereum, and then in some cases, back to fiat currency. The problem here lies with the transaction fees involved for these conversions, because they can add up fast, especially if you wish to carry out multiple transaction per day.

TenX plans to solve this by offering a debit card, that allows users to spend their cryptocurrencies at any regular point of sale system, this card is linked to a mobile wallet stored on their smartphone. Users can even spend their crypto assets directly via their smartphones at selected locations. Even today in the early stages of the project, the card is usable in over 200 countries, at over 36 million points of sale.

The key point to note here is that the cryptocurrencies stored in the TenX wallet are not converted to fiat currency until they are spent. This conversion then happens in real time. This also allows up to real-time currency conversions and the best possible foreign exchange rates and the lowest transaction fees.

The product has already completed a closed beta testing phase, with over 1,000 users testing the app in the real world, the total transaction volume during the beta phase was over $100,000. The beta tested version supported Bitcoin only, but the final platform aims to support Ethereum, along with ERC20 tokens and Dash in the short term, with support for additional cryptocurrencies planned in the long term. A public beta version is scheduled for release in Q4 2017, with a fully operational platform scheduled for Q2 2018.

Users in EU countries, along with select other European countries can now order TenX debit cards direct from the TenX website itself. There are plans to roll out the service in other countries, including the USA, in the coming months. With any payment platform like this, there are a number of compliance issues that have to be resolved - especially one that wishes to use the VISA debit card standard like TenX

There have been some issues however, with unprecedented demand for the cards themselves, which has in-turn caused a large backlog of orders. Currently the backlog stands at around 3 months, which is a major issue that will have to be resolved if the platform is going to have any sort of wider adoption.

TenX tokens (known as PAY) are used to incentivize usage of the platform. Users earn a 0.1% reward every time they use the app to spend their crypto assets, this reward is denominated in PAY. Currently this reward is distributed on a monthly basis, although there are plans to make this distribution as frequently as every hour in the future.

Holders of PAY tokens also receive a 0.5% reward based on the total transaction volume of the platform for the month. This reward is then multiplied by the number of PAY tokens each user has, so the more tokens one holds, the higher their reward.

During the ICO period, 51% of the total amount of PAY tokens were distributed to investors, with an additional 29% held back for further development of the platform. The team's long-term goal is to make 80% of the tokens available to the public, with the rest held by the founders and early developers.

One thing I particularly like about the TenX project is the team's commitment to wider cryptocurrency education through their YouTube channel. Cryptocurrency is still very much in the infant stages of its lifecycle, and any educational resources aimed at the general public can be looked at in a positive light.

The success of TenX going forward will depends on a number of factors. The first is competition, they aren't the only "cryptocurrency debit card" player in town. Monaco could be considered their main rival at this stage, although I'm sure that other similar projects will pop up in the near future. The second is the speed at which they can support various currencies in the app and card itself. Support for the big 3 cryptocurrencies (Bitcoin, Ethereum and Litecoin) would be huge for short term gains, and support for all ERC20 tokens would also be a positive as we move beyond 2018.

Storj (STORJ)

Price at Time of Writing - $0.678
Market Cap at Time of Writing - $70,896,782

Available on:
BTC: Binance, Bittrex, Poloniex
ETH: Binance, Bittrex, Liqui, Gate.io

Where to store: Storj is an ERC20 token so can be stored in MyEtherWallet

Storj (pronounced: storage) plans to take on the multi million dollar cloud storage industry with a decentralized blockchain solution. The team estimates that with a decentralized solution rather than a traditional model, cloud storage can be up to 10x faster and 50% less expensive.

Traditional cloud storage like say Dropbox, involves users uploading their files to a single, central server. Whereas with a decentralized model, these files are first encrypted to ensure their security, and then globally distributed across a set of storage nodes using blockchain technology.

The major problem that traditional centralized cloud storage companies face is that because there is one point of failure for the network, the network can suffer periodic downtime. Using a decentralized model, with the data effectively being stored in thousands of different locations, the network will not suffer from the downtime issues.

The other main issue that centralized storage faces is the security of the data itself. Once again, because there is a single point of entry to the server, there is also a single point of failure. This means no matter how good the encryption is, hackers could eventually get a hold of data. With a decentralized model, because the files are spread across thousands of different nodes

Another innovative function is the ability for users to effective rent out their unused hard drive space to users on the Storj network. This is known as Storj Share and users, known as "farmers" will be paid for their space in Storj tokens.

The Storj network is currently up and running, with a transparent pricing model, based only on what you use. Storage costs $0.015 per GB, per month with no minimum usage. So 100GB of storage would cost $1.50 per month. The platform has already attracted 25,000 users along with 19,000 farmers. An enterprise level model is also up and running, with an agreement already signed with a Fortune 500 company back in 2016.

One area that Storj may face trouble with is the hosting of illegal content via their service. The decentralized and encrypted nature of the platform makes it impossible to know exactly what kind of files are being hosted. The Storj team recognize this and are putting their faith in the userbase to use the service "within society's legal and ethical norms" and the ability for users to "graylist" certain content.

For example, those offering storage space could decide they do not want any pornographic material hosted using their space. You could argue that this is a centralized measure, but it should be noted that this only affects files hosted publicly, those hosted privately will be unaffected. Graylists will also be a strictly optional, opt-in required feature.

The coin has already received its fair share of support from big names in the Ethereum blockchain space, including Vitalik Buterin himself. This combined with a working product, make it an intriguing proposition as we move into 2018 and beyond.

Storj has also targeted an expansion into China to compete in their often difficult to penetrate cloud storage market. Regulations requiring overseas providers to partner with local companies caused Amazon to eventually sell $300m worth of its Chinese cloud storage assets to its local partner. Storj has partnered with Shanghai based startup Genaro in its own bid to expand into the large Chinese market.

Monaco (MCO)

Price at Time of Writing - $6.48
Market Cap at Time of Writing - $63,811,823

Available on:
BTC: Bittrex, Binance, Liqui
ETH: Bittrex, Binance, Liqui

Where to store: Monaco is an ERC20 token so can be stored in MyEtherWallet

Based out of Switzerland, Monaco aims to bridge fiat and cryptocurrency with an all-in-one debit card and mobile wallet app. The project should be looked at slightly differently to other cryptocurrency projects, as this one isn't strictly about cryptocurrency itself. You can look at Monaco more like a fintech project utilizing the cryptocurrency space.

Using their fair usage model, users won't be charged monthly or annual fees for holding the card. Monaco currently users VISA debit cards and the VISA payment platform so has access to over 40 million merchants worldwide. The project received official partnership with VISA in September 2017 and Monaco is now registered under the VISA Program Manager initiative which allows them further say in areas such as cashback rewards for their clients.

There are numerous features such as the card always using the local currency. So if you're someone who travels a lot, you'll have access to the official inter-bank exchange rate, rather than the consumer rate which is often 2-3% higher. Anyone who travels frequently will be able to understand that these savings add up quickly. Research has demonstrations this could represent savings of between $60-80 per $1000 spent.

The card also offers cryptocurrency cashback up to 2% with all purchases. Cashback cards are nothing new and have been around for decades, but Monaco represents the first one in the cryptocurrency space. The cashback will be in the form of Monaco (MCO) tokens. The cashback program is planned to offer higher rewards (of up to 10%) once wider adoption occurs.

The Monaco app can also be used to send instant payments to your friends and family, this can be done in multiple currencies including Bitcoin and Ethereum. On average, this will save 4% for international currency conversions when compared to regular banks.

Rollout of Monaco cards continues to rely on local compliance checks. The first cards will be shipped to those in Singapore after passing national governance tests in late October 2017. Over 17,000 cards have already been reserved and users can reserve their own by downloading the Monaco app for either Android or iOS. Demand is expected to be high and the Monaco team have already ordered over 500,000 physical cards.

Like most early stage projects, it hasn't been all smooth sailing for Monaco. A post-ICO price peak of $24 has been followed by steady declines throughout the year. This is partly due to initial ICO hype wearing off (pretty much every 2017 ICO has suffered from this), the other part is due to an issue with the smart contract mechanism in place. The original smart contract had to be re-worked in order to gain SEC compliance

Growth of Monaco is based firmly on passing compliance protocols across various markets. For example, their roadmap targets US approval within the first half of 2018, with European approval expected before then. Before then, news of Monaco being listed on more exchanges is what the community is looking for.

The team have experience in the payments space, for example the CFO is a former executive at MasterCard and they have advisers with previous experience at Visa and AWS.

The issue with Monaco going forward is that there is *a lot* of competition in the cryptocurrency debit card payments space already. I mentioned TenX earlier in this book, a project with similar intentions and there are other projects such as the UK based LBX along with TokenCard and Exscudo. There's no reason that a few of these cannot co-exist, but it will gradually be harder and harder to find a USP within the industry. Selling points like better exchange rates and cashback are effectively a race to the bottom and there may have to be significant additions to the Monaco project for it to be the consensus leader in the space. We are still in the very early days of cryptocurrency though, and once the card itself rolls out - there are sure to be interesting developments both as a technology, and as a financial asset. Monaco is definitely one to watch as we enter 2018, with potential industry wide ramifications going into 2019 and beyond.

Aragon (ANT)

Price at Time of Writing - $1.67
Market Cap at Time of Writing - $57,369,782

Available on:
BTC: Bittrex, Liqui
ETH: Bittrex, Liqui

Where to Store: Aragon is an ERC20 token so can be stored in MyEtherWallet

Aragon aims to use Ethereum blockchain technology to remove the needs for unnecessary intermediaries in the business world. This concept of Decentralized Autonomous Organizations (DAOs) is a common one in the blockchain space. The number of third parties needed to create and maintain a company leads to market inefficiencies, lower profits, and hampers the ability of that company to provide the best possible product or service for its customers.

The aim of Aragon is to provide everything a person needs to run their organization. This includes services such as payroll, accounting and governance. This leads to greater company transparency, greater cost efficiency and the ability to safely alter a contract without the mound of excess paperwork that comes with traditional contracts.

The ease at which users can perform usually complex tasks like issuing company shares is a huge bonus for small organizations. The fact that all this is transparent as well acts as a built in fraud prevention system. This also applies to raising capital, using Aragon's stock sale voting, it has never been easier for companies to access the capital they require to run their business. Running all this on a publicly accessible blockchain makes budgeting, dividend sharing and general accounting practices incredibly simple.

The Aragon team is headed up by Luis Cuende, who has had a storied history in the blockchain space. Named Europe's best young programmer in 2011 and elected to the Forbes 30 Under 30 list - he previously worked on Blockchain startup Stampery

The test currently has an alpha product available, and 3,000 organizations have been built using the test network. A public beta version is currently scheduled for February 2018.

The main hurdles to overcome for Aragon going forward will be the adoption and trust from wider public, especially with regards to issues like contracts and arbitration. Any bugs in the network regarding this will need to be ironed out before a public release of the Aragon network. However, with 3,000 DAOs already on the testnet, this phase of the project continues to shine positive light on Aragon both as a vision, and as a legitimate platform going forward.

There are similar projects in the works, which isn't necessarily a bad thing as it shows that the general demand is there. Colony is another project that is more focused on the day to day operations of a company and could eventually be used as a module within the Aragon network as Aragon supports third party modules.

District0x (DNT)

Price at Time of Writing - $0.039
Market Cap at Time of Writing - $23,255,100

Available on:
BTC: Binance, Bittrex, Liqui
ETH: Binance, Liqui, Mercatox

Where to store:
District0x is currently an ERC20 token and can be stored on My Ether Wallet. You can view how to add DNT as a custom token on https://etherscan.io/token/district0x

District0x has the goal of breaking the internet down into smaller, more manageable pieces. If you've ever seen the movie The Hunger Games, you'll remember each district was focused on a single task: District 7 was the lumber district, District 8 focused on textile production, District 9 with grain etc.

District0x plans to do the same thing with the blockchain technology and Decentralized Autonomous Organizations (DAO). Each district will have its own payment and invoicing system, along with complete self governance. The venture will use the Ethereum blockchain to run smart contracts.

What District0x has done to make to the process user friendly, is combine different necessary (like smart contracts and payment processing) elements into a package, so it's not essential for users to completely understand the technology behind the platform. You can think of this as similar to how Wordpress works for web development. At the core of every district is the ability to operate a market or a bulletin board application.

Currently, there are over 100 district ideas in play. Theoretically, it would allow an individual such as you or me to implement their own version of AirBNB, Craigslist or Uber, without having to go through a middleman like the current system has to. This in turn reduces transaction fees and makes the overall cost lower for all parties involved. There are no fees to create districts, which makes them available to everyone. Currently, refundable deposits are required to put forward a district proposal, once the district passes quality control checks (ensuring the district is not there for malicious intent), the deposit is refunded to the district creator.

One such idea already running is Ethlance, an online freelancing platform similar to Upwork or Fiverr, but without the large transaction fees. Interestingly enough, the District0x team has actually hired developers via Ethlance to help them execute the project.

Another promising proposal is ShipIt, which focuses on the multi-billion dollar shipping industry. The idea is to create a decentralized maritime logistics platform. The sheer number of transactions in this industry alone (trucking, forwarding, warehousing etc.) make this a perfect foil for a blockchain solution.

The framework is in place, however the team needs to do more to gather traction, plus a larger user base to utilize their own districts. The current team is small, with just 10 members, plus an additional adviser, but there will certainly be additions in the future as the project continues to grow. Progress reports are frequent and developments are regular posted on GitHub.

One interesting approach the District0x team are employing is creating a free "education portal" to inform the wider public about the platform, and the real world functionality of districts. They are doing this are they believe the current limiting factor is a general ignorance of the potential of the platform. The portal is scheduled for rollout in Q4 2017.

District0x tokens (DNT) can be used to fund project and stake voting rights in different districts, the more tokens one has, the greater of a say they have. The one issue here is a possible abuse of a "pay to play" system.

The decentralized element of District0x means there is no single point of failure, for example there is no single server that all of the individual districts run from. This ensures that targeted hacking attacks cannot take down the entire network.

Supply wise, there are 600 million DNT available, with a total projected supply of 1 billion. It should be noted that in the white paper, the District0x team does reserve the right to add additional coins to the total supply, however this is contingent on the exchange rate between ETH/USD. For example, if ETH's value declines significantly vs. USD, the team can add additional coins to account for this fluctuation. This isn't necessarily something to be concerned about (financial hedging occurs all the time in fiat markets), but it's definitely something worth nothing.

Listing on larger exchanges will help spike the price in the short term. The team are in ongoing discussions with large exchange Bittrex, and a listing on there could easily see price rises of 100%. Long term prices will be largely determined by the number of popular districts that are set up using the platform. The next two planned district launches are Name Bazaar and Meme Factory.

Request Network (REQ)

Price at Time of Writing - $0.066
Market Cap at Time of Writing - $42,266,398

Available on:
BTC: Binance, Liqui
ETH: Binance, KuCoin, EtherDelta

Where to store: REQ is an ERC20 token so can be stored in MyEtherWallet

Request Network aims to become a decentralized payment network allowing both businesses and individuals to request money from anyone. The project aims to bring blockchain technology into the payment provider space, and act as competition to PayPal and Stripe. Request has already received industry plaudits as well as investment from US based startup investment group YCombinator.

Current centralized payment providers and networks take a commission of between 1.5% and 6% per transaction depending on the platform and the type of payment. Request Network aims to lower this fee to as little as 0.05% per transaction, with an average fee of 0.2% per transaction. This represents huge savings to the consumer and the merchant. Request also allows payment in cryptocurrency as well as fiat currency.

By utilizing Ethereum technology, all payments requested and made will be available on a public ledger for anyone to see. This level of transparency lowers the degree of fraudulent payments and fraudulent refund requests that currently plague traditional networks like PayPal and Stripe. This also has residual effects for areas like time sensitive money back guarantees or warranties for items.

Another advantage Request has versus traditional platforms is the transparency leads to lowering auditing costs. For example, in 2014 online Microsoft paid Deloitte over $45 million in auditing fees, and Bank of America paid over $100 million. With Request's public blockchain ledger, audits would effectively be carried out in real time and would represent a far less expensive option than hiring a third party to manual check that the transactions are valid.

Request Network is actually part of the 3,000 companies that are built on the Aragon testnet, which shows the interaction between blockchain projects. Request has also partnered with another blockchain project, Kyber, to improve the automatic currency conversion element of the platform. The Kyber partnership has great real world use potential as the merchant can specify payment in any cryptocurrency of their choosing, and the payee can still pay with their preferred cryptocurrency.

Request also recently introduced continuous payments, which allows users to be paid by the hour (and in theory, by the second). This is an ideal model for contractors or freelancers who work on an hourly basis rather than per project.

The team continues to deliver on the roadmap, with the latest update, known as "Colossus" being delivered ahead of schedule in Q4 2017 rather than the initially anticipated Q1 2018. Q1 2018 will see the

"Great Wall" update, with a launch of Request Network on the Ethereum main net for the first time. The Great Wall update is of particular interest as this is when the "Pay with Request" button will be available to those who want to use it alongside traditional methods like "Pay with credit card" and "Pay with PayPal"

The payments sector is huge, and PayPal alone has an annual revenue of over $10 billion. If Request Network can capture even a small fraction of this, then there is potential for enormous growth. Alongside massive opportunity does come a certain amount of competition though, OmiseGO being the most well known one in the cryptocurrency space. There are also Populous and MetalPay, both of which have similar visions to Request.

A Low-Risk (But Still Highly Profitable) Way to Invest in Cryptocurrencies

For those of you familiar with traditional investments, then you'll likely to be aware of Exchange Traded Funds or ETFs. For those unfamiliar, and ETF is a security that trades like a regular stock, but instead of buying shares in one company, you are buying an aggregate of many companies. ETFs have an inherent advantage over single stocks in that by diversifying your risk over many companies, you are less likely to see sudden drops in price.

Based out of Slovenia, and active since November 2016, Fintech start-up Iconomi is currently running a blockchain based digital asset management platform using Ethereum technology. Known as Digital Asset Arrays (DAA), these are similar to ETFs and Index funds, as you are buying an aggregate of multiple cryptocurrencies instead of just one or two. Initial investments can be made with ETH or BTC, although there are plans to support fiat deposits in the coming months.

Their BLX blockchain index is the first passively managed array of digital assets, compromising of over 20 different cryptocurrencies, with the highest weight being in Bitcoin and Ethereum. The portfolio is re-balanced on a monthly basis, and different cryptocurrencies are added and removed based on performance. What's more is the BLX has currently outperformed both Ethereum and Litecoin over the past 6 months. There is also a more conservative fund which is composed of 60% Bitcoin, 20% Ethereum as well as 4 other ERC20 tokens. The fund have a 2-3% annual management fee, plus a 0.5% exit fee.

This could well be a good option if you're looking to invest in a multitude of cryptocurrencies, but don't want to deal with the hassle of signing up for multiple exchanges, and keeping track of various wallets. Iconomi currently offers 15 different DAAs, ranging from conservative, heavily Bitcoin based ones, to more risky ones featuring a multitude of smaller cap cryptocurrencies. Of course, like any investment, there are inherent risks involved, but if you're a more risk averse investor, who still wants to be a part of the cryptocurrency market, Iconomi is worth checking out.

Determinants of Cryptocurrency Growth Patterns in 2018 and Beyond

Coinbase

Regardless of your personal opinions on Coinbase as a cryptocurrency exchange, it still functions as the vast majority of user's first entry into the cryptocurrency market. It's accessibility and the ability to make purchases via debit and credit card means it's ideal as a "my first cryptocurrency exchange". Currently Coinbase allows the buying and selling of Bitcoin, Ethereum and Litecoin in exchange for fiat. However in November 2017, Coinbase announced that it would list ERC20 tokens in 2018, and any of the ERC20 below tokens being listed on Coinbase is sure to have a positive effect on price going forward. This also applies to other major exchanges such as Bitfinex and Bittrex, but Coinbase is the milestone here.

Market adoption

The later half of 2017 alone saw the cryptocurrency marketcap more than double to over $300 billion at the time of writing, and we are still very much in the infancy of cryptocurrency. Further investment by new players and a constant influx of new money into the market leads to bullish conditions. According to Forbes magazine, less than 0.5% of the world currently owns any form of cryptocurrency (and the vast majority of this will be Bitcoin).

We could look at this as a similar situation when the technology boom was in 1994, where email was the biggest use case, way before today's social media, video streaming, and online retail services. One could look at Bitcoin as the email of the cryptocurrency market. How does this relate to Ethereum? Well, in Ethereum's case, the vast majority of DApps aren't close to any sort of mass adoption, and it will likely be years before the market has matured.

Regulation

Regulation in various forms can have both positive and negative effects for the market as a whole. Ethereum itself was hit hard when headlines of "China bans ICOs" hit the front pages in late September. However, the news turned out to be temporary and the entire market recovered and surged in October and November. Large scale regulation in the US, China or Russia would indeed have a negative impact on both price and the technology future of Ethereum based projects.

Neo

Neo is the cryptocurrency project most similar to Ethereum in terms of being a platform that other blockchain companies can build on top of. Ethereum has a much wider adoption currently, but Neo is based out of China, and following on from the above point - Chinese government regulation in favor of a "domestic coin" could hurt Ethereum's adoption potential in the Chinese market. For example, an announcement that all Chinese ICOs must be built using Neo is plausible, and as China represents a large part of the cryptocurrency market, this will in turn have a negative effect on Ethereum. That being said, the above is an extreme scenario, and there is no reason that Ethereum and Neo cannot co-exist.

Futures Market & Institutional Investing

Institutional investors will play a big part in the growth of Ethereum as a tradable asset, and the release of an Ethereum futures market, where traders can bet the future price of Ethereum, will signify that it is maturing. As of yet, only Bitcoin futures can be traded, but as Ethereum matures more as an asset, there is no doubt that a similar market for trading ETH will emerge.

Moving to Proof of Stake

One of the largest technological challenges surrounding Ethereum is the move from a Proof of Work (PoW) mining algorithm to a more environmentally friendly Proof of Stake (PoS) one. The original PoW method is similar to the one used by Bitcoin, in that computers solve cryptographic puzzles (or complex mathematical equations) in order to validate a transaction and create a block. This method requires increasing amounts of computing power to mine cryptocurrency, and can leads to issues such as the vast majority of the mining power being concentrated in the hands of just a few miners (for example, someone running a large scale mining operation). It is this kind of centralization that Ethereum seeks to avoid. There is also the issue of electricity use, both Ethereum and Bitcoin are currently estimated to use over $1 million worth of electricity *per day* in their mining process, which is more electricity than a moderately sized country than Ireland or Denmark.

A PoS mining algorithm differs because it allows holders of ETH to deposit or "stake" their coins in order to validate the next block. The public blockchain tracks who holds ETH, and how much of it they have staked. Therefore, you don't need expensive hardware to participate in the mining process. Mining rewards are proportional to how much you have staked, so someone staking 10 ETH would get 10x the rewards of someone staking 1 ETH. PoS also has the advantage of shortening network transaction times, and making them more consistent. So instead of an average transaction time of 15 per second, the 15 transactions confirmed every second, like clockwork. PoS also allows ETH to be used as an asset and could be looked at like a savings account, because if you staked your ETH on the a network, you would essentially receive interest from mining rewards.

Ethereum's initial move will be to a Hybrid PoW/PoS algorithm in the "Casper" update to the platform. At the time of writing, the Casper update is live on the Ethereum TestNet, so the code isn't finalized but it can be tested for security and safety issues.

A full move to PoS is scheduled in Q1/Q2 2018 in the "Metropolis" update. A smooth transition to PoS will leads to a fairer Ethereum mining ecosystem in the long run, but like any big transition of this kind, there are challenges in the execution. Naturally, any safety or security breaches will lead to negative results for Ethereum, as will technical issues such as users not being able to stake their ETH. As the technology is still very much in it infant stages, these are the kinds of areas that we must be extra cautious of when considered investing.

Adoption in Asia

In June of 2017, South Korea overtook the US and China as the largest Ethereum market in terms of daily trading volume. Roughly $200 million of Ethereum is traded everyday on BitHumb, Korea's largest cryptocurrency exchange. Continued adoption in Asia is part of Ethereum's growth plan for 2018 and beyond, with a Chinese office opening next year, and a growing number of partnerships with Chinese companies in the works.

Conclusion

Ethereum has changed the way we look at financial transactions, auditing and the idea of a middleman. Our previous reliance on banks and other financial institutions has been put into question, and we are now moving forward towards a decentralized financial world. These multibillion dollar corporations and industries are facing disruption, and actual competition, for the first time in over a century.

For consumers, cross border payments at a near-instant transaction time, and far lower transactions fees are making the global economy smaller and more accessible.

Beyond Ethereum, blockchain technology has an additional laundry list of benefits ranging from transparency in elections to easily accessible medical records between parties.

As a commodity, no other financial asset, cryptocurrency or otherwise has produced better returns for investors over the past 12 months.

For those who believe in Ethereum, and Vitalik Buterin's vision for a better world, long may these returns continue.

I hope you've enjoyed this book and that you're now a little bit more informed about how Ethereum works, and more importantly, how it can work for you. Whether you're planning on investing for the long-term - I wish you the best of luck.

Remember, trade rationally and not emotionally. Never invest more than you can afford to lose, and for the love of God - don't check the charts 15 times a day.
Now, if you're ready to make the next step and get involved in the market. I have a small gift for you.

If you sign up for Coinbase using this link, you will receive $10 worth of free Bitcoin after your first purchase of more than $100 worth of cryptocurrency.

http://bit.ly/10dollarbtc

Finally, if you've enjoyed this book I'd really appreciate it if you left a review on Amazon.

Cryptocurrency: What you need to know about your taxes to save money and avoid a nasty surprise from the IRS

By Stephen Satoshi

Introduction

OK, so you've been buying or trading cryptocurrencies for the past few months or years and now you want to know exactly how this affects your tax situation.

To be frank, a year ago I had no clue either, so I did a research deep dive, contacted various institutions and people of note and found something fascinating...no one had any idea how it all worked! In fact, in 2015, the IRS discovered that only 802 people in the entire United States had declared any cryptocurrency related gains or losses on their tax returns. This has led to the IRS demanding Coinbase hand over customer records, which we will expand on later on in this book.

Fortunately, in the past 12 months, we have had some concrete developments in cryptocurrency tax laws. Now we have the ability to at least construct an outline as to how this all works, and what exactly you are liable for when buying and trading cryptocurrencies.

I should note this is **not** tax advice. Everything expressed in this book is my own personal opinion and nothing more. Please contact a tax professional before you submit your tax returns.

One more thing, the content here is focused on the US market, your local tax laws may well differ.

Anyway, let's get cracking shall we?

Stephen

Some important things to know at the outset.

Early data from credit monitoring firm Credit Karma shows that less than 100 people out of a sample of 250,000 filings, actually reported cryptocurrency gains or losses on their tax return last year. This amounts to just 0.04% of the sample size paying their cryptocurrency taxes to the IRS. While obviously not all of those doing the filing would have held cryptocurrency, it's safe to say the actual number is a little higher than 0.04% of all American citizens. The latest estimates have around 7% of US citizens owning cryptocurrency in one form or another.

In another survey of 2,000 cryptocurrency owners, 57% said that they realized gains on their coins, but an even higher number (59%) stated that they had not reported any gains or losses to the IRS.

This combined with other factors like online tax providers (such as TurboTax) not integrating cryptocurrency taxation shows up that it's not just the citizens who are behind on crypto taxes, it's the authorities and tax based businesses as well.

What this tells us is that people, in general, are confused about how exactly they should file their taxes for cryptocurrency and therefore, more education in this area is needed, and that's what I hope to be able to provide in this book.

Let's start off with the basics, shall we? What class of asset does the IRS consider cryptocurrencies to be exactly? Well, you may be surprised to learn that cryptocurrencies are not considered securities or stocks. Therefore there are a large number of tax laws that do not apply to cryptocurrencies. But there are an equal number of laws that *do* apply and make this is a rather complex issue. So if you're getting excited and thinking that crypto is "tax-free" then think again.

So what are cryptocurrencies considered? Well according to IRS note 2014-21, any digital currency, or in their own words "virtual currency" is considered "property" for tax purposes. It should be noted that at the time of writing, this is the only official statement the IRS has made about cryptocurrency. Oddly enough, the Securities and Exchange Commission (SEC) made a contrary ruling in 2017 when they decided that cryptocurrencies *were* indeed a currency.

The IRS ruling means your cryptos can be considered business property, investment property or personal property. In practical terms, and the big thing to note here is that any gain or loss is recognized every single your exchange your property, in this case, cryptos, to purchase goods or services.

Therefore if you're somehow who pays with cryptocurrency frequently, then you may well have more tax preparation to do than someone who merely buys and holds, or exchanges their cryptocurrency for fiat. This can make for an accounting nightmare if you haven't kept track of your cryptocurrency purchases. So I would advise you to do that as a bare minimum going forward.

The reason for this is that the IRS considers this two separate transactions. The first of which is the sale of your coins, and the second of which is using the proceeds of that sale to make a further purchase. Therefore, if you've bought Bitcoin at any time before January 2018, then it has most likely increased in value, and thus you will have to pay capital gains tax on it.

Let's use an example. You spend $4,000 on furniture at Overstock.com and you pay using Bitcoin (Overstock was actually the first major retailer in the US to accept Bitcoin as a method of payment). Using November 2017 figures, we'll say that Bitcoin was worth $8,000 at the time of the transaction, so you spent 0.5BTC on the furniture.

Now here's where it gets confusing, if you bought your Bitcoin back in early 2016 when BTC was trading for just $200 a coin, then you have a capital gain of $3,800 ($4,000-$200). Using the standard capital gains tax rate of 15% you have a $570 tax bill on your hand.

However here's where it gets even dicier. Even you spend your Bitcoin or any other cryptocurrency within a year, then you may be subject to the short term capital gains rate of 39.5% (this rate is scheduled to fall to 37% in 2018). This is on the top of the sales tax you have already paid for the goods themselves, so you're essentially undergoing a double tax hit.

This has huge ramifications not only on a personal level (no one wants to be taxed twice) but also on a widespread cryptocurrency adoption level. And we haven't even begun to discuss how this affects day traders, how can make multiple cryptocurrency transactions per day. We'll expand on this point later on in this book.

We have to remember as well that this is the IRS we are talking about. One of the most powerful institutions not only in America but in the entire world. The fact of the matter is this - if they want to find you, they will.

However, there are moves to make things easier for those who like to pay with cryptocurrency. A bi-partisan bill has been introduced by representatives that would only require you to report cryptocurrency purchases with a value of greater than $600. This makes more sense going forward, but it remains to be seen just how quickly this becomes written into the tax law.

How does my tax bracket relate to capital gains?

The formula for this simple for long term capital gains. So if you held your coins for a period greater than 12 months. It should be noted that these tax brackets are federal tax brackets, you state income tax level does not affect your capital gains.

People in the 10% and 15% tax brackets pay 0%.
People in the 25%, 28%, 33%, and 35% tax brackets pay 15%.
People in the 39.6% tax bracket pay 20%.

Hypothetical Scenarios:

Julie bought 1 Bitcoin on March 4th, 2017 for $1000. She then sold her 1 Bitcoin for $3000 3 months later on June 4th. Therefore her taxable gain is now $2,000.

If she was in the 15% tax bracket she would pay $300 ($2000*15%).
If she was in the 25% tax bracket she would pay $500 ($2000*25%)
If she was in the 39.6% tax bracket she would pay a whopping $792 ($2000*39.6%)

But say Julie keeps her Bitcoin for 1 year and sells on March 4th, 2018 for the same amount of $2,000. Her capital gains now look like this.

If she is in the 10 and 15% tax she bracket pays $0
If she is in the 25%, 28%, 33%, and 35% tax brackets she pays $300 ($2000*15%).
If she is in the 39.6% tax bracket she pays $400 ($2000*20%)

So by keeping her Bitcoin for a year, she saves almost $400 in taxes for the exact same transaction. So if you have no reason to sell (and remember, cryptocurrency is a long term investment so unless you literally need the money to eat you have no reason to sell), then you are better off keeping your coins for over 1 year to trigger the tax savings.

Now there is no way of telling if the price of cryptocurrency will be greater or less in one year than it is today. But if you have long term belief in the technology behind cryptocurrency, and thus its long-term viability as an asset as opposed to a short-term speculative vehicle, then it is well worth holding onto your coins.

What about if I sell for a loss?

If you have sold cryptocurrency for a loss at any time, this is, of course, deductible on your tax return. This is known as an "above the line" deduction, in the same way that interest of your student loan is deductible.

It should be noted that the maximal in capital gains losses you can deduct each year is $3,000. This is proportional to your income in the same way capital gains is. If you have more than this then you can roll it over to the next year until the remainder is cleared.

So for example, if you buy Bitcoin at $10,000 and it crashes to $5,000, at which point you sell, then you have a loss of $5,000. You would be able to deduct $3,000 in this tax year and then $2,000 in the next tax year, provided that these are your only losses.

What if cryptocurrency is re-classified as a foreign currency?

This is a perfectly plausible scenario. If this were to happen then any gains would be exempt from the capital gains tax, and more important there would be no more short term capital gains penalties. You would simply be taxed at your regular tax rate. This has a particular benefit to day traders who are currently at the mercy of short term capital gains rules.

However, there are additional advantages in the case of transactions for goods and services. Under the foreign currency exemption for personal transactions (so not business or investment ones), gains under $200 are tax free. If cryptocurrencies continue to be adopted on a consumer level, where the vast majority of the day to day purchases will be under $200, then this will be a big win for those who like to spend their coins.

The biggest issue we have in cryptocurrencies gaining foreign currency status is that because they are not minted or produced by a foreign bank - are they technically foreign at all? I would err on the side of caution for now, and go by the rules that the IRS has in place.

What if my job pays me in cryptocurrency?

This will only apply to a small percentage of readers, however, that percentage is increasing at a rapid rate. Year by year there are more and more people working in exchange for crypto. This especially applies to those working on ICO projects who are paid in tokens by the founders in lieu of fiat currency.

Luckily, the way you calculate taxes for services rendered is pretty simple. If you sell goods or services (such as your own skills) for cryptocurrency, your tax basis is their fair market value at the time your cryptocurrency was received.

So if you received 10ETH for a project when ETH was $500=1ETH then your tax burden would be the equivalent of $5000. Obviously, you should always keep track of the date you received your coins. You should also be consistent with which exchange you use because choosing multiple exchanges for the benefits of better rates is unfortunately going to run foul of IRS regulations.

What if I have not sold my coins yet?

OK, so assuming you haven't sold any coins or traded them for any other coins. You have simply bought them for fiat and held. Then you would have zero tax events and you do not have to report anything to the IRS. Once you do sell or trade those coins, then it becomes a tax event and you would have to report any gains or losses made. So if you're a pure HODL'er, then don't worry about anything just yet, the IRS will only want to know when you sell your coins.

Let me make one thing clear at this point. **This is the only way to avoid realizing gains.** Any other suggestions are just patently false.

It should be noted that once you do sell them, it doesn't matter if you keep the money on an exchange or if you cash it out to your bank account. It still counts as sold at the time of sale. So you can't get around the IRS by keeping your money in Coinbase for example.

What if my friend/family member/dog gave me cryptocurrency as a gift?

I would be willing to bet that cryptocurrency gifts were at an all time high last year and that more people received Bitcoin, Ethereum or Litecoin in 2017 than in all other years before them combined.

What you need to be concerned with is the basis of these coins when they were purchased. Hopefully, there has been a capital gain in the time when the gifter purchased them for you and when you received them.

The confusing part of this is if they were purchased for a higher price than their value when you received them. So in other words, if you have inherited a loss from the gifter. In this case, you can use the value at the time you received them, not at the time of purchase. This particular regulation leads you to have the best possible tax situation with gifting.

If you haven't sold yet then you don't need to worry, but this does affect you when to do decide to sell. So as unflattering and impolite as this may be, it's worth asking your friend their purchase date and the purchase price of the coins that have gifted you. This will ensure any future filings are indeed correct.

Let's do a few examples to clarify this.

Steve buys 1 Bitcoin for his friend Mary at $1,000. By the time Mary receives them, they are only worth $800. So to begin with, Steve's basis is $1,000 in this situation.

Scenario 1 - Mary sells for at $1,200. As she has profited, she inherits Steve's basis of $1,000 and she has a capital gain of $200.

Scenario 2 - Mary sells at a loss for $600. She cannot inherit Steve's basis so uses her own of $800 so her capital loss is $200.

Scenario 3 - Mary sells for $900. She still cannot inherit Steve's basis and a loss, so she uses her own for $800. Therefore her capital gain is $100, however as it is less than Steve's basis, it does not have to be reported as a gain or a loss.

The sale can be disregarded in this case, because there is no gain from the initial basis. This is all very confusing, which is why it is vital that you get the purchase price and purchase date from whoever gifted you the coins.

What if you are the gifter?

Like other gifts, giving cryptocurrency as a gift is not a taxable event because the recipient inherits the tax basis. So don't worry if you bought Bitcoin or Ethereum for your family and friends this holiday season, you're in the clear. Of course, if you exceed the gifting limit ($14,000 for 2017 tax year) then obviously you will have to file. Note that if you are married and you and your spouse file together, you can give up to $28,000 or $14,000 per person.

There is also the lifetime gift exemption of $5.4 million but obviously, that doesn't apply to the vast majority of readers.

How does the IRS know about my cryptocurrency?

Well, this question isn't easy to answer, the short answer is that someone told them. Don't worry, there are no crypto snitches out there reporting you without your knowledge. There are a number of ways this can occur.

The most common is that the IRS requests the data from an exchange. They can do this with exchanges based in the US, and also exchanges based in countries which share tax treaties with the US. The biggest one of these is obviously Coinbase, and its sister site GDax, which is based in the US and is therefore subject to the demands of IRS.

They would report you gains in the form of form 1099-K. We discuss under what circumstances a 1099-K would be filed by Coinbase later on in this book.

The second way, and probably the most common way for the regular investor would be if your bank account was flagged for one reason or another. This is known as a Suspicious Activity Report (SAR) and many banks will file one of these because of cryptocurrency transactions. Banks tend to be cautious types so many times they will file a SAR based on frequent cryptocurrency transactions or transactions for large amounts. There is no hard number for the filing to be enacted but you can safely assume that any single transaction over $5,000 has triggered this. Obviously, the larger and more frequent your transactions, the more likely you are to be flagged. It should be noted that SAR filings are often done to avoid money laundering investigations so you shouldn't be worried if one is filed against you. Just pay the amount you owe and you can go on your way.

The third way is that you volunteer the information to the IRS yourself. Now there are significant penalties for failing to report income, so I recommend you report your gains within the appropriate reporting period. Now if you're behind, don't worry too much because the confusing nature of cryptocurrencies may well lead the IRS to be more lenient in this particular domain, but it goes without saying that you should file any back taxes as soon as possible.

The fourth and final way is indeed if someone reports you. If you're the kind of person who has a lot of enemies this is somewhat plausible. But for many it won't apply. One lesson you should learn is to not brag or discuss large cryptocurrency holdings you may have, because people can and do get jealous, and as such, one may report you. This applies even more so on public internet forums where the information can potentially be seen by thousands of people.

How to invest in cryptocurrencies tax-free

This is a big one that many investors overlook because it's not very well published, and your regular accountant probably isn't even aware of it. But the good news is it's pretty simple and easy to execute even for a technophobe.

It is completely possible to add Bitcoin, Ethereum and other cryptocurrencies to your retirement portfolio such as your IRA. It goes back to the IRS ruling we discussed previously where cryptocurrencies are ruled as personal property. Therefore the IRS doesn't consider it to be "collectible" and as such, there is no limitation in adding it to your retirement account.

There are two ways to invest in crypto using an IRA

The first of which is to use what is known as a "captive" IRA, so basically your provider will buy the cryptocurrency on your behalf and then you can store and access it as you wish. This is similar to how most IRAs work and if you use a financial advisor to handle your retirement affairs you will likely be familiar with the process. The drawback of this is that your account handler may not directly buy cryptocurrency and may instead buy an alternative form that is executed in cash, such as purchasing shares of the Bitcoin Investment Trust which actually trades Bitcoin at anywhere between a 20 and 50% premium in relation to its actual market price.

The second way of doing this is a self-directed IRA. If you already have an IRA dedicated to holding real estate or other alternative asset classes, you may be familiar with this one. The advantage here is that you will directly own your cryptocurrencies yourself. However these types of accounts are trickier to set up and therefore you must ensure you get everything right the first time round, or otherwise, you may get into hot water with the IRS down the line if everything is not in order.

To set up a self directed cryptocurrency IRA you must have your cryptocurrency stored in a wallet, in other words, not on a cryptocurrency exchange. However, this cannot be a personal wallet so you cannot use a hardware wallet like your Ledger Nano S for example. Thus you must work with your provider to set up a separate wallet which is purely for your retirement funds. I would seek advice from your provider to ensure everything is set up correctly.

The other option is that you can create a separate LLC for the sole purpose of holding the wallet and then be responsible on the balance sheet for all transactions in and out of the wallet. If you haven't done this before I wouldn't recommend it for a first timer, because the added complication of a cryptocurrency wallet can make it confusing to those without experience in the area.

FBAR Requirements

Now the FBAR applies to income stored outside of the United States. If you ever held more than $10,000 outside of the USA on a single day you are required to file your FBAR online. How this affects cryptocurrency is if you have ever had more than $10,000 worth of coins or cash on an overseas exchange, then you must file. This particularly affects those who trade regularly on Binance or other non-US based cryptocurrency exchanges, and have held a significant amount of money on there.

OVDP & Streamlined Domestic Offshore Disclosure

Note if you suspect you are not compliant with these regulations for the previous year,s you can file an IRS voluntary offshore disclosure and get back into the IRS' good books. The best way to do this is with the Offshore Disclosure Volunteer Program (OVDP), this program is designed to facilitate compliance with the IRS and the DOJ. The program is open to any US taxpayer with offshore holdings or financial accounts. The main requirement for this program is that you are not currently under IRS investigation. The reason for the previous necessity is that by being a voluntary program, you must not be "forced" to enter it and if you are already investigation than that would constitute force. The standard OVDP application includes 8 years of tax return filings and 8 years of FBAR statements as well as other supporting documents.

The second one of these programs is most applicable to most people who this ruling affects. It's known as the Streamlined Domestic Offshore Disclosure. Despite it's strangely contradictory name, it deals with foreign accounts and foreign held money. Once again, contact an offshore disclosure attorney if you do wish to file.

If you have a significant amount and are behind on declarations, I would recommend investing some of that money and hiring a well experienced offshore disclosure attorney.

What about coins that were airdropped or I received as part of a hard fork?

Like most other cryptocurrency related tax issues, hard forks are a confusing one. According to Robert Crea from law firm K&L Gates "It's something new—it doesn't fit neatly into a dividend or stock split or even mining."

Crea's colleague Elizabeth Crouse then explained what this could mean for your tax liabilities.

"From the IRS's perspective, whenever you get something new you didn't pay for, it's accretive—it's income," she says. "When the Bitcoin Cash shows up in someone's account, that's probably a taxable event. The question is what's it worth."

As seen above, the main coin in question that we have to look for here is Bitcoin Cash (BCH). As a result of a hard fork, anyone holding Bitcoin on August 1st received an equivalent amount of Bitcoin Cash.

The question now is whether you would have to report this to the IRS and pay it as a capital gain, based on the price at the time of distribution (roughly $277 per BCH). Or the other scenario where you would only pay based on when you sold BCH.

The IRS is yet to make an official judgement on how exactly airdrops work though, and when contacted by various news agencies, simply referred back to their initial statements that conclude that cryptocurrency is considered property.

In this case, you would have to report your income based on the price of the coin at the time. In other words, just because you got your BCH for free, doesn't mean the IRS considers it to have zero value. In other words, it's a taxable event.

Now this gets dicey for those of your holding your Bitcoin in a Coinbase or GDax wallet because you would have received your Bitcoin Cash on January 1st, 2018, when the value of Bitcoin was much higher.

The other big hard fork event, that will affect those of you who have been in the market for longer, is the July 2016 Ethereum hard fork when Ethereum holders received Ethereum Classic (ETC) as a result of the hard fork after the notorious DAO hack.

Then there is the case of air drops. Many coins over the past few years have airdropped into wallets on certain exchanges. Tron, for example, airdropped 500 TRX into Liqui wallets in September 2017. With this example, you inherit the cost basis of the "gift" at the time you received it. As many of these air drops had little value at the time you received them, it won't be an issue for the IRS. This is unlike BCH which did have significant value at the time it was distributed (approximately $277 per BCH), which is more likely to trigger a tax liability.

Of course, once again this only applies when you sell your coins. Simply holding them is not a taxable event.

Can I actually pay my taxes *in c*ryptocurrency?

Is it possible to minimize your tax burden by paying in Bitcoin or Ethereum? Does the IRS accept crypto as a form of payment? Unfortunately, the answer to both of these questions is a resounding no. The IRS does not currently accept tax payments in anything other than US dollars.

However, at a state level, there may be some changes to this. For example, Arizona is the first state looking to pass a law that allows its citizens to pay state income taxes in Bitcoin as well as other sanctioned cryptocurrencies. This follows the lead of a number of municipalities in Switzerland which passes laws allowing their citizens to pay taxes in cryptocurrency.

If the bill passes it will be introduced by 2020 at the earliest so we're still a little ways off. Interestingly enough, the legislature states that Arizona would not hold the payments in cryptocurrency after they are made and would convert them back to fiat for their own use.

It is an encouraging sign though and we may well see other states follow suit in this respect. I would hesitate to think that federal allowance of tax payments in cryptocurrency is any way close though due to the increasingly complicated nature of passing federal laws versus state laws.

What do I do if I haven't reported anything thus far?

OK so first things first, relax. Unless you have holdings ranging into 6 figures, it's unlikely the IRS or any other government agency is going to come kicking your door down.

Your best option depending on your holdings would be to contact a good tax attorney and accountant. If you do have significant holdings (6 figures plus), and you haven't been compliant for multiple years, I would urge you to spend more money and hire the best you can afford, because it will make the process a lot smoother going forward. The IRS is not an organization you want to mess around with and therefore you should absolutely do your utmost to be compliant.

Also, be wary of any company that promises cheap and quick offshore incorporation as a means of hiding assets or lowering your tax burden. Many of these companies can and will set up foreign bank accounts for you, but just because your money is going into a foreign account, does not mean you do not have to pay tax on it, as is the often misquoted information online.

Thirdly, everyone's situation is different, there is absolutely no one size fits all solution for this and thus do not believe everything you read on internet forums or social media. A good tax attorney and accountant is the only way you will truly get accurate information for *your* situation.

If you have low level holdings of only a few thousand dollars then you can still self report. Remember to keep track of all your crypto transactions, and if you haven't done so already, start doing this going forward.

Does taxation affect the price of cryptocurrencies?

This issue came to the forefront around December 2017, when a lot of first time crypto investors and traders realized that tax season was coming.

Therefore, there was a lot of speculation that tax season was actually affecting the day to day price of crypto. While some believed that many investors were pulling their money out of the market after December 31 but before January 31st to in order to pay their taxes, and spread their burden across multiple years. Others simply speculated that it was a coincidence and that the US market isn't the biggest player in the crypto world. However, a similar pattern has emerged for the past 3 years so the theory may well have some merit.

What is interesting is that this is actually a different pattern to the stock market which tends to do well in January as institutional investors reestablish their positioning as they move into the new year. Either way, it's an intriguing pattern to monitor going forward.

Needless to say, you can't let short term price fluctuations like this affect your long term investing strategy, so unless you are a day trader then it's best not to worry about minutia such as this.

What about ICOs - are they tax-free because they are used to raise capital?

While this would make sense and would be in line with the 2017 SEC ruling that cryptocurrencies are a currency, the answer is actually no.

While conventional capital raising methods are considered tax exempt by the IRS. ICOs don't work in the same way. Therefore the proceeds of an ICO will be considered taxable income. The amount would be determined by the value of cryptocurrency received (in other words, the donation cryptocurrency rather than the new token) on the date the ICO ended. So if your ICO received 1000BTC and it ended when 1 BTC was worth $1000. You would have $1,000,000 of taxable gains.

The other thing to note is that unless you formed a corporation before you begin the ICO, you will be personally liable for the gains received. Obviously, if there are co-founders like most ICOs then you are considered a partnership for tax purposes and you will be responsible for an equal share of the net income made from the ICO.

Therefore if you are a developer and are planning to conduct an ICO then you should definitely consider forming a corporation beforehand. Income will then be taxed at a corporate rate rather than a person rate which has far reaching benefits for the people involved.

One interesting thing to note is that by conducting your ICO earlier on in the tax year, you may be able to acquire some extra benefits such as being able to spend the proceeds on deductible expenses. This includes operating costs, salaries and other items like office rent.

There is a lot of speculation that forming an offshore company can have a number of tax benefits, especially when it comes to legally avoiding US taxes. Needless to say, offshore tax laws are extremely complex, depending on various factors such as the jurisdiction where your incorporated the company, your tax residency and a myriad of other factors. They are difficult for even a seasoned tax accountant to navigate, so ensure that you have everything straightened out before you decide to go this route.

Beware of companies offering quick fix solutions like incorporation and bank account set up offshore, many of these companies will tell you that you will be completely compliant with US tax, but then you can find yourself in hot water down the line when it turns out there were certain things they *didn't* tell you in regards to your personal tax status. Often their advertising will use easy selling points like "0% tax rate", but it would be wise to investigate this fully before you do pull the trigger on any arrangement.

This is especially true if you reside in the US, then your income from an offshore company will still be subject to US taxation. Foreign owned companies will also have to deal with FBAR requirements that we previously discussed in an earlier chapter. You also have state taxes to be concerned with as your state will probably want some of your gains as well.

What if I make capital gains one year but lose the money the next year?

Here is a tricky situation, but certainly something we should all be aware of in the case of a market crash. If you make gains in one tax year, you will be required to pay them even if you make large losses the following year.

This can be troublesome in the case of a large year-long correction or bear market like we saw in 2015. There were a notable number of investors who made large gains in the prior year but as they expected this to continue, didn't take profits and kept much of their holdings in cryptocurrency. They went on to make some serious losses the following year and by the time their tax bill was due, they found they didn't have the money to pay it.

Obviously, we can't predict the way the market is going to go, but we can take some steps to ensure that we aren't left out of pocket. The biggest lesson from all this is that you should take intermittent profits for yourself no matter how good the market is doing because trust me, you'll thank yourself the next year if the market does take a turn for the worse. Make sure you can cover any tax burdens, and don't leave it to the last minute to withdraw your money because chances are a lot of people are doing the same thing, and thus it could cause a short term dip.

There are some exceptions to the rule but these will be made on an individual basis by the IRS themselves. So if this does apply to you, and you believe you could qualify for one, I recommend speaking with an accountant and seeing what can be done about your situation.

How are my cryptocurrencies taxed if I mined them?

Yet another area in which there is no real hard legislature right now is in the field of cryptocurrency mining. The IRS has made one ruling on this in Notice 2014-21 Q9 which states that anyone who mines cryptocurrency is "subject to self-employment tax on income derived from those activities."

In terms of how much your mined cryptocurrency is actually worth, the official IRS ruling right now is that each coin mined is given the value that it had when it was awarded on the blockchain itself. In other words, the value on the day it is mined, is the basis for that coin going forward.

For example, if you mine 1 Bitcoin when the value of BTC is $500, then its basis going forward is $500. So if you then sell it for $700 a year later, then your capital gains is $200.

When it comes to the subject of expenses and electricity, mining expenses are deductible if you have incorporated yourself into a mining business. Obviously, if you are a mining business, electricity would be a significant proportion of your monthly expenses and therefore there is no reason at all why they would not be a legitimate deductible. It should be noted that you will also have to make note of the square footage of the room your mining rig is housed in, as this is often how electricity expenses are factored when there is a multi-use situation. It should also be noted that you cannot write off electricity for an entire room (like your living room) just because there is a mining rig housed there. Trying to do this is an easy way to get the IRS on your case. Other mining expenses such as depreciation of your mining rig and its parts would also be deductible.

If mining is just a hobby for you, you must still pay additional self employment tax on any amount earned which is greater than $400 in a single year.

Gains made from mining pools or cloud mining would be subject to the value of your payouts as well as money initially invested. Once again, consult a tax professional to get a better handle of the situation.

However, on a strict consumer level, this is probably not a deductible. This is quite a gray area and I would recommend speaking to a professional for greater clarification on this subject.

Are crypto-to-crypto transactions considered "like kind" exchanges?

This is where it gets murky, although the logic would dictate that these kinds of transactions are indeed "like kind" exchanges and thus would not be a taxable event, this officially is not the case for the time being.

Unfortunately, the guidance from the IRS regarding this is over 3 years old now, when cryptocurrency and high volume cryptocurrency trading was far less common. So at the moment, we will have to treat crypto-to-crypto exchanges as not being like kind and therefore every single trade will be a taxable event.

So what does this mean for your returns? It means that any gains or losses can be written off against each other for that particular year, but cannot be moved over to another year. So for example, if you make $20,000 in capital gains one year, you cannot use these to offset a $10,000 loss the following year.

The other important thing to note is wash-sale rules. Designed so that traders do not fraudulently claim losses, this applies more to cryptocurrency than you might think. Wash-sale applies if you sell an investment at a loss, then re-invest in that same asset, in this case, the same coin, within 30 days of investing.

Let's do an example.

Say you buy 1 bitcoin at $20,000, it dips to $10,000, then eventually surges to $25,000. You sell 0.2 BTC at $5,000, which is a capital gain of $1,000 which you'd be responsible for short term capital gains tax.

However, if instead, you sold your bitcoin when it hit $10,000 and repurchased it, you'd reset your cost basis to $10,000 and claim a $10,000 loss on taxes.

When the price increases to $25,000 and you sell your 0.2 BTC, it would be a $3,000 capital gain, but combined with your paper loss of $10,000, you'd still be looking at a $7,000 capital loss. For wash-sale rules to apply, all these trades must have occurred within a 30 day period of the initial purchase of Bitcoin.

Wash-sale rules currently only apply to stocks and securities, which cryptocurrencies are not considered as the IRS labels them as property. So in theory you could apply these to your tax return and benefit.

However, under regular tax law, you would have to prove these trades were done for some other purposes other than just to benefit on your taxes. This is known as the Economic Substance Doctrine, so it is completely plausible that the IRS would not allow you to use these as a tax write off. The IRS uses this to fight against illegal tax shelters that long use this trick to provide additional tax benefits for their owners.

You can use the idea of market risk to argue to the IRS that these losses were sustained as a result of market volatility and nothing else. This is because the IRS considers you personal economic benefits at risk rather than just the potential tax benefits. Of course, any transactions over the 30 day period would not run afoul of any of these rulings and thus you don't need to be concerned with them if that is the case.

The Coinbase Form 1099-K

We discussed this earlier in the book and now we'll cover it in grater depth. You may have received a form from the IRS in the mail within the past 3 months, this was likely Form 1099-K which relates to your cryptocurrency holdings which you **sold** in exchange for fiat value within the past tax year.

If you have received this it is likely that you have had a Coinbase account for a period longer than 12 months, and your sales of cryptocurrencies exceeded $20,000. The $20,000 number is based on federal law that third parties must report sales over this number to the IRS. Therefore, this is a form that Coinbase has to send to the IRS, as it strictly relates to transactions on third party networks. So in this case, it will only include transactions on Coinbase and its sister website GDax.

This form does not give the IRS an indication of your total cryptocurrency holdings, or those on other sites outside of Coinbase or GDax. Nor does it give the IRS access to your wallet address on those two websites.

The one thing to note is that the form relates to your gross payment amount. This particularly relates to traders, especially day traders making many transactions. Therefore every single transaction is recorded and totaled up. In the case of Bitcoin, if you sold BTC at $10,000 twice - this would trigger the $20,000 threshold, and thus you may well have received the form, even if your net gains were well below this amount. This will also *not* take any transactions fees into account.

So if you sold your cryptocurrency for a loss, it would not take this into account. Therefore don't be surprised if the payment amount on the form is higher than your actual trading gains.

Let's do an example:

January - you buy BTC at $8,000 and sell for $7,000 (a $1,000 loss)
February - you buy ETH at $500 and sell for $1,500 (a $1,000 gain)
March - you buy LTC for $1,000

The number on the form would be $8,500 ($7,000+$1,500), which is higher than your actual gains. This form only relates to the sale amount, so your purchase amounts won't even be displayed and thus the IRS does not have data into your actual trading profits.

It should be noted that if you have not received one of these forms but have been trading significant amounts, then it is your responsibility to file a 1099 form to the IRS. You won't be able to use the excuse of "I thought Coinbase would do it for me" either, it's very much up to you to take the initiative in these kinds of dealing with federal tax authorities.

How to generate transaction reports on Coinbase & GDax

If you're a frequent trader and you do make a lot of transactions, when you have to file your taxes, you'll need to make sure you note down every single one of these transactions. It will make it a lot easier to you square things away with the IRS.

Below is a step by step guide on how to find an accurate number of all your cryptocurrency transactions in the past year using Coinbase & GDax.

Instructions for Coinbase:
1. Click "Tools"
2. Click "Reports" in the sub menu
3. Click "+ New Report" button
4. Set Account to "USD Wallet…" and Time Range to "Last Year"

Instructions for GDax:
1. Navigate to the menu in the top right
2. Click "Accounts" in the sub menu
3. Click "USD Account" in the menu on the left
4. Click "Download Receipt / Statement"
5. Set Time Range to "Custom" from 01/01/2017 to 12/31/2017

How can you minimize your cryptocurrency tax burden?

So first things first, this applies to regular investors rather than frequent traders, who obviously will not be able to take advantage of many of the tax laws here. I should also note I am talking about legal ways to lower your overall tax bill. Not illegal ways to avoid paying tax.

The big one is to hold on to your coins for at least 12 months after you buy them. This will allow you to be in the long term capital gains bracket which will always be below 20%, whereas the short term capital gains will be taxed at the same rate as your regular tax bracket.

The second one is mainly for peace of mind purposes, but try to use as few exchanges as possible so it's easy for you to track all your trades. Being able to download your entire trade history from Coinbase or GDax is very simple, but other exchanges, such as EtherDelta, do not have any trade records at the time of writing. It's unlikely that the IRS will accept "well the website doesn't record trades" as an excuse, so try to use exchanges where you can have a record of all your trades where possible.

As previously mentioned as well, if you received coins as a gift that are now worth less than their value when you received them, you will be able to write some of these off as a capital loss. So ensure when you receive them you discuss with the gifter the date they were purchased and the value of the coins at that date.

Depending on your income bracket you may also be liable for an additional 3.8% Net Investment Income Tax. Consult the IRS website for further details.

Can you register yourself as a self-employed trader to get a better tax deal?

There are a number of advantages to being a self-employed trader in the eyes of the IRS. The main one being, if the IRS considers your trading a "business" then your gains and losses become ordinary.

Registering a trader is extremely difficult though and your registration must be renewed twice a year to qualify for the benefits. There are a number of advantages and disadvantages to doing this. The may disadvantage being that your losses are no longer deductible because this is considered part of your day to day business and thus regular capital gain rules no longer apply.

However, just being on Binance a lot is not going to cut it come tax season. So if you do want to register yourself I would recommend consulting a tax professional if you want to go this route.

What about altcoins with no official conversion to fiat

In the case of many altcoins that don't have direct fiat trading pairs, you would use the USD value of the fiat equivalent that you traded them for. For example, if you bought 50XMR for 20 BTC and that 20BTC was worth $10,000 at the time, then officially you bought $10,000 worth of currency during that transaction.

This applies when you go to sell as well. It doesn't matter if the final sale was against another altcoin or not, the transaction will be recorded in US dollars. Obviously, this represents a great difficulty for a lot of people, so if you have been trading frequently I would seek out professional help from a tax firm.

Were there any changes in the crypto tax laws between 2017 and 2018?

So as we previously stated, there has only been 1 official ruling on cryptocurrency by the IRS. This was back in 2014, and nothing much has changed since then.

So like-kind exchanges still apply, you will pay taxes on crypto-to-crypto exchanges when you eventually convert these to fiat. Obviously this implication will have more effect on frequent traders and day traders then your regular buy and hold investor.

There are new federal tax brackets, which will affect your capital gains and these are listed below.

Rates for Individuals in 2018.
10%   - Up to $9,525
12%   - $9,526 to $38,700
22%   - 38,701 to $82,500
24%   - $82,501 to $157,500
32%   - $157,501 to $200,000
35%   - $200,001 to $500,000
37% - over $500,000

Rates for married couples filing jointly

10% - Up to $19,050
12%   - $19,051 to $77,400
22% - $77,401 to $165,000
24%   - $165,001 to $315,000
32%   - $315,001 to $400,000
35%   - $400,001 to $600,000
37%   - over $600,000

How are other countries dealing with cryptocurrency taxes?

While we wait for US tax law to evolve to be at a happy medium with cryptocurrency gains, it is interesting to see just how other countries are handling the problem.

Germany, for example, considers cryptocurrency to be foreign currency and trading in cryptocurrencies is considered a private sale. They also do not have any long term capital gains tax on cryptocurrency, so if you buy 1 ETH on June 1st 2016 and sell it for a profit on June 1st 2017, then you would not have to pay any tax on your gain.

Denmark is another progressive crypto country. In its goal of making the Nordic nation the world's first cashless state, cryptocurrency trades are not taxed and there is no capital gains on Bitcoin either.

In January 2018, the Portuguese tax authorities announced they would not be levying any taxes on profits made by trading cryptocurrency. The government of Belarus also announced that as of March 2018 there would be no taxes on cryptocurrency for its citizens for the next 5 years. This is to encourage the adoption crypto as well as to promote blockchain and smart contract technology. Serbia is another nation that is completely tax free for cryptocurrency profits, including profits made from crypto mining.

However, other countries are less friendly towards their citizens' bank accounts when it comes to cryptocurrency, for example, in Germany the short-term (less than 1 year) capital gains tax can be as high as 46%. In France, the situation is even worse and this number can top 60% in some cases.

Then there's the rather bizarre case of the few select crypto millionaires who are trying to construct their own "cryptocurrency utopia" in Puerto Rico. By establishing residency on the Caribbean island, which is a U.S. territory, they are aiming to avoid state and federal taxes. Puerto Rico has become somewhat is a tax haven in the past decade due to no federal personal income taxes, no capital gains tax and favorable business taxes — all without having to renounce your American citizenship. Which makes it an ideal tax haven for any US citizen.

There are talks of many of these men building lavish mansions with their own docks and airstrip for private planes. These men include Bryan Larkin, a crypto billionaire who was one of the early adopters of Bitcoin mining with an estimated personal fortune of around $2 billion. Another notable figure is Reeve Collins, one of the co-founders of the controversial US Dollar tether, which is a cryptocurrency pegged to the value of the US dollar, used for exchanges between altcoins. Needless to say, the project is in the early stages still and many of the group spend the majority of their time drinking at hotel bars rather than building mega mansions. It will definitely be interesting to see if it ends up as a cryptocurrency utopia or if the opposite happens and it turns into a Lord of The Flies situation.

Conclusion

Well there we have it, I hope I've cleared up some questions and that you've come out of this book with more knowledge about the general cryptocurrency tax situation than before.

We've covered everything from capital gains and losses, to how mined cryptocurrencies are taxed as well as gifting. We've also gone over the different forms that are filed and the various ways the IRS will be aware of your cryptocurrency tax situation, so I hope I've been able to address the vast majority of concerns you had before buying.

Remember, everyone's personal tax situation is different, and there is no one size fits all solution, no matter what anyone tries to tell you. It should be noted that anyone trying to tell you that their one size fits all solution works for you, is probably just trying to get your money.

If you have a single take away from this book, let it be this. The only person who will be able to help with your own situation is a qualified accountant or tax attorney. This is one area I would recommend paying more money and hiring the best you can afford, especially if you have made a lot of more with crypto.

I wish you the best of luck in your ongoing cryptocurrency journey. We all hope the IRS can get a better grip on the crypto tax situations as we go forward, but it may well be a few years before we get some better guidelines and more streamlined processes. In the meantime, just make sure you keep up with tax compliances and file on time every year.

And as always, I hope you make a lot of money with cryptocurrency and that it affects your life in a positive way.

Thanks,
Stephen

Marijuana Stocks: Beginners Guide To The Only Industry Producing Financial Returns as Fast as Cryptocurrency

By Stephen Satoshi

Introduction

Outside of cryptocurrency, the marijuana industry in the fastest growing asset class on Earth. In 2017 alone it grew by more than 30%.

That growth is showing no signs of slowing down and legal marijuana is projected to be a near $25 billion industry in the US alone by 2020. Between the US and Canadian stock exchanges, there are now over 220 securities which can broadly be described as "marijuana stocks".

And that's even with the US federal government listing Marijuana as a schedule 1 drug. That's in the same category as cocaine and methamphetamine. It may also surprise you to discover that despite this rapid boom, there is still only 1 single federally approved growing facility in the entire United States.

However, a number of factors in the coming year indicate that this is all about to change.

You see, 29 states now allow legal use of marijuana for recreational purposes, medical purposes, or both.

And the ball is already rolling for further state by state legalization.

64% of US citizens now support legalizing the drug nationwide, that's compared to just 25% when the same question was asked in 1995. 70% of citizens are opposed to a federal marijuana crackdown, according to a poll conducted by Vice. Among younger people, that number is now at a staggeringly high 94%. It goes without saying that the average American's view of marijuana has drastically changed in the past 20 years.

Nationwide legalization of medical marijuana in the USA is now a matter of *when* not if.

And that's not even considering Canada's move to legalize recreational marijuana. The country has already legalized medical marijuana nationwide, and this next move could have an even bigger effect on the market as a whole once the bill passes, which is currently projected to be in the summer of 2018. Canada has its own list of marijuana stocks which offer a tremendous money making opportunity.

No wonder it's been dubbed "the green rush".

Marijuana doesn't just have great investment potential, there are a huge number of economic and social benefits as well. The positive effects are already being seen in early adopter states like Colorado. The first state to approve recreational marijuana use, saw a 30% year-on-year rise in legal sales since 2012. This resulted in $200 million extra dollars in the state's bottom line from tax revenue. Colorado is using this money for good, as much of the money is being reinvested into educational programs and drug-abuse initiatives.

These are exciting times ahead for marijuana both on a medical and recreational level. And there are so many different ways to profit from this. These aren't just limited to the growers and distributors of the plant. Everything from real estate to biotech to a company that manufacturers tiny plastic tubes will be covered in this book. We'll also be doing an analysis of 12 different highlighted marijuana stocks and their different business models.

I hope you enjoy this book and that the information inside proves valuable to you.

Thanks,
Stephen

So just *how* legal is marijuana these days?

One of the more confusing elements of the booming marijuana industry is the legality of it all. In the USA, while marijuana is still illegal at a federal level, different types of marijuana availability is decided on a state by state basis.

As previously noted, recreational marijuana, available to anyone over the age of 21 in the same vein as alcohol is currently legal in 8 states. Medical marijuana, available to anyone over the age of 21 with a doctor's prescription, is legal in 29 states. Now here's where it gets confusing with medical marijuana is being illegal at a federal level. So technically, possessing marijuana is still a federal crime in these states, even if you have a medical marijuana card. This leads to some confusing legislature such as jobs being able to fire employees for off-the-clock marijuana use. Landlords can also evict tenants for marijuana use, even if their state allows it. What we should be concerned with most as an investor is the main law that affects medical marijuana companies. This is the law that means many of these companies cannot get access to full banking and credit due to the federally illegal nature of their business, the law was put into place to prevent drug dealers from laundering money through banks. We'll be going on to discuss how this affects marijuana businesses later on in this book.

Below is a full breakdown of the exact legality of marijuana and cannabinoids on a state-by-state basis.

States That Have Legalized Industrial Hemp Production
- Alabama, Arkansas, California, Colorado, Florida, Georgia, Hawaii, Illinois, Indiana, Kentucky, Maine, Michigan, Minnesota, Mississippi, Montana, Nebraska, Nevada, New Hampshire, North Carolina, North Dakota, Oregon, Pennsylvania, Rhode Island, South Carolina, Tennessee, Utah, Vermont, Virginia, Washington and Wyoming.

States That Have Legalized Hemp Oil/CBD Hemp Oil
- Legal in all fifty states, though CBD Hemp oil is still illegal in Idaho, Indiana, Kansas, Nebraska, South Dakota and West Virginia.

States That Have Legalized Medicinal Marijuana
- Alaska, Arizona, Arkansas, California, Colorado, Connecticut, Delaware, Florida, Hawaii, Illinois, Maine, Maryland, Massachusetts, Michigan, Minnesota, Montana, Nevada, New Hampshire, New Jersey, New Mexico, New York, North Dakota, Ohio, Oregon, Pennsylvania, Rhode Island, Vermont, Washington, Washington DC and West Virginia.

States That Have Legalized Recreational Use of Marijuana
- Alaska, California, Colorado, Maine, Massachusetts, Nevada, Oregon and Washington.

It is also predicted that a further 5 states: Vermont, New Jersey, Michigan, Oklahoma and Utah - will each legalize adult recreational marijuana by the end of 2018.

Supply and Demand

One obvious, yet often overlooked factor in the marijuana market is the supply and demand of the plant. This has historically been difficult to quantify due to the previous illegality of the drug, and thus a lack of consistent evidence. Many investors naturally assume that legalization across more and more states will lead to increased demand, which is true.

However, something that is also true is that supply is actually outstripping demand. For example, in California, locally grown supplies are up threefold from 2006 to a staggering 13.5 million pounds a year. In the past 2 years, the wholesale price of marijuana has plunged from around $2,100 per pound to $1,600 per pound. This is not only due to increased competition as more and more growers enter the market every year. There is also the technological advancement in growing techniques, which is further lowering wholesale prices. Great for the consumer, but obviously not so great for the growing companies. Until federal nationwide legalization, it is also difficult for these growers to be able to sell their excess harvest to other states due to the different laws in place. Therefore there is no option to take advantage of geographical arbitrage by growing in states with lower land prices, then selling in states with wealthier consumers.

The interesting caveat to this is that the current fear North of the border in Canada, is that supply will not be able to meet demand is nationwide legalization does occur in the summer of 2018 as is expected. Current estimates don't favor producers, and many believe that it will be at least 2 years before they are able to consistently meet the demand for marijuana across the country. Other estimates are less optimistic and have this figure at nearer 4 years before demand can be met. Marijuana producers are scrambling to agree on a deal on a state-by-state basis and we are also seeing companies work together in order to try and streamline their processes so they can meet demand.

Marijuana Real Estate

It's not just growers and sellers that are profiting from this "green rush", the real estate market is being turned on its head. As more than 20 states have legalized medical marijuana, as a result, an under reported yet significant part boom is the form of real estate. This being the land that marijuana growers, factories and stores utilize. Even celebrities are getting involved, including former Heavyweight Champion boxer Mike Tyson has just purchased a 40-acre ranch in a remote California which will be dedicated to growing operations, as well as a luxury marijuana resort for cannabis enthusiasts. Tyson plans to use the ranch to provide jobs for military veterans in the local community.

You see, Cannabis sales are higher per square foot than department stores by 5 to 1. Drug stores by 1.5 to 1, and narrowly beating out Whole Foods. In fact, Marijuana sales per square foot are closer to that of Costco than any other entity. This combined with the numerous red tape and bureaucracy that marijuana businesses face has led to a significant premium in the average price of real estate for a marijuana business versus a conventional business.

For example, in Denver, the marijuana industry pays on average a 50% premium for warehouse buildings. Sometimes this premium can as much as 2 or even 3 times higher than non-marijuana businesses! Colorado is one of the big winners when it comes to the marijuana real estate boom, and over one third of new industrial tenants are now marijuana businesses.

The biggest opportunities to be had is in states that newly legalize medical and recreational marijuana use. For example, states like Michigan and New Jersey both of whom are on the brink of legalization. However, bills can stall, as we have seen in states like Maine. So, therefore, there is a significant element of risk in trying to "jump the gun" and get a head start on the marijuana real estate boom. There is also the issue of zoning laws and the areas that these businesses are allowed to operate in.

One interesting potential development is how federal legalization would impact real estate with regards to interstate transportation. Right now, all legal marijuana sold within that state must be grown in the same state in avoid to not violate federal drug trafficking laws. However, a nationwide legalization would result in this not applying, and thus companies could take advantage of parts of the country with lower land prices. The biggest losers in this scenario would be East Coast producers who traditionally have the highest land prices of all the legal marijuana states.

This isn't the first time real estate has made its mark in an unfamiliar industry. Let's take a look at McDonald's for instance. Not only is McDonald's and its' Golden Arches one of America's most iconic companies, it's also one of the best performing stocks of the last 30 years. Outperforming IBM and Coca-Cola over the same time period. Many investors shun McDonald's for its low-cost, low-brow business model of offering cheap food to the masses. However, what people really overlook is the *business* of McDonald's.

You see, in investment terms, McDonald's is really a real estate company. A large chunk of their annual profits comes from buying land cheaply, then leasing it at higher prices to its franchisees. One of the simplest business models imaginable, but one that has continued to produce profits, hand over foot, for the past 50 years. Founder Ray Kroc was even quoted as saying "We are in the real estate business, not the hamburger business."

And now, the marijuana industry is undergoing a similar phenomenon. Marijuana businesses are prevented from receiving bank loan or mortgages under federal law. Therefore, nearly all marijuana businesses are forced to rent their buildings at a premium. So it is the landlords who are making a killing off of this.

We've even seen support from institutional investors, in January, a little known ETF, the ETFMG Alternative Harvest ETF moved its focus from Latin American real estate to the thriving marijuana industry. The fund made some big plays, including acquiring over 300,000 shares of Turning Point Brands.

Although it should be noted that the majority of Alternative Harvest holdings are in the growing and distribution sector, that doesn't mean more of a real estate based portfolio can't be counted out in the future. After all, their initial focus was on the Latin American real estate market, so the fund managers have previous expertise in that sector.

It's large swings in focus like what we have seen from Alternative Harvest that indicate that the market is undergoing something of a boom. We may well see further emphasis on this sector as we move forward into 2018 and beyond. Needless to say, there is a certain hysteria around marijuana real estate right now, and many investors are clamoring to get their piece of the pie.

Big Tobacco vs. Cannabis Industry

Big Tobacco is one of the main detractors from the medical marijuana industry. This is the same set of companies that vehemently denied for years that tobacco was dangerous to one's health. It was only the result of a multi-state lawsuit that got them to do so. Funnily enough, there were reports of the tobacco industry gearing up for legalized marijuana as far back as the 1970s. There is even a handwritten memo from the President of Philip Morris Tobacco George Weissman stating "While I am opposed to its use, I recognize that it may be legalized in the near future...Thus, with these great auspices, we should be in a position to examine: 1. A potential competition, 2. A possible product, 3. At this time, cooperate with the government." Philip Morris also formally requested marijuana samples from the Department of Justice so they could carry out their own testing.

The more intriguing part of this memo is the section saying "We are in the business of relaxing people who are tense and providing a pick up for people who are bored or depressed. The human needs that our product fills will not go away. **Thus, the only real threat to our business is that society will find other means of satisfying these needs.**" The last sentence is where the cannabis industry comes into play. Will tobacco companies actively try to put a stop to increasing legalization, rather than trying to enter the market themselves? Only time will tell with this one, however, given their history of opposing marijuana, we may well see this in the near future.

The other option is that big tobacco will look to diversify its own interests with investments in marijuana firms. For example, Imperial Brands (formerly known as Imperial Tobacco), one of the largest tobacco corporations, recently added Simon Langelier to its board of directors. Langelier is the chairman of PharmaCielo, a Canadian based manufacturer of cannabis oil extracts and other marijuana based health products. The tobacco industry in the US is declining around 4% year on year, and the companies may look to marijuana to help offset some of these expected drops in revenue. We have already seen of these companies diversify into the growing e-cigarette industry, and it is likely that we will see some small scale ventures into the marijuana market within the next 18-24 months. Whether this will result in direct takeover bids for marijuana firms is unknown, but it's something we can't count out at this stage.

Big Pharma vs. The Marijuana Industry

Legal marijuana's biggest enemy, in terms of a specific industry, is the pharmaceutical industry. Big Pharma has a long documented history of opposing any form of marijuana legalization, especially for companies focusing on the medical benefits of marijuana.

In 2016, a $500,000 donation was made to an organization opposing Arizona's recreational marijuana initiative. Donations of $500,000 to major political candidates are not uncommon at all, but ones of this size to a group fighting a signal issue are very rare. That $500,000 came from Insys Therapeutics, who manufacture Subsys, a powerful and extremely addictive Fentanyl based painkiller, targeted at cancer patients. This donation ended up playing a key part, as Arizona's initiative was defeated by the narrow margin of 51-49.

What makes this even more interesting is that Insys is now developing its own line of synthetic THC based drugs. So to make this abundantly clear, this pharmaceutical company not only donated money to help block legalization of recreational marijuana, it then released its own synthetic alternative. It should be noted that in December 2016, former CEO Michael Babich and six more Insys executives were arrested in an alleged bribery case revolving around pressuring doctors to prescribe Subsys, along with defrauding insurance providers. This was done with the motivation of promoting Subsys as an alternative to traditional painkillers and to try to capture market share.

Then you have the case of the 2014 Community Anti Drug Coalition of America (CADCA), where speakers pleaded against the legalization of marijuana. One of the main sponsors of this program was Purdue Pharma, the company that happens to manufacture Oxycontin. Over 1,000 deaths per year in the United States result from overdoses from prescribed Oxycontin. This number soars to over 100,000 when we account for a worldwide scale. Abbott Laboratories, the maker of Vicodin, is another large contributor to CADCA. It is estimated that Big Pharma spends upwards of $20 million per year in lobbying anti-marijuana initiatives.

Early estimates have put medical marijuana's competition as having the ability to cost Big Pharma between $4 and 6 billion per year in direct loss of sales. Washington, for example, has seen a decrease in Medicare prescriptions since the legalization of medical marijuana. Phizer, one of the largest drug companies on the planet as produced data showing that medical marijuana could take as much as $500 million out of its bottom line revenue.

Where Big Pharma's motivations lie to clear to see, the issue is a financial one, rather than a moral one. They are fully aware that nationwide legalization would eat into their market share, as customers seek alternatives to mass manufactured chemical drugs. This competition would lead to lower prices, which is the last thing the pharmaceutical industry is interested in.

Therefore it is likely we will be seeing more companies follow the lead on Insys, in manufacturing their own synthetic THC and CBD based drugs, which could bypass federal restrictions and therefore be sold in regular pharmacies across the country, rather than only in specialist cannabis stores. The potential market size for this is huge, as it is now estimated that over 100 million Americans now depends on some form of painkiller on a daily basis. This includes both doctor prescribed medications such as Vicodin or Percocet, as well as street drugs like Heroin. One thing marijuana enthusiasts have long since spoken out against is the possibility that Big Pharma could use its own pockets to corner the market with these synthetic cannabis drugs, as the general population will view them as "safer" due to their presence in regular pharmacies.

It will be interesting to monitor drug developments in the next 18-24 months from this larger pharmaceutical companies, as they seek to get their own share of the ever growing medical marijuana market. I would predict that we will be seeing more and more synthetic cannabis based drug options emerging from the traditional pharmaceutical companies.

Cannabinoids

You may have seen reports of companies who are focused on "cannabis medicine", what these companies do is utilize cannabinoids to create drugs and formulas to treat various diseases.

For those are you who aren't familiar, cannabinoids are the chemical compounds found in the marijuana plant itself. The main ones being THC, the psychoactive compound, which creates the "high" marijuana is known for. The other main compound is CBD, unlike THC, CBD is non-psychoactive, so you can take pure CBD based products and not feel a "high". Because of this distinction, CBD is legal in more states. There are also other compounds such as CBN, CBG and CBC.

There are a number of biotech companies which focus more on the cannabinoid side of things, by developing pharmaceuticals using these compounds as a major or periphery ingredient. The growth of stocks like these is largely dependent on FDA approval for their drugs, and if you've been in biotech for a while, you'll know this is a slow process.

One of the largest players in this market is the UK based GW Pharmaceuticals. Their main cannabis related product is Sativex. A spray that can help alleviate the symptoms of Multiple Sclerosis. Currently, Sativex has regulatory approval in 16 markets, with 12 more pending. Another drug, Epidiolex, aimed at treating child-onset epilepsy is currently in the pending approval stage as well.

Other significant players in the cannabinoid markets are MedReleaf, Tilray and OrganiGram, all three of these companies are based in Canada are produce CBD based drugs which aid treatment of various health ailments. We'll discuss both MedReleaf and OrganiGram in greater depth later on in this book, as both companies have some very exciting prospects up their sleeves.

"Non-Marijuana" Marijuana Stocks

There are a number of companies that you may well be aware of, and may even hold in your portfolio already, which actually have significant ties to the marijuana industry. As such, I have dubbed these "non-marijuana" marijuana stocks due to their primary business being in different industries.

One such example of this is Scott's Miracle-Gro. A long-time leader in the traditional home and garden care market, a market that usually produces slow, steady, unspectacular returns. Scott's has been a long-time favourite among many US households and known for their TV commercials.

However what you may not have known about Scott's is that 11% of their sales are now derived from a subsidiary company, Hawthorne Gardening Co. Hawthrone focuses its efforts on the medical marijuana industry, and has been steadily acquiring smaller marijuana businesses over the past few years. There additional focus of the business is on the technological side of things, mainly in Hydroponics, which is the act of growing plants in water enriched with minerals and nutrients. In 2017, Hawthorne's sales tripled, and those numbers are projected to continue rising as we move forward.

Even if sentiment completely reverses regarding marijuana and legalization, Scott's can still fall back on its bread and butter business of traditional lawn care, which makes up 89% of the business in total.

The other issue we can look at is the potential for Big Pharma companies to try to acquire some of these cannabis producers as a hedge against their own day-to-day business operations. These companies have very deep pockets, especially compared to even the bigger marijuana firms. We may see some of the pharmaceutical giants make takeover plays for cannabinoid based biotech firms in the next few years.

Marijuana Industry & Red Tape

Now here's where the state legalization vs. Federal legalization issue gets hairy. Because banks have to comply with federal laws regarding issues like money laundering, this directly affects the day to day marijuana business. You see, as a result of this confusing status, many marijuana businesses have zero access to credit. Some can barely get access to more than a basic checking account. This is because it is entirely possible for a bank to be charged with money laundering if they deal with marijuana businesses. Although I should note at this time, there have been zero instances of this. At the time of writing it is estimated that one third of licensed marijuana vendors have been denied a bank account.

There are also no tax breaks for marijuana businesses. In a similar law that was aimed at preventing illegal drug dealers from deducting business expenses, marijuana companies are now feeling the effects. A strange caveat to this is that businesses such as prostitution and contract killing can still claim deductions. I know what you're thinking, and you are correct hitmen can claim business expenses. The ramifications for this are large across the industry, basic business expenses such as rent, advertising, wages and utilities (a big one for the growers) are not allowed to be claimed by owners of marijuana businesses.

Where this hits home on the bottom line is that many marijuana businesses are looking at effective tax rates (the percentage of their *pre-tax* profits) of 70%, as opposed to the much lower 30% for other businesses. In terms of the larger conglomerates, it is estimated that many US businesses pay an effective rate as low as 12.5%. What's worse is that marijuana businesses can be on the hook for federal tax evasion if they don't comply with these laws. We should remember that it was a federal tax evasion charge that ended up bringing down Al Capone's entire empire in the 1930s.

There is hope though, in 2017, a bi-partisan act introduced by Senator Ron Wyden and Senator Rand Paul would allow marijuana businesses to make the standard business tax deductions. However, the bill is currently stuck in committee though, and it may well be years before it is able to be passed and enacted.

What's more is, many of these businesses are forced to operate in cash. This gets even more absurd when you consider that even though marijuana is still illegal at a federal level, due to tax code 280E, which requires drug dealers to report their illicit profits for tax purposes, the IRS collects roughly $3 billion per year from marijuana vendors. This leads to a number of stories where marijuana vendors are having to pay the IRS in cash at their local office. Marijuana is certainly beneficial to the IRS and industry growth would lead to even more revenue down the line. Data shows that legal marijuana could lead a 6 fold increase in federal tax revenue.

Why could this all go wrong?

All investments come with a certain amount of risk, and it's always good to analyze the contrarian view of the situation, so we will do so here. Here are a number of factors that could mean this all ends in disappointment. I should note before we begin this section, that this is all speculation. Thus you should take it with a pinch of salt.

Industry Consolidation

The astounding growth rate for the industry thus far, and the continued predictions of 26% per year for the next 3 years. However this does mean we're yet to see any sort of industry consolidation, many of these smaller companies especially will be absorbed into the larger marijuana conglomerates that will no doubt be formed within the next few years.

On the flipside of this though, investing early in these smaller companies could well lead to big gains if they are bought out, rather than run out of business by these larger firms.

Penny stocks

Many of these smaller marijuana stocks are defined as penny stocks as they trade under $5/share. Therefore they can't be listed on the NASDAQ or New York Stock Exchange. Many of them will list on Over The Counter (OTC) exchanges, which have lower requirements and monitoring standards than the bigger exchanges you'll be more familiar with.

This makes them more liable to misinformation and less than stellar business practices. I would exercise caution to these tiny marijuana based stocks, as like other penny stocks, they are more likely to be manipulated than larger ones.

News flows slower in the OTC world as well, so investors looking for up to date information regarding important metrics like cash flow, may well be left in the dark for a longer period than they are comfortable with.

The other factor is the vast majority of penny stocks are companies with less than solid fundamentals in the first place. Most penny stock companies are losing money every year, which is a big part of their low price. Others do not yet have a working product and are banking on future approval in order to their stock increase price.

When researching these stocks, you will see phrases like "expansion phase" "potential revenue" and "impressive management team" rather than talk of consistent profitability or market share. There will also be a group of people shilling the stock on message boards or in private Discord groups. You'll see phrases like "get on the train", "10X by the end of the month" and other fear of missing out type language. If you've been involved with cryptocurrency at all, you'll see the same patterns and language associated with that market.

Like any penny stock, these microcap marijuana companies should be looked at as a speculative gamble, rather than a long or even short term investment. If we want to look at some historical precedence, let's take a look at 6 nanotechnology companies that were previously listed on OTC market. Nanotechnology was another big boom industry in the mid 2000s, and many investors made speculative plays.

JMAR ($JMAR): Down 100% from its peak
Biophan ($BIPH): -99% from its peak
US Global Nanospace ($USGA): -99% from its peak
Industrial Nanotech ($INTK): -96% from its peak
Natural Nano ($NNAN): -99% from its peak
mPhase ($XDSL): Down -99% from its peak

If you had invested $1,000 in each of these companies, so $6,000 total, you would currently have **15 cents to show for your initial investment.** So if you are not an experienced investor, or you don't have deep pockets, I would urge you to stay well away from these microcap companies for the reasons listed above.

Jeff Sessions

Attorney General Sessions is one of the biggest critics of the marijuana industry. Sessions has been previously quoted as saying "good people don't smoke marijuana" and "My best view is that we don't need to be legalizing marijuana." Needless to say, statements like these don't fill the room with confidence when it comes to the issue of nationwide legalization.

Sessions also strongly believes the gateway drug theory, that many opioid addicts were exposed to the ideas of illegal drugs via marijuana and thus marijuana is the direct cause of their addictions. Despite a large number of academic studies that have long since refuted this theory, Sessions continues to stand by his views.

What is more concerning is that these statements were made, despite increasing amounts of data supporting the medical and social benefits of legalized marijuana. For example, in 2015 there were 20,101 deaths resulting from opioid related overdoses. Contrast this to a grand total of ZERO deaths from marijuana related overdoses. You can't really argue for stronger data than that when it comes to legalization, and yet here is one of the most powerful men in the country using phrases like "historic drug epidemic".

The positive of this is in the form of the President Donald Trump himself. During his campaign, he stated multiple times that he was a supporter of medical marijuana, and said the issue should be decided at the state level. Trump's views on drug legalization are well documented in the past, and he was even quoted in a 1990 Miami Herald interview as stating "We're losing badly the War on Drugs. You have to legalize drugs to win that war. You have to take the profit away from these drug czars."

However, there is a possibility that Sessions could try to override this by repealing the Rohrabacher-Farrr Amendment. Needless to say, the man who said "I reject the idea that America will be a better place if marijuana is sold in every corner store." is going to be one of the largest hurdles to overcome.

Canada backtracking on legalization

For the Canadian stocks talked about in this book, the path appears to be smoother, but that doesn't mean bumps in the road can't happen. Whilst recreational marijuana legalization is scheduled for summer 2018, a lot can happen between now and then. Originally supports had hoped for an announcement for July 1 2018, which happens to be Canada Day, but Prime Minister Trudeau ruled that out in December 2017. Any further delays could lead to decreased industry confidence, which will no doubt have a negative effect on market sentiment and share prices of Canadian based stocks.

Public Sentiment Regarding Legal Marijuana

The sentiment is an overlooked part of analyzing a market. General public opinion is a huge factor in both the short and long-term growth of an industry. Often, short-term price changes are decided mostly on sentiment rather than any fundamental changes with a company or industry. We have seen this multiple times with cryptocurrency and the price volatility associated with that particular industry.

In February 2018, Marijuana Business Daily released their "Marijuana Business Factbook", an almanac of statistics relating to the marijuana industry and its potential growth going forward. The big takeaway is that they have now upgraded their projection from 3x growth to 4x growth by 2021.

The second biggest indicator that we could be poised for solid long-term gains is the public opinion poll carried out in the research. 59% of Americans now favor legalizing marijuana, a number that continues to creep up every year. In addition to this, only 32% of Americans are now fundamentally *opposed* to legal marijuana. Once again, going by age, the younger generation is more fervent in their support.

In total, there have been 5 major opinion polls in the past year alone, and their results all say the exact same thing. The majority of the US population is in favor of legalization, both on a medical and recreational level. One survey, by Quinnipac, solely focused on medical marijuana, and a whopping 94% of respondents supported the idea.

An Analysis of 12 Marijuana Stocks

In this section we take a look at a number of marijuana stocks, the companies behind them, and how they plan to capture their part of the marijuana market. Not all of these are pure play stocks, so not all of their revenue is directly tied to marijuana, but all of worth investigating, to say the least. As always, I am not recommending you buy any of the stocks listed here.

It should be noted that although a number of these are Canadian stocks, some do trade on OTC exchanges in the United States.

Scotts Miracle-Gro ($SMG)

Price at time of writing: $89.13

Probably the most well known of the "marijuana stocks" in this list. We should note off the bat that the marijuana component only makes up around 10% of Scotts total business, but this is an ever growing proportion. We previously mentioned the 2015 purchase of General Hydroponics, which will be a key factor in Scotts expansion into the marijuana sector going forward. General Hydroponics provides both consumer and industry indoor growing solutions, which will be huge if recreational marijuana is legalized on a wider business, and could result in a rise in the company's important to Scotts bottom line..

A dip in price at the beginning of 2018 was to be expected, as the lawncare business that makes up 90% of Scotts revenue is extremely seasonal. As the hydroponic portion of the business grows this will likely even out as the nature of hydroponics make it a seasonproof growing tool. Grow wise, further expansion into other aspects of the marijuana business may well be on the cards, and a company like Scotts has deeper pockets than most, thus would be able to afford any short term losses as a result of growing pains that these new ventures can often cause.

Another area of interest for long term investors would be Scotts extremely strong fundamentals and track record within the sector. The company is now 150 years old and has been a household name for many years before legalized marijuana was on the radar of most Americans.

GW Pharmaceuticals

Price at time of writing: $126.06

The biotech giant from Britain is one of the more well known "marijuana stocks" although unlike many of the others here, they do not participate in the growing or distribution market. GW's usage of marijuana is in the manufacturing of drugs known as cannabinoids, in which marijuana is a key component.

Their current flagship product is Sativex, the first cannabis based treatment to receive FDA approval in the United States. Sativex helps treat the symptoms of Multiple Sclerosis (MS) including pain relief, bladder control and involuntary muscle spasms. The success of Sativex has helped GW rise into the ranks of one of the top performing biotech stocks of the last few years.

GW is now betting big on Epidiolex, a CBD based drug that will help epilepsy sufferers, particular those with child onset epilepsy. In discussions with insurance providers, it is planned that if approval is gained, the drug will be available to over 200 million Americans on their healthcare plans. As previously discussed, developing new drugs can take a long time when you factor in everything from lab development, multiple testing phrases and the huge amount of red tape that comes with trying to get FDA approval.

GW received good news though in December 2017 when they revealed that the FDA had approved their New Drug Application for Epidiolex. This doesn't mean they have the all clear to manufacture and sell the drug yet, but it is certainly a step in the right direction. If the FDA approves the drug in the middle of 2018, the timeline will mean that the drug could be on the market within 3 months.

There is another cannabinoid in GW's pipeline as well, the lesser reported Cannabidivarin (CBDV) which is being developed to help treat epilepsy in adults. There have already been tested on CBDV in treating symptoms of autism in young children. However the development is in the early stages and therefore will have no bottom line impact on GW's revenue this year, and approval by the end of next year is also unlikely.

GW's strong fundamentals have led to some financial analysts labeling it "the most secure marijuana stock". Whilst biotech as an industry operates different to pure marijuana stocks, there may be additional benefits as any federal rulings on recreational marijuana use are unlikely to affect the development of cannabinoid based drugs. Overall, compared to some of the riskier plays here, GW offers the conservative investor an easy entry point into the marijuana market.

Kush Bottles ($KSHB)

Price at time of writing: $5.50

Kush Bottles is a marijuana company, that doesn't actually deal with the growing or handling of the plant at all. The California firm provides and distributes the materials needed to grow marijuana and marijuana products at an industrial level. This includes everything from child-safe packaging, labels, vape pens, cannabis pipes and other paraphernalia. Their flagship product is a plastic tube to safely store a pre-rolled marijuana joint. While this may seem fairly inconsequential, pre-rolled joints are a big feature of legal marijuana that did not exist when it was still illegal. Every marijuana dispensary worth its salt features pre-rolled joints heavily, and being able to capture this part of the market could mean big things for Kush Bottles going forward. Currently, the firm boasts over 4,000 legal marijuana customers, and in a sales presentation July, stated they sold over 1 million of their pre-rolled tubes to dispensaries every month.

The company is still very much in its early stages, with only $18.8 million in recorded revenue in 2017. However, the firm is not up to it neck in debt like many smaller marijuana companies which can be seen as a big positive. In its first 3 years of business, the firm has acquired 3 competitors already in the form of Dank Bottles, CMP Wellness and Roll-Uh-Bowl.

Growing pains will be in line with many other marijuana firms regarding basics like tax deductions and banking regulations.

Cronos Group ($MJN)

Price at time of writing: $9.20CAD

Cronos Group takes a slightly different approach to the industry. Rather than focusing its effects on cultivation or distribution of marijuana, the firm acts as an investment group for Canadian medical marijuana companies. The firm currently owns 3 marijuana companies outright and has partial holdings in 3 more.

Cronos is betting big on the proposed legalization in summer 2018. Legalization would give a boost to all of its companies, and the diversified nature of its investment mean it can withstand additional competition in certain parts of the industry such as growing. Competition is still a concern industry-wide, and short-term effects could be an increase in advertising spend as it fights for market position. However, this should not be a concern for those looking to hold long-term.

Another thing to note is that Cronos and its subsidiaries are not yet profitable, so investors can expect additional share issuances. The amount of shares in play has increased by a factor of 10 within the last 4 years, and with each new issuance comes a devaluing in the current value of shares. In terms of short-term viability, Cronos has a lot of eggs in the legalization basket, so it may be worth holding off on pulling the trigger until that matter is sorted out.

Emerald Health Therapeutics ($EMH)
Price at time of writing: $6.53 CAD

The Canadian pharmaceuticals company, formerly known as T-Bird Health Inc. is another company with more of a focus on the medical marijuana space. The company producers cannabis oils, dried cannabis as well as marijuana based health solutions in capsule form.

The firm is more research based than other medical cannabis producers and makes an effort to identify the most important qualities in each marijuana strain, before isolating those properties and creating new products from them.

Growth towards the end of 2017 was fueled by a purchase of additional growing space and the company was also given a recent upgrade to Tier 1 by the Toronto Stock Exchange. This indicates solid financial reporting practices and generally shows the company is well run.

One additional point of interest with EMH is their adoption of blockchain technology. Blockchain technology is the underlying digital ledger which allows cryptocurrency to function securely among other things. EMH will be using the technology to help develop supply chain and ecommerce solutions in a joint venture with DMG Blockchain Solutions. The venture will be named CannaChain Technologies and as expected, will focus its initial efforts on the legal cannabis industry.

Medical Marijuana Inc. ($MJNA)

Price at time of writing: $0.11

Famous for being the first publicly traded marijuana company in the United States. The stock has been trading for over 4 years, which makes it a grandfather in a space seeing new firms pop up every week. The firm operates in both the marijuana and industrial hemp fields. This includes selling hemp oil, CBD oil and other cannabinoids aiming to treat various health ailments.

Because none of these oils are THC based, MJNA operates more on the legal side of things than other companies. CBD oil, for example, is legal in all 50 states. However, recent FDA rulings may complicate this matter, as the FDA wishes to regulate CBD based products due to them containing miniscule amounts of THC. This continued fight led to share prices tumbling more than 70% in 2017, and there doesn't seem to be much potential good news on the horizon for the company.

The company operates a number of subsidiaries, which has led to small calling it a small scale marijuana ETF. The interesting structure of these companies and exactly how their profitability works is a factor that could lead to investor caution. There is also their large numbers of shares issued (3 billion at time of writing) which may also be a factor in looking elsewhere for solid marijuana investments. As such, MJNA looks at this stage to be a highly speculative play at best, and one probably suited more towards serious investors with much experience in penny stocks.

MedReleaf ($MEDFF)

Price at time of writing: $18.00 CAD

MedReleaf is another Canadian company just spends more of its focus on the medical marijuana side of things. As a manufacturer and producer of cannabis oils and dried cannabis, it targets those holding medical marijuana cards. Their 2017 IPO was North America's largest marijuana IPO yet.

The medical marijuana industry in Canada continues to grow at a rate of 10% per month, that's right, not per year but per month. Cannabis oils are growing even faster than that at a rate of around 16% per month. Oils have a much higher margin than dried cannabis, and therefore MedReleaf is able to grow its earnings at a much higher rate than competitor companies who only focus on the dried plant. The company controls roughly 45% of the cannabis oil market in the country, and with their expanded production facility, this percentage could well go even higher.

This has led the company to post decent financial numbers in the past few years. Although the company is not yet as profitable as others like Canopy and Aphria, it continues to be well run and has not yet diluted shares to raise capital like some of its competitors.

MedReleaf's growth plans include expanding their Bradford production facility to 86,000 square feet. This will allow the company to keep up with the ever increasing demand, especially if the legalized recreational marijuana bill passes this year. Their focus on higher margin products, and positioning to take advantage of any proposed legalization makes MedReleaf a very exciting prospect to watch. Most marijuana companies aren't profitable and are betting on the future rather than the present. MedReleaf is one of the rare exceptions to this rule.

Organigram Holdings ($OGRMF)

Price at time of writing: $3.30

Based in New Brunswick, Organigram is one of only two companies (the other being marijuana giant Canopy Growth) with a license to produce marijuana in the province. Why this is important, is that New Brunswick is the only Canadian province with fully legal recreational marijuana use. This led to an almost 200% increase in the number of patients that Organigram serves, with this total projected to rise further in the next 12 months. All of this comes before nationwide legalization currently scheduled for summer 2018.

With estimated produce levels topping 65,000 kilograms a year, the firm shows that it means business. All this comes from just a single production facility, which Organigram plans to expand in 2018. As well as moving into higher margin strains of marijuana. The company also has a dried cannabis sales arm, although the growth of that element of the business has been slow.

This makes Organigram a prime target for a buyout from one of the larger corporations. With a market cap of $400 million, along with its previous connections and licenses, one of the bigger firms may well be taking a look at Organigram as a way to enter New Brunswick. The company also has an agreement in place to supply Prince Edward Island with 1 million grams a year which will work out in an additional $7-9 million in sales.

Potential problems include the ability to scale their operations that quickly, especially when marijuana companies are in somewhat of an arms race to increase their production yield as fast as possible. Being first to market when the recreational legalization deal is made will be huge, and Organigram is competing against some heavy hitters in this respect. Their current agreements alone though make them well worth checking out.

Update: A February press release noted that OrganiGram had received additional licenses to expand their production facilities. Construction of a new facility with estimated 65,000 kilogram yield per year is now due to begin in April 2018. This is very positive news for the company going forward.

Canopy Growth Corp ($TWNJF)

Price at time of writing: $22.35

Canada's Canopy Growth Corp is a big player which currently holds around a 20% market share.

Canopy has been quick to expand, and last year purchased Mettrum Health in a deal which included 2.4 million square feet of land with the capacity for growing marijuana.

Obviously, the big external factor will be whether Canada passes legal recreational marijuana in the summer of 2018 as is expected. Currently, there don't seem to be too many hurdles in the way, and Prime Minister Justin Trudeau is leading the charge himself. One important factor to note is that the proposed tax rate for the newly legalized marijuana is much lower than any of the state tax rates we have seen in the United States so far. This will allow marijuana to be priced at more competitive rates, and eliminate competition from the black market, which has been a thorn in the side of some states like Washington.

This is combined with the number of Canadian medical marijuana increasing by a staggering rate of almost 10% per month. Canopy's Canadian presence is one of the factors that helped it overtake GW Pharmaceuticals as the world's largest marijuana stock by market cap in November 2017.

Canopy also exports dried marijuana to many European countries that have legalized the drug including the Netherlands.

One factor to watch with Canopy is if the new legislation brings about an influx of competition in the space. While this is to be expected, it remains to be seen what effect this will have on Canopy stock prices going forward. Needless to say though, for the time being, Canopy can safely say it holds the position as King of the Legal Marijuana industry.

General Cannabis Corp ($CANN)

Price at time of writing: $4.12

General Cannabis Corp has a wide range of business including consulting, advisory, marketing, and management services to the marijuana industry. Their holdings include a 3 acre property in Colorado, as well as a branding and marketing firm that targets the marijuana industry.

Their website doesn't really tell you more than that, using terms like "trusted partner" and "turn your dreams into reality." rather than making more concrete statements about what the company can do for potential clients. The homepage also features a stock ticker, and the company Instagram account, which are two facets of business that don't usually appear side by side.

The balance sheets are rather alarming with less than $300,000 in assets and over $4.5 million in liabilities. That ratio alone is frankly terrifying. The company also made a $9 million loss in the past year with just $2 million in gross sales. With numbers like this, it's hard to say just how much of a future the company has, and it obviously cannot continue to make big losses like this. Overall, I can't see much upside for General Cannabis Corp and its investors going forward.

Aphria ($APH)

Price at time of writing: $16.08CAD

Aphria concentrates on providing hydroponic solutions for medical marijuana. The company currently has a partnership with the Canadian government and this is part of the reason the stock tripled in price during 2017. The company currently has around 40,000 patients and a fledgling nationwide distribution system.

Aphria is one stock that defies industry norms in terms of producing positive revenue growth and ending the financial year in the black. Strong fundamentals like this make the stock a promising one to monitor as we go forward. Revenue increased by 62% last year and the last quarter's earnings were also positive. The ability to not only promise a product, but actually deliver on a profitable one, is something that could well indicate strong long term potential.

The company also acquired Broken Coast Cannabis for $230 million (note: this was a largely stock funded deal with only a small fraction coming in cash), which gives them better access to Canada's West Coast. Late January also brought news of the acquisition of Nuuvera in a huge $826 million cash and stock deal. The deal was made with the intention of moving growth beyond the Canadian borders, and international expansion seems to be on the cards. Nuuvera was already working with parties in Germany, Israel and Italy to explore distribution opportunities for newly legalized medical marijuana. The Italian market alone is worth around $9 billion annually and Nuuvera is one of the few foreign companies with a license to export goods to Italy. This aggressive growth strategy is one that may put Aphria into the big leagues in an industry that is consolidating at rapid rates.

February brought news of an international supply chain agreement with Cannabis Wheaton. This will help both companies advance their distribution strategies in order to keep up with the ever increasing demand.

This may be bigger news for Wheaton than Aphria in the short term due to the company's smaller size, but working agreements like this show that co-operation on future projects, which may have more benefit to Aphria, is on the cards.

Corbus Pharmaceuticals ($CRBP)

Price at time of writing: $7.05

Corbus is focused strictly on the medical side of the marijuana equation. It's currently betting big on its drug Anabasum. Anabasum aims to treat sclerosis and has done well in initial trials. There are also plans to trial the same drug in relation to Lupus.

After a meteoric rise at the beginning of 2017, with prices soaring over 500% in the first 3 months, the stock began to cool off towards the end of the year. Like most smaller cap companies, Corbus is yet to be profitable. Current cash flow analysis indicates the company has enough money to continue its day-to-day operations into Q4 2019. Although this could be extended with a stock offering.

The obvious concern is whether Corbus is a one trick pony, and as of right now, that's probably a correct assumption to make. If Anabasum doesn't get approved then its back to square one, and with a lack of profitability, that may well be it for Corbus. However, if Anabasum continues to produce positive results and ends up getting FDA approval, then Corbus will move on to bigger and better things, much to the delight of investors.

Marijuana ETFs

At the time of writing, there are 3 approved marijuana ETFs in North America, with two more scheduled for launch in February 2018. For those of you looking for a more low-risk, hands off option for investing in marijuana stocks, one of these ETFs may be exactly what you are looking for. That's before the obvious advantages of ETFs like only paying 1 commission vs. Upwards of 15 commissions if you were to buy the individual stocks.

In December 2017, ETFMG Alternative Harvest ETF became the first ETF to list on a US stock exchange. We have previously mentioned this ETF and discussed how their decision to pivot from Latin American real estate to the marijuana industry may be cause for concern. The move comes with buying popular marijuana stocks such as Canopy, Aurora and GW Pharma.

The price action after the move was heavily in the positive direction, just take a look at this chart from Bloomberg after the decision to buy marijuana stocks occurred.

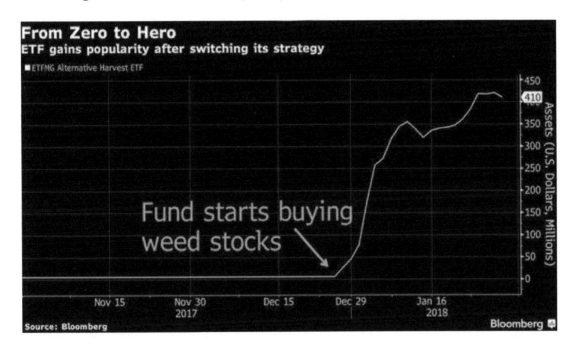

What you may not know about this ETF that's been in the news so much over the past 2 months is that it's Custodian Bancorp is considering dropping the ETF due to its drastic switch in the business model. This move also appears to be based on the uncertain future of federal level marijuana legalization. There is, of course, the probability that if Bancorp does drop the ETF, that another bank will step in and fill its shoes. However, if they cannot find a replacement, the ETF will have to be liquidated.

Switching focus is not necessarily uncommon for an investment group to do, however, it is the complete industry pivot that is something we must examine. As indicated by the graph above, the fund remained relatively flat before the move to marijuana, so their track record in other industries isn't something we can verify. The next 6 months will be interesting and it remains to be seen if they can replicate their initial short term success.

Horizons Marijuana Life Sciences ETF ($HMMJ)

Price at time of writing: $18.76CAD

Launched on the Toronto Stock Exchange in April 2017, this ETF has been one of the top performers since the beginning. Posting gains of over 85% in 2017, although it has experienced some pullback to start 2018.

The fund focuses more on the medical marijuana industry and has a policy of not buying any companies that focus strictly on recreational marijuana in the US or Canada. However, this view is likely to change depending on how quickly legalization occurs in both countries. You can certainly expect investments in recreational marijuana companies if legalization goes through in Canada this year as expected.

The fund holds 30 stocks, which is generally considered a low number for an ETF, and as such your diversification is lower than other ETFs, making it naturally a riskier proposition. Another factor to examine is the proportion of the fund that is held in the top 20 stocks. In the case of HMMJ, the top 10 (not 20) stocks make up over 80% of the fund, which is somewhat concerning for the low-risk investor. The top 4 holdings are naturally the large Canadian medical marijuana companies, namely Canopy Growth Corp, Aurora Cannabis, Aphria and MedReleaf.

Some investors would like to see additional diversification in form of biotech companies and cannabinoid firms, although these companies tend to be in the slower growth rate sphere due to the long process of their drugs receiving approval, and therefore aren't without risk themselves.

HMMJ is certainly the most fundamentally sound marijuana ETF, and with a management fee of 0.75% plus sales tax, it's not an expensive one for the retail investor to get involved with either. If you are looking for a lower-risk way to enter the marijuana market, this could well be it.

Horizon Marijuana Growers ETF ($HMJR)

Price at time of writing: Not yet launched

Another ETF by Horizon, this one focuses on the growing and cultivation part of the industry in particular. This particular ETF consist mainly of small cap companies with upside potential and aims to take advantage of increased demand for marijuana across Canada pending the legalization of recreational marijuana.

One interesting thing to note about this ETF is that 20% of the holdings will be made up of overseas companies, in the first instance, this will be growers from Australia. This could certainly help negate some of the risks that comes with banking on summer 2018 Canadian legalization. The first group of holdings has CANN Group as the largest with 7.24% with its Australian growing company AusCANN making up a slightly lower portion of the fund.

The fund will have a 0.85% management fee. So if you're someone who has huge faith in the demand for growers, then this ETF might be a smart play for a low-risk investor who doesn't want to go in on just one or two individual companies.

Evolve Marijuana ETF ($SEED)

Price at time of writing: Not yet launched

Scheduled for Launch on February 12th 2018, this will be the 4th ETF in North America and will trade on the Toronto Stock Exchange. Evolve Funds Group CEO Raj Lala stated the fund aims to take advantage of "a 60-per-cent compounded annual growth rate in the next few years." It is unclear just which sector of the market the ETF will target, but they have stated they will be investing in both domestic and global marijuana companies. The initial focus will be on the Canadian market, but as legalization gets more traction worldwide, expansion beyond its borders will occur. You can fully expect that the big Canadian companies like Aurora, Canopy and Cronos Group will be among the initial portfolio of holdings.

It has also been stated that the fund will have a management fee of 0.75% per year. Evolve has a strong track record and their first venture into the marijuana market will be an interesting one to monitor. Another Marijuana ETF, run by Redwood Investments is due to launch around the same time period.

Can non-Canadian residents buy Canadian stocks?

As you may have seen, a large number of these stocks are listed on the Toronto Stock Exchange, Canada's largest stock exchange. Some are also listed on US regulated exchanges, which means you can buy them using a local broker, or broker who supports US stocks if you are based outside of the US.

You can also buy Canadian stocks from many online brokers including TD Ameritrade, Schwab and E-Trade, however, there may be higher commissions than US stocks when using these sites. Some of the commissions can be as high as $19 per trade. I advise you to check your broker's rates for Canadian stocks, and it may be easier to call them on the phone than dig through the website looking for rates. At the time of writing, only Schwab uses the same rates for both US and Canadian stocks.

It should be noted that some online brokers do not directly buy Canadian stocks, they instead purchase pink sheets as a proxy for the stock. These pink sheets will have a 1:1 value, but trading volume will be lower than the volume on Canadian exchanges. So this is something to look out for if you are planning on buying or selling large amounts, and I would recommend double checking with your broker before executing any trades.

The other thing to note is if you are using a US broker, you may be looking for a different stock symbol than the ones listed in this book. These symbols will usually be 5 letters long, so make sure to check your particular stock's corresponding US symbol before you accidentally buy shares of the wrong company.

Should I still invest in Marijuana Stocks if I'm fundamentally against marijuana as a drug?

Obviously, some more socially conservative investors will have an opposition to marijuana stocks. Many of these companies will fall into the same category of "sin stocks" as alcohol and tobacco companies, and if you are morally opposed to investing your money in these kinds of companies, that's OK.

On top of that, as we have previously discussed, marijuana still remains illegal at a federal level, and there are a number of ramifications that come alongside this decision. It should be noted, that obviously any publicly traded marijuana stock is conducting its business within the eyes of the law, this goes for small cap stocks traded on OTC exchanges as well as larger cap ones on the NYSE or the Toronto Stock Exchange.

However, that doesn't mean you have to miss out on one of the hottest asset classes in the past 10 years. There are still a number of companies that are focused more on the beneficial side of marijuana. These would be companies more on the biotech side of things that are focused on utilizing marijuana and components like CBD, to cure help diseases.

Firms such as GW Pharmaceuticals fit this bill well, with their epilepsy drug Epidiolex. We should reiterate at this point that CBD, unlike THC, does not have any capacity to alter one's mindstate, so users will not experience a regular marijuana "high". There is also InSys Pharmaceuticals, who we have discussed previously, and their subsidiary company SubSys which is developing a drug called Syndros to assist in helping weight loss associated with chemotherapy.

Other companies like Scotts Miracle Gro have a small marijuana element to their business and as such, can be solid plays without needing to tell your friends you bought a "pot stock". These are just a few options if you wish to get a part of the pie, without committing yourself to a pure marijuana stock and going against your own individual moral code.

Conclusion

Well there we have it, an introduction to the exciting world of marijuana stocks, and the potential benefits of investing in them. Like I said before, this market is projected to triple in size in the next 3 years, and there is enormous opportunity across many factors of the industry. From growing to manufacturing and distribution and real estate, marijuana is going to make a lot of people rich in the few years.

Like any industry, there is risk involved, and I urge you to do additional research on top of what you've read in this book. There are also a number of external factors to consider, many of these are out of the control of the companies they will affect, so it would be wise to monitor any legalization news closely.

Marijuana is still in the early stages as an asset class, so as such many of these companies should be looked at as more speculative plays, similar to cryptocurrency in this respect. Therefore they should not make up a significant portion of your portfolio.

I hope you've enjoyed what you have read in this book, and if you do decide to invest in marijuana stocks, I hope you make a lot of money.

Finally, if you learned something from this book, I'd appreciate it if you left a review on Amazon.

Thanks,
Stephen

Stock Market Investing for Beginners: The Keys to Protecting Your Wealth and Making Big Profits In a Market Crash

By Stephen Satoshi

"Be fearful when others are greedy, and greedy when others are fearful." - Warren Buffett

Introduction

Since the end of the previous market crash in 2009, the S&P 500 is up over 290%. President Donald Trump is predicting a "middle class miracle" which will be fueled by tax cuts. It might seem like sunshine and roses out there for the stock market, and for the financial outlook of the United States.

However, those in the know, are sensing a very different financial future in America.

You see there are a growing number of signs that indicate that a horrific financial event may be on our horizon. This event isn't a something that is potentially a decade or two away either.

In fact, many experts are predicting a full scale crash within the next 3 years.

Which fortunately gives you just enough time to get your affairs in order.

You see, we've been through this before.

We had the 2008 crash fueled by the sub prime mortgage crisis, which then led to the housing market crash. We had the DOTCOM bust in the early 2000s, and the initial tech stock crash of 1990 preceded by the junk bond crash before that. These are just the major events in our lifetime. And we've not even begin to discuss the great depression of the 1930s, an incident that rocked America's economy to the very core.

What we learned from each of these horrific financial events is that a select small group of investors not only manage to weather the storm successfully, but actually come out even stronger than before.

In this book you'll learn not only how to balance your portfolio to minimize the impact of a crash, but you'll also discover the assets which thrive when traditional markets fail. In addition to learning about how to diversify your portfolio with non-traditional assets. How to legally store some of your wealth offshore. As well as further steps you can take to prepare for a financial crisis, which goes beyond mere finances and asset protection.

Because after all, this could be a game of survival.

So without further ado, let the games begin.

Stephen

What are the major indicators that tell us a downturn is coming?

I should note here at the outset that this is not a political book, and I have done my utmost to leave politics out of it. However, there are certain government acts and policies that do and will have real effects on America's financial future over the next few years, so to not mention them would be a disservice to my readers.

Many of these won't be known to you if you live in an affluent part of the country. The New Yorks, Californias and Washington DCs if you will. However, those in the heartland of America will be starting to witness these with their own eyes sooner rather than later. And what hits the heartland first, eventually spreads to the richer areas of the USA.

Wages

The average US worker hasn't experienced real wage growth in 30 years using inflation adjusted measures. In fact, there are fewer working age citizens in employment now than there were in 1975. These are the people who played a major part in Trump winning the election. Unfortunately, the President sold them short on his promise to "Make American Great Again" not by any nefarious means, but because he simply doesn't have the ability to do so, nor does he have the support in Congress to pass any of his more ambitious plans.

Trump's tax plan promised to increase take home pay for the middle class. However, study's by the bipartisan Tax Policy Center indicate that whilst the plan is a net positive for business owners, it is near worthless for employees who will see their taxes actually *increase* under the plan. This leads to increased personal and national debt. Where this is frankly terrifying is that this debt will increase *exponentially*, and exponential growth of anything is not sustainable.

Quantitative Easing

You've probably heard of quantitative easing (QE) by now. Put simply, QE is when federal banks introduce new money into the overall money supply and use this money to buy stocks and bonds. This then causes inflation, which most economists agree is necessary in small amounts in an optimal economy. The theory behind QE is is that price levels are expected to lag behind monetary inflation and thus everyone has a marginally better standard of living than before. QE is usually performed to prevent potential deflation in an economy, where people's money becomes worth more than the year before, and results in a scenario where citizens actively hoard their money without spending it. In an ideal economy, this is bad because no one is paying for goods and services.

Now how does this all relate to an impending financial crisis? Well, the Fed is currently reducing its bond holdings by $10 billion per month, a number that will rise to $50 billion per month at the end of the initiative, that's $600 billion per year less on the Fed's balance sheet. This currently decrease will lead to an increase in interest rates, and in an economy which is more reliant on debt than ever, eventually leads to the bubble bursting.

But enough with the down and gloom, what we can do is act. You can prepare your portfolio is be as "recession proof" as possible. In later chapters, I'll discuss specific assets that can protect you when traditional markets are turned on their heads. We'll also be talking about proper precautions you should take to be ready for a worst case scenario.

Housing Demand vs. Supply

This ties into our point about wages, and we saw this one come to prominence during the last market crash. A house is obviously the biggest asset that the majority of people own. So when the supply of housing begins to outstrip demand, this generally indicates that the economy is slowing down, wages aren't keeping up with house prices, and that people have less disposable income than before. This not only happened in the 2008 crash, the recessions in the 70s, 80s and 90s were all preceded by an oversupply of housing.

How to prepare for a stock market crash

One vital thing to be aware of is that a stock market crash *will* happen. It's not a matter of if, it's a matter of when. It could be next week, it could be in 3 years time, but it will happen. On average a significant market downturn occurs once a decade. The last major downturn was in 2007 and 2008, so we're right on cue for the next one.

Live within your means

No one magically starts spending beyond what they can afford. These habits creep up over time. So if you haven't got a handle on your finances, meaning you don't know exactly how much is going out and coming in each month, then this should be your first port of call.

More importantly, identify and cut back on unnecessary expenses, especially recurring monthly ones that you don't need or don't use, like magazine, newsletter or physical product subscriptions.

Minimize debt obligations

Simply put, stop financing things you don't need. Having a mortgage is one thing, but financing multiple cars when you can buy a used model for a fraction of the price, and having huge monthly credit card bills are things you can and should avoid. Owing money to multiple people doesn't get any easier in the event of a market crash.

Cash on hand

This is what you'll need for a nightmare scenario if you (God forbid) lose your job. The latest reports indicate that a staggering 69% of Americans have less than $1,000 in savings. Hopefully, this isn't you, but if it is, concentrate on banking a good proportion of your paycheck into a rainy day fund for emergencies.

Your ideal safety net should be a minimum of 1 year's worth of living expenses accessible right now. That means in nothing more than a regular savings account. You should save your money as aggressively as possible to get to this point. 2 years is even more optimal if there is a true financial crisis. You don't need anything more than 3 and at that point you're better off having your excess money in other forms

Acquire multiple streams of income

Having a solid second stream of income is a Godsend should your primary stream be taken away from you. Anything from ecommerce to real estate investments to niche market likes restoring classic cars can be a healthy extra source of cash each month. This second stream of income, no matter if it's a mere $500 a month, will be vital if you are unfortunate enough to lose your job as a result of a market downturn.

Ensure the majority of your investments have stop losses or trailing stops

We'll cover this in more detail later on in the book, but at the very least you should have stop loss orders on your major holdings. That way you limit your exposure in the event of an all out crash.

How diversified should you be?

We've come a long way since Benjamin Graham's groundbreaking book *Security Analysis* in 1934, and while the legendary investor is still right about many things he wrote in that text, his diversification strategy of 50% stocks 50% bonds is a bit outdated to say the very least.

The assessment wasn't necessarily incorrect because at the time, both stocks and bonds were overwhelmingly cheap, after all, we have to remember the book was written off the back of the 1929 crash, and there were few other assets available to consumer investors other than gold.

We've seen additional diversification since with cash and commodities being two more emerging asset classes. This led to politician and Libertarian icon Harry Browne recommending a 25% split between cash, stocks, bonds and commodities. This included annual rebalancing based on market factors.

We can break this down even more and discuss diversification within each asset. For example with cash, should you only own domestic currency or foreign currency as well? Many analysts now recommend owning at least a few thousand dollars worth of foreign currency as an insurance against a collapse by the dollar.

Now, if you live outside the US, having a few thousand in US dollars is going to come in handy in more ways than one. I should note that due to changes in international money laundering regulations, it is now much harder to open foreign bank accounts as a US citizen, so I would recommend exchanging your money for cash bills as this will be the easiest way for you to get your hands on foreign money.

Within commodities, you have gold, silver, oil among many others. Gold and silver have traditionally held strong during financial crises, and I would always recommend owning the physical property rather than gold shares or mining contracts. Remember, tangible assets you can hold in your hand always do well when paper assets like stocks are performing badly.

There are other stores of value to think about like art or antiques, tangible assets that you can liquidate easily if needed. Real estate is another, and owning at least one house is key (remember if you're still paying for it, you don't own it - yet). There's also farmland ownership as both a beneficial tax strategy and legitimate investment vehicle. Big time investors like Jim Rogers, for example, are extremely bullish on farmland as an asset class. Then there's the opinion of Dr. Marc Faber, who recommends farmland for a somewhat different reason "when the war comes, the bombs will predominantly fall on urban areas."

Cryptocurrencies could be considered a brand new asset class all to themselves. They are a speculative one, and one with a lot of market volatility, but definitely something worth owning. Even if they make up a tiny portion of your own portfolio. Within cryptocurrency, you don't have to get too diversified if your move is purely a hedge. Owning some Bitcoin and Ethereum will do for this purpose. While we don't have any real data on how cryptos will perform during a crisis as Bitcoin has only been around as an asset since 2010, we can predict they will be negatively correlated or uncorrelated to traditional markets. Needless to say, with continued institutional involvement, cryptocurrencies have never been more legitimate as an investment vehicle and it won't be long before all the best investors portfolios will at least contain *some* cryptocurrency. We'll be doing a deep dive into cryptocurrency later on in this book.

How to save huge on blue chip stocks

One of the best ways to profit during a market crash is to utilize cash secured put options on blue chip stocks. Now if you aren't aware what options are, they are contracts that give you the right, but not the obligation to buy or sell a stock at a certain price, at a certain date.

If you don't have previous experience with options or options trading then I recommend staying away until you are more familiar but if you do, they are a useful tool to have in your arsenal during a market downturn. Essentially you make a cash offer on a stock at well below the market rate. This the equivalent of finding a beautiful property in a great location and then making a lowball offer to buy it should it ever hit the market. Your offer may never be taken up, but if it is, you've just secured a great deal on a premium property, and now you can apply this same strategy to stocks.

Now I should note at the outset that any trading with "options" in the name has a certain amount of stigma within the investing community. We are not talking about riskier naked put options here, but a more conservative investment strategy. If you believe in the long term potential of the stock, but think there will be a dip in the price in the short term, then cash secured put options are a great way to capitalize on this. Essentially you have a right, but not an obligation to buy these stocks at the lower price.

Your worst case scenario here is that you own a stock you previously wanted to own at a lower price. As these are blue chip stocks that we believe in the long term potential of, we are not assuming the traditional risk of the stock going to zero yet being obligated to buy at the higher price. However, this is still lower than the loss you would have taken if you had just purchased the stock outright at the higher price in the first place. Alternatively, the option expires worthless if the stock is still above the strike price at the date the option expires and you make a premium on the option itself in the short term.

For example, if Coca-Cola (currently trading at $43) is on your radar, you can wait until the price drops to $36 and then make an offer to buy at $33. This gives you a chance at a 25% discount from the current price and then sets you up for a strong long-term position in one of the world's most well known brands.

The one important thing to remember with cash secured puts is that you must have enough liquidity in your account to cover the entire trade. 1 option equals a minimum of 100 shares so be sure of this before you execute any trades.

Why you should consider short selling stocks

Shorting has long been a technique that the consumer level investor has overlooked and left to the "big boys" on Wall Street. For those of you unfamiliar with the term, short selling or "shorting" just refers to betting against a stock. So essentially you are betting that the stock will go *down* instead of up.

How the technical process works is that you borrow a certain number of shares from the original owner, then you sell your position the same way you would normally buy stocks, except you are selling instead of buying. At the consumer level, your brokerage platform does this automatically for you when you enter a short trade.

Some people have a moral opposition to shorting because they feel it is bad form to want a certain company's share price to go down. Really though all you are doing is spotting overvalued businesses or ones who business model is flawed in one way or another. This is how a few select investors got rich by shorting Enron in 2000. The most famous example, which is fantastically documented in the movie *The Big Short,* is Michael Burry's Scion Capital fund which began shorting the housing market in 2005 and made huge profits from the subprime mortgage crisis in the next 3 years. Burry was mocked at the time, yet his fund made investors over 400% returns in under 8 years, with his housing market bet one of the most profitable calls.

Now, I'm not suggesting you start shorting everything in sight. This would be a great way to lose money in the long term. However, shorting can be a useful hedge in terms of market turmoil, and will negate some of the losses that your portfolio will no doubt suffer.

Knowing when to short is key, and there is one pattern you should familiarize yourself with to capitalize on this opportunity. This is known as the "lower high" pattern. This is when a stock has rebounded after a dip but then peaks at a lower level than the previous peak before reversing once more. This signifies that the market is turning and we are in for a prolonged downturn.

Obviously the lower high can potentially come before a higher high, so you should set a hard stop loss above your initial short position, this is so your losses are minimal if the market does continue to rise.

If this all sounds complex, you can actually buy shorting ETFs. The two easiest ones are the ProShares Short QQQ (PSQ) which acts as an inverse of the Nasdaq 100, and the ProShares Short Financials (SEF) which acts as an inverse of the Dow Jones financial index. In other words, when these indexes go down, share prices of these ETFs go up.

For example in the 2008 crash, the PSQ was up 69% in a little over 3 months. Just a small position in this would have saved your big losses on other parts of your portfolio.

Stocks that traditionally do well during market downturns.

If you're not holding some of these, they are a great hedge when the market turns bad. Others are also solid, low risk, long term holds regardless of market conditions.

Retail

The first group of these are the giant low-cost retailers, ones that sell pretty much everything under the sun. The reason for this is demand for everyday items doesn't waver much during recessions. On top of this, those who traditionally shop at higher end retailers are hit, and therefore take their business to these lower end stores. Walmart is the big one of these, during the 2008 crisis, Walmart sales grew by 6.5% and stock prices rose 10.5% on the year, all while the S&P 500 dropped by over 30% in the same time period.

Following on from this you have the bargain basement retailers. These stores absolutely thrive when people are stretching their dollars. One such stock is Tanger Factory Outlet Centers, and their performance can be summed up in the words of CEO Steven Tanger "In good times, people love a bargain, and in tough times, people need a bargain." Outlet stores like these are also less prone to having their market share eaten away by ecommerce. If there's one area that Amazon hasn't yet penetrated, it's the deep discount market across all sectors. Consumers will still head out to their local discount store to get the cheapest toilet paper and snacks, rather than order them online.

Dollar Tree is another one stock that falls into this category and has boasted strong performance in market downturns. Discount clothing retailer Ross was yet another stock that significantly outperformed the S&P in 2008. These both could represent solid plays if you're looking to recession-proof your portfolio.

Resources

When stocks go South, resource commodities go in the other direction. Gold, silver and other mining companies thrive during bad economic periods as demand for their commodities increases. In fact, since the rise of cryptocurrencies, both the silver to gold and platinum to gold ratio are at all time lows. Both of these commodities traditionally perform very well in recessions, are tremendously undervalued at this time, and as such mining firms for these should certainly have a part in your portfolio. What's more is, the market tends to overreact to the companies themselves when you look at company valuations vs.

Valuations of the commodity they are mining. Therefore a 30% increase in gold prices could see a 50% increase in the share price of mining companies.

Precious metals have always been a global hedge against currency deflation and market crashes, and it is unlikely anything will change regarding this during the next recession.

Relaxation

You're probably thinking, "what the hell is this guy talking about?, who on Earth is relaxing during a market crash?" Well then answer me this, why did Anheuser Busch InBev grow by 39.4% in 2008? They provided the cheapest mass market beer, which in turn provides self medication and a brief escape from reality from many folks who are down on their luck. No matter what the economic conditions look like, people are still going to drink.

Even though this was the year when Anheuser Busch was bought out by InBev, revenues still grew by 5% from the previous year. Then we have the big entertainment stocks like Disney and Viacom, which also tend to do well during the lean years, because people still watch TV and although they may cut back their movie spending, that tends to be more of the Mom & Dad date night movies than the family friendly ones, which still receive decent box office numbers. After all, there's no way people aren't taking their kids to see the latest Avengers or Thor movie.

We can also add adult entertainment to this. The adult industry thrives during these years, as more people spend nights in than out of the house. Unfortunately, from a social perspective, porn usage rises with unemployment. So with increased lay offs during recessions, we also see increased click rates on adult websites, and increases in share prices of many of the adult entertainment companies.

Others

As well as stocks that thrive, we have the market neutral industries such as health care, and pharmaceuticals, as well as, tax prep services and life insurance companies. No matter what the prevailing market conditions, people will always have to do certain things. These are paying their taxes, then they will get sick, and then they will die. Usually in that order, but not always. These stocks tend not to be affected by whether the economy is going up or down and often make decent long-term holds because of this.

How to use trailing stops

Trailing stops are one of the most simple, yet underutilized investment protection tools for the consumer investor. They require a little more vigilance in the initial set up stage but the pay off for having them in place can be huge. Especially in the case of a sharp market downturn.

A trailing stop is the same as a regular stop loss order, one placed to automatically sell a stock if the price dips to a certain point, except the trigger price automatically moves in line with the stock should it move higher.

Therefore, if the stock continues to increase in price, your trigger price for the stop loss increases as well. For example, if you buy Hershey at $100, and set a stop loss at $90. You can make this a $10 trailing stop and so if the stock goes up to $105, your new stop trigger price increases to $95. Then if it goes up further to $110, your new stop trigger price is $100. At this point the worst that can happen to you if that you will break even if the stock falls back to $100, any further upward moves will see your trailing stop increase further and move you into guaranteed profit territory.

If the market falls, the stop price doesn't change, and as such you have locked in any profits. This is a great way to benefit from a rising market, while still lowering your overall risk to your portfolio.

Trailing stops aren't just available for regular stocks or ETFs, many brokers also offer them on options and futures as well. These are a great instrument to have on any long-term holds, plus any new plays you may be making in the coming months.

Holding assets offshore

There is some confusion about the legality of holding assets offshore. Due to constant negative media attention, and headlines of "tax dodging" and "tax evasion". Many people falsely believe that holding any assets outside the United States is federal tax evasion and a felony, but this couldn't be further from the truth.

The crux of the law is this, as long as you declare all of your foreign held income, and pay the necessary tax on it, everything is completely fine in the eyes of the IRS. In other words, as long as you are not explicitly "hiding" income, you will have no problem with tax authorities. I should note at the outset of this part of the book, that this is not a tax evasion strategy of any kind. All methods discussed in this section are my personal opinion and not professional tax or investment advice.

Thanks to significant changes in international money laundering regulations since the last market crash, opening foreign bank accounts is now extremely difficult for US citizens. Even countries with relatively lax banking laws often hold US citizens as persona non-grata. This is because foreign banks don't want dealings with US government bodies like the IRS.

There are a number of ways around this however and it is possible and relatively simple in fact, to open gold and silver bullion accounts offshore. You can use services such as BullionVault to store precious metals in the UK, Canada and Switzerland for example. The service has no contracts so there are no penalties for early withdrawal for example. One thing I particularly like about BullionVault's service is that you can spread your investments around multiple storage facilities without paying extra to do so.

If you are going to use an offshore gold service, be sure to check that they do not use your gold as a lending device. The other thing to check is that your gold is held off the company balance sheet as an insured, allocated asset. So in other words, if the company holding your gold goes under, creditors will not be able to reclaim your personal property as part of any bankruptcy settlement on the company itself.

Holding offshore real estate is another option. Whilst many offshore deals can be tricky due to local legislation, it is worth looking into. One thing I would recommend is buying in cash if possible with offshore deals due to the sometimes less than stellar reputation of banks in these local countries. Being in contact with a good *local* attorney is vital as well, as your attorney in your home country will not be able to offer anywhere near the same level of service in foreign jurisdictions. This includes important yet often overlooked factors like setting up local corporations is necessary and deciding whether said corporation should be held in your name or in a trust. Also, buying in local currency will get you a much better deal than a marked up property valued in US dollars.

So how do you get started? The first thing to do is decide whether you have enough assets worth protecting. There's no point spending thousands of dollars on a qualified tax specialist to minimize your tax burden if said burden is not a significant amount in the first place. If your total assets (not including your primary residence) are under $100,000 then looking offshore would not be for you.

Secondly, make sure you understand everything that is going on. This doesn't mean knowing the ins and outs of the tax codes of multiple countries, but you should at least have a grasp of where your money is going, and what purpose this will serve for your benefit. This is what separates the good offshore tax planners and wealth managers from the bad. If the person you are dealing with can't explain to you in plain English exactly what is going on, then it should be considered a red flag. Lastly, stay away from one size fits all solutions that promise to "take all your money offshore so you don't have to pay taxes". This firms largely center around charging huge amounts of money to open foreign companies in your name, and then leave you at the behest of the IRS when it emerges that you are not being tax compliant. Every situation is different, and thus you should have a tailored solution for your own.

Stocks which need a growing economy to make money

There are certain stocks that only thrive during boom periods. As such, when consumers no longer have any excess funds to spend on things that aren't considered "necessities", these stocks are the ones often hit the hardest. If you have these in your portfolio, this isn't necessarily an indication to get rid of them, but their exposure should be hedged at the very least and I recommend making portfolio readjustments based on this.

Airlines

Airline stocks traditionally do terribly during recessions. Recreational air travel is something many people cut back on during the lean years. International and domestic vacations both get hit hard, as do the share prices of the major carriers. In addition, it's an industry with very high fixed costs which doesn't benefit from the recession in the slightest. It should be noted that discount carriers are less at risk as their model is always to keep prices low and make it up on the backend with extras.

It's estimated that airlines won't be hit as hard during the next recession due to industry consolidation. This has been happening ever since the deregulation of airlines in 1978 and we've gone from having over 400 carriers in the US to just 68 today with the big 4 (American, Southwest, Delta and United) making up around 70% of the market. Holding a large percentage of your portfolio in airline stocks is still not a great move though

Restaurants

Eating out is another big cut back from consumers during periods of economic downturn. The hardest hit is often the low to mid range casual dining chains that focus less on alcohol and more on food. Chains like P.F. Chang's, Red Robin are ones to watch.

Once again, the bargain chains are less prone to market conditions. So don't go dumping your McDonald's stock yet (it could be argued that McDonald's are in the real estate business and not the restaurant business as it is). Takeout businesses like Dominoes Pizza are also less affected because their convenience model is one that still holds strong during bad times.

High end luxury items

Stocks that fall under this umbrella would be ones like Apple and GoPro, those that sell technological luxury with high price tags. Although people still buy these goods during lean years, they tend to delay their purchases and therefore the balance sheets of these companies don't look as good, causing the share prices to fall. On average, people replace their phones every 2 years for example, if they delay this to 3 years, this makes a significant impact on Apple's bottom line during a recession.

Another example of this would be Nike. If Nike customers decide they can wait another 6 months for a new pair of sneakers, this sends ripples throughout the company and in turn, leads to lower share prices. Some of the larger companies may be able to mitigate some of the risk through their international operations, but the US numbers will still drag their prices down during bad periods.

Why you absolutely must buy stocks when no one else wants to

One of the biggest factors which singles out the best investors from the masses, is their willingness to go against the crowd. To be fearful when others are greedy, and more importantly, to be greedy when others are fearful.

The latter part of the above sentence allows you to make big gains for relatively little risk. This allows you to make large gains on blue chip stocks, which have little downside and goes against the conventional "wisdom" that you must make big risks in order to get big rewards.

First, let me give you an example of what I'm talking about. In 1939, a now legendary investor named John Templeton made million by directly doing against the market. For context, the market was in freefall, millions of Americans were living in abject poverty, and what's more, Hitler's Germany had just invaded Poland, the event in which began World War II.

Market fear was at an all time high. Stock prices were at 5 or even 10 year lows. Negative sentiment was everywhere. Templeton shunned this negativity and bought $10,000 worth of stocks, the equivalent of around $170,000 today. He was no stock picking genius, he just noticed that nearly every blue chip company was greatly undervalued because of underlying market sentiment. Within 4 years he had made a 300% profit.

Fast forward to the 2008 financial crisis, banks were failing left, right and center, and this was having a snowball effect on the market as a whole. Stocks were down across the board. Some as much as 50 or even 80%. Now ask yourself this. Were these companies really now worth just 20% of their value 1 year prior? Had their business models been impacted that much? For some, the answer is maybe, for the majority the answer is a flat no. There was never a better chance to buy blue chip stocks than in 2008. Starbucks, for example, rose 1900% in the next 9 years. Apple rose 966%. Ford was another that experienced huge gains over the coming decade. Once again, had these companies had their business models impacted by the financial crisis? No, everyone else was just panicking.

Let's use another example, the 2010 BP oil spill fiasco. If you don't remember this incident, it was the largest oil spill in world history. Over 4 million barrels of oil made their way into the Gulf of Mexico, causing an environmental disaster. BP wasn't even the primary operator of the rig, it was a mere part owner, but it was BP that made the headlines, and was made the scapegoat of the incident. In the 2 weeks following the incident, BP stock fell over 50%, from $59 to $27. Now ask yourself this, was BP now really worth less than half because of one incident, albeit a serious one. The answer was of course no. Investors who bought at the bottom made 80% profits in less than a year.

If everyone in a market is pessimistic, this usually represents a great time to buy. So long as the business models of this companies doesn't change. Obviously, if cars are banned tomorrow, then Ford might not be the best buy. But bad market conditions don't make for doom and gloom everywhere.

During the next market crash, many blue chip, household name stocks will lose large percentages of their value based on nothing more than overall sentiment. If you can separate market overreaction from strong fundamentals, then you will set yourself up to make massive profits when the overall mood turns positive again.

Why you should consider farmland as a hedge

In the last decade, a very interesting investing phenomena has been quietly occurring across the United States. Institutional investors have been slowly accumulating millions of acres of farmland around the country. In fact, the University of Illnois' Investment Fund now has 10% of their $1.8 billion holdings in farmland. What's even more intriguing is that these holdings have outperformed the rest of U of I's portfolio by a factor of 2. This isn't just an American phenomenon, in England, the price of farmland has risen 800% in less than 20 years. Farmland investing is not something we saw during the 2008 crisis, so it can be considered a relatively new vehicle to hedge against a potential financial crisis.

So first of all, why is this happening? The main reason is demographics, the average age of today's land-owning farmer is 58. Many of this farmers are being offered sale-leaseback deals which gives them an injection of cash before retirement. Large institutions, on the other hand, want to take advantage of rising land prices by buying as much of this land as they can, and farms represent a great way to do this.

Secondly, the worldwide population continues to increase and is expected to peak at around 9 billion people by 2050. Tat leaves the area of available farmland per person at a continued decline for the next 30 years. This coupled with the inevitable increased demand for food has sparked this farmland rush.

Like regular real estate, investors can increase the value of the land they own. With farmland this is actually very easy, for example, investors can turn raw land into crops or pasture or converting low end crops to high end crops if the soil permits it. There's also, of course, the option of improving the standard of the buildings or infrastructure. You can also make money from selling the water rights on your property if that is an option.

So does this mean you have to give up your comfy suburban life and become a farmer? Don't worry, you don't have to. Living a labor intensive life is not for everyone, and it takes a fair amount of financial capital to even get started. There are a number of funds that allow you to get access to farmland. Cresud Sociedad (CRESY) owns over 1.25 million acres of land across Latin America and pays dividends of 3.2%. Other options include the Market Vectors Global Agribusiness ETF and Cozan Ltd. Which is the world's largest producer of sugarcane and ethanol.

Agricultural investments are certainly not short term plays, but they can be useful long-term investments. If they are not part of your portfolio right now, then you should consider them as you move forward. Remember this, in an economic downturn, that land is going to become extremely valuable, and even more so in an all out financial crisis. Plus, who doesn't want a farmhouse to escape to if it all out chaos breaks out?

How to hedge with cryptocurrency

Cryptocurrency not only represents a fantastic opportunity to build real wealth quickly, it also represents a useful hedge against traditional financial markets. They are a good hedge because they show zero correlation with the stock or bond market. Bitcoin, in particular, may well live up to its moniker of "digital gold" due to its fixed supply and deflationary nature.

The most common objection to cryptocurrency that many investors who are unfamiliar with it have, is that it is not "backed" by any central bank and therefore it must be worthless. However, this couldn't be further from the case and I'm going to show you why.

Blockchain Technology

The most important thing to understand with cryptocurrency is the blockchain technology that makes all of this possible. Blockchain technology allows for a permanent, incorruptible record of all transactions that have ever taken place, free from human errors or data loss.

One important thing to remember is that these transactions do not always have to be financial, they can be in the form of legal contracts, auditing consumer goods and file storage. However, in the case of cryptocurrency, these are financial transactions.

So we don't have to rely on a bank to tell us that a transfer of funds has taken place, we can see it for ourselves. This alone gives inherent confidence in how cryptos work because no single party can disrupt them. As we saw in the financial crisis of 2008, banks can and will mislead their customers and investors, a situation like this would just not be able to happen in the crypto market.

For a more in-depth look on how to profit from blockchain technology, in ways that go beyond merely investing in cryptos, check out my book *What the World's Best Blockchain Investors Know - That You Don't*

Things to be aware of when investing in cryptocurrency

First and foremost, cryptos are volatile. We've seen coins gain 100% in a few hours, 1000% in a few days and 10000% over the course of 1 year. The inverse has also happened with entire market drops of 20% or even 30% in a day. Therefore they should only make up a small percentage of your portfolio. Because of this volatility, I also do not recommend you set stop losses with cryptos, because it is very easy for them be triggered. Instead I recommend just taking smaller positions than you would normally do, this is because cryptocurrency is a true "never invest more than you can afford to lose" asset.

The second thing to be aware of is storing your cryptocurrency properly. This goes beyond storing it on an exchange, because exchanges are hosted on central servers and are therefore vulnerable to hacking. The best storage options would be a paper wallet or hardware wallet such as the Ledger Nano S. For full instructions on setting up a Bitcoin paper wallet go to.

http://bitaddress.org

Or http://bitcoinpaperwallet.com

How to buy your first cryptocurrency

It's actually much easier than you think to buy cryptocurrency. In fact, if you've ever bought anything online you can buy Bitcoin, Ethereum and Litecoin just as easily.

Coinbase

Based in the US, and currently largest currency exchange in the world by number of users, Coinbase allows its users to buy, sell and store cryptocurrency. The platform is undoubtedly the most beginner friendly exchange for anyone looking to get involved in the cryptocurrency market. Using the platform, once your ID is verified you can buy cryptocurrency within minutes using a debit or credit card. They currently allow trading of Bitcoin, Ethereum, Bitcoin Cash and Litecoin using fiat currency as a base.

Known for their stellar security procedures and insurance policies regarding stored currency. The exchange also has a fully functioning iPhone and Android app for buying and selling on the go, very useful if you are looking to trade.

If you sign up for Coinbase using this link, you will receive $10 worth of free Bitcoin after your first purchase of more than $100 worth of cryptocurrency.

http://bit.ly/10dollarbtc

Other exchanges

If you want to buy additional coins, you will have to do so by trading your Bitcoin, Ethereum or Litecoin in exchange for these other cryptocurrencies. The best exchange to do this and the one I personally recommend is Binance, which currently has over 100 different cryptocurrencies, each with Bitcoin or Ethereum trading pairs.

Once you've bought your coins you can keep them on the Coinbase website, or you can store them in a paper or hardware wallet, which I personally recommend.

The top 10 cryptocurrencies explained in 1 paragraph

These currencies were the top 10 by market capitalization at the time of writing (18th February 2018). Source: Coinmarketcap.com

Bitcoin (BTC)

The original and most well known crypto was born in 2009 and is a decentralized digital currency that functions as a peer-to-peer cashless transaction system. Each transaction is publicly verified on the blockchain. Bitcoin has the largest network effect of any cryptocurrency and is accepted for goods and services in over 170 countries.

Ethereum (ETH)

While Bitcoin can only be used as a store of value, Ethereum has many other functions. Ethereum has the ability to execute smart contracts, contracts that self-execute based on a number of factors. For example, you can set up a smart contract where John pays Susie 1 ETH if her account balance is less than 10ETH at the end of the month. Many other cryptocurrencies are built using Ethereum's network, which is what gives the crypto a lot of its value. Currently around 80% of the top 100 currencies are built using the Ethereum network.

Ripple (XRP)

Ripple focuses on lowering payments in the banking sector via the use of the Ripple network. Designed primarily for financial institutions like banks, Ripple is often referred to as "the banker's coin". Using Ripple makes cross-border payments cheaper than traditional methods like SWIFT. Utilizing lightning fast technology, Ripple can process payments is approximately 4 seconds. The currency was the biggest gainer in 2017 where the coin saw a rise of over 34000%.

Bitcoin Cash (BCH)

Formed as a result of a hard fork in Bitcoin's code in August 2017, Bitcoin Cash was born as a result of trying to fix the scaling problems the original Bitcoin faced and continues to face. Bitcoin Cash uses larger block sizes to try and reduce transaction time. The figurehead of the project is the somewhat controversial Roger Ver. As of February 2018, Bitcoin transaction fees were lower than Bitcoin Cash for the first time ever.

Litecoin (LTC)

Litecoin has been dubbed the "silver" to Bitcoin's "gold". Like Bitcoin, it's purely a method of transaction. However, it's a faster, more lightweight currency that processes transactions 4 times faster than the Bitcoin network and with lower fees. Litecoin benefits from being the lowest priced coin on Coinbase which is most user's first entry into the cryptocurrency market.

Cardano (ADA)

An ambitious cryptocurrency project with a team of academics behind it. Cardano essentially aims to solve all the problems that other major coins face. They use a proof-of-stake mining system which is more energy efficient than proof-of-work used by Bitcoin. The one drawback for Cardano right now is that there is no working product, so their technology is still largely in the theoretical stages. Some have sarcastically named it the "$16 billion whitepaper" due to the lack of product and high market cap.

Neo (NEO)

Dubbed "the Ethereum of China", Neo was one of the biggest crypto success stories in 2017. It too can run smart contracts and decentralized applications on the platform. Neo's access to the Chinese market can it a huge advantage when it comes to other cryptocurrencies. China has had a tumultuous relationship with cryptos and Neo having its home base there may be hugely beneficial going forward.

Stellar (XLM)

Stellar is another coin that focuses on payment processing. With a particular target on the third world, and underbanked countries rather than banks and other financial institutions. The project received a lot of attention in late 2017 and received funding from IBM. You can think of Stellar as a more decentralized version of Ripple.

EOS (EOS)

A decentralized infrastructure to run applications. Kind of like a programming language or video game engine that is reusable for different purposes. EOS is very excited for programmers and the eventual aim is to make it accessible to regular folks as well. The goal is to make decentralized apps mainstream, so normal users can benefit from them without even needing to understand how blockchain technology works.

Dash (DASH)

Rounding out the top 10 we have Dash, short for Digital Cash. Another coin focused on payment transactions, but with a twist. Dash can be used anonymously using its DarkSend protocol. There are also significant passive income opportunities that can be had by hosting a Masternode, which keeps the Dash ecosystem running. However, at the time of writing one of these nodes works out at about $60,000.

For more information on cryptocurrency along with a fundamental analysis of 12 different coins, check out my bestselling primer to the subject *Cryptocurrency: Beginners Bible*

What part should crypto play in your portfolio?

I recommend cryptocurrency make up no more than 20% of your overall portfolio, and this number should decrease as you get closer to retirement age. For example, if you are 65 or older, crypto should make up no more than 10% of your overall holdings.

I believe everyone should hold Bitcoin as part of their crypto holdings and there are a few reasons for this. The first of which is that currently, the entire market is loosely tied to the performance of Bitcoin itself. If Bitcoin is performing badly, the media headlines are focused on this and money goes out of the market. Conversely, when Bitcoin is performing well, this is what leads new money to flood into the market, as we saw in November and December of 2017 when Coinbase became the most downloaded app on the app store. The other coins tend to grow when Bitcoin's price is stagnant.

I believe in holding some Ethereum as well, because 80 of the top 100 coins by market cap are built on the Ethereum platform. You could also hedge this with some Neo if you wanted to bet big on China. There are also coins which focus on the supply chain management sector, in which blockchain technology will see its first widespread adoption cases. The main ones of these are VeChain, WaltonChain and Modum, with smaller projects like Ambrosus also worth investigating.

Are there any cryptocurrencies I recommend you avoid? The only ones I would lump in this category would be any coin that seemingly operates a pyramid scheme or guaranteed returns investment program. I previously warned readers about BitConnect and DavorCoin before both of these operations pulled exit scams causing prices to fall by over 95%. FalconCoin is another one that falls into this category and you should stay well away from.

I do recommend researching any coin you plan on investing in. Going in blind with the hope of quick huge returns is an easy way to lose money in this market. Coins with legitimate use cases and long term potential should be where your money goes.

Why you should have a grab bag ready

In a worst case scenario situation, when you need to leave home immediately, you absolutely must be prepared. This could be anything from a natural disaster like an Earthquake or Hurricane. To a terrorist attack on your neighborhood. Or even attacks by local militias in the case of a civil war. While all these scenarios are unlikely to happen to you personally, this is an insurance type situation. Hopefully, you will never need it, but if and when you do, you'll be glad you have it.

This means having a bag ready to go by the front door that you can literally grab and go at a moment's notice. The bag itself should be small, no larger than an overnight sized backpack (55L), preferably even smaller than that (around 40L). You don't want to be weighed down by its contents either. Here are 11 things this bag must contain.

1. **Identification**

In the case of police checkpoints, checking in hotels and motels, you will need some form of government ID. You should also keep photocopies of these as well. This applies to all members of your family

2. **Cash**

You'll need emergency cash in case the ATM network is affected like in the case of a cyber attack. Remember, cash is king in these kinds of situations. I recommend having at least 1 week's worth of cash, stored in different compartments in the bag. There are additional ways to keep it safe in the case of concealable belts and bras so consider spending $20 and having one of these.

3. **Medicine and first aid materials**

If you or your family take prescription medication, have an extra bottle or supply in your bag. Remember many prescription drugs lose effectiveness after 2 or 3 years so be sure to replace this regularly. In addition a small first aid kit with band aids, antiseptic ointment etc. Can be very handy in a disaster scenario. Keep an epi-pen around as well, even if no one in your family is diabetic.

4. **Contact details of friends and family**

Chances are your cellphone will be on your person, but if the battery goes dead, you should have hard copy addresses and phone numbers of your immediate family so you can get in touch with them if need be. Remember, pay phones are still in existence.

5. **Swiss army knife and other multi-tool**

You'll need a can opener for food, screwdrivers and knives for miscellaneous tasks. A Swiss army knife is a life saver in these kinds of situations. Pro tip: Get one with a torch on to save you having to carry a separate torch.

6. **Food and water**

This is space permitting but you should ideally have at least 24 hours worth of food and water in the bag. You can buy canned goods and meal pouches with a 25 year shelf life from supply stores like wisefoodstorage.com

Regarding water, this is a tricky one as ideally you want 1.5L per person per day, and that amount adds both a lot of weight and a lot of space. As an alternative, you can buy bottles with built-in filtration systems that remove the need for bottled water. These can be used with any water source you come across. You can also use water purification tablets for this purpose.

7. Basic hygiene provisions

Toothbrushes, toothpaste, some deodorant, toilet paper, disinfectant alcohol spray like Purell, and wet wipes. Just the bare necessities to make the next day or two slightly more bearable if you end up being stuck without a shower.

8. Local area map

If your phone dies or the GPS stops working, you'll need to go old school. So if you don't know how to read one, probably best learn now.

9. Cold weather clothes

Remember, if it's hot you can always take clothes off, but if it's cold you'll need something on top. One thick sweater for each family member should suffice, perhaps a wooly hat each if you have space because we lose most of our body heat through our heads.

10. Mini AM/FM radio - preferably with shortwave capability

If all cell towers are down, the radio network will be your best way to keep informed of what's going on. Find out the emergency radio frequencies and have them written down. Ensure you radio is a wind up model as well so you don't have to rely on an external power source.

11. Whistle

This might be your most important tool of all. If you immediately need to get people's attention in an emergency, then this will be your best friend.

I should also note that due to the controversial nature of the topic, I have deliberately not discussed firearms in this section.

The New Economy and Barter items

In the case of a total financial collapse, the way we look at money is going to be turned on its head. This could be as a result of hyperinflation like we saw in Zimbabwe and more recently in Venezuela.

For the initial period, we'll be no longer relying on our platinum cards to take care of day to day transactions. We'll be going old school instead. Cash will be very much king, but we should also discuss barter items as well.

Physical Gold & Silver

Not the paper gold your might buy in an ETF. I'm talking real, tangible gold and silver that you can hold in your hands and see with your own eyes. Gold has had intrinsic value for hundreds and years, and the same goes for its younger brother silver. In the event that a government introduces a new fiat currency, for example, these metals will hold their value.

This doesn't just include physical bars and coins. This can be in the form of jewelry as well.

Stores of Value

We've already discussed gold and silver, but there are other physical stores of value that would hold up well against a currency collapse. For example watches, jewelry, art and real estate all have inherent worth in their physical form. Obviously, it's easier to liquidate a watch than it is an entire home, but both will perform well even if the is a dire fiat currency situation ongoing.

Cryptocurrency

If you're unfamiliar with cryptocurrency then this might seem like a strange pick. However, we've already seen this in action in cases like Venezuela, where many citizens turned to Bitcoin in an attempt to negate the crippling effects of the country's hyperinflation. For example, the case of engineer John Villar who purchased vital medical supplies online using Bitcoin to help treat his sick wife. This was after stifling shortages within the country's own health service.

Bitcoin and other cryptocurrencies can be transacted merely by scanning a code on a smartphone, with the receiver getting the funds within a matter of minutes or even seconds. This makes them far more liquid and fungible than other items such as gold for example. You can also spend fractions of cryptocurrencies without difficulty. So this could well be a new way of bartering that we see during the next financial crisis.

Day to Day Bartering Items

Medical Supplies

Arguably the most vital of the short-term bartering goods is medical supplies. Nothing becomes more necessary in a short space of time than things like insulin, antibiotics, blood thinners and painkillers. Lower on the spectrum you have non-emergency items like antiseptic, rubbing alcohol and iodine. Even beyond bartering, having these on hand may well make you a hero to someone else during a crisis, and that alone is why they are well worth keeping around.

Salt

Salt has been long used as a barter item for over two thousand years, dating all the way back to Roman times. Not only is it a vital mineral for our bodies, it's also the number one key ingredient in cooking and preserving food. Stored in an airtight container, salt can last for decades so I would recommend having a few kilos in the house for both personal use and as a potential bartering opportunity.

Batteries

An item that's relatively light and you can keep a lot of around but one that proves invaluable in a disaster scenario. People need batteries to power flashlights, radios and walkie talkies, so having some spares on hand is going to make you very popular indeed.

Gasoline

It might seem abundant now, but what many of you may not know is that gas was actually rationed during World War II. People were only allowed 3 gallons per week, and it sent "black gold" prices soaring. Keeping a few spare gallons will be of huge benefit to you during a worst case scenario type situation as people require fuel for their vehicles as well as if they are running any generators to power their homes. If you really want to go all out you can learn to make your own biodiesel.

Conclusion

Hopefully this book has given you a better understanding of how you can protect your portfolio, your wealth and your family in the case of a significant downturn, or even an all out crash. And in some cases, how you can even come out ahead when the market turns bullish again.

By diversifying your assets, and incorporating some alternative investments into your portfolio, you can hedge against any losses your traditional investments may incur when the market turns bearish. From farmland to rare metals, to cryptocurrency, adding these to your portfolio can massively negate any losses your stocks or bonds may incur.

We've also discussed potential "worst case scenario" type options and how you can adequately prepare yourself for these. We pray that these are just hypothetical, but these are the types of situations that if you don't plan your strategy in advance, you will wish you had. Having a go bag ready by the door containing all your essential items will be something your family thanks you for if anything does go down that requires you to need it.

I hope you've enjoyed this book, and that you've learned some new things after reading it that you can apply to your own asset protection strategy. If you have then I'd really appreciate it if you left a review on Amazon.

I wish you the very best for your financial future,

Stephen Satoshi

Cryptocurrency: The 3rd Generation - Ultra Fast, Zero Transaction Fee, Futureproof Coins that Need to Be on Your Radar

By Stephen Satoshi

Introduction - Cryptocurrency as we move into 2018 and beyond

Wow, what a year 2017 was for cryptocurrency. We saw Bitcoin hit peaks of $20,000 for one coin, Coinbase became the #1 most downloaded app in the Apple store and cryptocurrency as a whole truly entered the mainstream for the first time. Now the hysteria is over (for the time being), we can examine some of the more interesting coins as we move into 2018 and beyond.

This is where cryptocurrency 3.0 comes in. If you're sat here wondering when we saw cryptocurrency 2.0, don't worry, there's a more in-depth explanation coming up. All you need to know now though is that crypto 3.0 is focused around fast, fee-less coins that allow for near instant peer-to-peer transactions. This represents the next generation of cryptocurrency, and many aim to solve some of the largest problems that plague coins like Bitcoin and Ethereum.

This book will not only allow you to uncover more details behind the technology that fuels the entire cryptocurrency market, but hopefully, also expose you to some more unheard of coins that represent interesting investment opportunities in both the short and long term. All of the coins mentioned here are pushing the boundaries of what we previously thought possible, even in a space that moves as fast as the cryptocurrency space.

It goes without saying that you should never invest more than you can afford to lose. Once again, I encourage you to do your own research beyond just reading this book, and if you do invest, I hope you make a lot of money with cryptocurrency.

Happy reading,
Stephen

The 3 Generations of Cryptocurrency

Cryptocurrency 1.0 - The Originals

The originals are the first generation of cryptocurrencies that focused solely on functioning as a peer to peer electronic monetary transaction system. These obviously started with Bitcoin back in 2008, and this tag could also apply to coins like Litecoin, Dash and Monero. This isn't to say these coins are outdated in any way. For the time being, Bitcoin is still very much the King in the cryptocurrency space. It does, however, indicate that they were designed for one purpose and function for one purpose only.

Cryptocurrency 2.0 - Smart Contracts and DApps

The next generation features cryptocurrencies like Ethereum and Neo, which are platforms that can run smart contracts, contracts that self-execute based on pre-agreed criteria being met, and also run decentralized applications (DApps). The value in these currencies comes from the network fee each smart contracts or DApp pays to use the network. You can think of these cryptocurrencies as almost like an operating system on your cellphone like Android, in which developers build applications to run on. They can have multiple purposes and can be used to run many different types of applications.

Cryptocurrency 3.0 - Beyond Blockchain

Where the 3rd generation come into this is that they actually go beyond blockchain technology. So if you're just getting your head around blockchain technology, I'm sorry, there's a new kid on the block that you absolutely should be aware of. These include coins like IOTA and RaiBlocks that can use this next generation of technology to provide near-instant, feeless transactions without the scaling problems that hamper many of the previous generation cryptocurrencies. This goes beyond just payment processing as well. It could also be used for the emerging machine-to-machine (m2m) economy, and for data integrity purposes. The one thing these currencies all have in common is that they use Directed Acrylic Graph (DAG) technology rather than blockchain, the key feature of DAGs being that they allow users to secure their own transactions, rather than having to rely on miners to verify them.

So is this the end of blockchain already?

In a word - no, blockchain technology is still very much here to stay. Platforms for building Decentralized Applications such as Ethereum and Neo aren't going anywhere anytime soon. The former accounts for around 70% of the new coins being launched this year being built on the platform.

Where DAGs and cryptocurrency 3.0 comes in is making poor cryptocurrency projects obsolete. Unless a project has a network effect like Bitcoin, and to a leer extent Litecoin - they will be hard pressed to compete in areas like transaction speed and transaction fee. It will be interesting to see just exactly how much of a market share coins like IOTA and RaiBlocks are able to capture in 2018 and beyond.

What is the Internet of Things (IoT)?

Before we move into specific cryptocurrencies and their use, it's important to briefly touch on the Internet of Things. Simply put, the Internet of Things consists of all physical devices that possess Wi-fi capability. This includes common household items that we all own let cellphones, all the way to newer devices that incorporate internet connections like air conditioners, refrigerators and coffee makers. The IoT also goes beyond households and into commercial grade items such as airplane engines and industrial machinery.

Where cryptocurrency comes into this is dealing with the inter-connectivity of IoT devices. Say for example, a car manufacturer is interested in gathering data from your morning commute in order to make the internal traffic monitor more advanced. With your permission, the manufacturer could gather this information from you, and you would be rewarded with cryptocurrency. Other companies could also purchase this data for their own usage, and be rewarded with cryptocurrency (once again, with your permission).

Cryptocurrency has a special advantage over regular fiat currency in that the decentralized nature of blockchain and DAG protocols makes this data far more secure and accountable than an old school centralized solution. This other part of this is that this new generation of cryptocurrencies that specialize in micro-payments, will be able to effectively handle millions of micro-transactions between devices in a small space of time. This is something that previous generation cryptocurrencies like Bitcoin and Ethereum are either not built to do, or simply cannot do due to the nature of their technology.

What is IOTA?

Tangle vs. Blockchain

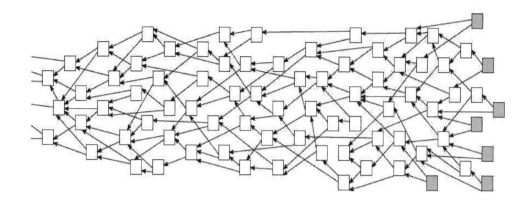

With a regular blockchain transaction. One party makes a transaction to another. This transaction then gets sent to a node, which a miner needs to verify in order to process the transaction. Those miners then get "paid" to verify the transaction.

Remember in school, when the teacher asked you to grade each others homework or tests? Saving them the work in the process. That's essentially how Tangle works.

With Tangle, every time a transaction is sent, another 2 are verified in the process. This removes the miners from the process completely, which has multiple benefits including lower fees (zero in theory), faster transaction times as well as environmental benefits like less electricity being needed to complete the transaction.

This also has a great number of uses when we talk about the Internet of Things (IoT).

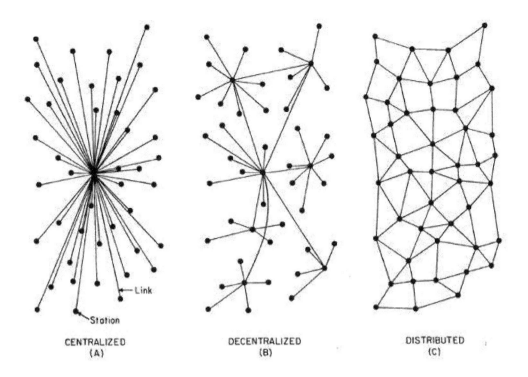

CENTRALIZED (A)   DECENTRALIZED (B)   DISTRIBUTED (C)

Another way of looking at this would be in the above image. Picture A being a traditional, centralized solution like a bank or government body. Picture B is a traditional blockchain solution, and picture C is a DAG or Tangle solution like the one utilized by IOTA.

Quantum-Proof

Since it's inception, one of the bigger issues that nearly all cryptocurrencies face is the threat of Quantum Computing. The theory is that in the future, a Quantum Computer (a computer that bi-passes the basic binary information regular computer use and can therefore solve problems much faster than current models) could brute force the private key for a cryptocurrency wallet and steal the funds.

The Tangle network is Quantum proof due to the cryptographic algorithm it uses.

IOTA vs. Mega IOTA

One thing to note that you may have seen when dealing with IOTA tip bots on forums is the notion of Mega Iota or MIOTA. Because IOTA can be broken down into tiny decimals units, the majority of the transactions are carried out for 1 million IOTA or 1 MIOTA. So if you buy IOTA on an exchange, you are actually purchasing 1 million IOTA or 1 MIOTA. All exchanges and market cap websites use MIOTA are the default quantity, So if you see IOTA being listed for $4.00 on an exchange, that is the price for 1 million IOTA or 1 MIOTA.

Mining IOTA

So as you may have guessed by now, there is no mining IOTA. The supply has already been created and is fixed at 2,779,530,283MIOTA. Instead of mining, in order to send IOTA, your "fee" is that you have to verify 2 other transactions. If you're worried about potentially having to manually verify these, you don't need to be, the algorithm takes care of it all for you.

Investment from Bosch

In December 2017, the IOTA project received investment from German based multinational Bosch. You may be familiar with Bosch for household gadgets, such as hair dryers and refrigerators, but this retail side is only a small part of their overall business. In fact, the company was granted more patents in Europe, than any other last year. These include patents for self-driving cars, and some of the technology used in the self-driving demo model of the Tesla Model S.

It should be noted that the Bosch investment came in the form of IOTA tokens and plans to help utilize the tokens alongside the company's current Internet of Things projects.

Potential Problems for IOTA going forward

As with any coin, or investment in general, it's important to realize the shortcomings and drawbacks of IOTA, even though we are still very much in the early stages of development.

Lack of support for traditional smart contracts

This is the main drawback of the platform when we compare it to say, Ethereum for example. Due to the way the Tangle network functions, there is no strict "order" of the blocks, like there would be in a standard blockchain setup.

Reusing Addresses

One of the more confusing parts of IOTA's current setup is the need for a sender to generate new addresses for every sending transaction they want to make.

It should be noted that the receiver of the transaction does not have to generate a new address and can receive multiple transactions to the same address, so long as that address **has not** already been used to send funds.

Current the best solution to this is to use the official IOTA desktop wallet, which generates a new receiving address every time you use a previous sending address. It is important to still double check any addresses that you are sending and receiving IOTA from.

The current centralized network setup and it's vulnerabilities

There is much debate in the cryptocurrency space whether IOTA's current setup makes it centralized or not. IOTA in its current form relies on a central "Coordinator" node which is run by the IOTA foundation themselves. This node is the node that all other transactions run through. The reason for doing this is to keep the network up and running in the early stages before the node is eventually removed in favor our IOTA users running their own nodes (which would come at a minimum cost to ensure upkeep of the network). You can think of the Coordinator as IOTA's training wheels. Yes, it isn't the final vision of what the network is supposed to be, but it is necessary to get it up and running.

The vulnerabilities associated with the network in its current form are well documented. As each transaction requires the user to verify 2 previous transaction in order for theirs to execute. A nefarious attacked would only require 33% of the hashpower of the network, as opposed to 51% with a traditional blockchain setup. While 33% is still a huge number when we consider the scale involved here, it is still a concern.

One of the IOTA co-founders described the potential for an attack like this as "possible, but not rational" in the sense that anyone trying to take down the network would suffer their own monetary consequences, and thus would have little incentive to do so. So the question here is one of theory rather than an actual security concern.

The Wallet

This is a current concern, but is not a major factor going forward. Compared to RaiBlocks, IOTA's wallet is somewhat buggy and difficult to use. Users have reported transactions being listed as "pending" for days at a time, and manual intervention being needed in order to get the transaction to finally complete. This seems to be especially prevalent when sending to the Android version of the wallet.

While this is a reasonably cosmetic drawback that can be fixed with future updates, it does affect short term adoption. After all, for day-to-day transactions, having a functioning wallet that is simple to use, is vital to the progress of the platform. This is especially true in IOTA's case as much of the overall project focuses on fast peer-to-peer transactions.

What is RaiBlocks?

Apart from IOTA, the other 3rd generation coin that received the most attention in 2017 was RaiBlocks. Coming seemingly out of nowhere in the final quarter of the year, RaiBlocks (XRB) saw a meteoric rise from $0.40 to a peak of over $33 in a little under a month, before a pullback to $16 in late January. Like IOTA, RaiBlocks is focused on peer-to-peer transaction with speed being the major selling point.

In terms of day to day usage, you could look at XRB like another "coffee shop coin", one that could allow you to spend small amount of money, without your purchase amount being eaten up by large transaction fees. Anyone involved in cryptocurrency in late 2017 will understand the pain of large Bitcoin transaction fees, which at one point reached about $40 per transaction. Even coins like Litecoin saw transaction fees increase by a factor of 10 during peak December periods.

RaiBlocks uses "accounts" to allow users to participate in the network. An account is the public portion of a key, or the receiving address for XRB coins. This also includes an account's transaction and balance history.

A basic transaction using the RaiBlocks network requires two separate transactions, a send transaction and a receive transaction which involves the recipient confirming the sender's amount. It should be noted that although both parties must be online for the transaction to go through, the recipient can confirm the transaction at a later date.

Block Lattice

Like IOTA's Tangle, RaiBlocks also uses its own cryptography that goes beyond a basic blockchain solution. This is known as a block lattice.

Within the block lattice, every transaction counts as a "block", so in effect, each user runs their own blockchain. They can send XRB using their private key.

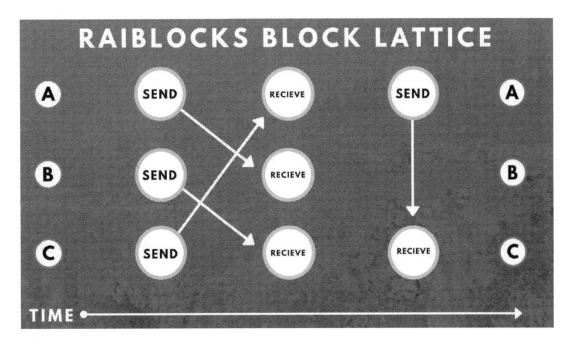

Image credit: fynestuff.com

Where the block lattice differs from Tangle is that users do not have to validate 2 transactions before their own transaction will validate. RaiBlocks transactions are self-validated so each transfer of funds requires both parties to confirm the send and receive function.

Delegated Proof of Stake

Like other DPoS networks, the more XRB one has, the more "voting rights" they have. This means any potential "conflicts" such as double spending are decided by votes.

The main issue with DPoS is if a majority of users are offline at a particular time, the network will be less secure during this time. But this is where the whole idea of delegation comes in. By delegating your voting rights to another user, you don't need to be online in order to "vote". This means users can have their XRB in offline storage (like a paper or hardware wallet) without it affecting their participation in the network.

The drawback of DPoS is if an attacker can somehow position themselves are a delegate and gather a large number of voting rights, they could potentially use these rights for evil intent. Similar to how a corrupt politician would operate.

Real World transaction costs

This is where RaiBlocks really shines - current transaction costs for the network are around $0.00035, which for comparison is around 100,000 cheaper than a Bitcoin transaction and 1,000 times cheaper than a Litecoin transaction.

Going back to the coffee shop example, using the current model, a vendor may have to pay anywhere between 3-5% in transaction costs to Visa or Mastercard. For a small business doing around $100,000 a month in sales, that amounts to up to $5,000 gone. RaiBlocks has the potential to drastically decrease costs for a merchant.

Rebranding

Let's face it, RaiBlocks doesn't exactly roll off the tongue. As such, a rumoured rebranding is tentatively scheduled for Q1 2018. The rebranding itself isn't the most important point here, but in how said rebrand is marketed. The current frontrunner name is Nano, and the domain nano.co has already been registered by someone close to the RaiBlocks project. It doesn't take a marketing genius to see that Nano is a far catchier and more marketable name than RaiBlocks is.

One major drawback for the name Nano is the potential for confusion with the popular hardware wallet Ledger Nano S. Other commentators have remarked that Nano is simply too generic of a name that has already been used for marketing efforts in other fields such as the iPod Nano.

In terms of historical precedence in the cryptocurrency space, The most successful rebranding in recent times for the cryptocurrency space is Antshares rebrand to Neo in Q2 2017. It's too early to say if the same overwhelmingly positive effects will be seen with a RaiBlocks to Nano or any other name rebrand, but it will certainly be an interesting development to watch as we move forward.

Can you mine RaiBlocks?

No, RaiBlocks is not mineable like say Bitcoin or Ethereum. There are a number of third parties websites that claim to mine RaiBlocks, but these actually mine different cryptocurrencies then "reward" miners in XRB, taking advantage of XRB's tiny transaction fee in the process.

Potential Problems for RaiBlocks going forward

Lack of Formal Code Review

The code that runs the RaiBlocks networked hasn't been formally reviewed yet so flaws could come up. However it should be noted that this is assuming the worst.

The code that runs the RaiBlocks network hasn't been formally reviewed yet so flaws could come up.

Ugly Wallet

It's kind of ironic that both IOTA and RaiBlocks, which are both meant to represent the new generation of cryptocurrency, both have poor web and desktop wallets as of the time of writing. What's more is web wallets somewhat defeat the point of decentralization, which both of these coins rely heavily on.

Coinbase gets a lot of flack for a number of reasons (some of them justified), but what it does very well is make cryptocurrency transactions extremely easy for non-technical people.

Both IOTA and RaiBlocks will have to make significant improvements in their own wallets as we move forward, and first mover advantage will be extremely important here.

IOTA has the edge with hardware wallets as well, being supported by the Ledger Nano S which is the current market leader in hardware wallets. The RaiBlocks team currently aims to be compatible with the same wallet by the end of February 2018, but it will need to be supported by March at the latest, which is the when the next batch of Ledger Nano S wallets will be shipped.

Lack of major exchanges

After being listed on Kucoin on January 5th, RaiBlocks is listed on 3 relatively minor exchanges. The other two being BitGrail and Mercatox. Of these 3 exchanges, Kucoin is the easiest to use, but still doesn't have a large userbase compared to the bigger exchanges. The addition of RaiBlocks on a much larger exchange like Binance will undoubtedly see positive short terms effects on price.

Talks of listing on Coinbase are premature of as the time of writing, but it remains to be seen how many coins Coinbase plans to add in 2018. I personally don't expect a potential Coinbase announcement until Q3 2018 at the very earliest.

Incentives for running a node

While each user can run a full node using their desktop wallet, this obviously costs money in the form of electricity, so what incentive does a user have to increase their electricity bill each month?

The obvious answer to this is anyone running a full node has a desire to be an active participant in the RaiBlocks network, and while this may be enough in the short term, it remains to be seen if there are enough long term benefits to keep users running nodes.

The other argument is that vendor participation in the form of exchanges running nodes, will be enough to secure the network. These vendors need nodes to secure XRB transactions for their own purpose. In the case of an exchange, network security is needed to process XRB to crypto exchange pairings.

Race for a fiat pairing

Like any cryptocurrency aiming to truly reach mainstream status, XRB needs a direct fiat to crypto exchange pairing to reach the masses. The ability to buy XRB in exchange for say US dollars or Euros could lead to a short term gain of at least 20-30%, with gain of over 100% not uncommon for a newly released fiat pairing.

The Ledger size

Another issue for XRB is that the ledger (chain) size is already nearing 4GB with only a handful of transactions. It has no proposed mechanism for reducing this and if not taken care of soon - will drive XRB into the same scaling wall as Bitcoin. This is something the team will have to address at a technological level going forward, especially as XRB becomes more widely adopted and used on a day-to-day basis by more people.

Institutional Appeal vs. Ripple (XRP)

While the RaiBlocks project doesn't necessarily focus on large scale institutional appeal such as acting as a payment processor for international banks, we should definitely examine the viability for smaller merchants versus the more widely known Ripple. It will be interesting to see if Ripple's network effects and adoption from large financial companies will trickle down to day-to-day merchants, or if they will stick to a system that is designed for them in the form of RaiBlocks.

It should be noted that even without an institutional appeal, RaiBlocks has a lot of room to grow in the short and medium as a strict person-to-person transaction mechanism.

How to Buy IOTA & RaiBlocks

As of the time of writing, neither of these cryptocurrencies are available in exchange for fiat currency. So there are some additional steps necessary in order to purchase them.

First steps: Purchasing cryptocurrency for Fiat

1. Create an account on Coinbase

Coinbase is still the easiest way for most people to get involved in the cryptocurrency market. Once you sign up (remember to use the link http://bit.ly/10dollarbtc to get $10 worth of Bitcoin for free after your first transaction)

2. Transfer your money to GDax

While Coinbase is without a doubt, the most accessible way for anyone to buy cryptocurrency, it does come with a price. There is an additional 4% fee for debit or credit card purchases (even higher in some countries), so if you are planning on buying a lot of cryptocurrency, these fees will add up fast.

There is an easy way to eliminate them though and that's by using Coinbase's sister site GDax, which has fees of just 0.25% for the taker and 0% fees for the maker. You can use your Coinbase login credentials to access GDax, once you've signed in, there is no extra verification process needed because you have already verified your account on Coinbase. Once you've signed in to GDax, click "deposit" and choose "Coinbase account" as the source of funds. There is no fee for transferring funds between the two platforms.

I should note that GDax is a full trading platform, so you are able to set buy orders below market price, limit orders etc. Unlike other trading sites, GDax will automatically fill orders at market price, so you won't accidentally buy Ethereum at $10,000 for example. Still, if you're not comfortable dealing with this, then I recommend sticking to Coinbase if you're only planning on buying small amounts.

3. Buy Bitcoin, Ethereum or Litecoin

You can either do this directly on Coinbase, or by transferring your money to Coinbase's sister site GDax which has lower transaction fees.
Once you have bought your coins, they will be automatically transferred to your wallet on the respective site. Remember, if you are buying purely for the sake of exchanging coins for the altcoins mentioned in this book, then I recommend buying ETH rather than BTC because the transfer fees will be much lower.

Buying IOTA

1. Create an account on Binance

Binance is the best exchange to buy IOTA as it has the most liquidity. It also has better uptime than rival exchange Bitfinex. Once you create your account on Binance, select funds from the dropdown menu and click on deposit and choose the coin you wish to deposit, Bitcoin or Ethereum. You can then send your coins from your Coinbase/GDax account to Binance. **Make sure you double check your address before sending**

2. Buy IOTA using Bitcoin or Ethereum

Once your Bitcoin or Ethereum transfer is complete (transactions take around 10 minutes), head on over to the Binance exchange. I recommend choosing the basic settings at first. Click on the trading pair you want, IOTA/BTC for Bitcoin and IOTA/ETH for Ethereum.

Select the amount of IOTA you want and hit the buy button. And boom, you've got your IOTA.

I should note that at the time of writing, the IOTA/BTC pairing has 6 times the liquidity of the IOTA/ETH pairing. This won't be an issue if you're only buying smaller quantities (<$1000 worth), but if you want to purchase larger amounts, I would recommend using IOTA/BTC

Buying RaiBlocks

RaiBlocks (XRB) are a little trickier to buy as the cryptocurrencies isn't listed on an major exchanges, although this will likely change by the end of Q1 2018. The exchange with the most volume right now is the little known, but safe, BitGrail, which accounts for around 60% of XRB's trading volume. BitGrail contains XRB/BTC, XRB/ETH and XRB/LTC pairings, although the latter two have relatively tiny liquidity compared to the first one. BitGrail also doesn't charge any fees to withdraw XRB.

The other large exchange is Mercatox, which accounts for roughly 30% of the total trading volume. It should be noted that Mercatox currently has a 1XRB withdrawal fee.

1. Send your coins from Coinbase/GDax to BitGrail

The process is similar to using Binance. Note that BitGrail uses "secondary" accounts to actually exchange your coins, so make sure your coins are transferred to that before wondering why your account is still showing a balance of 0.

2. Buy RailBlocks using BTC/ETH/LTC

Search for your appropriate pairings and click on "place an order" for the quantity you want. Your order may execute immediately or you may have to wait a short while. If there is a delay, it is usually to find sufficient matching "sell" order(s) for your buy order.

Note that BitGrail requires two factor authentication to execute each order, so have your cellphone close buy if you don't want to face any delays.

How to Setup an IOTA Wallet

Storing your IOTA is, as is the case with all cryptocurrencies, best done off an exchange. So in order to do this you'll need to setup your own IOTA wallet, which is a relatively simple step by step process.

Currently IOTA does not have any hardware support, but there is an ongoing community project to make it compatible with the Ledger Nano S hardware wallet.

1. Download and install the IOTA wallet from https://github.com/iotaledger/wallet/releases
2. Choose "Light node". Pick any from the list.
3. Make the seed. It means make a string of random 80 uppercase letters and mix somewhere inside the number 9. By doing that the string will consist of 81 characters. It will serve as your seed/private key. Keep this safe. Everyone who knows the seed can come and transfer money from your wallet. Under no circumstances gives your seed to anyone.
4. Login with your seed. If you want to get IOTAs from someone, press "RECEIVE", generate your receiving address, attach to the Tangle and give that address to someone you want to get money from. If you have issues connecting to the Tangle, try changing nodes.

How to Securely Generate an IOTA seed

A seed is an 81 character long string of alphanumeric characters that you need to secure your IOTA balance within your wallet. It is absolutely vital that you do not lose your seed as it acts as a backup to your account.

In January 2018 there were some reported incidents of user accounts being compromised and seeds being "stolen". This had nothing to do with the security of the network itself and more to do with people using online generators which were setup by nefarious parties looking to steal keys. Once again, the **only** way to properly secure your cryptocurrency is to take everything offline as do it yourself.

To properly generate a secure seed, follow the instructions below.
1. Open this page in your browser: IPFS file (or go to http://bit.ly/IOTASeed)
2. Turn off your Internet connection - **this step is vital**
3. Follow the instructions on the page to generate a seed (move your mouse around on the screen)
4. Once a seed is generated, change a few of the generated letters as an extra security precaution
5. Save your new seed in a secure location - I recommend writing it down on paper and storing that paper in a safety deposit box. Although you can use secure password applications like KeePass
6. Don't ever lose your seed

Note, do not use the following websites to generate seeds, as they have been compromised:

http://iotaseed.io

Other interesting 3.0 Cryptocurrencies

ByteBall (BYTE)

Price at Time of Writing: $689.75 (note: on exchanges, the price is denominated in GigaBytes, or 1,000,000,000 BYTE)
Market Cap at Time of Writing: 1,000,000 GBYTE

Available on:
BTC: Bittrex, Upbit, Cryptox

Where to store:
The official desktop, iOS, Android and Linux wallets are available on http://byteball.org

Byteball is an intriguing cryptocurrency that despite it's high $ value (more on that later), is a coin with huge growth potential in 2018 and beyond. Like IOTA and RaiBlocks, Byteball doesn't use a traditional blockchain structure, instead opting for a DAG structure like the one pictured in the image below.

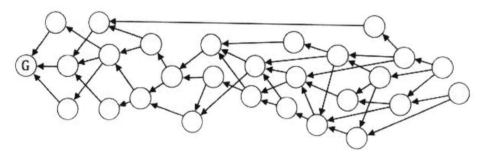

Image credit: Byteball.org

Like a blockchain structure, transactions are non-reversible and publicly available. However, unlike blockchain, there are no blocks or miners so to speak. Each new transaction is simply added to the end of the chain and this new transaction confirms the previous transaction in that particular unit. This prevents a two-tier system where miners, or in the case of Bitcoin, large mining farms, can profit from each transaction by charging a higher and higher fee each time. Like other DAG based cryptocurrencies, Byteball aims to keep fees to a minimum and transactions times fast. Current transaction fees are tiny, at around $0.000002 per transaction at the time of writing, and in terms of speed, the average transaction time is currently around 15 seconds.

Where Byteball has carved out a USP for itself is with conditional payments in their desktop wallet. The sender can set a condition in the form of a smart contract, in which the receiver only gets the money if that condition is filled. If the condition is not met, the money is returned to the sender.

This has a multitude of uses including peer to peer insurance, prediction markets and peer to peer betting. There are a number of already pre-programmed contracts that run concurrently using the Byteball desktop wallet and are synced to specific Slack channels for those events. One such channel is the

#prediction_markets channel where users can bet on the results of certain sporting events versus other users.

Another huge plus for Byteball is that the wallet also has the ability to send cryptocurrency directly to an email address, even if the recipient doesn't have a Byteball wallet yet. This worked out great for PayPal who did the same thing years before to encourage adoption of the platform. There is also the option to send a message to a users Facebook Messenger or Whatsapp account, along with various other social media networks.

This is known by the Byteball team as "textcoin", as coins are sent and received via all forms of text media. In order for the end user to not have to pay a fee to receive their coins, the sender adds a small amount to cover a temporary address that stores the coins before they are transferred to the recipients newly created address. If the sender accidentally types in the wrong email address or phone number, the coins can be retrieved using a "claim back" link within the wallet. You can think of the entire process as like PayPal without the third party keeping control of your money. This is one area where Byteball has the potential to outperform other coins, especially when compared directly to IOTA and XRB that both suffer from less than stellar wallets in their current form.

There is also a built-in privacy feature in the form of what is known as "Blackbytes", which have the same value as Byteball Bytes, yet are not visible on public databases.

Distribution of Bytes is done uniquely based on the amount of Bitcoin (BTC) or BYTEs one holds in the official Byteball wallet. In the cryptocurrency space this is known as an airdrop, because users don't have to do anything to receive the tokens, except for already holding tokens or having an account on certain exchanges. The reason for an airdrop is to ensure uptake on the wallets themselves.

Once again, we can liken the similarities to PayPal in this case. In the early days of the platform, anyone who signed up was given $10, and any referrals made by that user were also given $10. This is slightly harder to do within the cryptocurrency space, due to the relative user anonymity, but Byteball has found a workaround solution to this.

All new Byteball users, who verify their identity (to prevent multiple registrations from one individual), will receive $20, minus $8 that the verification requires. So the individual is left with $12 net in BYTEs after they have registered. Referrals for new users are also worth $20. This entire project aims to utilize Metcalfe's Law, that the total value of any network is the square of the number of its users - something we can see with large social media sites like Facebook or YouTube, or even with Bitcoin in the cryptocurrency space.

Currently around 64.5% of the total BYTEs have been distributed, with the next planned distribution date on March 2nd 2018. BYTEs will be distributed to those holding BTC and BYTEs in the official Byteball wallet.

One of the more confusing elements of the Byteball project, is how BYTEs are measured within the system and on exchanges. The price per coin may seem high at first, especially for a so-called "low market cap, high potential" coin. However, it is important to remember that this price is for 1GBYTE or 1 billion BYTE. As mentioned in my previous books though, this can be seen as a negative in the short term, as investors like to own a whole of something rather than a fraction.

It's possible that as the price of GBYTEs increases, that exchanges may move to a lower number in the form of MBYTEs (1 million BYTE) or KBYTEs (1 thousand bytes) as the displayed value of BYTE. However, the big question will be if the Byteball team officially decides to switch to either one of these are the denomination for the tokens, because until they do - the high $ value listed on exchanges is going to be a turnoff for some investors.

IoT Chain (ITC)

Price at Time of Writing: $2.96
Market Cap at Time of Writing: $113,187,626

Available on:
BTC: Huobi, OKEx, Bibox

Where to store:
The current iteration of ITC is an ERC20 based token and thus can by stored in any Ethereum compatible wallet including MyEtherWallet.

Dubbed "the IOTA of China", IoT Chain is a virtually unheard of cryptocurrency project with the potential to make a big splash in 2018 and beyond. After receiving funding from large Chinese blockchain incubator FBG Capital, the project came to prominence in the English language media in January 2018 after an article in the Huffington Post.

The project is centered around building a secure operating system for IoT devices. In short, they will prevent hacking from getting access to your personal data by hacking your refrigerator or air conditioning unit for example. IoT devices and services currently make about $300 billion a year as an industry and at growth rates of a staggering 30% a year, this is projected to reach $3 trillion by 2020. In practical terms, we're talking multiple IoT devices in every single home in the Western world. So in terms of potential market adoption, the scope is there for sure.

The current problem the IoT industry faces is that much of the user data stored on centralized servers owned by the merchants themselves. For example, if you have a smart refrigerator made by Bosch, then all your data is stored on Bosch owned servers, which makes it vulnerable to cyber attacks. A decentralized solution to this would increase the security of your data as there would be no single point of entry, and thus there would be no single point of failure either.

The setup of ITC and the token's value comes from user data being shared with third parties (with their consent) to provide improved products and services. This would allow quicker and more efficient product designs, redesigns and interactions between products. This could also be applied to users themselves, who would receive payment in exchange for their "feedback" on how their devices are performing. This solution will be marketed as more of a "plug and play" for manufacturers rather than using something like IOTA, which would require specific technical knowledge.

One interesting thing to note is that unlike many other cryptocurrency projects, there was no ICO to raise funds. All of the $15 million initial investment came from private funding groups, including the one mentioned in the paragraph.

The project currently runs on the Ethereum network, however there are future plans to move the entire project over to ITC's own blockchain.

The main drawback of ITC right now is the lack of availability on Western exchanges. It is possible for investors to buy using Chinese exchanges, but to be frank it is a hassle. A listing on even a small Western, English language exchange (like Cryptopia or Liqui) would mean positive short term price effects for sure.

It should be noted that the main network is not scheduled for release until December 30th 2018, and test networks are not yet released at the time of writing, although these are planned for Q1 and Q2 2018. As such, ITC may well be a slow burner for the first few months of the year, but may well pick up steam as we move towards the end of the year and into 2019.

PascalCoin (PASC)

Price at Time of Writing: $2.81
Market Cap at Time of Writing: $46,277,013

Available on:
BTC: Poloniex

Where to store:
Windows and Linux desktop wallets are available from http://www.pascalcoin.org/#wallets with mobile wallets scheduled for future release

PascalCoin has the claim to fame of being the first, and at the time of writing, only cryptocurrency to successfully execute over 100 transactions per second in a real world environment. This would allow for exponentially larger block sizes than traditional cryptocurrencies. For example, PASC can theoretically sustain a blocksize of 5.4GB, compared to only 1MB for Bitcoin and 8MB for Bitcoin Cash. The coin is coded in the Pascal language, which it is also named after.

The coin centers around the concept of infinite scaling and a unique technology known as SafeBox, which acts an alternative to blockchain technology seen in first and second generation cryptocurrencies. Whilst other coins and mining models use old block data to fund new transactions, PascalCoin does things slightly differently.

The coin solves scaling issues by only storing a recent transaction history. In their own terms, PascalCoin stores the flow of transactions rather than the entire history. In essence, the blockchain Although PascalCoin does not store the infinite history of transactions, it still retains the full cryptographic security of the entire history. This is because the balance of the ledger is still stored, so you can still see which transactions took place and for how much.

Another interesting feature of PascalCoin is the account system. These are similar to traditional bank accounts but with cryptocurrency instead of fiat currency. Every user can purchase an account for 1 PASC (although some "premium number" accounts do cost more), and this account will be given a publicly available name for those who want to make deposits. This would be searchable within the PascalCoin wallet system. This system also limits the number of addresses that can be created (1 per user), which allows the technology to be able to scale without the issue of theoretically unlimited accounts clogging the network.

In terms of proven transaction speed, there have already been successful executions of 46,000 operations on a 5 minute block (153 transaction/second). For example, Bitcoin currently processes around 7 transactions/second. Other cryptocurrencies may claim more transactions/second in a perfect environment, Vitalik Buterin himself said 100,000/second is theoretically possible on the Ethereum network, however PASC has already recorded the above number in a working environment.

Future plans for the coin include privacy measures being implemented using ZK-Snarks algorithm, once this is running, users will have the option of complete anonymity.

In the short term at least, wallet updates with a more intuitive GUI will be a big step for the coin going forward, as well as, the release of mobile wallets.

Note: There is a copycat coin floating around trading as PascalLite (PASL), this coin is not affiliated with PascalCoin in any official capacity

HDAC (DAC)

Price at time of writing: Still in ICO stage
Market cap at time of writing: Still in ICO stage

Available on:
There are no exchanges released yet, but the first listing is expected in February 2018.

A very new cryptocurrency project coming out of South Korea, HDAC can be looked at as similar to IOTA. Having raised over 15,000 BTC so far, it currently ranks as receiving 3rd biggest funding for an ICO in history.

The project is headed up by Dae-Sun Chung, whose family are one of Korea's most successful business families in history. His grandfather founded the Hyundai Group, which currently consists of over 200 global companies. Dae-Sun founded Hyundai BS&C in 2008 which operates the IT & Construction arms of the Hyundai business.

One interesting element to this particular project is the aim of giving IoT devices the ability to make automatic payments on behalf of their owners. This would combine the use of smart contracts to ensure that payments are only processed if all associated criteria are met.

Users will be given the flexibility to choose their own transaction fees and create their own smart contracts. While neither of these is a new innovation, it remains to be seen if they can be bundled in a way that allows them to be easy enough for everyday usage.

In the short term, the first exchange listing is expected in February 2018, which will be the first time users can buy and sell DAC tokens on the open market. Which exchanges it will be listed on are still unclear, although it is unlikely that the first ones will be the larger exchanges like Bittrex or Binance.

Supple wise, there is no limited supply like most other cryptocurrencies. This is done to prevent any chance of rapid inflation or deflation. Currently, 85% of the initial total supply will be distributed by HDAC's own Eco Proof of Work (ePoW) algorithm over the course of the next 175 years. Although it should be said that not much has been disclosed about exactly how this unique take on Proof of Work is eco-friendly, outside of a few sentences on the official website. It will be interesting to see if the project continues with this particular mining model or switches to a different one as it progresses.

There have been some hiccups so far as part of the ICO funds had to be refunded due to the technical errors and users donating less than the minimum amount of 0.1BTC. These should be looked at as relatively minor in the big picture, however it does not indicate a good start for the project as a whole. It does say something that they managed to raise over 15,000BTC in a time period where ICOs are under more scrutiny than ever.

Overall, the HDAC project is one in the extreme early stages, so I would advise caution if you are interested in investing. The next few months will be interesting to monitor as it moves out of the ICO stage and into the exchange stage. I wouldn't expect any product updates for the first few quarters of the year, but by the end of 2018 we should be able to gather a clearer vision of where this particular project is going. Their goals are large, so that alone makes it worth tracking, but it remains to be seen if the team will be able to successfully put their vision into play.

Factors to Consider Before Investing

While larger cryptocurrencies like Bitcoin, Ethereum and Litecoin have long track records and multiple real world functions, some of the coins mentioned in this book do not - hence their lower price.

There are a number of different variables to investigate before you undertake any investment, and cryptocurrency has its own set.

Proof of Concept (PoC)

In other words, does the technology have a working model, or is it still in a theoretical stage. Obviously more mature coins will have a higher value, with the more theoretical coins being a bigger risk. As the different coins here are in different stages of their life cycle, that is up for you to decide.

The Development Team

Who are the developers and what is their track record? Particularly within the cryptocurrency and blockchain space. Another thing to consider their record within the particular industry they are targeting, and if they have industry connections are not. The third item to consider, is what % of the overall coin supply is held by the developer team. Due to the rise in ICOs in 2017, we now see coins that masquerade as blockchain projects, when in reality their use of blockchain technology is slim, and their coin has no actual utility. They are simply using the ICO as a way to raise money, without having to give up any company equity. One easy way to identify if an ICO is more than likely a cash grab, is to see what % of the total coins will be delegated to the development team. Anything more than 20% is too high for my liking. For example, the RaiBlocks development team retains about 7,000,000 XRB which is around 5% of the overall total.

The Utility Of The Coin

Ideas are great, but if the coin token itself doesn't have usage, then the true potential of the project must be questioned. This is especially true in the case of certain coins where the theory and market potential checks out, but the question of "why can I just use Bitcoin/Litecoin to do the same thing" is often raised. The coins mentioned in this book each tick this particular box, as their utility comes from the ability to process micro transactions, both in an IoT setting and in a human-to-human one.

The Roadmap

Roadmaps are important for short-term gains because they set out development targets for the coin. If these goals are reached and the products/platforms move from alpha to beta to a fully launched product, then that only means positive things for the coin and its value.

Which exchanges is the coin listed on
Many of these coins are still only available on smaller exchanges. Once the coin is listed on larger exchanges, with Coinbase being the biggest and most accessible, the coin has greater visibility and this leads to a rise in value. This one most affects RaiBlocks in the short term, with its lack of accessibility on

any major exchange. The follow up point to this would be offline storage capabilities, such as in a hardware wallet like the Ledger Nano S. IOTA currently is supported by the Ledger Nano S whereas the other coins discussed are not at the time of writing.

The mining algorithm used - or lack of one

You may have noticed by now that these coins do not utilize traditional mining structures like Proof of Work. As such, the incentives for participating in them is slightly different. For example with the case of RaiBlocks, users can run nodes to secure the network and help process transactions.

Best websites to stay informed with unbiased cryptocurrency news

FUD (Fear, Uncertainty & Doubt) is an important acronym for every potential cryptocurrency investor to know. In a space that moves as quickly as cryptocurrency, any news, be it positive or negative, has a big effect on coin prices. FUD is the engineering of either lies, or misrepresentation about certain cryptocurrencies, spread with the intent of driving down the price. It is different from actual criticisms about a coin and the technology, such as Bitcoin's scaling issues, because FUD is only spread with bad intentions.

For example, rumors of the death of Ethereum founder Vitalik Buterin, caused the price to dip 30% in a matter of hours. This is a classic example of nefarious players trying to spread FUD. The news had no actual basis and eventually were revealed to have begun on anonymous chat website 4chan.

Therefore it is more important than ever that you get your cryptocurrency news from reputable sources. These sources are rarely mainstream media outlets who do not employ cryptocurrency experts, and what prefer to report on hot takes and try to gather soundbites rather than news with any basis.

The two best websites for staying up to date on cryptocurrency news in my opinion are http://coindesk.com and http://cointelegraph.com - both these sites are cryptocurrency focused, and their writers have extensive experience in the space.

If you're looking at investing in ICOs, I would recommend utilizing https://icorating.com/ as an impartial third party analysis. So far they have rated 85 different ICOs based on criteria such as development team, minimum viable product (MVP), the project whitepaper and if the project has any partners or advisors. What I particularly like about icoratings is their methodology is listed on the website for anyone to see, whereas other sites appear to merely apply a numerical rating to an ICO without any basis behind it.

A word on the Weiss Ratings Cryptocurrency Report

One of the more interesting developments in Q1 2018 was the release of Weiss Ratings Cryptocurrency Report by Weiss Research on January 24th. This is the first report of its kind and aims to provide a similar report to those given to Fortune 500 companies. The computer model uses four factors to determine a rating, those being: Risk, reward, technology, and fundamentals. The first two are based on volatility, which is obviously something cryptocurrencies vastly differ from traditional financial institutions.

While Weiss Research was considered a reputable financial research firm for many years, their track record in the past 10 years has been somewhat questionable. For example, their employment of Larry Edelson as a contractor and the founder himself Martin Weiss have come under scrutiny from regulatory agencies. Weiss and Edelson were the subject of SEC charges in 2009, and ended up settling and returning nearly $2.5 million in investor funds. The charges were based on "unregulated investment advisory and the distribution of materially false and misleading marketing materials."

Many have speculated that these reports could lead to short term price movements. For example, a cryptocurrency receiving an A grade would experience a bump in price, and one receiving a C grade or worse would be the subject of a price decrease. As such, many have called this a mere publicity stunt to bring notoriety for Weiss Research.

It should be noted again that cryptocurrency in its current state is unregulated, meaning anyone can offer formal investment advice. This includes Martin Weiss and Weiss Research. As a caveat, I should remind readers that everything in this book is my own opinion and **not** financial or investment advice.

Another thing to note is that many of the larger ratings agencies such as Moody's and Standard & Poor have had their records called into question since 2008 when they rated subprime CDOs as AAA (the highest possible rating), this was before the market crash which was primarily caused by these same CDOs.

A warning about a possible exchange scam

At the time of writing there is a proposed IOTA/fiat and XRB/fiat currency exchange in the works. However, it should be noted that the founder has a chequered past.

SCExchange, which is poised to launch on December 31st 2017, promises to accept fiat currency in exchange for IOTA, among other cryptocurrencies.

The founder, a 19 year old from Ireland, has already perpetuated one scam, with his previous project Creative Nations, which promised better revenue distribution for video creators than YouTube. The platform ended up not paying creators at all, reportedly stealing huge amounts of revenue in the process. Many former employees have reported to not being paid either.

As one former CreativeNations employee stated

"The company vanished one day without paying me the last wages which were owed to me or even telling me that I lost my job."

The exchange currently is not regulated by authorities is any country. Which is a huge red flag, and even more of one when you consider the plans to support fiat currency deposits from many countries including the United States and Japan. At the time of writing, and with the founder's questionable track record. I can only recommend staying well away from SCExchange for the time being.

Recommended Cryptocurrency YouTube Channels + An Update on BitConnect

This is an additional section that I'll be starting in this book and will include in future books going forward. This is because many of you (myself included) enjoy consuming information in video form as well as from the written word.

However, unfortunately there are a lot of bad actors in the cryptocurrency niche, including those who are using their large following to promote cryptocurrency scams and pyramid schemes. In my previous book *Cryptocurrency: Top 10 Trading Mistakes Newbies Make - And How To Avoid Them* I warned readers about BitConnect, and why I believed it to be a ponzi scheme.

Since the release of that book, BitConnect announced it was shutting down, causing the value of its native BBC token to fall by 95% in a matter of hours. Unfortunately, thousands of people were heavily invested in BitConnect and at the time of writing, it seems nearly all of these people have failed to recover their money.

There is another similar company operating now called DavorCoin, which is promoting itself as a cryptocurrency lending platform. DavorCoin exhibits much of the same red flags as BitConnect, so I would advise readers to stay well away.

Back to a more positive note, the following YouTube channels are ones I personally subscribe to and feature solid, unbiased cryptocurrency information and more importantly **do not promote** any scam cryptocurrency schemes or projects. I should note that I am not affiliated with any of these channels in any way.

Boxmining - Michael provides daily cryptocurrency market analysis, and his ability to speak Chinese gives him unprecedented access to interesting Chinese cryptocurrency projects such as WaltonChain.

Crypto Bobby - Has a bunch of interviews with figures behind major cryptocurrency projects.

Coin Mastery - Objective analysis of many different cryptocurrency projects without the hype

Doug Polk - Doug has taken it upon himself to call out scammers in the cryptocurrency space, doing us all a public service in the process.

Ameer Rosic - The founder of BlockGeeks, an online cryptocurrency education platform, he focuses more on the big picture and blockchain technology as a whole. His videos tend to be on the longer side and provide a more in-depth analysis.

Conclusion

Once again, thank you for purchasing and reading this book. One of my main motivations in writing these is to separate fact from fiction and give an honest, unbiased view of the various cryptocurrency projects out there. I hope you've come out of this with more knowledge than you had going in.

I encourage you to do your own research outside of what you read here, and don't invest in a coin based on the opinion of one person or one website. The recommended YouTube channels on the previous page will help you to do this.

Remember, the cryptocurrency market is volatile, and dips of 30%+ in a day are not uncommon, but if you only invest what you can afford to lose, you can ride these bad times and still be there for the good times to come - which believe me, there will be a lot of. Cryptocurrency is still a highly speculative asset, and I would recommend that it make up not more than 30% of your overall investment portfolio.

I wish you the very best in your cryptocurrency journey, and if you do decide to invest, I hope you make a lot of money with cryptocurrency.

One final word, if you have enjoyed this book, I'd really appreciate it if you took 2 minutes to leave a review on Amazon

Thanks,
Stephen

P.S. If you sign up for Coinbase using this link, you will receive $10 worth of free Bitcoin after your first purchase of more than $100 worth of cryptocurrency.

http://bit.ly/10dollarbtc

Cryptocurrency: FAQ - Answering 53 of Your Burning Questions about Bitcoin, Investing, Scams, ICOs and Trading

Introduction

Hi,

For those of you already familiar with my books, the format of this one will be a little different. I won't be doing any in depth analysis of any particular coin. Nor will I be discussing any trading or investment strategies to employ.

Instead, I decided to do a question and answer format for questions I received from my email list, as well as some popular ones I found online that seemed to be asked over and over again. Some of these will be low level beginner questions, and I've decided to cover those first so the more experienced cryptocurrency investors can skip over them and move on to the more advanced section.

These questions were wide ranging and included topics like "Does coin X have greater potential than coin Y", as well as questions about government regulation, potential institutional adoption, the future of ICOs and much, much more.

I'd like to thank everyone who submitted a question, and I hope my answers cleared up any queries that you had.

I hope you enjoy this book, and if you do, I'd really appreciate it if you left a review on Amazon.

So let's get to it.

Thanks,
Stephen Satoshi

Bitcoin

What's the easiest way to buy Bitcoin?

We'll get the most basic one out of the way. The best way for a completely new investor to invest in Bitcoin is to use Coinbase.

At one time, the most downloaded app on the App store, Coinbase allows users to buy, sell and store cryptocurrency. Coinbase is undoubtedly the most beginner friendly exchange for anyone looking to get involved in the cryptocurrency market. They currently allow trading of Bitcoin, as well as, Ethereum and LiteCoin using fiat currency as a base. As of January 1st 2018, you can now buy Bitcoin Cash on Coinbase as well. Known for their stellar security procedures and insurance policies regarding stored currency. The exchange also has a fully functioning iPhone and Android app for buying and selling on the go, very useful if you are looking to trade.

Once you are signed up and complete the identity verification procedures you can buy Bitcoin with your credit or debit card instantly.

Coinbase also recently launched the Coinbase Vault, which is a secure way of storing your cryptocurrency while still having it accessible to trade. The vault uses double email address + phone verification in order to access your funds. If you're planning on holding long-term, I still recommend offline storage - but as an intermediary option, the Vault is a step in the right direction.

If you sign up for Coinbase using this link, you will receive $10 worth of free Bitcoin after your first purchase of more than $100 worth of cryptocurrency.

http://bit.ly/10dollarbtc

Note, if you're going to be trading Bitcoin, I recommend doing so on Coinbase's partner platform GDax, which has lower fees.

I'm new to cryptocurrency how can I get started?

My personal recommendation would be to check out my Cryptocurrency: Beginners Bible book. It explains all the basic concepts behind cryptocurrency and blockchain technology and offers a primer to Bitcoin as well as 12 other of the more well known coins including Ethereum, Litecoin and Neo. There's also information about safely storing your coins.

How much Bitcoin does the Mt. Gox Trustee have? Could he dump it all at once? If he does will it cause a crash?

One of the more recent negative cryptocurrency stores came out in early March of 2018. For those of you who haven't been in the space for long, I'll catch you up on exactly what Mt. Gox is.

Mt. Gox was, at one time, the biggest cryptocurrency exchange in the world. At its peak, the Japanese exchange was handling over 70% of all Bitcoin transactions worldwide, which is a far higher number than any exchanges today.

The exchange was hacked in June 2013, which resulted in 850,000 Bitcoin being stolen by hackers. Roughly 5% of the total world supply of Bitcoin. This led to Mt. Gox filing for bankruptcy in February 2014 and CEO Mark Karpeles was arrested and charged with fraud and embezzlement by Japanese authorities.

Now, Mt. Gox was back in the news in 2018 when the bankruptcy trustee, sold over 18,000 Bitcoin (worth approximately $180 million) in one day, in order to pay creditors from the bankruptcy filing. Now, the trustee still holds over 166,000 Bitcoin, which if sold on the open market could cause massive downward pressure on price. Now, there has been a lot of speculation that the trustee is not allowed to sell more than a certain amount of Bitcoin per quarter, in order to keep the market somewhat stable. So it is doubtful that a huge sell off would occur any time soon, however, even selling as much as 10% of the holdings in one day would be concerning. Any further sales would also require approval from the bankruptcy court.

Many commentators have asked why the trustee didn't sell the Bitcoin at auction, like other bankruptcy assets are often sold, or why they didn't sell at an OTC desk like the FBI did with their seized Bitcoin from the Silk Road case. Either way, it is worrying that so much Bitcoin is in the hands of one person, whose sole goal is to extract as much fiat currency as possible from it.

Is it too late to buy Bitcoin?

It depends on exactly how you define "too late". If you're looking for 10000% gains in under 5 years then yes, it probably is too late. Some investors believe Bitcoin will eventually rise above $100,000 per coin, and a couple of more optimistic people have already put public statements out that they expect Bitcoin to reach $1 million per coin in the long run. Obviously these estimates are on the very bullish side, but the optimism is still there.

Where I believe Bitcoin can really shine is as a digital store of value - a "digital gold" if you will. It has already shown itself to be uncorrelated to the stock market, so could be a useful hedge against uncertain financial times during a market crash. The big factor in determining if Bitcoin can ever really reach this status is if volatility decreases as we move forward. Investment Banks have previously been reluctant to recommend such a volatile asset to their clients, and although we are seeing institutional adoption increase - this volatility will hamper further adoption.

Regardless of this, I believe Bitcoin has a place in all cryptocurrency portfolios because of its market leader position and influence on the price of other cryptocurrencies.

Can Bitcoin make banks disappear?

I think there's some level of confusion on this topic, which is why it deserves an answer here. In the original whitepaper, the "vision" for Bitcoin was as a trustless, peer to peer method of monetary transaction, which didn't require a third party (such as a bank), to verify said transactions, as the blockchain would do this.

The key thing to note with Bitcoin is that you yourself are your own bank. If you hold your private keys, the codes needed to actually spend your coins, then no one else has access to this, including a bank.

The real question emerges when we take into account Bitcoin's limited supply and deflationary nature. If people view Bitcoin as a method for day to day transactions, then we could see it eat into the market shares of banks. But if instead its position in cryptocurrency is indeed as a store of value, or "digital gold", then this is unlikely to affect banks going forward.

Other coins though may well do this. For example, if we see a scenario where Litecoin or Nano becomes the defacto day to day currency for people, and Bitcoin is looked at as a long term hedging asset. Then banks could well be in trouble.

In terms of making banks obsolete, this is unlikely in the near term at least. Banks will still be present as a service provider for insurance, personal loans, mortgages and such. Many banks are already developing their own blockchain solutions, and while this hasn't led to bank created coins yet, I wouldn't rule out the possibility that we will see some private bank-owned cryptocurrency experiments within the next 5 years.

Can you buy a fraction of a Bitcoin?

This is a big question from new investors in the cryptocurrency space, especially those who have only ever invested in stocks before. It may seem daunting when you see Bitcoin prices at $6,000, $9,000 or even $19,000 when the amount you wanted to invest was much smaller.

Fortunately, you can buy just a fraction of a Bitcoin. In fact, you can buy amounts as small as 0.0000001 Bitcoin. So even if you only want to test the waters with a small amount, this is entirely possible. All you have to do is set the dollar amount you want to invest in the Coinbase app or on the website and it will show you the fraction of Bitcoin you will receive in return.

Will the price of Bitcoin increase forever?

This is an interesting question, posed by a forum user. Due to the limited and fixed supply of Bitcoin (21 million), it is designed to be deflationary. In other words, it's value should theoretically increase indefinitely. Just like fiat currency's value would decrease indefinitely as more money is printed by central banks.

We won't truly know the answer to this question until all 21 million Bitcoin are in circulation, which is not scheduled to be until 2140, if the current mining difficulties do not change.

That, of course, does not take into account government regulation which could significantly affect the price one way or another. This is part of the reason why cryptocurrency as a whole is so volatile.

Then there is the big "what if" question regarding cryptocurrency becoming defacto day to day currency. For example, if the price of goods and services is measured in Bitcoin rather than fiat currency, then its primary use is no longer as a store of value, but as a regular currency. Therefore people will be encouraged to spend their Bitcoin, and the deflationary nature would pose problems.

Will the price of Bitcoin keep dropping?

This question relates to the early 2018 correction in which Bitcoin lost roughly 60% of its value in just 2 months. This will be alarming to all the new investors in the space, however, for those of us who have been around a while - it's nothing new.

In 2011, Bitcoin lost 94% of its value. Then in 2014, it lost 86% of its value. In 2017 alone we saw dips of 30% over 5 times, and yet these dips were then followed by even higher highs.

This is an all too familiar pattern in the Bitcoin world. Yet this time it has been receiving more media attention than before. For a medium term view, technical analysis shows there are support levels (people waiting to buy) for Bitcoin at $7.2K, $6K and $4.8K. If these levels are breached then I would start to worry as the support levels below them aren't as clear. However if these levels can hold, in other words, if more sellers don't emerge, then we will likely see an upswing again.

The big rises will come when we see increased adoption levels from Wall Street and institutional money coming in. Otherwise we could potentially be in for a full year of sideward movement like we saw in 2015.

When is the best time to buy Bitcoin?

The best time to buy Bitcoin was in 2010, the second best time is today. Cryptocurrency is far too volatile to try and time the market, so unless you are an experienced investor with a good grasp of technical analysis - your best option is to simply buy and hold.

You will need to get used to large upswings and downswings in price. For example, those who bought at the very top in late December are down roughly 60% at the time of writing. But those who bought 1 year ago are up roughly 500%. So once again, time in the market beats timing the market. So if you only invest what you can afford to lose, and can hold steady through the bad times, then you can receive large gains in the long run.

Cryptocurrency Investing

Why is the market so volatile?

A great question, and one all new investors in the space are wanting to know. There are a number of reasons for this and I'll explain them one by one.

The first is that this is the first asset ever to be born in the internet age. An age of instant gratification, an age of being able to do everything at the click of a button. Although online brokerage accounts for stocks have been around for some time now, the market as a whole was born in an age of stock tickers, and slow information. Cryptocurrency is the only market that is online 24/7 365, and thus, traders are always moving prices one way or another. Cryptocurrency trading is also a lot cheaper than trading other financial instruments, Binance, for example, takes 0.1% from all trades, whereas stock trading can be much more costly in terms of transaction fees.

The second one is the size of the market. Even at its peak of $800 billion in January 2018, that's still tiny compared to other financial markets. The global market cap for stock, for example, is around $80 trillion. Thus, it only takes a small amount of new money to move the market one way or another, especially if that money is institutional. $10 billion may seem like an enormous amount to you or I - but it's a drop in the ocean for large banks and hedge funds. This kind of money has the potential for huge effect on price one way or another.

The third is that because we are still in the early adoption stages of the market, any news, be it good or bad, tends to have a significant repercussion. For example, we saw a rumor of Ethereum founder, Vitalik Buterin's death cause the market to crash by 20%. Then we saw a fake news piece of "China bans cryptocurrency" cause another significant crash. In turn, 10 or 15% spikes in a day are the result of a US congressman speaking positively of cryptocurrencies.

These are the three big factors which contribute to volatility, and ones you should always be aware of, especially if you plan on trading frequently. For those of you planning to buy and hold, it will prepare you for days where we see red lines everywhere - but don't worry, these don't tend to last for long.

How many different coins should I own?

That is entirely up to you. As stated in previous books, I have always recommended having the majority of your portfolio in Bitcoin and Ethereum if you plan on investing for the long term. However, these are less likely to produce the 1000% gains we've seen in the past as they are now more mature assets than the rest of the cryptocurrencies.

In terms of other cryptocurrencies projects, I encourage you to do your own research on coins, and not blindly invest because of some hyped up marketing language on their website.

Another thing to remember is that the price of a coin is not an indicator of its potential growth. Market cap is a far more important indicator. For example, I see many new investors look at the price of Ripple and think "wow it could rise to $100 and I'll be rich". Ripple has the third biggest market cap right now at the time of writing ($27 billion), roughly one fifth of Bitcoin's market cap. Therefore at $100 per XRP, it would have a market cap of $3.9 trillion, which is 10X the total cryptocurrency market cap right now and just isn't realistic in this lifetime.

Generally speaking, coins with a market cap below $100 million can be considered smaller projects, with those below $20 million being looked at as microcap high risk projects.

How often should I take profits?

Everyone's financial situation is different, so I can't make any blind recommendations or a set period of time when you should take profits.

I still always recommend intermittently taking gains for yourself, and if you initial investments rise enough, you can be in a position where you cash out your initial investment and simply play with house money so to speak. This is probably the best position you can be in.

Will there ever be a chance to make 10000% returns again - or has that ship sailed?

We have to remember that we are still very much in the infant stages of cryptocurrency and blockchain technology. There is still only a small amount of money that has come in from Wall Street and other big institutional funds.

One thing to note is that the current value of the cryptocurrency market is roughly equivalent to what the Nasdaq value in the late 1980s, so we are still WELL before the Dotcom boom if you want something to compare it to.

There will be many projects that absolutely explode in the next few years. What those projects will be is another question entirely.

What evidence is there that institutional money really is coming in to the space?

Not all institutional investors take the same line as Warren Buffett or Charlie Munger. Even if the soundbites coming out are on the negative side, we must remember that these large investment banks and hedge funds are spending hundreds of millions of dollars gearing up to offer cryptocurrency to their clients. It is now not a matter of if, it is a matter of when. Here are just three examples of positive sentiment towards cryptocurrency from these giant financial firms.

Global investment management fund Blackrock Capital, whose assets are in the trillions of dollars, is headed up by Larry Fink - who is very bullish on cryptocurrencies. Fink has gone on record as saying *"I'm a big believer in the potential of what a cryptocurrency can do."* Chief Investment Strategist Richard Turnill also stated *"We see cryptocurrencies potentially becoming more widely used in the future as the market matures."*

Wellington Capital Management, another trillion dollar firm is sizing up cryptocurrencies. In a report to investors in February, the firm stated they were looking at companies connected to cryptocurrency. The report then went on to say *"Various Wellington teams are already positioning portfolios to take advantage of mining and blockchain implementations by, for example, investing in select chipmakers making components."* So it's not just talk anymore, money is beginning to come in.

Goldman Sachs owned Circle Internet Financial Ltd bought Poloniex, one of the largest cryptocurrency exchanges in the world, for over $400 million. A 9 figure buyout, from a company owned by an investment bank, is a surefire sign that institutional scale money is coming in.

What will government regulation mean for the cryptocurrency space? Is it a good or a bad thing?

The key thing to note is that at the federal level at least - cryptocurrency is not disliked.

Governments want to regulate crypto, to some degree, so they can monitor fraud, and they will take the necessary steps to do this. Now, whether these steps conflict with your moral views towards decentralization is one thing, but regulation is a positive price in terms of price action. Institutional money will only come in if the regulation question is sorted, that is certain.

What is your personal portfolio?

While I won't disclose my exact portfolio of holdings, I will say that it consists of roughly 75% BTC and Ethereum and then the other 25% is split between smaller cap coins. I utilize dollar cost averaging while investing to minimize volatility.

Who are these "whales" people keep talking about?

Good question, simply put, a whale is an individual with high net worth. In the cryptocurrency space, their net worth is measured in cryptocurrency rather than fiat. For example, the top 300 Bitcoin addresses control roughly 25% of the total Bitcoin in circulation.

If you trade regularly you can spot whales by their ability to manipulate the price of coins for their own benefit. They can do this by putting up large buy and sell walls, and also providing huge surges in trading volumes. You must watch out for this if you plan on trading coins with low volume anyway, as these are more easily manipulated. The first major "whale incident" for crypto trading occurred in 2014 when one user sold 30,000 Bitcoin for a price of $300 each. Fortunately, the market was able to recover quickly.

Will there be a crypto ETF within the next 12 months?

This is a big one, both institutional and consumer investors would love to see a cryptocurrency ETF available. The SEC has already rejected 2 Bitcoin ETFs in 2017 due to the volatility issue and the issue of custody. The latter is a case of an independent third party being able to secure the coins within these ETFs so that money managers cannot make off with investor funds. This happens with all other ETFs, but as cryptocurrency doesn't work in the same way as regular ETFs, we are still trying to find a solution that makes all parties happy.

However, as further regulation occurs, and the custody issue is sorted, we will no doubt see more warming towards both a cryptocurrency ETF and a Bitcoin ETF. Whether that will happen in 2018 is uncertain, but I would predict that we will see both of these ETFs within the next 24 months. Obviously one or both of these would be huge for the market.

What is the US stock market's effect on the cryptocurrency market and vice versa?

Thanks to email subscriber Angel D for this one. Now, this is a topic I've looked into very closely over the years, and I can say with a certain degree of certainty that there is zero correlation between the two. In fact, many investors are now looking at the crypto market as a hedge against the stock market.

What do think of owning masternodes as a way of earning passive income?

Thanks to email subscriber Eugene H for this one. This was actually a multi-part question but I condensed the answer into one.

Owning a masternode essentially means you host a certain coin's blockchain on your personal machine. This means you help support the running of the network. This method is an alternative to mining coins.

The majority of masternodes have a minimum amount of coins you must own in order to run one. This is to ensure that the node owner has a significant financial stake in the system, and thus, has less of an incentive to conduct nefarious activity on the network itself.

The big incentive for owning a masternode is that you are rewarded in the form of dividends, these range between 3 and 10% depending on coin. Dash for example offers 7.54% return. PIVX is another decent masternode coin with a 5.74% return, with Navcoin having one with 5% dividends. Be wary of any coins offering ridiculous ROI (at the time of writing, I see one coin offering a 778% annual ROI), these are bonafide scams.

However, the big limiting factor with masternodes is that many of them are just way too expensive for the regular investor. DASH masternodes are around $400,000 a WaltonChain one would be around $130,000 and VeChain around $35,000.

Obsidian represents a good median investment level opportunity for masternode as the 10,000 ODN required would only set you back around $1,400 at the time of writing - with 10% returns. However, you are also taking a risk on a low market cap coin - so you returns could be theoretically worthless.

ROI is obviously important, but there are other factors you should take into account before investing in a masternode for a certain coin. One issue is what percentage of masternodes are owned by a few owners. If only a few parties own the majority of the nodes, they could theoretically band together to attack a coin if they chose to. The other factor is how stable the overall coin value is. Say if you buy a masternode for $10,000 and then the coin's value drops by 50% in the next 3 months, you returns from hosting the node have been drastically reduced. That is why I would only invest in a masternode for a coin you are have already been invested in for a significant period of time.

As a decent middle ground, or if you want to earn passive income without a huge invesment, I like Neo's model of paying out Gas to Neo holders.

How do you choose the coin you invest in?

Thanks to email subscriber Claudio S for this one. Unfortunately, the answer is very boring. It involves painstaking research - Namely the coin whitepaper, YouTube videos by other crypto commentators, checking out GitHub pages and LinkedIn pages for developers.

After that, if I'm still confident (I'd say for every pick there are 5 coins that don't make the cut) then I move forward.

Which coins should I buy if I'm just getting started?

Thanks to email subscriber Jerri C for this one. If you have less than $500, I wouldn't recommend spreading yourself too thin and only starting with one or two coins. You can't go wrong with Bitcoin or Ethereum for these purposes.

If you did want to look at smaller projects, I like Binance Coin (BNB), Ambrosus (AMB) and Jibrel Network (JNT) right now.

ICOs

Are ICOs dead in 2018?

2017 was undoubtedly the year of the ICO. There were 435 successful ICOs with a grand total of over $5.6 billion raised by ICOs throughout the year.

However, they were fraught with talks of scams, development teams running off with the money, and poor execution. As well as projects that didn't really utilize blockchain technology using an ICO as a way to get around SEC regulations for IPOs and raise capital quickly.

The latter point is the most concerning going forward. If cryptocurrency is to progress then we absolutely must stop ICOs being used as a substitute for Kickstarter and Crowdfunding campaigns.

Cryptocurrency at its core is trustless, transparent and decentralized, and many of these ICOs go against one or more of these principles. On top of this, we have seen far too many new investors straight up gambling by throwing their money at these projects with the hope of a quick 10X return.

What we should see is the overall number of projects reduced, but the quality of them rise. This means more projects with a working product, even if its just an MVP, as opposed to a website and a poorly written whitepaper. I'm also intrigued to see how ICOs on Neo and Stellar perform compared to the Ethereum ICOs we saw so many of in 2017. Hopefully, these projects will be able to attract new money into the market while using said money to properly advance their project and give rewards for said investors. We need ICOs to be a viable option if the market is to grow as a whole, due to mass scale cryptocurrency mining being an environmental and logistical problem. ICOs also offer startups a useful way of raising capital while also building a user base at the same time, which the current venture capital model does not.

We may also need additional regulation to prevent poor quality ICOs from being able to get off the ground. Regulation and cryptocurrency are two words that have often been disassociated with one another, but I don't believe regulation would be bad if it weeds out the scammers and only allows legitimate projects to raise funds.

There's also the issue of geographical regulations, for example, China banned its citizens from participating in ICOs in Mid 2017, a move that shocked the market and caused a big dip. If certain projects cannot receive investment from certain countries, then this hampers the goal of payments being truly borderless and again goes against the very essence of cryptocurrency.

So no, I don't believe we will see any "death" of ICOs in 2018 any more than we will see a "death" of cryptocurrency as a whole. The entire ICO craze does need to be cleaned up, and hopefully the market will be able to do some of this "weeding out" process itself as investors become more sophisticated and selective with the projects they choose to invest in, rather than blindly throwing their money at the next flashy ERC20 token.

Why do so many ICOs fail?

Good question, and one that isn't exclusive to cryptocurrencies alone. The vast majority of new startups, blockchain or otherwise, will fail within the first 3 years.

Last year we saw a huge boom in ICOs, with 435 different ones being run, and I would estimate that at least 80% of these will fail in the long term. ICOs garnered tremendous popularity last year, and many of them had no business being in the cryptocurrency space at all. Due to this, we saw a record number of poor quality ICOs. Many of these were never going to be able to execute their projects, and thus, have quickly fallen by the wayside.

In 2018, I predict the overall quality will improve, and we will see more longevity from this next batch of ICOs than we do from many of the 2017 ones.

What are some red flags to look out for before investing in an ICO?

This is an area I've touched on in previous books but it's a vital topic and one which you must be aware of if you don't want to invest in poor quality ICOs.

The biggest red flag is also the one that most people overlook, and that's the whitepaper. You should always read a coin's whitepaper before investing in an ICO. This is the document which lays out, in full, how the coin will work, and how exactly the token itself will be used.

Whitepaper red flags include: Poorly translated whitepapers, plagiarized parts, incomplete white papers which don't offer an explanation on topics. The biggest one of all being no whitepaper available. I would **never** invest an ICO which didn't have a whitepaper available.

The second is the team behind the project. What is their track record? What background do they have with blockchain projects? What background do they have within the industry they aim to disrupt? All these are vital questions that we have to look at. We've even seen cases where poor quality ICOs are using pictures of celebrities as their team members online avatar (see below). Unfortunately, this project still managed to raise over $800,000 before performing an exit scam.

I've previously suggested we will see a decrease in the number of ICOs this year but that we will see an increase in the overall quality of them.

Altcoins

What is Ripple?

Ripple focuses on lowering payment costs in the banking sector via the use of the Ripple network. Designed primarily for financial institutions like banks, Ripple is often referred to as "the banker's coin". Using Ripple makes cross-border payments cheaper than traditional methods like SWIFT. Utilizing lightning fast technology, Ripple can process payments in approximately 4 seconds. The currency was the biggest gainer in 2017 where the coin saw a rise of over 34000%.

Many cryptocurrency purists have been against Ripple day 1 due to its connection with big banks and its centralized nature. The other main criticism lobbied against it was that it is not necessary to use the XRP token to use the Ripple network and thus the token is inherently worthless.

However, Ripple is the coin with the most partnerships with big financial institutions right now, and thus has first mover advantage when it comes to full scale adoption. There are also ongoing rumors that it will be the next coin to be added to Coinbase, which could well result in a huge rush of money coming in because as discussed before, investors see a price of $0.61 and believe it has unlimited room to grow, despite its already large market cap.

Is Steemit/Steem a pyramid scheme?

Now this is an interesting one, for those of you who aren't aware, the Steem itself is based on the social media platform Steemit. Users can publish content such as blog posts and long form articles, and this content is rewarded in the form of digital currency. Similar to how Reddit users receive upvotes, Steemit users receive Steem tokens known as Steem Dollars. The theory behind this being that the financial incentive ensures that users strive to produce quality content.

The elephant in the room is that the Steem founders currently own 80% of the tokens. There has been a lot of rumbling that the large sell orders on Poloniex for Steem tokens are coming from the founders themselves. They also have much higher voting power on the platform than any other user, so in theory, could just transfer huge amounts to their friends by upvoting certain posts. One of the biggest criticisms lobbied at the platform is that all the highest upvoted posts (the ones receiving the most money), are pro Steemit posts. This combined with the ability to instantly cash out your Steem already leads to way too much selling pressure.

Which leads us to a followup question of "how can it be workable long term?"

They will have to continue to "print" more Steem to pay for new content, that much is certain. The initial supply inflation was 100% per year, for comparison Bitcoin's was 100% for the first year and is currently projected to be 5% for this year. New users are suffering because their posts are simply not gaining enough traction for them to build a following, which is an issue we have seen with multiple social networks including YouTube and Instagram. Then there is the issue of bot accounts upvoting content from fellow bot accounts which can be boiled down to rich making each other richer. So I can see the argument for a "pyramid" like dependency where new users have to come in Steem to be worth anything, and if new users don't think it's worth it to post content anymore - then we could indeed see a sharp drop in Steem's value.

Essentially, the biggest problem for the platform right now is the conflict between the promotional material pertaining to "being paid to post" and the actual distribution of rewards on the site. Too much voting power is in the hands of too few users right now, and this can influence price in a number of ways.

That being said, I don't believe the project is a "pyramid scheme" in the traditional nefarious sense of the word. Their token economics may not be the best, and the concentration of wealth is concerning. But this can be fixed with a rework in their reward algorithm. The team have accomplished a lot, and their large user base should be admired. But the long term potential for the project is not without scrutiny, and without fixing some element of the reward system, I can't see how the project will pan out 5 or 10 years down the line.

Where is best place to buy altcoins like Ripple, Stellar and Neo?

If you've been in this space for a while, you'll now understand that there are many more investment options than just the 4 coins on Coinbase.

The most popular of these is Ripple, with Stellar and Neo being two more large projects within the top 10 that have received a lot of publicity in past 6 months. However, it is hard for investors to buy these for fiat currency, so we must buy them using cryptocurrency like Bitcoin, Ethereum or Litecoin.

I personally recommend Binance (use the QR code if you are reading the paperback edition of this book) if you are looking to buy, sell or trade any altcoins. They have by far and away the best customer support of any cryptocurrency exchange. In addition to allowing Ethereum trading pairs for all coins. There are currently over 100 coins you can trade on Binance and they have very competitive trading fees of just 0.1%

I should note I no longer recommend Bittrex as they have stopped allowing registrations from US customers. Other exchanges I have personally used to buy smaller altcoins are Liqui and Cryptopia.

Is Dogecoin a joke or a real cryptocurrency?

One of the oldest coins around, Dogecoin started as a fun project and ended up with actual monetary value. Because of the coin's ability to facilitate micropayments (usually a few cents) - Dogecoin's value largely comes from an internet form of "tipping". The most prominent example of this is holders donating Dogecoin to Reddit users for posts they enjoyed reading.

The coin was never meant to be a long term investment, or be a trading tool against other currencies. The community's price slogan of "1 doge = 1 doge" is an indicator of this. So unless you're planning on using it for tipping or just as a fun introduction to cryptocurrencies, I wouldn't buy a ton of Doge expecting it to rise anytime soon.

If I buy XRP, am I investing in cryptocurrency or Ripple Labs?

Thanks to email subscriber Roberta K for this one. There is a big distinction to be made here, if you buy XRP tokens on Binance or wherever, you **are not** buying shares of Ripple Labs. They operate as a separate entity, and XRP tokens are merely the native token of the Ripple protocol. XRP is what is destroyed to cover transaction fees of banks using the Ripple network.

So the value of XRP is indeed linked to the success of the Ripple payment network, but it is not a linear ratio. The Ripple network has the ability to operate without XRP if necessary.

Which coin has the fastest transaction time?

Speed is one of the most imperative factors in examining a coin, especially the ones aiming to be payment facilitators. For example, Bitcoin transactions take an average of 10 minutes to complete, and the network itself can process roughly 7 transactions per second. Ethereum's network is sightly faster at roughly 20 transactions per second.

The Visa network on the other hand processes roughly 7000 transactions per second. Ripple is the current leader in the crypto world for this and processes roughly 1,500 transactions per second on its network - which makes it roughly 10 times faster than PayPal for example. Other coins like Stellar Lumens and Nano pride themselves on fast transaction times but don't have the volume of the Ripple network to put these to the test.

Then there are a number of other projects that claim to be able to process transactions faster. XtraBytes (XBY) for example has patent pending technology that the team claim could process "up to 100,000 transactions per second". Other coins like RChain claim speeds of 40,000 transactions per second. Though I should note these are purely theoretical or have only been achieved in a pure low volume test environment - thus have not been "battle tested" so to speak.

Do you believe in technicals or fundamentals when analyzing a project?

Thanks to email subscriber Munish M for this one. I am a long term value investor first and foremost. I would rather invest in a great project at an OK price than try to make a quick buck because of some short term price action on a project I feel is just "OK". This market is so volatile that I believe in the best projects, even if they have 50% dips, we've seen it for so many of the good projects, and they always come back stronger.

Is Electroneum (ETN) a scam?

Another scam question, these appear to be very popular. Electroneum boasts about being the first British cryptocurrency. The ICO raised the expected hard cap amount well before the deadline. However, since then, the project has been hit by a number of developments which are a cause for concern for those who participated in the ICO.

Part of the hype surrounding the project was that mobile mining was possible, with numbers of 70ETN per day using a Samsung Galaxy S8 claimed. Many users are reporting rewards closer to 1ETN per day. Obviously, some room for error is expected, but for that estimate to be wrong by that amount is concerning. Either the development team exaggerated the potential reward pool, or the technology is not working as they would have hoped. There was also a security breach in November that had a number of users concerned about the team's technical ability to deal with situations like this. Lack of exchange listings have also been cause for concern, as a listing on Kucoin continues to be delayed for unspecified reasons. Perhaps the most concerning of all is that updates from the team themselves have been getting *less* frequent in recent months.

That being said, I haven't seen any nefarious acts from the team themselves and I doubt outright scam would be the right word to use, it seems to me that the project is just going through growing pains right now. Mobile mining is a fairly novel concept and one that remains to be seen whether it is viable in the long term. I'd still say the project is one to keep tabs on, but one you should monitor closely if you are already holding ETN.

Is Monero (XMR) really just for drug dealers and criminals?

One of the biggest gainers of 2016, and currently the number 11 coin by market capitalization, Monero has gotten a bad reputation over the past year due to its complete anonymity for those using it. Bitcoin, on the other hand, is "pseudo-anonymous" in the sense that you could trace transactions back to a person if you can identify one of their transactions. Monero came to mainstream attention in 2016 after it was revealed to be the currency of choice for users of AlphaBay, an underground drug dealing website. Monero proved itself to be truly private after law enforcement officials simply could not work out just how much XMR the AlphaBay owner had in his possession.

The thing is though, you don't need to be a criminal kingpin or even a small time drug dealer to have the need, or want, for privacy. The biggest one of these being that privacy makes you less vulnerable to cyber attacks. For example, we know exactly how much Bitcoin the largest wallets in the world hold, and the identities of some of these wallet owners are known, which in turn makes them a target for thieves. Monero on the other hand makes this impossible, and thus, keeps the owners safety as a priority.

This isn't the first time the crypto space has had accusation like this levied at it. Bitcoin was previously under scrutiny during the days of underground drug market Silk Road. However, it has seen cleaned up its act and it is now estimated that less than 1% of Bitcoin transactions are for illegal goods or money laundering. There are also a number of other coin which claim to be anonymous but don't quite deliver on this promise on the same level as Monero - namely ZCash and Dash.

What kind of asset do the US government consider cryptocurrency?

Now, this is a confusing one as it has certain tax implications. So cryptocurrencies are *not* considered securities like regular stocks. Nor are they consider to be commodities like gold and silver. They are actually considered to be property of all things. That means they are still under the same short and long term capital gains but do not fall under wash sale rules like regular stocks. You can however still write off losses.

Which cryptocurrency projects have working products right now?

I took this to mean projects that are out of the alpha and beta stages and have full use of their platform online available for the public (or their industry) to use.

We'll start with the coins that are fully functioning. We have the coins which are purely payment orientated like Bitcoin, Monero, Ripple, Dash. These are work as intended as peer to peer transaction systems. Then we have to include the big smart contracts platforms like Ethereum and NEM. As well as the coins which are linked to exchanges like Binance Coin and KuCoin Shares. Now we have these out of the way, we can look at some more interesting uses of blockchain technology, we are already implemented.

Navcoin's mobile wallet is now out of the beta stages and allows currency transfers with optional private payments.

Basic Attention Token has their brave browser up and running, although it remains to be seen what kind of long term adoption they will get when competing against Chrome and Safari.

DENT (not to be confused with Dentacoin) have a working mobile app which allows users to top-up and earn free mobile data. Currently, it works in the US and Mexican markets but more countries are planned for later this year.

WABI has RFID and counterfeit protection rolled out in multiple department stores, with over 1000 stores planned across China by the end of the year.

Bounty0x, kind of blockchain version of Fiverr/Upwork/Mechanical Turk which offers crypto rewards in return for doing small tasks, is already up and running with 381 jobs currently online.

Will Ethereum overtake Bitcoin this year?

This is probably the most popular question I've seen in the past 3 months. Will "the flippening" as many call it, happen in 2018? For this to occur, we'd need to see Ethereum's price go to roughly 20% of Bitcoin's, and thus, due to Ethereum's larger supply, the overall market cap would be bigger. At the time of writing, if Bitcoin stays at around $8,500, we'd need to see Ethereum at $1,600 for this to happen.

Now the closest we've come to this before is seeing Ethereum/Bitcoin ratio at around 0.12 in June last year. That was before the late 2017 bull run where Bitcoin once again took off and ran away from the pack so to speak.

For Ethereum to overtake Bitcoin in the next 12 months, we'd need both overwhelmingly positive news for Ethereum, in turn with some negative sentiment towards Bitcoin. The former could be achieved with implemented the Casper protocol which would see Ethereum move over from a Proof of Work model to a Proof of Stake one, however, this looks increasingly unlikely to happen before 2019 now.

We would also need to see success from more of the ERC20 tokens. If you're not aware, 80 of the top 100 cryptocurrency projects right now are running on the Ethereum network, which is a big part of what makes Ethereum so successful. Many of these projects are still in the early stages of development, so if we can see the teams hit their roadmap targets, and receive more attention, then this will, in turn, lead to positive move going forward.

The third factor is that of trading pairs. Will more traders switch from Bitcoin pairings to Ethereum pairings for buying altcoins? If you're new to the market, you might not be aware that until 2017, it was pretty much impossible to buy altcoins with anything other than Bitcoin as a trading pair. Now, the major altcoin exchanges all feature Ethereum pairings for the vast majority of the coins they offer. Binance, for example, now has ETH/ALT pairings for 101 out of the 104 coins it offers. That being said, traders still seem to favor Bitcoin pairings, mainly because the ones doing the large trades have accumulated a large amount of Bitcoin, and thus that is the coin they have the necessary liquidity in to perform such big trades. If we start seeing more volume for Ethereum pairings then will lead to a push in the price of Ethereum.

The second part of this whole equation is that we would probably need some negative Bitcoin news. However, this then poses another problem in that whenever Bitcoin's price drops significantly, it pulls the rest of the market down with it, including Ethereum. The theory behind this is that when we have bad news regarding Bitcoin, people convert their Bitcoin back to fiat rather than putting it in altcoins. This is also the reason we see altcoins go down when Bitcoin goes on a run because new money entering the market only goes into Bitcoin. Historically, altcoins have performed best with Bitcoin's price has been stagnant for a while, as this is when new investors move their money from Bitcoin into other crypto ventures.

So you can see it's not quite as simple as just waiting for Ethereum to overtake Bitcoin, a number of stars would have to align so to speak. I still think it's entirely possible in the long run that Ethereum could be the number one cryptocurrency, but I don't see it happening in 2018.

Could Litecoin be worth more than Bitcoin Cash?

This is another, could coin X be worth more than coin Y question which I received via email. Looking at market capitalization at the time of writing. We have Litecoin worth roughly 60% of Bitcoin Cash in terms of market cap.

Both of these coins have hurdles to overcome going forward. Litecoin, which positions itself as a cheaper, faster Bitcoin, has growing competition from other coins which focus on the microtransactions space, with Nano being the biggest threat right now. Litecoin does have first mover advantage, and if their payment processor Litepay is adopted by a lot of companies, then we could see a push for Litecoin. Litecoin also has the advantage of "being the cheapest coin on Coinbase" and as such, receives a lot of new money that comes into the market during bullish periods.

Bitcoin Cash, on the other hand, has a more questionable future ahead. It saw a run at the end of last year, in what was one of the most exciting days in 2017 where the price soared from $800 to over $2100 dollars in a day and reach the #2 spot in terms of market capitalization. However, recently, Bitcoin transactions have actually been faster *and* cheaper than Bitcoin Cash transactions, which was the latter's big selling point. It was added to Coinbase in January 2018, but without the network effects that Bitcoin has, I really can't see a clear path for Bitcoin Cash going forward unless the team undergoes a full rebrand, which could even end up hurting it even more.

Long term, I am more bullish on Litecoin as a potential project, so I can certainly see the market cap being worth more than Bitcoin Cash.

Why are there so many supply chain tokens?

This could be rephrased as "why are there so many cryptocurrency tokens" - but we'll focus on the supply chain side of things.

Supply chain management is one of the initial areas in which blockchain has a real world use case. Whether it is medicine, food or other consumer goods, blockchain technology can help prevent fraud, counterfeit goods while ensuring safe transportation from one party to another. For manufacturers, it combines with the Internet of Things economy and helps monitor various transport conditions to ensure the product is delivered both on time, and in the required condition.

Blockchain's publicly verifiable ledger means that anyone can see that there has not been any tampering with a product during the transportation stage. In other words, they can see that the carton of milk they are buying really is milk. This might not seem to be a big issue for those of you in the West. But in China, counterfeit food is a real problem. We've seen baby formulas laced with Melamine, lamb which was actually rat meat and a statistic that up to 70% of the wine in the country is falsely labeled. Needless to say, in China at least, fake food has now become an epidemic.

Hence why we have so many coins focusing on the supply chain sector. We have Modum out of Switzerland, which monitors medical goods. We also have Chinese products like WaltonChain, which focuses on RFID technology, as well as, Wabi and VeChain. And also smaller ones like Ambrosus. These projects are also competing with traditional companies developing their own blockchain solutions for supply chain management.

The important thing to remember is, there won't be one "winner" when it comes to these tokens, the supply chain sector is so broad that many different tokens can peacefully co-exist without eating into each other's market share.

Unlike pure payment coins, which usually compete directly against each other, we could also see a number of these supply chain tokens collaborate with one another, to share technology, and help develop a better solution for consumers and manufacturers alike.

What's the difference between Bitcoin and Bitcoin Cash?

So by now, we're all familiar with Bitcoin, but some of you may be wondering exactly what Bitcoin Cash is, and its role in the cryptocurrency economy.

Bitcoin Cash (BCH) emerged as the result of a split or "hard fork" in the Bitcoin technology on August 1st 2017. The end-goal of Bitcoin Cash is to function as a global currency, in the founder's words, to be what Bitcoin was supposed to have been in line with the original vision for Bitcoin outlined in the 2008 whitepaper.

The split occurred out of problems with Bitcoin's ability to process transactions at a high speed. As the network continues to grow, so do waiting times for transactions. BCC aims to run more transactions, as well as, providing lower transactions fees. One of the major solutions to this issue is increasing the size of each block so that more data can be processed at once. Bitcoin Cash increases the block size to 8MB, as opposed to the 1MB size of Bitcoin.

However, as of the time of writing, Bitcoin actually had lower transaction fees than Bitcoin Cash, so it seems like the change hasn't really worked. You also have to consider Bitcoin's network effect, in other words, how many people are aware of it and use it on a regular basis - which is obviously much more in favor of Bitcoin than Bitcoin Cash.

Listing on Coinbase did help Bitcoin Cash in the short term, but it remains to be seen if the two coin can co-exist in the long run. If I was a betting man, and I had to put all my money on one coin surviving, I'd choose Bitcoin.

What do you think of APPICS (XAP)

Thanks to email subscriber Mike D for this one. APPICS is the first ICO built on top of the STEEM platform, and operates in the same vein. It is a social media platform that rewards participation with cryptocurrency. However, APPICS sees itself as more of a competitor to Instagram as it will focus on the mobile space and the sharing of pictures and videos.

The main concern is that it will use the same token economics as STEEM, which is that "power users" are given a large number of XAP tokens and thus have large voting power. I previously expressed my dislike of this model in discussing the STEEM platform itself, and the same potential for manipulation occurs in the APPICS model as well. APPICS furthers my concern with their use of "judges" for each category. A pre-selected social media influencer or influencers will have a large holding of XAP tokens and can use these to select content they believe is worthy of big rewards. This is anything but a decentralized model and could almost be called blockchain nepotism.

APPICS also promises to integrate point of sale shopping for its tokens, in other words, you can directly spend tokens in stores which accept them.

At the time of writing, the coin is currently in the final stages of its ICO which the aim of raising around $18 million. The website doesn't have much information beyond what I've written here, with a basic whitepaper and a limited FAQ section.

Overall, it's a good concept, but there is a lot of competition in the incentivized blockchain social media space. I can see the idea being attractive to content creators, but just how much they will be able to encourage user adoption of the platform I'm not sure.

Miscellaneous Questions

Could the Rothchilds bring down cryptocurrency?

Thanks to email subscriber Mark M for this one. The Rothchild's, and other world's financial elite do not have a hold on cryptocurrency as they do not control a large portion of any of the funds.

It's plausible that they could manipulate a smaller token for their own gain. Others have rumored that as Ripple focuses on the banking sector, the financial elite owns large portions of this. However, these are just rumors and I wouldn't hold put too much thought into them.

Will blockchain technology cause people to lose jobs?

Blockchain technology is game changing in the level of trustless automation it will provide. The negative side of this is that it could well impact the job security of those working in certain industries.

The biggest ones in the early stages will be low level financial positions such as bookkeepers and mortgage lenders. Blockchain could easily streamline these processes and eliminate the need for a human being. There are also impacts for those in the banking and security industries for the same reason. Supply chain management is another area in which blockchain technology has the potential to greatly impact.

Now, I wouldn't go as far as some commentators who cry that "all accountants will be made obsolete within 10 years", but there will definitely be a downsizing in certain industries.

How do you spot a cryptocurrency scam?

Like any space that has money flowing into it, there are a number of bad actors and people with nefarious intentions. Cryptocurrency is no different in this respect. In the past 6 months, there have been a number of high profile scams. The most notable of which was Bitconnect - a cryptocurrency lending platform.

Bitconnect claimed they had a cryptocurrency trading bot which made investors guaranteed returns of 40% *per month*. Now, we must remember that Bernie Madoff, who ran the largest pyramid scheme in Wall Street history, was only delivering investors 8-12% *per year*. Any project with promises of "guaranteed returns" should be avoided.

How the scam worked was the same way all pyramid schemes worked. It funneled money from new investors into the pockets of older investors. And when the money stopped coming in, the project collapsed upon itself. In December, Bitconnect received cease and desist letters from various authorities and then pulled an exit scam causing the price to drop roughly 95% in just a few days.

There have been a few "successors" to Bitconnect in the form of Davorcoin and Falcon coin. Both of which have the same model of promising investors guaranteed returns. Fortunately, both of these have since shut down and had less of a lifespan than Bitconnect. There will doubtless be another pyramid or Ponzi scheme that pops up like this in the near future, so stay well away from any project that promises guaranteed returns.

Why does Warren Buffett keep badmouthing cryptocurrency?

There are a few Warren Buffett quotes floating around regarding Bitcoin and cryptocurrency as a whole. Including ones such as *"I can say with almost certainty that they will come to a bad ending."* as well as calling Bitcoin *"a mirage"*.

What we need to remember is that Buffett earned his wealth from investing in fundamentals, and in his own words "only investing things I understand". In the same interview with the first quote above, he finished with *"I get into enough trouble with the things I think I know something about. Why in the world should I take a long or short position in something I don't know about?"*.

Over the years, Buffett has been famously reluctant to touch new technology as an investment, preferring more to focus on companies with a long standing history. His self-admitted previous "misses" so to speak include Amazon, Apple and Google. The latter of which he apologized to investors, for not recognizing the potential of Google, at a Berkshire Hathaway annual meeting in 2017.

So it's not that Buffett is so bearish on cryptocurrencies and blockchain technology as a whole, he just doesn't understand them, and thus investing in them would go against his entire investment philosophy.

Why do so many cryptocurrencies rebrand?

That's a very good question, in the past year we've seen two high profile coins rebrand. First, we had Antshares rebrand as Neo, then we had RaiBlocks rebrand as Nano.

One of the big reasons behind this is that many projects see rebranding as an opportunity for increased adoption of their platform. For example <Word>Chain is seen by some analysts as juvenile and amateurish, while others see it as limiting investment to within the cryptocurrency space.

There's also the case of logo rebrands. In the Antshares example, the logo changed from a cartoon ant which could have been drawn by a 13 year old, to a more slick green logo. Nano's logo change also used the name to represent the unique block lattice design of the network, whereas the previous RaiBlocks logo could have been a default Symbol in MS Paint.

Other see rebranding as merely a chance for a coin to get its name into the media again. Especially during a down period in the development cycle. Both Nano and Neo received large bumps in price after rebranding so there could be some credence to this theory.

Is mining cryptocurrencies profitable for the average person?

The answer to this is simple. In 99.9% of cases, if you live in a country where you *do not* have access to dirt cheap electricity, then mining cryptocurrency will be a net negative. That is without considering the large investment you require up front to get your hands on the latest mining equipment like top of the line ASIC rigs. The most successful mining operations are all ones that have invested a minimum of 7 figures up front, and often this figure is in the tens of millions of dollars.

You are much better off buying and holding coins if you are a beginner. If you have financial trading experience than trading can also be profitable.

Are people *really* getting rich with cryptocurrency?

Yes, without a shadow of a doubt, more regular folks have gotten rich with cryptocurrency than with any other financial instrument in the past 20 years. We are currently witnessing the birth of a new asset class not seen since the days of the DOTCOM boom.

How long is "long term" in cryptocurrency?

Cryptocurrency isn't like a stock where we'd consider long term to be 10+ years. The stock market moves much slower, and the cycles themselves move extremely quickly. The majority of this is because cryptocurrency has always been around in the internet age. The age of interconnectivity where everything can be done at the touch of a button. Whereas stocks and bonds were formed at an age of having to call brokers. There's also the wild card of having a 24/7 365 market in cryptocurrency, something that no other financial asset possesses.

When the Nasdaq crashed in 2003 after the dotcom boom, it took almost 15 years for it to return to the highs seen in the year 2000. Conversely, when Bitcoin had its first big "crash" in 2013, it returned to new highs within just 2 years. So needless to say, the crypto market moves *a lot* faster than traditional financial markets.

Therefore when we're talking long term with cryptocurrency, we're often talking about periods of no more than 18-24 months. This applies to both price cycles and development roadmaps for newer cryptocurrency projects.

What are the best YouTube channels?

The following YouTube channels are ones I personally subscribe to and feature solid, unbiased cryptocurrency information, and more importantly **do not promote** any scam cryptocurrency schemes or projects. I should note that I am not affiliated with any of these channels in any way.

Boxmining - Michael provides daily cryptocurrency market analysis, and his ability to speak Chinese gives him unprecedented access to interesting Chinese cryptocurrency projects such as WaltonChain.

Crypto Bobby - Has a bunch of interviews with figures behind major cryptocurrency projects.

Coin Mastery - Objective analysis of many different cryptocurrency projects without the hype

Doug Polk - Doug has taken it upon himself to call out scammers in the cryptocurrency space, doing us all a public service in the process.

Ameer Rosic - The founder of BlockGeeks, an online cryptocurrency education platform, he focuses more on the big picture and blockchain technology as a whole. His videos tend to be on the longer side and provide a more in-depth analysis.

<u>Coin Bloq</u> - This is a new one that I've just started following, they do in depth, level headed reviews of some more obscure ICOs and altcoins.

Where are the best places to store my coins?

There are 3 options to store your coins. You can keep them online on an exchange, which I only recommend if you are holding small amounts. The important thing to note with exchanges is that you do not hold your private key, the exchange does. This is still the case if you use the Coinbase Vault as opposed to the regular Coinbase wallet.

Your private key is what you need to spend your coins and transfer them out of your wallet. Therefore if the exchange gets hacked, your private key can be stolen by hackers.

The other options, in which you do hold your private key, are to take your coins "offline" in either a paper or a hardware wallet. Both of these represent a more secure long-term storage solution.

Paper Wallets:

Paper wallets are simply notes of your private key that are written down on paper. They will often feature QR codes so the sender can quickly scan them to send cryptocurrency.

Pros:
- Cheap - your only cost is the paper you print them on
- Relatively simple to set up
- Your private keys are not stored digitally, and are therefore not subject to cyber-attacks or hardware failures.

Cons:
- Loss of paper due to human error
- Paper is fragile and can degrade quickly in certain environments
- Not easy to spend cryptocurrency quickly if necessary - not useful for everyday transactions

Recommendations:
It is recommended you store your paper wallet in a sealed plastic bag to protect against water or damp conditions. If you are holding cryptocurrency for the long-term, store the paper inside a safe.

Ensure you read and understand the step-by-step instructions before printing any paper wallets.

Bitcoin:
http://bitaddress.org
http://bitcoinpaperwallet.com

Ethereum:
http://myetherwallet.com/

Litecoin:
https://liteaddress.org/

Hardware wallets:

The Ledger Nano S is still the best of the hardware wallets on the market. Plus, they are finally back in stock after a 3 month drought on the official website. Note, only buy your Ledger Nano from the official site (http://ledgerwallet.com) as a number of counterfeit models which steal your private keys have popped up on third party websites.

What are the biggest problems facing businesses who want to accept cryptocurrency?

I found this one on Reddit and thought it'd make a good discussion topic. Many business owners are now seeing adoption for crypto increase, and examining how accepting it as a payment method could benefit their business.

The big issue right now though is volatility, no one wants to accept something that could lose 50% of its value in less than a month. There are workaround solutions to this, for example, BitPay is a point of sale operator which converts cryptocurrency to fiat at the end of every working day. However, BitPay had its own issues with slower transaction times.

Transaction fees are also an issue, which is why coins focusing on micropayments like Nano and Ripple may well have an advantage in this area.

What is the cryptocurrency tax situation?

The cryptocurrency tax situation is a complicated one, and depending on where you live will vary tremendously. The big thing to note is that if you have simply bought and held to this point, you have not incurred any taxable events.

There is also the question of short and long term capital gains tax. In other words, you owe more if you sell an asset within 1 year of buying it than you do for selling it after holding for more than a year.

Although I am not a tax advisor, I have written a brief introduction to the various cryptocurrency tax scenarios which is available on Amazon.

Conclusion

And there we go, answers to all of your burning cryptocurrency and blockchain questions.

First of all, I'd like to thank everyone who submitted questions via email or on various forums, it was great fun answering them all, and I hope my answers can benefit many more people as a result of this book.

As per usual, I'll finish with my standard recommendations of doing additional research on top of what you read in this book, and never invest more than you can afford to lose.

I wish you the best of luck in the cryptocurrency market, and I hope you make a lot of money.

Finally, if this book has proved useful to you, I'd appreciate it if you took 2 minutes to leave it a review on Amazon.

Thanks,
Stephen

Introduction

So you've decided to take the plunge into the cryptocurrency fast lane. You're looking for those gigantic returns you've read so much about. Well, you've come to the right place. Trading is without a doubt the quickest way to get rich with cryptocurrency.

From the outset though, let's make something clear. Trading is incredibly risky, and you are liable to lose money if you don't know what you're doing. The entire point of this book is avoid making giant mistakes, that losing traders always seem to make. So you can mitigate some of the risk by directing your attention to learning the right trading principles to set you up for long term trading success.

These aren't just technical principles, and I won't have you studying 500 chart patterns for 3 years before investing your first dollar, pounds or euros. There are significant mental preparations you need to make before you begin trading. This applies to cryptocurrencies, as well as any other financial trading situation. You'll also need to learn the principles of money management, and how to correctly use your bankroll to give you the biggest chance of long term trading success.

It is advisable to spend a significant portion of your time studying trading theory before you spend time trading your hard earned coins. Remember, at its very core, trading comes down to two factors, and two factors only.

1. Making money

2. Keeping what you've made

As we're currently in one of the biggest bull markets ever seen, many people are doing number one quite well. However, what remains to be seen is if they'll keep their money once the market turns bearish, and our beloved cryptocurrencies start to drop in price (which is a matter of when, and not if - this is a financial market after all).

Trading is the ultimate rush, it's a game played against one another via a computer screen, where it's your mind against another person, your money against theirs. Some days you come home a conquering hero, and other days you'll be left beaten, demoralized and broken. Hopefully, you'll be having more of the former than the latter after studying this book, and you'll become a consistently profitable trader going forward.

And as per usual: **Only invest what you can afford to lose**

Finally - if you enjoyed this book, I'd appreciate it if you left it a review on Amazon.

I wish you all the best in your trading endeavors,

Stephen

Trading vs. Investing

For the vast majority of people, buying a coin and holding it for the long term is a smarter move than actively trading one or multiple coins at once. You see, cryptocurrency trading is rife with uninformed "traders" who simply buy and sell on a whim and inevitably end up broke, even in the current bull market conditions. Luckily for you, if you take some time to study the basics, you can outwit and outtrade these people and take consistent profits for yourself.

Trading Cryptocurrency vs. Big Board Stocks or Penny Stocks vs. Forex

If you've dabbled in trading securities before, then you'll probably be familiar with some of the concepts discussed in this book. However, there are a few major differences between trading cryptocurrency and trading traditional stocks or even penny stocks.

The main one of these is that the cryptocurrency market is open 24/7 365. There are no weekends off, there are no market closures at 1PM for holidays or anything like that. As such, traditional trading advice such as "the best time of day to trade" falls by the wayside here. Price movements can happen while you sleep because the Chinese market is already up and trading, or there is a large volume of buy order coming in from Korea. Events like this aren't uncommon, and you need to be aware of these factors before committing to trading.

Mistake 1: Falling for Pump & Dump Schemes

Opt-In Pump & Dump Emails

Another thing to be aware of. These are a hangover from the mid 2000s when penny stock trading was all the rage, and scammy stock promoters would send out emails to their list promoting a certain stock. Either because they were paid to do so by the company, or the promoters had already invested big themselves. They then wait for the email recipients to invest and push the price up even more, before dumping their shares on the market for a profit, leaving the email recipients holding large losses.

Unfortunately, due to the lack of regulation by the SEC, companies regularly do this for cryptocurrency as well. That is why I recommend you don't subscribe to any of these types of emails, whether a free or paid service. Your trading should be done based on market condition and technical analysis, which we'll go into in more depth later on in this book.

Technical Analysis

Mistake 2: Not utilizing technical analysis

Why Technical Analysis is vital in any form of financial trading

1. Future trends follow past trends

Human beings are a predictable bunch, and we generally do the same things over and over again. This also applies to trading, because certain patterns emerge and repeat themselves, and we can use the patterns to somewhat accurately predict price movements.

2. We're all looking at the same charts

Individual human beings are less good at predicting things than a group of humans predicting the same event, the "wisdom of the crowd" if you will. How this relates to cryptocurrency trading is that as there are thousands of us looking at the same chart, we will generally come to the same conclusion and make similar moves to one another.

3. The current cryptocurrency price includes all available data

Even data that isn't widely or publicly available will be factored in (this is the advantage that so-called "insiders") have over the rest of the trading population. Thus, we can assume that the current price of the cryptocurrency is correct.

All technical analysis can be broken down into 2 main chart patterns:

Continuation Patterns - Where the price of a coin is expected to keep trending the same way it is currently moving

Reversal Patterns - Where the price of a coin is expected to reverse from its current trend (I.e. a coin's price is expected to stop falling and start rising)

The following are some of the basic, and most essential chart patterns you need to know. You can get by with an in-depth knowledge of these, and having a deeper knowledge of the basics charts is better than having surface level knowledge of many charts.

For more in-depth reading on technical analysis, I having a recommended reading list at the end of this book.

Support & Resistance

If you're going to learn one technical tool for trading, make it support and resistance levels. These horizontal trend lines are the lifeblood of all technical analysis.

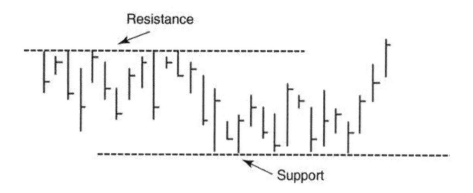

Support Level:

A support level for a coin is a price in which traders do not think it will fall below. They believe there is enough demand at that price that investors will continue to buy, and this will prevent any further declines in the price. Support levels can be identified using charting patterns.

If you're just starting out, study longer term historical data and use this to identify previous support levels for a coin. So with the case of Bitcoin, use 6 month or 12 month graphs rather than 1 week graphs.

Resistance Level:

Resistance level is simply the opposite of a support level. It's a price where traders don't believe there is enough demand to break through and go higher, therefore more traders will be selling at this particular price. Resistance levels are calculated slightly differently than support levels due to the nature of human psychology. For example, round numbers often have a psychological effect e.g. Bitcoin @ $10,000 or ETH @ $300 and this creates a resistance level in itself. You can also use the reverse of the techniques you used to find a support level on a chart.

For both support and resistance levels, look for at least two or three price action zones in a single chart. Once you identify this price action zones, you can draw a straight line to indicate support and resistance levels. Generally speaking, the more a coin hits a specific support or resistance level, the stronger the price move will be once it does finally break through.

Once a stock breaks through it's resistance level, it's not uncommon for the previous resistance level to become the new support level and vice versa. Understanding this helps your risk management as you continue to trade more frequently.

Candlestick Charting

Candlestick charting, also called Japanese candlesticks is one of the best ways to determine support and resistance levels in a coin. Candlesticks take into account the opening, closing, high and low price of that particular day for a coin.

There are literally hundreds of different candlestick patterns you can learn, but there are a few that are absolutely vital to know, so those will be the ones we discuss in this book. One more thing to point out when studying candlestick charts. Red or black candlesticks represent downward movement, whereas white or green candlesticks represent upward movement.

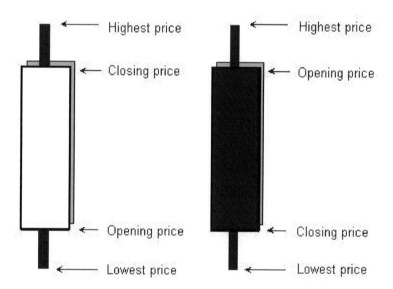

Doji

Doji's are characterized by a very small difference between opening and closing price and look like plus signs on a chart. The Doji pattern represents indecision in the market, these are usually found near support and resistance points, because market participants aren't sure if the coin will break these levels.

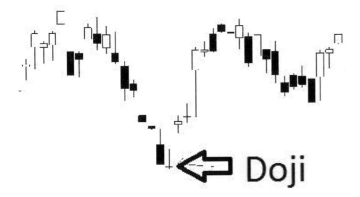

When analyzing candlestick charts, you should use daily charts that go back at least 3 months and try to identify patterns.

Channels

Channels are plotted with 2 parallel lines on a candlestick or line chart and denote continued support and resistance levels as a coin is trending in upwards or downwards fashion. Channels are useful because they help us form multiple ideal entry and exit points for a particular coin going forward. This is a big plus if you plan on trading frequently.

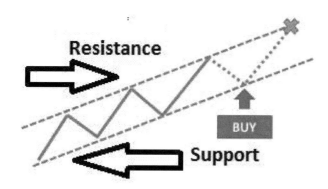

Head & Shoulders Pattern

One of the most important patterns to recognize is the head and shoulders reversal pattern. Simply put this indicates that the trend of the coin is about to reverse. So in the example below, the price is expected to drop. If the chart is inverted, we would expect a rise in price going forward.

The expected price movement (denoted by m in the picture) can be calculated as the inverse of the price between the neckline and the head, which is why it is crucial that you measure the neckline correctly.

Note, the majority of the time, the chart will not be a perfectly aligned head and shoulders, but the general pattern is enough to go on.

Double Top & Double Bottom

A double top (bearish), and its inverse the double bottom (bullish), are made up of 2 consecutive peaks with a trough in-between. Most of the time the first peak will be slightly higher than the second peak and be accompanied by a higher volume as well.

It is also not uncommon for there to be a triple top or triple bottom pattern if there is not enough volume to break through resistance or support levels. Like most patterns, once a breakthrough occurs, the previous support level becomes the new resistance level and vice versa.

The double top is one pattern that newer traders often misinterpret, especially when looking at short term charts. Remember to focus on volume at the support/resistance levels before entering a trade.

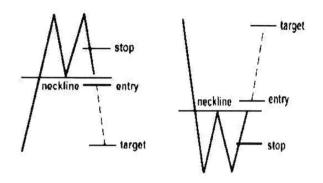

Double Top and Double Bottom

Triangles

We could probably write an entire book just on various triangle based patterns, but we'll stick to the basics here. The three types of triangle pattern are the symmetrical, ascending and descending triangle.

Symmetrical Triangle

A symmetrical triangle is a continuation pattern that signals a price is going to keep moving in the same direction after a brief trend reversal. The two points of the triangle start from the support and resistance lines then converge. The price of the coin has been trading between these two lines and then will continue to trend in the previous direction once these lines meet.

Ascending Triangle

An ascending triangle is a bullish pattern that signals the price will keep moving upwards after a period of bouncing around the resistance line, but not dipping low enough to hit the support line. The line is drawn from the previous resistance and support lines, and will converge at the resistance line. If there is enough volume, the price will break the resistance line and continue to rise.**Descending Triangle**

The opposite of the ascending triangle is a bearish pattern, except this time the lines converge at the support level. Enough volume at this level will result in a breakthrough to lower prices.

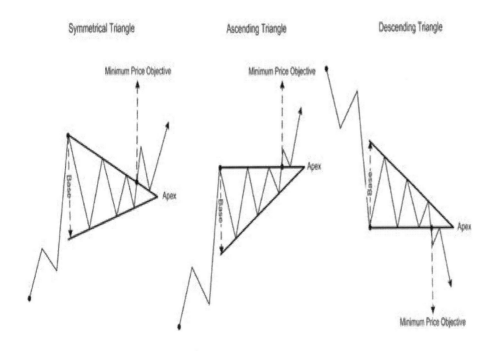

Flag Patterns

Flag patterns are similar to triangle patterns that appear during consolidation period (small reversal from previous price movements). They are represented by two parallel lines following a of a sharp price movement (which acts as the flag "mast") Following a flag patterns, prices continue to trend in the same direction they were moving previously.

The slope of the flag will be the opposite direction to the predicted price movement, so a downward sloping flag will signal a continued bull movement, and an upward sloping flag will signal a continued bear movement.

Like triangle patterns, the buy or sell signal comes when there is enough volume to break through the previous support or resistance level.

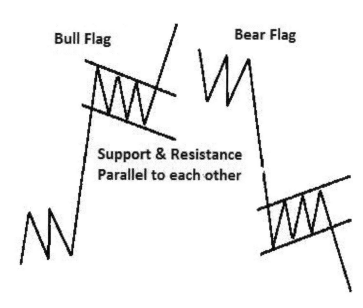

The Baseball Cap

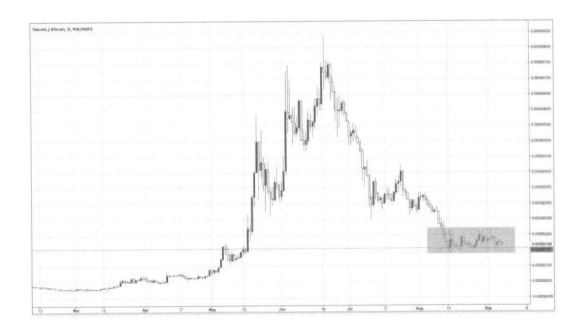

The Baseball cap is a consolidation pattern where a new support level forms after a dip in price. This new "floor price" means the price has stabilized for the time being, and due to the cyclical and high volatility nature of cryptocurrencies, this is usually followed a sharp increase in price. Like in the chart below. If you study the baseball cap pattern enough, then you can time you buys correctly - and therefore if you're going to learn one pattern well - make it this one.

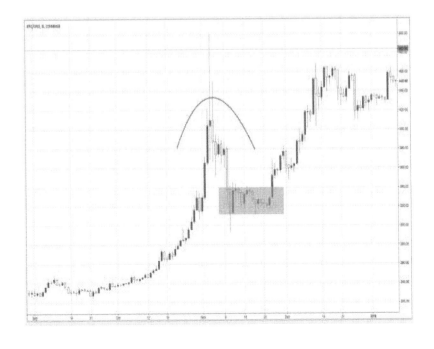

Trading Volume

Mistake 3: Not factoring volume into technical analysis

Another technical factor to take into account is the trading volume at a particular point in the chart. Ideally we want to see significant volume for upward trends, and lower volume for downward trends. If we see a downward trend accompanied by large volume, we can assume that this is not a weak trend and the price will continue to fall. Similarly, if we see volume is steadily decreasing on an upward trend, then this trend is likely coming to an end in the near future.

Limitations of Technical Analysis

Technical Analysis is just one tool that a trader needs in his arsenal. It is absolutely not the be all, end all of trading. Think of it as a guideline to making money, rather than a direct pathway.

The biggest factor is that we just don't have that much data available on the cryptocurrency market. Bitcoin has only been trading for 7 years now, and most other cryptocurrencies for less than 3. Unlike stocks where we have data for tens of years for individual stocks and the market as a whole.Sometimes, if you dive too deep into the technical side of trading, you lose your instincts and even your common sense. Even if your charts are saying hold, you should probably sell if your position is up 100% over the past 3 days. After all, what goes up, must come down. Developing solid trading instincts is something that does take time, but the more trades you make, you'll start to subconsciously notice things.

Remember, if you are unsure of a trade based on your analysis, look at the bigger picture and add another timeframe to your chart to see if the same patterns emerge.

Trading Mindset/Trading Psychology

One of the biggest hurdles new traders have to overcome is acquiring the mindset of a successful trader. This is even more prevalent in the cryptocurrency market because its sheer volatility allows the potential for large losses in addition to large gains. These losses can be demoralizing for even seasoned pros, but the important thing to remember is to know that these losses will come (professionals estimate a 55:45 win/loss ratio for even the best traders), and how to deal with them when they do happen. Acquiring a successful mindset is the single most important skill a trader must possess. Moreso than any technical tools. We must remember that we as humans have our own built-in biases, and even delusions, and many of these will hamper our trading ability. So the following is a list of important mindset and trading psychology factors that you must be aware of if you're going to become a successful trader.

Why Paper Trading is Useless

For years now, common trading advice has been that you should paper trade (trade with fake money) to get a hang of reading charts and learning when to buy and sell. However, I think this advice is limited at best, and potentially harmful.

You need to make mistakes with real money on the line, and you need to learn from these mistakes. Your brain and emotions simply don't react the same way if you know, deep down, that any losses you make are just on paper. To put it simply. You need to lose money to truly find out if trading is for you.

From then on, it's up to you how you react to these losses. Are you freaking out and trying to recoup them as soon as possible? Are you up until 4AM trying to get back some of the previous day's lost cash? If the answer is yes, then trading probably isn't for you. However, if you can accept that everyone has bad days, and learn to analyze your mistakes and decipher where exactly you went wrong, and most importantly, learn from them - you may well wind up as a successful trader in the long run.

Paralysis by Analysis

So, you've spent your time reading and studying charts, now it's time to go to CEX.io or your preferred trading website and deposit money into your account. So you do so, and begin looking at charts, and waiting…and waiting…but you just can't seem to pull the trigger. This happens to a lot of new traders, especially those who are naturally risk averse. You want everything to go perfectly and you want to start out on a good note. However, this is trading, and as previously mentioned, you need to make mistakes in order to get better.

This is also why you need proper money management in trading, because say you lose on 8 out of your first 10 trades (not uncommon by any means), you'll need to have properly managed your bankroll in order to be able to fight another day.

Knowing when not to trade

Mistake 4: Trading for the sake of trading

One of the more important qualities of a good trader is restraint. In other words, being able to understand that there are days where you don't need to make a trade. Maybe there are no obvious patterns appearing, maybe it's just a slow day in the market. Either way, you need to learn to take days off. This is good for preventing trading burnout as well, especially in the cryptocurrency market that is 24/7.

Accepting that the market is always right

One of our great cognitive biases as human beings, is believing we are better than we are at certain things. For example, are you an above average driver? I bet 90% of people will answer yes, but statistically, only 50% of people can be above average at anything, that includes trading as well.

What I'm getting at, is we often make excuses for our bad trades, such as the old classic "the market is wrong." The market will move in ways you don't expect, and if anyone had figured out a way to truly predict market direction, they would be a retired trillionaire by now. Your technical analysis will not influence the market, it will only help you make better decisions.

Accepting that you are wrong

Following on from the above point. The market isn't wrong, you are. You need to be able to accept that you will be wrong on many trades, even multiple trades in a row. Remember, judge yourself by your results, and not on any perceived "clever moves" you may have made. You will always have losers, but you need to be able to take a step back and accept this in order to move forward.

Taking Intermediate Profits

If your profits are only on paper, you haven't made squat. You need to convert some of your gains back to fiat from time to time. Taking profits helps you mitigate your need to even more money on paper, which leads to greed taking over, which inevitably leads to losing money in the long run. If you enter a trade at $70, with a plan to exit at $80 because you see resistance there, then exit at $80. Don't let the coin go to $80 and then revise your plan and hope it goes to $100. There is no greater force that turns winning trades into losers, than that of greed.

Survivorship Bias

In my original book *Cryptocurrency: Beginners Bible* I talked about survivorship bias, and how seemingly everyone had made money with cryptocurrency. Well this is because winners speak up, and losers stay quiet. If you spend any time in the trading community, you'll be constantly surrounded by stories from traders who turned $300 in $50,000 in just a few weeks. Or a 19 year old kid from Russia who made $200 million in under a year. Of course success stories exist, but there doesn't mean there aren't as many, and in the case of trading, even more silent parties who lost money trading cryptocurrency. So the lesson here is to only measure yourself against yourself. If you're making continuous profits, then you're doing something right.

Recency Bias

You're only as good as your last trade is something that many traders suffer from, especially if they have a run of losers. This leads to negative mental energy, and a loss of confidence in oneself. What you need to learn to do, is not focus on these losses, but look at the bigger picture. Instead of focusing on your next trade, focus on your next 100 trades. By focusing on the next 100 trades, you remain committed to your trading fundamentals as opposed to chasing short term results and dopamine hits.

7 Common Cryptocurrency Trading Myths

Mistake 5: Believing any of these myths

1. Cryptocurrency Trading Isn't Regulated therefore isn't safe

This is one of the oldest cryptocurrency myths that still lingers around the market today. Cryptocurrency trading may not be regulated in the same way traditional securities trading is, but that doesn't mean the exchanges don't follow regulations. Coinbase and GDax are both registered in the United States and therefore need to comply with SEC guidelines. Other exchanges need to comply with their local jurisdictions as well.

2. You need to know everything about blockchain technology to trade cryptocurrency

Knowing the ins and outs of the coin you're trading might be helpful, but it's certainly not essential. In fact, an argument could be made that it is more beneficial *not* to know that much about your coin, to avoid making an emotional attachment.

Keeping up to date on cryptocurrency market news as a whole is advisable however. The two best sources for unbiased cryptocurrency news are.

http://coindesk.com

http://cointelegraph.com

3. You need to know every single chart pattern every recorded

You'd be much better off knowing the basics well, then having a broad but limited knowledge of hundreds and hundreds of different chart patterns. This is especially true when starting out, as you'll start to see patterns everywhere, even when they really aren't there, and as a result - make poor trades.

4. Leaving your coins on an exchange is perfectly safe

Exchanges are centralized, and therefore, are vulnerable to security exploits and hacks. From Mt. Gox in 2014 (which was handling 70% of the world's bitcoin transactions at the time) to Bitfinex in 2016, exchange hacks do happen. It's best to transfer any funds you are not using at the time to a safe, offline storage solution like a paper or hardware wallet.

5. You should follow one person/one source's cryptocurrency trading tips

Following a single person's advice is a good way to lose money, even if that person themselves is profitable, because there will be a delay in their trades and your trades. This means your margin will be lower, and thus you are less likely to make consistent profits over time.

A compounding factor to this is paid trading advice or paid newsletter subscriptions. These are often nothing more than pump and dump schemes by those running them. Unfortunately, as much of the cryptocurrency world is still unregulated, these schemes often go unpunished.

6. **You should try to hit a home run with every trade**

An important part of trading is knowing *when* to take profits. The newbie trader often mistakes the critical mistakes of going for just that extra 1 or 2% more, which often never appears and suddenly your gains have quickly turned into losses.

7. **You can act as a perfect trader if you just learn the fundamentals**

Unfortunately, as humans we have these little things called emotions. Fear, excitement, greed, all of these play a big part in our trading mindset and our subsequent trading actions. Mastering your emotions is a huge part of being a successful trader, and we'll look into this in more depth later on this book in the trading mindset and trading psychology section.

Best Cryptocurrency platforms for traders

Cex.io or http://bit.ly/cexsatoshi

With trading fees ranging between 0.1% and 0.2% per trade, CEX.io has some of the lowest fees in the crypto trading sphere. An added bonus on zero deposit fees for bank transfers and cryptocurrency deposits makes this a favorite among crypto traders.

Bitfinex

Bitfinex offers the best liquidity of any cryptocurrency exchange on the market today. They also offer margin trading. Their fees are slightly higher than Cex.io, and the tiers needed to access lower fees are also higher. But Bitfinex still remains one of the premier cryptocurrency exchanges for trading today.

GDax

GDax is a subsidiary of Coinbase, so falls under the same SEC regulations a Coinbase does. The ease of transfers from Coinbase to GDax make it preferable to those who would rather keep their funds all on one single web ecosystem. Fees are slightly higher than both Cexio and Bitfinex, but the ease of transfers may outweigh these higher fees for some traders. GDax fees range from 0.1% to 0.25% for "takers" (buyers) 0% fee for "makers" (sellers).

Poloniex

Poloniex offers a wider range of cryptocurrencies than other exchanges listed here. So if you're looking at trading some lower cap altcoin pairs, then Poloniex might be the best option for your trading.

Coinigy

Based out of Wisconsin, Coinigy is a rather interesting concept in that it's not an exchange itself. But a desktop application that gives you access to 45 different cryptocurrency exchanges from a single account. They also have 75 different technical indicators available. Although the interface might be overwhelming at first for new traders, more experienced traders may enjoy the sheer range of options available. Their pro account costs $15/month and allows for unlimited trading with no additional fees, which is extremely cheap if you plan on trading at high volumes. They also have an Android app if you want to trade on the go. At $15/month the expense is worth it, even for a novice trader because the charting features by themselves are extremely helpful if you're just starting out.

Mistake 6: Trading on the Wrong Exchange

Where not to trade cryptocurrency

You should stay away from any exchanges that could potentially be closed down by government regulators, these include Chinese exchanges. I would also not recommend Coinbase for trading, as the fees are higher than the other exchanges listed, however for a first time buyer, Coinbase is still the most accessible cryptocurrency exchange.

Where to store your cryptocurrency - Wallets & Cold Storage

Mistake 7: Storing your cryptocurrency on an exchange

Once you've successfully bought some cryptocurrency, be it Bitcoin, Ethereum or another altcoin, you'll need somewhere to safely store it.

Your cryptocurrency wallet is akin to a regular fiat currency wallet in the sense that you can use it to spend money, in addition to seeing exactly how much money you have at any given time.

However cryptocurrency wallets differ from fiat currency wallets because of the technology behind how the coins are generated.

As a reminder, the way the technology works means your cryptocurrency isn't stored in one central location. It is stored within the blockchain. This means there is a public record of ownership for each coin, and when a transaction occurs, the record is updated.

You can store your cryptocurrency on the exchange where you bought it like Coinbase or Poloniex, it is advisable not to do this for a number of reasons.

1. Like any online entity - these exchanges are vulnerable to hacking, no matter how secure they are - or what security measures they take. This happened with the Mt. Gox exchange in June 2011

2. Your passwords to these exchanges are vulnerable to keyloggers, trojan horses and other computer virus type programs

3. You could accidentally authorize a login from a malicious service like coinbose.com (example) instead of coinbase.com

Cold storage refers to any system that takes your cryptocurrency offline. These include offline paper wallets, physical bearer items like physical bitcoin or a USB drive. We will examine the pros and cons of each one.

Cryptocurrency wallets have two keys. A public one, and a private one. These are represented by long character strings. For example, a public key could be 02a1633cafcc01ebfb6d78e39f687a1f0995c62fc95f51ead10a02ee0be551b5dc - or it could be shown as a QR code. Your public key is the address you use to receive cryptocurrency from others. It is perfectly safe to give your public key to anyone. Those who have access to you public key can only deposit money in your account.

On the other hand, your private key is what enables you to send cryptocurrency to others. For every transaction, the recipient's public key, and the sender's private key are used.

It is advisable to have an offline backup of your private key in case of hardware failure, or data theft. If anyone has access to your private key, they can withdraw funds from your account, which leads us to the number one rule of cryptocurrency storage.

The number one rule of Cryptocurrency storage: Never give anyone your private key. Ever.

Therefore, with your trading funds, it's advisable to keep any excess funds offline, a hardware wallet is an ideal way to do this because unlike a paper wallet, it is much simpler to transfer your funds between the hardware wallet and your computer in order to fund your trading account.

Paper Wallets:

Paper wallets are simply notes of your private key that are written down on paper. They will often feature QR codes so the sender can quickly scan them to send cryptocurrency.

Pros:

- Cheap - all you need a printer and some paper

- Your private keys are not stored digitally, and are therefore not subject to cyber-attacks or hardware failures.

Cons:

- Loss of paper due to human error

- Paper is fragile and can degrade quickly in certain environments

- Not easy to spend cryptocurrency quickly if necessary - not useful for everyday transactions

Recommendations:

It is recommended you store your paper wallet in a sealed plastic bag to protect against water or damp conditions.

If you are holding cryptocurrency for the long-term, store your paper inside a safe deposit box.

Ensure you read and understand the step-by-step instructions before printing any paper wallets.

Bitcoin:

http://bitaddress.org

http://bitcoinpaperwallet.com

Ethereum & ERC 20 tokens:

http://myetherwallet.com/

Litecoin: https://liteaddress.org/

Hardware Wallets

Hardware wallet refer to physical storage items that contain your private key. The most common form of these are encrypted USB sticks.

These wallets use two factor authentication or 2FA to ensure that only the wallet owner can access the data. For example, one factor is the physical USB stick plugged into your computer, and the other would be a 4 digit pin code - much like how you use a debit card to withdraw money from an ATM.

Pros:

- Near impossible to hack - as of the time of writing, there have been ZERO instances of hacked hardware wallets

- Even if your computer is infected with a virus or malware, the wallet cannot be accessed due to 2FA

- The private key never leaves your device or transfers to a computer, so once again, malware or infected computers are not an issue

- Can be carried with you easily if you need to spend your cryptocurrency

- Transactions are easier than with paper wallets

- Can store multiple addresses on one device

- For the gadget lovers among you - they look a lot cooler than a folded piece of paper

Cons:

- More expensive than paper wallets - starting at around $60

- Susceptible to hardware damage, degradation and changes in technology

- Different wallets support different cryptocurrencies

- Trusting the provider to deliver an unused wallet. Using a second hand wallet is a big security breach. Only purchase hardware wallets from official sources.

The most popular of these are the Trezor (bit.ly/GetTrezorWallet) and Ledger Nano S wallets. For altcoins that are not supported by these wallet, you can create your own encrypted USB wallet by following online tutorials.

Money Management while trading

Mistake 8: Not having a money management game plan

One of the most overlooked, but undoubtedly most important skills while trading is learning how to manage your bankroll.

You can think of trading cryptocurrency as akin to playing poker in this respect. If you put 50% of your holdings into one hand, then it only takes 2 losing hands in a row to wipe you out.

What's more is, when you lose money, you need to make more on your next trade in order to get back to your initial position. For example, if you lose 50% on one trade, you need to make 100% back on your next trade to break even. That's why trading with only a small amount of your holdings on a single trade is the smart way to go.

So no, you should never go "all in" on one single trade, no matter how much of a sure thing you think it is. The higher % of your total holdings you use for an individual trade, the higher your overall risk. In fact, the reason so many traders is that they don't anticipate losing a number of trades in a row. The holds true no matter how good you are at identifying chart patterns, or any other learned trading skill. Without proper money management, you will eventually go broke.

So let's just numbers. Because of the high risk element of trading cryptocurrency, I personally recommend that you do not risk more than 1-2% of your account on a single trade. The more active trades you are making at one time, the lower risk per trade should be. When you are starting out, I advise you risk no more than 0.5% of your account for your initial trades. This sounds low, but big dips do happen, and these can add up quickly, therefore we want to lower our risk as much as possible.

One more thing, cryptocurrency trading is a cash only undertaking. Under no circumstances should you borrow money from family, friends or financial institutions to trade. You don't want to start your trading career already owing people money, this has a huge negative effect on your state of mind and will cause you to make bad trades.

Risk/Reward Ratio

This is a vitally overlooked factor in trading. As we previously mentioned, if you lose 50% on one trade, you have to make up 100% on the next trade in order to break even. Therefore, you should enter all trades with a reward:risk ratio of at least 2:1. In other words, you must expect to make at least twice what you are willing to lose on the trade, because this will cover your losses from losing trades in the future. For example, if you are willing to lose $100 on a trade, you must be trying to gain $200 from that same trade. A higher reward:risk ratio allows you to have more losing trades, because your higher profits from winning trades make up for your losses on losing ones.

How many trades should you have open at once?

This is largely dependent on how much time you can spend looking at charts per day, but generally, you shouldn't have more than 5 or 6 open trades at a time. When you're starting out then one or two will be enough to cause your brain to work overtime. Remember to set stop losses if you want to manage multiple trades at once.

Which cryptocurrencies should you trade?

That's entirely up to you, however you should beware of coins with very low market caps and liquidity levels, as these are more susceptible to market manipulation and organized pump and dumps from nefarious parties.

I would recommend everyone start out with Bitcoin, purely because the market has the most liquidity.

Keeping a Trading Journal

Now, I'm not talking about a trading diary where you complain about your week's trading woes. I'm talking about logging your trades in an excel spreadsheet or a google doc. You can learn so much just from looking at your past trades, and you'll learn a hell of lot more from your losers than you will your winners.

As a thanks for downloading this book, I've including a handy trading journal for you to log you trades.

You can download the free spreadsheet at http://bit.ly/SatoshiTradingSpreadsheet

What causes price movements?

We have to remember here, that we are trading cryptocurrencies and not traditional stocks, and as such, the metrics for determining price are different.

The big difference is that there is limited fundamental analysis we can do on a coin when compared to traditional stocks. For example, we don't have earnings reports to look at or quarterly profit/loss statements. We also don't have to be concerned with potential mergers occurring between cryptocurrencies. Apart from, having a working product already, how fast the transaction fees are and scalability of the project, there really isn't much in the way of fundamental analysis. Both of these factors are more important for long term investing than they are for short term trading.

Market Sentiment

Overall market factors play strongly in the growth of individual cryptocurrencies. We are dealing with a singular market after all. For example, when Mt. Gox was hacked in 2014, and 850,000 Bitcoin were stolen, the entire market dropped as a result.

The second part of this equation is how mainstream media often misreports cryptocurrency price movements, being all too quick to cite a "plunge" or "crash". It's now getting to the report where media reports citing a "crash" happen on days where the price is still UP over the previous 24 hours.

Bitcoin's network effect is now so strong that many mainstream sources see Bitcoin as the be all, end all of cryptocurrency. Remember, buy the rumor, sell the news.

Bitcoin's price

The cryptocurrency market is still largely in its infancy, and as such, news regarding Bitcoin still greatly affects the market as a whole. At the time of writing, Bitcoin makes up roughly 56% of the overall cryptocurrency market cap, so any major Bitcoin price movements are reflected in the market as a whole. So even if you're trading smaller altcoins, it's wise to keep tabs on the price of Bitcoin as well.

Some commentators make the claim that Bitcoin and altcoin prices are inversely related, so if Bitcoin goes up, altcoins go down and vice versa. Whilst there is some data that backs up this theory, it isn't the entire story.

99% of people's first entry to the cryptocurrency market is into Bitcoin, this is even more so for institutional traders who move into cryptocurrency, because Bitcoin has the most liquidity, and therefore is an attractive market to enter. Therefore new money coming into the market is usually followed by investors moving their funds from altcoins into Bitcoin.

Asia

Mistake 9: Overlooking Asia' influence on the markets

One area to watch from looking for news to potentially affect trades, is any news coming out of Asia, particularly China and South Korea. These two countries have the highest volume of trades between them, more so than the USA, despite investors having to pay a premium (many South Korean exchanges trade cryptocurrencies for between 8-10% higher than US or European based ones). Any government clampdowns on exchanges or changes in legislation regarding cryptocurrency, is bound to have a negative effect on price. An example of this was the temporary ban on Chinese citizens investing in ICOs, which caused market prices to drop sharply. This was further compounded by the South Korean Financial Services Commission taking the same steps.

Stop Loss/Stop Limit Orders

Mistake 10: Not utilizing stop loss/stop limit orders

Stop loss and stop limit orders are both risk management tools that allow you to both prevent excessive losses on a trade, and also lock in any unrealized profits on an open trade. Both of these are relatively simple tools, but you would be amazed by just how many traders (usually the unsuccessful ones) fail to use them in their trading strategy,

A stop loss order is a level or particular price you set to automatically sell your position in a stock, or in this case a coin. For example, if you buy Bitcoin at $1000, you can set a stop loss order at $900, so that if the price falls to $900, you will automatically sell your position at that level, providing there is enough liquidity to fulfill it.

To use the second example above, say you make the same buy order for Bitcoin at $100, but it then increases to $110. You can set a stop loss at $105 to lock in your previously unrealized profits from this trade.

Effectively, you sell your position automatically once this level has been reached, which allows you to not have to monitor charts 24/7. This helps you in cases where a stock falls rapidly and prevents you from facing huge losses in open positions. The one drawback of relying solely on stop loss orders is that, if the volume is not there at your stop loss price, and the price continues to fall, your order will not execute and your position will still be open.

You can also use stop losses when shorting coins to prevent losses if the price increases after you place your short-sale.

A stop limit order is slightly different because you set both the maximum and minimum level you are willing to buy a particular coin. Let's say you want to buy Bitcoin at $95, but it is currently trading at $100, you can set a limit order so you automatically buy once it hits $95. But you can also set the order to automatically sell at $120 if it reaches that level. By doing this, you can step away from the computer, and providing the stock reaches those levels, the trade will execute automatically.

What you should set your stop loss at depends on your risk persona. Traditional trading advice recommends a 2% stop loss for each order, however with cryptocurrency's volatility, this may well be too conservative a measure and will result in excessive losses. I advise you to experiment for yourself and decide on your own personal stop loss point.

Note: For both stop loss and stop limit orders, you can employ a strategy of placing many smaller stop losses, which total up to your position in the coin - this prevents issues like a lack of volume to fulfill them. This isn't always necessary, but it worth doing as a precautionary step.

Margin Trading

Disclaimer: Margin trading is extremely risky, only do this if you can afford to lose everything you invest. Never ever short on margin in the cryptocurrency market.

If you're unaware of what margin trading is, Investopedia sums it up with this analogy

"Imagine this: you're sitting at the blackjack table and the dealer throws you an ace. You'd love to increase your bet, but you're a little short on cash. Luckily, your friend offers to spot you $50 and says you can pay him back later. Tempting, isn't it? If the cards are dealt right, you can win big and pay your buddy back his $50 with profits to spare. But what if you lose? Not only will you be down your original bet, but you'll still owe your friend $50. Borrowing money at the casino is like gambling on steroids: the stakes are high and your potential for profit is dramatically increased. Conversely, your risk is also increased."

Many cryptocurrency exchanges allow you to trade on margin, which is essentially borrowing money from the exchange in order to trade. Bitfinex allows for 3.3:1 margin trading, so for every $1 you have in your trading account, you can trade up to $3.3 on margin in the cryptocurrency markets. This is by no means the largest margin offered either, Kraken for example allows for 5X leverage on Bitcoin. BitMex, another exchange, allows for 100X margin, meaning you can literally borrow $100 for every $1 of your own money.

The reason exchanges allow margin trading is because the overall trade volume is higher, and therefore their fees are higher as well.

As a new trader, you should never trade using leverage. You are too inexperienced to be able to handle the potential losses that margin trading brings. Drops of 20 or 30% are not uncommon in crypto markets, and those drops are magnified when you are margin trading and can potentially wipe out your entire trading account.

Trading on margin also makes you vulnerable to flash crashes, such as in June 2017 when Ethereum fell from $360 to $13 for a brief period on GDax. Anyone trading on margin would have seen their funds wiped out in an instant.

Cryptocurrency Trading Bots

If you're not familiar with trading bots, they are automated pieces of software that perform technical analysis on stock, bonds or in these case, cryptocurrency. Ever since the boom in online trading, these bots have been synonymous with scams, pyramid schemes and other guaranteed money losers for those who use them.

The cryptocurrency world is no different, and I can safely say that the majority of trading bots on the market today are either completely useless or an outright scam.

Bonus Mistake 10.5: Believing "too good to be true" trading software or services

Cryptocurrency Bot & Trading Software Scams

CryptoRobot365

After defrauding hundreds of users, and receiving countless negative testimonials from those who never recovered their money, it's safe to say CryptoRobot365 should be well and truly avoided. To make matters worse, not only will you lose money, but your personal information may also be at risk.

The first warning sign is that this bot isn't registered with any regulated brokerages. The second being that although the software is advertised as free on signup, the actual minimum amount needed to have any access to the trading bot is a deposit of $250. The third sign being a fake "Best 2016 Performance Robot" icon on their website, when the site has only been registered since July 2017. The final nail in the coffin is that their testimonial page features a ton of fictitious testimonials using fake pictures and identities.

Unfortunately, as of the time of writing, the site still runs Google ads under popular keywords including "cryptocurrency trading bot". If you see it listed during a Google search, stay well away.

CryptoTrader.co

CryptoTrader.co's website opens with a man named Dave Richmond informing us that he can help us make $5,000 per day with his revolutionary new trading software. The software is apparently so good that he's turned 43 people into a millionaire last year! Notice any warning signs yet? Me too.

Like the above website, CryptoTrader.co also suffers from misinformation regarding how long the site has been functioning. The claims of making 43 people millionaire last year don't exactly hold up when the site has only been online for a few short months. The site also has no brokerage license or legal authority of any kind.

So with zero reviews on any independent websites, a website filled with a whole bunch of lies. An a frontman who appears to be a paid actor, CryptoTrader.co is definitely a no go as far as trading software websites.

Any person who approaches you with a trading bot

Occasionally if you hang out in enough cryptocurrency trading groups on social media or Telegram, someone will message me saying they have this great bot for sale at a surprisingly low price. If it looks too good to be true, it probably is. So stay well away from these low level scammers.

The only trading bot I recommend

HaasBot (http://bit.ly/HaasSatoshi) by HaasOnline is the only auto trading platform I recommend using. In a sea of scams and dodgy platforms, its nice to see a group with an ethical foundation.

The reasons for this recommendation are as follows: First of all, they refer to the operation as a trading platform rather than a trading bot. What they are actually selling is a software that numerous bots can be used with.

HaasOnline is completely upfront about what their bots *can* and more importantly *cannot* do. They don't make any vague guarantee about always beating the market like other bot or trading automation software does. Most importantly, they don't make any guarantees about monetary returns.

The software uses transparent technical analysis methods to perform trades. The bot uses this analysis to trade 24/7, and will add small amounts of volume needed to execute trades. There are also a number of safety features built in, to protect your investments.

Currently the bot supports over 500 different cryptocurrency pairings. Plus it is compatible with major cryptocurrency exchanges including Bitfinex, BitTrex and Poloniex. Where it may shine the most is with its built in arbitrage bot, which takes profits from the small difference between various pairings.

The team behind HaasOnline are based in the Netherlands, and there is a public figurehead in founder Stephen de Haas. In a discussion on popular Bitcoin forum bitcointalk.org, de Haas answered the questions "Can I get rich with this software?" in a frank manner.

"It's possible, but I can not guarantee this. As i stated before with speculation there is a risk involved. The main power of this simple trade bot is that it operated 24-hours a day. Meaning the bot will work for you when you are sleeping or working. This gives you the advantage of making more trades and possibly result in much higher profits."

Quality does come at a cost however, with the cheapest option being 0.09BTC (roughly $1000 at the time of writing), and the most expensive option being priced at 0.24BTC. However, this investment could be deemed as worth it by those looking to trade serious cryptocurrency volume, but can't dedicate 12+ hours a day to studying charts. The team also offers full, limited time refunds to those who use the software but for whatever reason do not like it.

Open Source Trading Software

There are a few open source platforms where developers have created their own trading bots for users to try free of charge. The two most popular of these are Gekko and ZenBot. Neither of these make any guarantees of profits, and were made more for experimentation than anything else. However as they are open source, and can be scrutinized by anyone, I'd thought I'd include them for those looking for a cheaper automated solution to their trading needs.

Trading Suicide

The following are moves that traders make that I consider trading suicide. Making any one, or more of these moves is generally a terrible idea, and **will lose you money** in the long run.

1. **Adding to a clear losing position**

Don't throw good money after bad. Let's say you've bought ETH at 300, and it's dropped to 270, but you're convinced it's going to rebound, do not top up your position. You may believe that by buying more at 270, your entry price averages out to 285, but you are unlikely to get back to this price before the stock drops even further. If you are clearly in a losing trade, close your position, get out, and live to trade another day.

2. **Focusing on single trades compared to long term profits**

Don't get attached to trades, especially bad ones. You may have thought you've done everything correctly, but sometime the market just knows better. Once again, get out, reset and live to trade another day.

3. **Checking prices of a coin after you've closed your position**

This is a subtle, yet deadly trading mistake that many losing traders make. It happens all too often, and leads to greed setting in for subsequent trades. Say you bought XMR at 180, and sold for 200, but you then see the price has gone up again to 215, and you start kicking yourself thinking "if only I'd held on a little bit longer", and you beat yourself up over your lost hypothetical profits.

The effect this has on your next trades is that it will cause you to hold onto positions for too long before closing, which inevitably leads to losses.

4. **Chasing a coin past your initial target entry price**

This is even more important if you're doing short term or day trading. You have a target entry price for a reason, because the charts say so. If for whatever reason you miss the entry price, then focus on another trade because your chances for profit has been drastically reduced.

5. **Being impatient with winning trades, and being too patient with losing ones**

Sometimes trades take time to play out, sufficient buyer demand may take a few days or even a week to appear, but as long as the price is moving sideways, you can keep the trade open. If you see downward movement however, it's best to get out as soon as possible and limit your losses.

6. **Not deciding if you want more fiat, or more cryptocurrency**

Cryptocurrency is unique in the respect that you can still make a good trade in terms of dollars, but you can lose money in terms of actual cryptocurrency gains. The best way to combat this, is to decide which cryptocurrency(ies) you want to make the most of, and focus on trading with that goal in mind, rather than flip flopping between USD gains and crypto gains.

7.   Not having a target exit price when you enter a trade

This is a surefire way to lose money. You need to have a target exit price or profit % based on your technical analysis, otherwise you will end up chasing gains for too long, and inevitably lose money. On top of target exit price, you should have a rough idea of how long you want to stay in the trade for.

8.   Trading in an unstable mood

This includes if you're under the influence of alcohol or narcotics. If you're in a bad mood, then don't trade. Your emotions will get the better of you, and you make stupid decisions and cost yourself money.

Conclusion

So there you have it. The biggest cryptocurrency trading mistakes that new traders make - and you can avoid them and become a profitable trader.

So remember, pick a trading strategy, and don't deviate from it.

Don't panic trade, and trade when you're in an unstable mood. Trade rationally, removing all emotion from the trade (as much as humanly possible anyway).

Only trade cryptocurrencies you're familiar with. So it's best to start with the ones with most liquidity like Bitcoin, Ethereum and Litecoin.

And trade on an exchange with low exchange fees, so your profits don't get eaten up the more you trade.

Utilize the spreadsheet I included to help you track your trades and identify patterns in your own trading.

I wish you the best of luck, and most importantly, I hope you make a lot of money with cryptocurrency.

Thanks,

Stephen

Additional Trading Resources:

The following are additional resources for everything from charting to trading psychology. Note, the majority of these are not cryptocurrency specific, nor am I affiliated with any of the authors.

Top 10 Trading Setups Explained by Ivaylo Ivanov - Focuses on traditional markets like stocks, but the lessons can be easily applied to cryptocurrency. The book shows you how to recognize overall market patterns and how to approach each one of them.

Technical Analysis of Stock Trends (9th Edition) by Robert Edwards and John Magee - If you're going to buy one "encyclopedia" of technical analysis, make it this one.

One Up on Wall Street by Peter Lynch - Lynch famously beat the market 15 years in a row. Much of his trading advice holds true today as much as it did when the book was first released. Note, the paperback version of this book is cheaper than the Kindle version for reasons unknown

Cryptocurrency: 13 More Coins to Watch with 10X Growth Potential in 2018

By Stephen Satoshi

Free Bonus!

As a gift to you for downloading this book I'm offering a special bonus. It's a free, exclusive special report detailing 3 microcap coins with huge growth potential in 2018. I guarantee you won't find these discussed in any mainstream cryptocurrency forums or newsletters. These 3 were picked as a result of weeks of research on microcap cryptocurrencies.

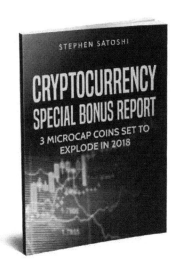

Grab the free report here!

Or go to http://bit.ly/FreeSatoshiReport

Introduction - Cryptocurrency as we head into 2018

2017 was undoubtedly the year that Cryptocurrency arrived on the world stage. The total market cap surged from $18 billion on January 1st to over $600 billion by the end of the year. Coinbase became the world's number one most downloaded app and saw transaction volume increase by a factor of 30.

Bitcoin hit $20,000 per coin very briefly in December. Ethereum went from $9 to over $700, and Litecoin finally broke out and hit $300 by the end of the year. Average returns for investing over the 12 month period range from 200% on the low end, to over 1000%. Frankly, if you put money into cryptocurrency in 2017, it was near impossible to lose.

One of the most startling statistics of 2017 was that if you had invested $100 into the top 10 market cap coins on January 1st, you would have seen returns of $43,000 over the course of the year.

But how does that affect us going forward? Will we have a repeat of last year and see gigantic market growth once more? We'd all sure like to hope so. It's likely though that the market will be a little more nuanced as we progress.

It's clear now that cryptocurrency isn't just "internet gimmick money", we are truly witnessing the birth of a brand new asset class. Institutional money is flowing into the market just as fast as consumer money. There are multiple cryptocurrency ETFs in the works and December saw the launch of Bitcoin futures on CME, the world's largest futures exchange.

But to those of us who are in search of projects with potential for huge growth, 10X, 100X or even 1000X growth, that we now know is completely possible within the cryptocurrency space, we have to dig a little deeper. That's why in this book I'm listing 13 coins with huge possibilities in 2018. Coins with exciting ideas, projects and use cases. Some of them may be more familiar to you than others, but every single one of them has been hand picked based on my own criteria, and you can rest assured that many other coins were discarded in the selection process.

I wish you the very best in your cryptocurrency investing journey, and I hope you make a lot of money.

Thanks,

Stephen

Factors that affect coin growth

Continued Adoption

It's easy to forget sometimes that we are still very much in the early stages of the market. Cryptocurrency may have quickly reached a $600 billion market cap, but that is still dwarfed by the $200 trillion market cap of stocks, cash, gold and bonds combined. And blockchain technology as a whole still has a huge amount of growing to do.

Adoption of coins both as payment methods for currency based coins, as well as, partnerships with larger corporations for non-currency based ones will lead to continued growth going forward.

Coinbase

Coinbase, the cryptocurrency exchange app ended 2017 having hit the number one download spot on the Apple store and Google Play store. The vast majority of the new players into the market (and that may well include yourself), got their start with Coinbase. The convenience of being able to buy and sell cryptocurrency on the go using a credit card is something that favors mass adoption. Especially when compared to previous years when complex wire transfer processes made cryptocurrency much harder for the average person to buy.

As you may know, however, Coinbase currently only deals with 3 cryptocurrencies. Namely, Bitcoin, Ethereum and Litecoin. However, Coinbase Co-Founder and CEO Asiff Hiriji stated in December 2017 that the platform plans to add more coins in the coming months. With rumors about which coins would be added driving up the price of a number of altcoins including Ripple and Bitcoin Cash.

Needless to say, the next coin to be added on Coinbase will see short term positive effects regardless of its long term potential. Much of the cryptocurrency buying public won't be able to wait to get their hands on the shiniest new coin. However, exactly which coins would be added is still largely unknown, although we can make some educated guesses into which ones *won't* be next in line.

Monero - Its status as a complete privacy coin conflicts with Coinbase's position as an SEC regulated entity and their anti-money laundering provisions. The same applies to coins like **ZCash.**

Neo - NEO is not divisible like other cryptocurrencies, and could technically be classified as a security which pays a dividend (in the form of GAS). This makes it hard for Coinbase to add it due to being bound by SEC regulations.

It should also be noted that there are multiple fake images online showing Dash, Monero and Ripple added to Coinbase. Please check the official website before buying or selling on other exchanges based on news of Coinbase additions.

Update: As of December 20th 2017, Bitcoin Cash was added to Coinbase

Bitcoin

Like it or not, Bitcoin's price still carries a lot of the new money being flooded into the market. Although this may prove to be less of an issue going forward as many first time buyers are now investing in Ethereum or Litecoin as their first venture into the cryptocurrency market, Bitcoin is still a major factor in determining overall market sentiment.

The cryptocurrency flowchart generally goes like this.

1. New investors buy Bitcoin with fiat currency as their first foray into the market > Bitcoin's price goes up

2. As Bitcoin's price goes up, altcoin holders move their money into Bitcoin > Altcoin prices go down

3. If Bitcoin's price falls, those holding Bitcoin cash out to fiat, signaling decreased market confidence > Bitcoin & altcoin prices go down

4. If Bitcoin's price remains stable, investors begin to look for new opportunities and begin researching and buying altcoins > altcoin prices rise

If you track the BTC vs. Altcoin patterns in 2017, this generally holds true. Altcoins perform best when Bitcoin prices are stable, and not moving much in either direction. Large movements in Bitcoin price generally have negative effect on altcoin prices.

Legislation

Cryptocurrency leglisation is still a hot topic, and one where we are still largely in the unknown. Poorly researched news articles with headlines such as "Chinese government bans Bitcoin" tend to be the ones that are the most read, even if their factual accuracy is debatable at best.

Cryptocurrency at its core ideals has always been a decentralized idea. In other words, the entire existence is predicated on moving away from control by a single central government. However, in practical terms, especially where investments and securities are concerned, there does have to be some form of recognition by governments, at a national level at least.

For US citizens, the number one short term concern would be senate bill including digital currencies as part of current anti-money laundering laws. These laws would force traders to reveal indentities in certain circumstances, which would obviously hamper the growth of privacy based cryptocurrencies such as Monero, ZCash and Verge. This is also a concern for both UK and EU citizens, whose governments are working on their own version of similar rulings.

Asian legislation is another area of concern, with China and South Korea being under the spotlight specifically. These two markets represent the largest portion of the cryptocurrency space, and government clampdowns from both of these countries have had negative effects on the overall market as recently as mid 2017.

Atomic Swaps

Atomic swaps are one of the most fascinating cryptocurrency developments as we move into 2018, and one that is sure to affect many coins going forward. Atomic swaps allow coin conversions, without the need for a third party. For example, if you own 1 Bitcoin and your friend owns 100 Litecoin, and you want to swap. Currently you would have to use a third party exchange to do so. Third party exchanges require both fees and a degree of trust.

However, by using atomic swaps, there is no need for a third party as both the sender and recipient could confirm the transaction themselves by using what is known as a hash-time limited contract (HTLC). An HTLC is essentially a one-time code that would be generated as part of the swap, that is required to verify its success. If the code is not entered by either party, the transaction will be reversed and both parties will receive their initial coins back.

Up to this point, we have only seen atomic swaps used in very limited amounts, because cryptocurrencies are running on different blockchains, and we need them to share the same cryptographic hash function. The implementation of Lightning Network would allow this to occur. Currently, successful atomic swaps have been carried out between Litecoin, Bitcoin, Vertcoin and a few other coins. Coins that are capable of atomic swaps may well have significant first mover advantage going forward.

Coin Prices & Fractions

I know what you're thinking, I bought this book just to be told the price of a coin matters?! First, let me expand on this rather obvious statement. Cryptocurrencies are unique in the sense that many of them (with notable exceptions like Neo) are divisible into tiny fractions. Bitcoin, for example, is available down to 8 decimal digits, so you could go on an exchange and buy 0.0000001 Bitcoin.

Why does this matter? Simply put, it's extremely confusing to new investors who have previously only bought entire shares of companies. Therefore, they would rather buy 1 of a certain cryptocurrency, than a fraction of another - especially if there are no other deciding factors between the two. It appears easier to buy a "whole" of one coin versus a fraction of another. Therefore, coins with a low $ price are inherently more attractive, even if they have a huge market cap and have less room for potential growth than coins with a lower supply and market cap, but a high $ price per coin.

For example, Ripple currently trades at around $0.50 per XRP, and is seen as "cheap" by many inexperienced buyers, despite its huge market cap. The same applies to Stellar Lumens which trades at around $0.28 per XLM.

Factors to Consider Before Investing

While larger cryptocurrencies like Bitcoin, Ethereum and Litecoin have long track records and multiple real world functions, some of the coins mentioned in this book do not - hence their lower price.

There are a number of different variables to investigate before you undertake any investment, and cryptocurrency has its own set.

Proof of Concept (PoC)

In other words, does the technology have a working model, or is it still in a theoretical stage. Obviously more mature coins will have a higher value, with the more theoretical coins being a bigger risk. As the different coins here are in different stages of their life cycle, that is up for you to decide.

The Development Team

Who are the developers and what is their track record? Particularly within the cryptocurrency and blockchain space. Another thing to consider their record within the particular industry they are targeting, and if they have industry connections are not.

The Utility Of The Coin

Ideas are great, but if the coin token itself doesn't have usage, then the true potential of the project must be questioned. This is especially true in the case of certain coins where the theory and market potential checks out, but the question of "why can I just use Bitcoin/Litecoin to do the same thing" is often raised.

The Roadmap

Roadmaps are important for short-term gains because they set out development targets for the coin. If these goals are reached and the products/platforms move from alpha to beta to a fully launched product, then that only means positive things for the coin and its value. However continually missed targets are a red flag.

Which exchanges is the coin listed on

Many of these coins are still only available on smaller exchanges. Once the coin is listed on larger exchanges, with Coinbase being the biggest and most accessible, the coin has greater visibility and this leads to a rise in value.

Mining Algorithm - Proof of Work vs. Proof of Stake vs. Proof of Signature

You'll notice later on when discussing individual coins that I talk about which mining algorithms are used. The two most popular are Proof of Work (PoW), used by Bitcoin and Proof of Stake (PoS), which will be used by Ethereum from Q4 2017 and beyond, and is currently used by a number of Ethereum based tokens. There is also Proof of Signature (PoSIGN), which is used by newer projects including Xtrabytes.

How to Buy Bitcoin, Ethereum or Litecoin

Gone are the days when buying cryptocurrency was a time consuming and somewhat uncomfortable endeavor. Nowadays buying Bitcoin and other popular cryptocurrencies is a similar process to exchanging currency when you go on vacation.

If you haven't purchased any cryptocurrency before, what you need to do first is to use fiat currency (USD, EUR, GBP etc.) to purchase cryptocurrency via an exchange. These exchanges function the same way as regular foreign currency exchanges do. The prices fluctuate on a daily basis, and like regular currency exchange markets - they are open 24/7. Exchanges make their money by charging a small fee for each transaction.

Some charge both buyers and sellers, some only charge a fee for buying. For security reasons, most of these exchanges will require you to verify your ID before allowing you to purchase cryptocurrency.

It is also important to note the type of payments each exchange supports. Some allow for debit/credit card payments whereas other only accept PayPal or bank wire transfers.

Coinbase

Currently largest currency exchange in the world, Coinbase allows users to buy, sell and store cryptocurrency. Coinbase is undoubtedly the most beginner friendly exchange for anyone looking to get involved in the cryptocurrency market. They currently allow trading of Bitcoin, as well as, Ethereum and LiteCoin using fiat currency as a base. Known for their stellar security procedures and insurance policies regarding stored currency. The exchange also has a fully functioning iPhone and Android app for buying and selling on the go, very useful if you are looking to trade.

Once you are signed up and complete the identity verification procedures you can buy Bitcoin with your credit or debit card instantly.

Coinbase also recently launched the Coinbase Vault, which is a secure way of storing your cryptocurrency while still having it accessible to trade. The vault uses double email address + phone verification in order to access your funds. If you're planning on holding long-term, I still recommend offline storage - but as an intermediary option, the Vault is a step in the right direction.

How do I buy these altcoins if I can not buy them in my local currency?

Buying altcoins can be confusing at first because the vast majority of them aren't available to buy in exchange for fiat currency. Therefore, there are a few steps to go through, but not to worry, because here is a step by step guide to buy altcoins.

1. Create an account on Coinbase

Coinbase is still the easiest way for most people to get involved in the cryptocurrency market. Once you sign up (remember to use the link http://bit.ly/10dollarbtc to get $10 worth of Bitcoin for free after your first transaction)

2. Buy Bitcoin, Ethereum or Litecoin

You can either do this directly on Coinbase, or by transferring your money to Coinbase's sister site GDax which has lower transaction fees. You can use your Coinbase login credentials to access GDax.

Once you have bought your coins, they will be automatically transferred to your wallet on the respective site. Remember, if you are buying purely for the sake of exchanging coins for the altcoins mentioned in this book, then I recommend buying ETH rather than BTC because the transfer fees will be much lower.

3. Send coins to your exchange of choice

I have listed which exchanges to buy these coins at, on the individual coin page under "where to buy". Create an account on that particular website and go to the "deposit" page. Once on the page select your respective coin's wallet (double check you haven't selected the wrong one), and generate an address

You address will be a string of alphanumeric characters similar to this

0x0ded6e1e425eeb3876269c6ae93df77944acf4eee4fe1d7ccd77b185dce1d207

Go to the send coins page on your Coinbase/GDax account and copy the above address into the "recipient" box, and click confirm. This will show your transaction fee as well (for ETH it is currently around $0.40 per transaction).

4. Use your coins to exchange for altcoins

Once the transaction has gone through and your coins are now showing up in your new wallet, you can exchange them for the altcoins of your choice. For example, if you want to buy XLM, you can select the XLM/ETH pairing on the exchange.

How to save up to $20 on each altcoin transaction

One of the major problems we face right now in cryptocurrency is the sheer strain on the network as it tries to keep up with increased demand. Transaction fees and transaction times have been dramatically increasing since Mid-November, and new investors are realizing the hard way when they try to transfer their coins from where they bought them, to another exchange.

Many websites give instructions of "Buy bitcoin first, then send to an exchange". However, this is fundamentally wrong and will cost you money. It is much cheaper to buy and send Ethereum for the purpose of exchanging it with one of the coins listed below. The same applies to Litecoin, but there are much fewer Litecoin/altcoin pairs available when compared to Bitcoin and Ethereum.

Currently the approximate transaction prices for each coin are as follows

Bitcoin: $17

Ethereum: $0.40

Litecoin: $0.13

Coins to Watch in 2018

WaBi (WABI)

Price at Time of Writing: $2.00

Market Cap at Time of Writing: $90,339,960

Available on:

BTC: Binance

ETH: Binance, EtherDelta

Where to store:

WaBi can be stored on MyEtherWallet or the Mist desktop wallet

WaBi is a Chinese based blockchain initiative that focuses on anti-counterfeiting for physical products. Born out of the 2012 Chinese milk scandal, that saw 6 children die and over 50,000 hospitalized as a result of fake baby milk formula, the project aims to battle the $500 billion counterfeiting industry.

WaBi's solution to this is linking products using RFID labels with a built-in anti-counterfeit measure. Using Walimai's anti-counterfeiting RFID technology allows consumers to verify the authenticity of the product using their smartphone. Blockchain technology comes into this by verifying product authenticity on a decentralized digital ledger that would allow anyone to see which products are authentic and which ones are not. This essentially creates a secure link between the digital and physical domains. This has ramifications for so many consumer goods industries including baby food, pharmaceuticals, alcohol, clothing and electronics.

This bold venture faces many challenges, especially as there are physical products involved, which in itself has its own set of hurdles. For example, deterioration of product labels, can the labels be securely attached for the entirety of the product's lifespan, and if not, can they be replaced with counterfeit labels?

However, after 3 years of development, the WaBi team has now successfully created a working product as of December 2016, and their tags feature both a unique encrypted product ID and geolocation data of the product source I.e. which factory it was manufactured at. So counterfeiters would have to be able to replicate both of these if they wanted to produce a fake version of the same product, which would prove near impossible unless they have access to the exact same factory where the authentic version of the product is produced.

There is also the issue of consumer trust, can consumers really be sure that the authenticity data is accurate? Well, that's where blockchain technology comes in. Because records are publicly available, and constantly updated in real time, there is no inherent reason not to trust them.

The next level of this trust is the facilitation of consumer to consumer or peer to peer sales. The problem with traditional peer to peer platforms like eBay, and newer ones such as social media based selling, has always been the prevalence of counterfeit goods. As this selling platforms are not under the same legal scrutiny as traditional ones, sellers of counterfeit goods often get away with it. By utilizing WaBi technology, a potential buyer can verify the authenticity of any product *before* the sale goes through, which ensures that all transaction and products are legitimate. The platform has already undergone testing in China, both in ecommerce and in physical stores.

The WaBi token itself will be given to customers every time they scan an item. There are plans for these token to then be used as a loyalty incentive for customers to purchase products with the token as opposed to cash.

2018 will see WaBi roll out to over 1,000 stores across China. Price action in the short term will largely dependent on the token being available on more exchanges because Binance alone is not enough to support increased token demand.

Neo (NEO)

Price at Time of Writing - $72.25

Market Cap at Time of Writing - $4,696,120,000

Available on:

Fiat: Yunbi (CN), Jubi (CN), Livecoin

BTC: Bittrex, Binance, Bitfinex

ETH: Bittrex

Where to store:

Wallets are available on the official Neo website

I previously discussed Neo in my first book *Cryptocurrency: Beginners Bible.* Since then the price has risen by over 900%, and a number of exciting new developments have occurred with the Neo project, so I thought an update would be appropriate as we move into 2018.

One of these earliest Chinese based blockchain projects, Neo, formerly known as Antshares prides itself on being open source and community driven. The coin has been compared to Ethereum in the sense that it runs smart contracts instead of acting as a simple token like Bitcoin. The project is developed by a Shanghai based company called ONCHAIN.

In a June 2017 press conference held at the Microsoft China HQ in Beijing, the Antshares founder Da Hongfei announced the rebranding to Neo as well as discussing other projects in the pipeline. These included collaborating with certificate authorities in China to map real-world assets using smart contracts.

Neo's base in China allows it unique access to the world's 2nd largest market and the largest cryptocurrency market. This of course is seen as a unique plus when compared to other cryptocurrencies. However current drawbacks include a limited number of wallets for the coin itself, and a lack of ICOs completed on the platform. As of December 2017, there has still only been 1 Neo ICO in the form of Red Pulse.

At the Microsoft China event - Srikanth Raju, GM, Developer Experience & Evangelism and Chief Evangelist, Greater China Region, Microsoft, said that ONCHAIN is "one of the top 50 startup companies in China." Support and positive press from a global powerhouse like Microsoft can only be a positive for Neo going forward.

Perhaps the biggest determining factor for NEO going forward is support from the Chinese government. While other cryptocurrencies suffer from legal battles with governments, Neo's relationship with the leadership has been low key if somewhat positive, with founder Da Hongfei attending government conferences and seminars on cryptocurrency and blockchain technology. After China banned Chinese citizens from participating in ICOs in July 2017, the entire cryptocurrency market took a hit. Neo has the potential to change this. For example, a future ruling that ICOs built on Neo are legal in China would likely see Neo's popularity increase on a worldwide scale.

One thing to be wary of with Neo is once again, a Chinese factor. This time it's the language barrier, as much of the news about the coin is published in Chinese originally, there is significant potential for mistranslations in the English speaking world. For example, "partnerships" with Microsoft and Alibaba (China's largest eCommerce company) have been overstated due to poor translations from Chinese news sources. That doesn't mean collaborations like this aren't possible in the future, but you should always be wary of news coming out of China, especially where unofficial translations are involved.

In the commonly held Neo versus Ethereum debate, there is no reason why one coin has to "win" against the other. Blockchain technology increases in popularity year by year, and there is no reason that both projects cannot coexist. In the short-term at least I would expect DApps to be built on both platforms.

The smart contracts running on Neo include equities, creditor claims, bills and currencies. This also includes the ability to issue what is known as "digital identities", this is paramount if things like financial assets need to be registered on the platform, because it acts a failsafe and holds people accountable if they break the terms of agreements they have set up. These identities will use internationally agreed upon standards, and as such will be compliant in the eyes of regulators. This may contradict many people's idea of completely private blockchain transactions, where identities of all parties are anonymous, but total privacy is not needed for *all* blockchain projects.

Neo has a number of developments planned for 2018, including NEOX, which will be Neo's version of atomic swaps and allow users to swap cryptocurrencies seamlessly without the need for an exchange. As of December 2017 though, this is still very much in the testing stage and the Neo team have not yet completed an atomic swap using NEOX. There are also several more ICOs planned for the platform.

It should also be noted for investing reasons, that one unique aspect of Neo, is that unlike most other cryptocurrencies, the coins are not divisible, so the smallest unit you can buy is indeed 1 Neo.

Gas (GAS)

Price at Time of Writing: $26.97

Market Cap at Time of Writing: $231,878,704

Available on:

Fiat: Coinnest (KOR)

BTC: Binance, Poloniex, OKEx

ETH: Poloniex

Where to store:

Note: Some exchanges will note credit your Gas if you hold Neo in their wallet. Binance definitely *does* credit it, but to make sure you should hold Neo in a non-exchange wallet.

If you've heard of Neo (or if you bought my first book back in August when it was trading at ~$7 as Antshares), then you've probably heard of Gas (previously Antcoins).

Gas is the token used to pay for transactions and service fees using the Neo network. So anytime someone sets up a smart contract, then Gas will be used as a means of payment for the network. It should be noted that the network is currently free as a means of garnering adoption in early stages, but this won't always be the case.

Essentially, Gas is the utility of the entire Neo ecosystem. Gas is what powers the Neo blockchain and allows the DApps built on it to function. Neo tokens on the other hand function more like shares in Neo as a whole.

You can earn Gas just by holding Neo in a wallet (so not on an exchange), currently if you hold 1 NEO, it would take approximately 22 years to generate 1 Gas. However, it may well be more profitable just to buy Gas itself. The thinking behind is the based on the Gas:Neo price ratio, which tends to hover between 0.3 to 0.5. However, many analysts believe the long term ratio will actually be closer to 0.8. This makes Gas an interesting play for higher potential gains than Neo itself. Especially as more and more DApps are launched on the Neo network, and these DApps require more Gas to function.

Right now the schedule of Gas produced by the Neo network is scheduled to end after 22 years (when all 100 million Gas tokens will be in circulation.) There is a caveat however as the Neo developers still reserve the right to produce more Gas tokens if necessary. The team also reserve the right to adjust the amount of Gas required to use the network, however, this should not impact the price of Gas in theory (as they can simply divide the required price into fractions).

Right now the main issues with Gas prices have been that it is not as widely available on exchanges as Neo. For many months Gas was only available to buy on Chinese exchanges, and even at the time of writing, it only available on Binance and Poloniex. So let's make this entirely clear, due to the laws of supply and demand - **it is completely possible for Gas to be worth more than Neo in the short term.**

Stellar Lumens (XLM)

Price at Time of Writing: $0.28

Market Cap at Time of Writing: $5,064,226,845

Available on:

BTC: Bittrex, Binance, Kraken

ETH: Bittrex, Binance

Where to store:

A full selection of wallets including mobile, desktop and web-based are available on

https://www.stellar.org/lumens/wallets/

XLM tokens are also compatible with the Ledger Nano S hardware wallet.

A late bloomer that saw some big price rises at the very end of 2017. Stellar Lumens is an intriguing project with a rather interesting history behind it.

Drawing obvious comparisons to Ripple, the Stellar network is focused on payment processing between large corporations and in the consumer to consumer space. The main difference however is that Stellar operates as a nonprofit organization that doesn't charge for use of the network. The initial funding for the project was from payment processor Stripe.

For example, you are an American who wants to send money to your friend who lives in Germany. Currently, you would have to pay large transaction fees to send Euros from your US bank. However, by using XLM (or Lumens, the currency of the Stellar network). You could send USD, and your friend could withdraw money in Euros, without having to pay huge currency conversion fees. The current base fee for a transaction is just 0.00001 XLM, which is just a fraction of a penny, which is paid for by the sender. Like other blockchain projects, transactions on the Stellar network are publicly available and verifiable to prevent fraud occurring.

The Stellar team also focus on social causes, such as making saw a banking system is available to those who don't currently have access to one. The reduced fees, especially for those who need to frequently send money overseas, is a big selling point in the third world countries this initiative is targeting.

2017 was a big year for the Stellar project, Forbes magazine dubbed it "Venmo, but on a global scale - and for larger bodies like banks and corporations." The coin was added to larger exchanges like Binance and is now compatible with well known hardware wallet including the Ledger Nano S.

In October, the team announced a formal partnership with IBM and KickEx to "develop a blockchain-based cross-border payments solution proven to significantly reduce transaction costs and increase transaction speeds." This announcement kick started a price surge for Stellar which continued for the remainder of the year.

Stellar's history is one that should be mentioned as well. It was founder in 2014 by Jeb McCaleb and Joyce Kim. McCaleb has history in the cryptocurrency space and was one of the founders of the Mt. Gox exchange, which at its peak was the largest cryptocurrency exchange in the world. McCaleb sold the exchange in 2011, shortly before the hacking incident that would result in Mt. Gox's bankruptcy.

McCaleb then moved on to Ripple, but was made to leave the team after the Mt. Gox incident which deterred major financial institutions from wanting to deal with the project. This is where it gets dicey, after being asked, McCaleb announced that he would be liquidating his 9 billion XRP that he accumulated for his part in the project. He proceeded to do so in one lump sum and resulted in XRP's price crashing. He was then taken to court by Ripple and ended up losing the case.

This doesn't necessarily mean anything for Stellar going forward, and the project has been free of any controversy thus far. However I do feel it is important to take a look at the backgrounds of prominent team members, especially those with a track record like McCaleb's.

Moving into 2018, the success of Stellar Lumens will largely depend on the continued adoption of the platform. Partnerships with groups such as SatoshiPay, a web payment system that helps online publishers monetize their content is one such initiative. As of December 2017, the network was processing roughly 30,000 transactions per day with an average transaction time of 4 seconds.

The network does have built-in inflation to deal with the increasing volume of transactions. Currently, this rate is set at 1% per year. 5% of all Lumens (5 billion) are reserved for operating the network.

Groestlcoin (GRS)

Price at Time of Writing: $2.14

Market Cap at Time of Writing: $147,727,132

Available on:

Fiat: Litebit.EU (EUR)

BTC: Bittrex, Cryptopia, Livecoin

ETH: CoinExchange

LTC: Cryptopia

Where to store:

Wallets are available from https://www.groestlcoin.org/downloads/

The rather strangely named Groestlcoin (pronounced "Grow-es-tul coin"), based off an Austrian word meaning quality and rigor, the coin has drawn comparisons to both Litecoin and Vertcoin. GRS is actually a pioneer in cryptocurrency in that it was the first coin to successfully utilize SEGWIT activation back in January 2017.

One of the key components of GRS is how easy it is to mine. If you've read any of my previous books, you'll know that I'm generally against at-home, consumer level mining for larger coins like Bitcoin and Ethereum, due high startup costs, electricity wastage and decreasing ROI year on year. However, GRS has seemingly found a workaround to this issue with their unique mining algorithm.

In their own words "You can mine with your old laptop and still turn over a profit", and power costs are far lower than mining larger coins, and the computer hardware needed is nowhere near as expensive.

In terms of actual use cases, GRS will function mainly for peer-to-peer transactions like Litecoin. There is also a privacy element (similar to Monero), by using the official Samurai wallet, users can use completely anonymous addresses with 256 bit encryption.

The coin also has a large number of available wallets (which many larger coins are still struggling with), including ones for less popular platforms like Blackberry and Linux. There are also plans to get hardware wallet support in early 2018.

One of the main determinants of the GRS price going forward will be the popularity of atomic swaps. This is a function where users can do coin-to-coin swaps for minimal transaction fees. Uptake of atomic swaps would allow users to exchange coins without having to rely on a centralized exchange.

Funnily enough, one of the sticking points in the GRS community is the name itself. There is a planned rebranding vote, with G2Coin being the most popular alternative suggestion right now. However, as of the time of writing, Groestlcoin remains the name, and GRS the symbol on exchanges.

Ultimately the success of GRS is in much the vein as the other "payment coins" such as Litecoin and Vertcoin. Can their features prove enough to reach wider adoption, especially in the face of mounting Bitcoin dominance in the space, which only appears to be getting stronger. After all, getting merchants or ecommerce stores to accept one crypto payment is one thing, but adopting 4 or 5 at once is whole other story. That being said, GRS is certainly one to watch based on the atomic swap factor alone.

Substratum (SUB)

Price at Time of Writing: $0.56

Market Cap at Time of Writing: $128,717,705

Available on:

BTC: Binance, HitBTC, KuCoin

ETH: Binance, HitBTC, EtherDelta

Where to store:

Substratum is an ERC20 token and can be stored using MyEtherWallet

Substratum is a blockchain project that focuses on the reallocation of unused computer resources. This has many applications such as web hosting and providing storage space for databases. Substratum aims to target both the institutional and consumer markets.

The main difference between this project and traditional cloud hosting services like Amazon Web Services or Rackspace, is that rather than paying for total uptime, users would pay per click on their site. So if you decide to host an unpopular website that doesn't get my traction, you won't be spending excess money on hosting that you don't need.

The platform also promises to be censorship free, so there would be no external monitoring or geo-restrictions in place. This is especially important in the times of net neutrality, where governments give internet service providers that right to charge more to access certain content.

The leads to the question of dealing with content that is deemed morally or legally bad such as terrorism or child pornography. As the network is decentralized, no single person or group has the ability to restrict what can or cannot be seen. Substratum users can vote to remove content from the network if it is deemed obscene or illegal. This voting system would be weighted so that it cannot be manipulated for personal gain by certain groups.

This is the area of the project that has come under the most scrutiny so far. Is a simple voting system enough or keep illegal content from being hosted? Following on, is there a potential workaround to this that doesn't involve a centralized body being in charge of what can and cannot be hosted on the network. Without a doubt, this is the biggest challenge the Substratum project faces in the short term.

Hosting on Substratum can be done by anyone with an internet connection, and hosts would be paid per click as well. The plans are for hosts to be able to run their service or "nodes" in the background without any disruption to their computer's performance. These nodes would be dynamic, so if you are not using your computer, it would allocate more resources to hosting, and vice versa.

For web users, they won't know the difference, it'll just be like viewing any other web page.

The SUB token (known as Substrates) can be used to pay for hosting on the network, but a unique element is that it is not locked into the Substratum ecosystem. By integrating with CryptoPay, users can convert any unused SUB, or SUB they earn from hosting, into different cryptocurrencies or fiat currency, directly through the Substratum website. This kind of dynamic payment system is useful when compared to other cryptocurrency projects that force you to be locked into their particularly token, with no way of converting it without going onto a third party exchange.

Going forward, there are plans to release a public beta version of the platform in Q1 2018, and it will be extremely interesting to see how this goes, especially when related to the points above about hosting dubious content. If it can find a way to effectively deal with this, then there is no doubt in my mind that this project has a lot of room to grow going forward.

Modum (MOD)

Price at Time of Writing: $2.26

Market Cap at Time of Writing: $41,207,269

Available on:

BTC: Binance, Mercatox, Kucoin

ETH: Binance, EtherDelta

Where to store:

Modum is an ERC20 token running on the Ethereum blockchain, therefore it can be stored in MyEtherWallet.

Based out of Switzerland, Modum is a blockchain project that focuses on the supply chain management sector. It aims to provide a monitoring solution for transactions involving physical goods. The first industry Modum is targeting in the Pharmaceutical industry, which spends an approximate $3 billion a year on supply chain monitoring. Modum believes their solution could reduce shipping costs within the industry by as much as 60%.

What Modum does is monitor environmental conditions in the transit of goods. As many pharmaceuticals need specific conditions in order for the product to maintain its use (such as being refrigerated during transportation), it is vital that these conditions are met, and if they are not, it is equally vital that one of the parties be held accountable.

By using smart contracts, Modum allows companies to do this passively. For example, company A is purchasing drug X, which will be shipped from company B's warehouse. Drug X needs to be kept under 4 degrees centigrade during transit to maintain usability. By using Modum smart contracts, company A can verify that the drug was indeed kept under this temperature during transit, and when it arrived at company A's headquarters, a notification will go out, and payment will automatically be released. All of this can be monitored on both desktop and smartphone applications, in addition to a full range of backend data analytics.

The pharmaceutical industry is a wonderful test case as it requires great deal of supply chain integrity, and features a large amount of automation. The industry also has some of the highest standards required for product safety and security, so it's definitely a case of starting at the deep end for the Modum team.

Modum's main challenge is finding adoption from companies who would rather use Modum's solution as opposed to building their own in-house blockchain. Large corporate entities including IBM and Microsoft, are both dedicating large amounts of money to blockchain solutions of their own. It is worth noting that Modum's aim isn't to compete which large scale logistics operators, but to partner up with them and potentially license Modum devices to these larger companies for a best of both worlds solution.

Modum has obviously drawn comparisons to other blockchain projects such as WaltonChain, WaBi and VeChain, however, this isn't necessarily a bad thing. Supply chain management may well be the first widespread use case of blockchain technology. Therefore it's more than possible that all of these coins can co-exist. Modum is the only one of these projects based in Europe, a continent that has a whopping $1.2 trillion pharmaceutical industry.

In the short term, Q1 2018 should see the release of the first of Modum's product line, and an official entry into the Swiss market. The Modum also plans to step up their marketing efforts, which have been relatively lacking thus far. In the longer term, a real time tracking device is currently scheduled for Q1 2019, making Modum a project with long term viability as opposed to just short term monetary gains. Beyond the next couple of years, there is no reason that Modum cannot branch out beyond the pharmaceutical industry into supply chain management for other industries such as clothing. In a world full of hype and talks of 10X price increases in 1 month, I personally like Modum as a long-term hold with actual industry disruption possibilities.

One more interesting thing to note is that although Modum raised approximately $13 million worth of BTC and ETH during their ICO, due to the recent market bull run, this value has actually doubled since. Seeing as the team confirmed in December 2017 that they didn't yet sell any of their BTC or ETH received in the ICO, they have a larger pot to play with going into 2018, which could well see an accelerated roadmap moving forward.

XtraBytes (XBY)

Price at Time of Writing: $0.15

Market Cap at Time of Writing: $65,083,510

Available on:

BTC: Cryptopia, YoBit, C-Cex

LTC: Cryptopia

Where to store:

XtraBytes can be stored in wallets downloaded from https://www.xtrabytes.global/#wallet

XtraBytes aims to provide a decentralized cryptocurrency without dependency on inefficient, centralized mining operations. The projects will do this by using a newly created mining algorithm known as ZOLT which uses a Proof of Signature (PoSIGN) consensus method, as opposed to Proof of Work or Proof of Stake. The project has gathered some steam within the past few months and was the subject of an article on respected cryptocurrency website cointelegraph.com titled "Has XTRABYTES Already Rendered The Top Cryptocurrencies Obsolete?"

While that may be an overstatement at this stage of its development, the project is certainly an interesting one with a huge vision. A network of instant transactions, that are scalable combined with decentralized applications (DApps) that you can program in any language is an appealing proposition.

One of the first apps planned for the XBY ecosystem is X-Change, a decentralized cryptocurrency exchange. This will allow users to trade directly on the blockchain itself, without having to register for a third party exchange. This prevents incidents such as a centralized server being hacked, and user funds being stolen, like was the case with Mt. Gox exchange back in 2014.

Another planned project is X-Vault, a decentralized data storage applications that would store user data in encrypted pieces or "shards" across the network. This would prevent anyone from being able to access user data because even if they could "hack" one part of the network, they would only be able to access a tiny portion of the data. There are also additional plans for a decentralized instant messaging service as well as a platform for designed and executing smart contracts.

Currently, the project has managed to perform over 1,000 transactions per second on the TestNet, with a theoretical maximum of over 10,000 transactions per second. For comparison, Ethereum currently does around 20 transactions per second, albeit on a larger scale. Visa currently handles around 1,800 transactions per second.

XtraBytes has a long way to go before it can compete with larger projects in a similar vein like Cardano and EOS. A successful launch of both X-Change and X-Vault, even in beta form is likely to have positive price action as we move forward. A concentrated marketing effort is also needed if the coin is to receive more traction. It is important to note that much XBY's technology is still either in testing or theoretical stage, which explains its lower price and marketcap compared to some of the other projects mentioned here. However, a project with as much potential as this one should absolutely be on your radar in 2018 and beyond.

RaiBlocks (XRB)

Price at Time of Writing: $3.28

Market Cap at Time of Writing: $436,917,146

Available on:

BTC: BitGrail, Mercatox, BitFlip

Where to store:

Online wallets are available from https://raiwallet.com/

Other desktop wallets are available on the official website https://raiblocks.net/

Currently hardware wallet support is planned for Q1 2018

RaiBlocks aims to use blockchain technology to facilitate peer-to-peer transactions in a fast, costless manner. RaiBlocks does this by using an unconventional blockchain variant known as a "block-lattice", in which easy user runs their own blockchain, known as an "account-chain", which allows for faster transactions. The ultimate goal is for XRB to become a fast, feeless way for a regular person to move their money around. This has led to XRB being dubbed "Blockchain 3.0" by some commentators.

Since each user runs their own account chain, both the sender and the recipient are required to confirm the transaction, unlike the traditional model which only requires confirmation from the sender. Although for convenience, the recipient of the transaction can confirm it at a later date, so it doesn't require them to be online at the time the transaction is sent.

One of the major advantages of this model is that transaction are infinitely scalable in theory because individual transactions settle regardless of other network activity. Therefore there is no "transaction queue", which we have seen with other cryptocurrencies, notably Bitcoin. This also means traditional mining algorithms like Proof of Work, are not necessary to verify the transaction.

Another major advantage of this model compared a traditional one, is the overall security of the network. In theory, one could take down the entire Bitcoin or Litecoin network without owning a single dollar worth of either currency. With XRB, you would need to own 51% of all the XRB in the world to coordinate such an attack, making it not only financially pointless but also a waste of time from a moral or ethical standpoint. After all, why would you want to take down a network that you own the majority of?

RaiBlocks price going forward will largely be determined by the team's ability to get on major exchanges. With the majority of the volume currently traded on BitGrail, which is a relatively tiny exchange when compared to giants like Binance and Bittrex. Long time price determinants will be mass adoption, both on a peer-to-peer basis, and for a consumer-to-business payment system. The latter is something many coins are trying to achieve, and it is unlikely there is space for all of them going forward. It remains to be seen how much of that space XRB will take up, and as such, it should be viewed as a speculative investment.

In terms of competitor coins, IOTA is the obvious one, as their missions are largely the same, and neither of them requires any kind of mining or mining resources. However, RaiBlocks does have an advantage in that their network doesn't require Proof of Work to maintain security, and thus their long term costs are much lower. Another major difference is that XRB allows you to reuse addresses for transactions, an issue that IOTA faced when a few users lost a lot of currency because they tried to receive IOTA at an address they had already used. It should be noted that nearly every other cryptocurrency allows you to reuse a wallet address, so this is very much an IOTA problem rather than a cryptocurrency problem. There is an additional project in Radix, but it is still largely under development and far behind the other two at this stage.

Nav Coin (NAV)

Price at Time of Writing: $2.63

Market Cap at Time of Writing: $163,670,064

Available on:

Fiat: LiteBit.eu (EUR)

BTC: Bittrex, Poloniex, Cryptopia

LTC: Cryptopia

Where to store:

You can download wallets from https://navcoin.org/downloads/ - by using these wallets you can stake your coins and earn 5% interest on them

Based out of New Zealand and dubbed "The world's first fully anonymous cryptocurrency", Nav coin is one of the older projects around having started in 2014 as a fork of Bitcoin with greater optimization. For example Nav transaction times are around 30 seconds as opposed to Bitcoin's 10 minutes, as well as optional anonymous transactions. Nav also has low transactions fees, which currently amount to around $0.03 per transaction.

Nav's anonymity element is interesting because it uses a different anonymity algorithm to other major privacy coins. The two major algorithms in use are CryptoNote/Ring CT, which is used by Monero, and ZKSnarks, which is used by ZCash. These algorithms are both relatively new, and have little literature or regulated studies performed on their security, which is paramount for any network that claims to be anonymous.

Nav on the other hand uses the RSA algorithm, which is the most studied of the three. The RSA algorithm uses 2048 bit length keys, which are near impossible to hack via brute force.

Nav uses Proof of Stake (PoS), as opposed to Proof of Work (PoW). Not only is PoS a more environmentally friendly way of mining, as it doesn't require giant mining farms, it also allows you to earn interest on your coins by "staking" these coins to help run the network. PoS would also require any network attacker to own 51% of the coins themselves in order to coordinate an attack on the network.

Nav's big development move going forward is the release of NavPay and Polymorph. NavPay is a mobile wallet that would allow anonymous transactions between wallets, nothing too special there right? However, when combined with Polymorph, this would allow anonymous transactions of coins through coin transfer programs like Changelly. This is convenient because it allows cryptocurrency to cryptocurrency swaps without having to register for many different online exchanges. You can think of this like atomic swaps, but with an added privacy element. So for example, you could anonymously exchange your LTC to BTC, using Nav as the intermediary currency. So even if your base currencies do not have a privacy element, you could use Nav as the go-between to take advantage of a private transaction.

QASH (QASH)

Price at time of writing - $0.98

Market cap at time of writing - $346,077,200

Available on:

Fiat: Bitfinex, Quoine (USD & JPY)

BTC: Bitfinex, Quoine, Qryptos

ETH: Huobi, Qryptos

Where to store:

You can store QASH using MyEtherWallet by adding it as a custom token. Alternatively, you can store it on the Qryptos exchange in the short term.

QASH (also known as the Quoine Liquid Token) is one of the most interesting cryptocurrency projects as we head in 2018. The Quoine Liquid Platform plans to become the world's premiere cryptocurrency trading platform by combining liquidity from multiple markets.

Currently the global foreign exchange market for traded fiat currencies stands at around $5-6 trillion per day. Cryptocurrency's average trading volume is around $3 billion per day, but continues to grow on a monthly basis. The biggest problem the cryptocurrency market faces however is limited liquidity, especially when we are talking about the lesser known cryptocurrencies. Most cryptocurrencies are only liquid in a few pairings, and this varies from exchange to exchange. For example, there may be a lot of BTC/Neo liquidity on one exchange, but little on another. This also applies to many less used fiat to crypto pairings such as Canadian dollars, New Zealand dollars and Philippine Pesos. Citizens of these countries should all be able to access the cryptocurrency market, but they are currently being limited by lack of volume from their respective currency.

The Quoine Liquid platform plans to solve this problem by aggregating various liquidity sources into one single giant tradable order book. In other words, by combining liquidity from multiple markets, there is now enough to be able to fill everyone's orders. This would also allow buyers to buy cryptocurrency in their currency of choice, without having to convert to a more popular fiat currency first. The end result of this is that users would be able to effectively trade on any global exchange, without having to register or hold funds on that exchange.

QASH aims to become the world's first prime brokerage for cryptocurrency. This means they would offer a multitude of services including securities trading, credit facilities including lending, and leveraged trading. Prime brokerages appeal to institutional clients as well as to consumer clients.

Where the QASH token comes in is as a means of payment for using all services tied to the Quoine Liquid platform, such as transaction fees, as well as a token that is tradable on the open market like other cryptocurrencies. QASH holders will receive a 5% discount for transactions on the platform, with no maximum limit. This is especially important when we factor in prime brokerages into this, because a 5% discount on a transaction of $50,000,000 (not uncommon for prime brokerages), represents huge savings to the client.

QASH will initially be built on the Ethereum blockchain using ERC-20 tokens. Going forward, the team plans to migrate the project onto their own blockchain in mid 2019.

One of the major advantages of QASH is that the Liquid platform is already complete and online. At the time of writing the platform supports 15 different cryptocurrencies. The platform is fully licensed and regulated by the Japan Financial Services Agency.

The big growth factor for QASH and the Liquid Platform going forward will be adoption from institutional clients. If their first to market approach is successful, they could see an influx of large clients from Asia and beyond and this would provide them with a significant advantage of their competition. This alone makes QASH a cryptocurrency to watch as we move into 2018.

Cardano (ADA)

Price at time of writing - $0.50

Market cap at time of writing - $13,003,955,572

Available on:

Fiat: Coinnest (ROK)

BTC: Bittrex, Binance

ETH: Binance, Bittrex

Where to store:

You can store Cardano using their official Daedulus Wallet https://daedaluswallet.io/ - please note, at the time of writing there is an unofficial Daedulus Wallet listed on the Google Play Store. **For safety precautions do not download any Cardano wallets from the Google Play Store**

Cardano aims to become the world's most advanced open source smart contract platform. It can also boast of being the first ever cryptocurrency project that has been completed peer reviewed by a group of academic researchers. Cardano is built using the Haskell programming language, a language that is not often used in cryptocurrency projects, but one that can be considered one of the more secure, and least prone to errors.

Cardano can be seen as the 3rd generation of cryptocurrency, in that the project aims to revolutionize how we see blockchain technology as a whole by developing what the Cardano team believes is a fairer and more balanced ecosystem. This is opposed to first generation cryptocurrency like Bitcoin that merely function as a peer-to-peer monetary transaction system. On important distinction to make is that while other cryptocurrencies began as, and continue to be a work in progress, Cardano took the decisions to work on the project behind the scenes, and bringing to market a protocol that would be able to handle future adaptation.

The project uses a unique Proof of Stake (PoS) mining algorithm known as Ouroboros, as opposed to a Proof of Work algorithm.

An important element of the Cardano project is what they term the "social element of money", in other words, how particular communities interact with their money. This makes sense if you think about the broader scale of different cryptocurrencies. For example, Bitcoin and Litecoin have very few technical differences between them, the same goes for Ethereum and Ethereum Classic. However, all 4 of these cryptocurrencies still maintain large communities supporting them and each of them have large market capitalizations.

Where Cardano comes in is the ability for users to propose changes in how their cryptocurrency of choice operates. This could be from voting on which projects the development team devotes funds to, to how different markets should be regulated. Cardano does this by utilizing a decentralized trust fund, which will be collected from transaction fees on the network. In theory, any user can request funds from the trust, and a ballot system would be used to decide whether the request is fulfilled or not. This would solve disputes such as soft or hard fork debates that have adversely affected both the Bitcoin and Ethereum communities.

One of the key elements of Cardano is a balance between the privacy of users on the platform and the needs of regulators such as government bodies.

Cardano is very much a long term project, and the roadmap signals that the full platform is not scheduled for release until early 2019. Investing in a project without a working product is a high risk move, and if you do choose to invest in Cardano, you should do your due diligence before allocating any of your portfolio towards it.

Bitcoin Cash (BCH/BCC)

Price at time of writing - $3,547.70

Market cap at time of writing - $59,829,341,444

Exchanges:

Fiat: Coinbase (as of 12/20/17), BitHumb (ROK), Coinone (ROK), Kraken

BTC: Bittrex, Bitfinex, Poloniex

Where to store:

There are numerous wallets available for all platforms on http://bitcoincash.org

Bitcoin Cash is also supported by both Trezor and Ledger Nano S hardware wallets.

I suppose we should probably talk about Bitcoin Cash. Especially for those of you who are new to the market and are wondering why on Earth there are now 2 Bitcoins on Coinbase (as of 12/20/17). I've already discussed Bitcoin Cash in my first book, *Cryptocurrency: Beginners Bible,* however as there have been a number of major developments since then, I felt it would have been a disservice not to provide an updated version of my summary.

Bitcoin Cash (BCH) emerged as the result of a split or "hard fork" in the Bitcoin technology on August 1st 2017. The end-goal of Bitcoin Cash is to function as a global currency, in the founder's words, to be what Bitcoin was supposed to have been in line with the original vision for Bitcoin outlined in the 2008 whitepaper.

If you held Bitcoin before August 1st (or to be technical, all Bitcoin holders as of block 478558), you will have been credited with an equal amount of Bitcoin Cash. Coinbase finally did this on 12/20/17, the same day that Bitcoin Cash was added. Your BCH will have been deposited directly into your wallet. It should be noted however that not all exchanges credited user accounts with BCH, so it's worth double checking yours.

The split occurred out of problems with Bitcoin's ability to process transactions at a high speed. For example, the Visa network processes around 1,700 transactions per second whereas Bitcoin averages around 7. As the network continues to grow, so do waiting times for transactions. BCC aims to run more transactions, as well as, providing lower transactions fees.

One of the major solutions to this issue is increasing the size of each block, so that more data can be processed at once. Bitcoin Cash increases the block size to 8MB, as opposed to the 1MB size of Bitcoin. This is in line with solving the problems of scalability that Bitcoin was facing previously. The technology itself worked in the short-term, with the first Bitcoin Cash block registering 7,000 transactions compared with Bitcoin's 2,500.

The success of failure of Bitcoin Cash will largely depend on Bitcoin's own adoption of the SegWit technology, and the ability to process transactions quicker to act truly as a currency - rather than a speculative asset. Detractors have also raised security concerns about Bitcoin Cash.

Bitcoin Cash has been widely adopted by many cryptocurrency exchanges. At the time of writing, there are only a few months worth of data available and thus, no one has been able to execute any long-term trends or technical analysis of BCH as a commodity. As further adoption continues, the price may well continue to rise. Early price rises for Bitcoin Cash have been largely driven by demand from South Korea, with over 50% of the total trade volume being seen on South Korean exchanges.

There are also now two divided camps within the Bitcoin movement, with the original Bitcoin (or Bitcoin Core) on one side, and Bitcoin Cash on the other.

Miners have been quick to adopt the currency as well due to its higher mining ROI when compared to Bitcoin. The decrease in mining difficulty (leading to greater rewards for mining) will continue to see for miners move their resources from Bitcoin into Bitcoin Cash.

As we move into 2018, arguably the biggest debate in the cryptocurrency community will be whether Bitcoin and Bitcoin Cash can co-exist, or if one will win out against the other. Once it was added to Coinbase, Bitcoin Cash once again reached near all time highs in value compared to Bitcoin, but 2018 will be a big year in determining if BCH is here to stay.

Note: Depending on your exchange, Bitcoin Cash may use the symbol BCC or BCH - double check before executing a trade

How to Identify Market Manipulation

When investing in any cryptocurrency, it's important to be aware of market manipulation in the form of coordinated pump and dump schemes. This is more prevalent with lower volume cryptocurrencies where manipulation is easier to perform.

It doesn't take much digging to find the groups behind these, a few Google searches bring up various groups on Telegram, a Russian cloud-based instant messenger app that encrypts users identities. These groups aren't exactly subtle about their intentions with names such as Crypto4Pumps and PumpKing. These groups coordinate mass buys of low cap cryptocurrencies to artificially inflate the price, then sell their holding at a higher price once the general public become aware of it.

The reason these schemes can exist is the lack of regulation in the cryptocurrency market. These schemes used to be prevalent in the form of email blasts, during the penny stock market craze back in the mid 2000s, before many of the largest groups were shut down by regulators like the SEC.

The groups release buy signals to their users ahead of time, who then prepare funds, before being alerted to which cryptocurrency to buy. Previous coins that have been targets of these include MagiCoin, Gnosis and Ubiq. Once the initial buys happen, the group moves to other channels to "spread the word" of a great buying opportunity.

The initial buyers are now ready to dump their coins at a profit, which then tanks the price of the coin. Leaving those who bought late at a huge loss.

So how can you avoid these? Simply look at volumes on exchanges, and if you see a tiny market cap coin with a giant increase then stay well away. Price rises of 50% in under an hour are not uncommon with these sorts of schemes. Most major exchanges allow you to sort by price increase in the past hour, and it's a metric worth looking at. So don't chase anything purely because you see a quick price rise and hope to get in on the action, chances are you are already too late. Remember to do your own research before investing in a coin, and invest without emotion or the hope of instant riches.

One big cryptocurrency to avoid - why you should be wary of Bitconnect

Bitconnect, which trades as BCC on many exchanges, should be avoided in my opinion. I make careful choices never to go out of my way to specifically recommend coins worth buying, and this book is my personal opinion and not financial advice.

However, I will take a stance against any cryptocurrency project that I believe gives the space a bad name, and Bitconnect does just that. Currently ranked #20 on CoinMarketCap.com with a total market cap of $1.7 billion, the project is heavily promoted on social media. Bitconnect has a huge a number of red flags around the project and I've laid them out below.

Red Flag 1: Bitconnect is a Bitcoin lending system that promises enormous gains for those who put money into the platform. Their website promises returns of 1% *per day,* which anyone with any understanding of finance will tell you is impossible to uphold in the long term without completely breaking the world's economy.

Red Flag 2: Bitconnect claims their trading bots will continuously make money in order to fulfill these returns, regardless of overall market conditions. If they really did have a bot capable of doing this, why would they need investors? Surely that complicates things and adds unnecessary risk for them?

Red Flag 3: A capital "lock up" period of 299 days. So every investor *must* keep their initial investment in the Bitconnect program for 299 days before being allowed to cash out. That seems fishy as other managed funds do not require this or any other sort of "minimum investment period".

Red Flag 4: No public blockchain transactions that can verify their trading bots effectiveness. This is blockchain after all, so why can't we see how well the bot is doing? Their marketing video doesn't mention the bot very much, because they concentrate more on how rich everyone involved in the project is.

Red Flag 5: Bitconnect was originally registered in the UK, but the company was shut down because it never filed any accounts.

Red Flag 6: Prominent cryptocurrency figures including Ethereum Founder Vitalik Buterin, Litecoin founder Charlie Lee, and billionaire blockchain investor Michael Novogratz have dismissed the project as a "Ponzi scheme" and "most likely a scam."

Red Flag 7: This is the big one. Their referral system. Bitconnect operates a 7 layer referral bonus system. A system where you receive a % bonus from your referrals, and a smaller percentage from their referrals, and then an even smaller percentage from their referral's referrals. Do you see where this is going? Does the phrase "pyramid scheme" spring to mind?

As usual, I encourage you to do your own research on top of what you read in this book. I would be extremely vary of any program in cryptocurrency or otherwise, that promises guaranteed returns, and for that reason along with the others listed above, I strongly urge you to avoid Bitconnect.

Cryptocurrency Golden Rules for Safety & Security

So now you've bought your coins, here's a guide on how to safely store them, as well as some general best practices to employ with cryptocurrency.

1. **Never give your private key to anyone**

Your private key is what you need to spend your coins, therefore you are the only one who should hold it. You should keep your private key secure, preferably written down on paper and stored somewhere safe (like a safety deposit box). If your cryptocurrency is stored on an exchange, you likely won't have a private key and will use your exchange password to sell your coins.

2. **Do not store your coins on an exchange long-term**

No matter how good or reputable an exchange is, because of their centralized nature they are still vulnerable to being hacked. If you have any significant amount of cryptocurrency you should store it either in a desktop, paper or hardware wallet. For each of the coins listed I have provided links to wallets you can store them in. For hardware wallets I recommend the Trezor or Ledger Nano S, although not all coins are compatible with these.

3. **Double check all links to websites (including ones in this book)**

Phishing scams are still rife in the cryptocurrency space, and unfortunately, some of these links slip through Google Adwords checks and therefore appear at the top of a Google search for that cryptocurrency or exchange. Make sure you check the URL you are typing in or clicking on, so you don't end up on binnance.com or mynetherwallet.com by mistake. This is even more important when it's a website that requires your username and password.

4. Don't reveal how much cryptocurrency you have

I see this a lot on social media this days with people posting about their 5, 6 or even 7 figure portfolios. Your identity can be traced back to you if someone really wants to, and if they know you have millions of dollars worth of cryptocurrency, they suddenly have a motivation to do so. To be on the safe side, don't post on the internet regarding the amount of cryptocurrency you own. Posting about which coins you own is perfectly fine though.

5. Get your news from reputable sources

When investing in cryptocurrency, it can often be hard to know who to trust. There is a lot of misinformation out there, and this leads to bad investing moves. Unfortunately, mainstream media is particularly bad at reporting cryptocurrency news, preferring to choose soundbites that are attention-grabbing rather than fact-filled. For example, December saw articles stating "CEO of Bitcoin.com sells all his Bitcoin" but many of these articles failed to note that Bitcoin.com is merely a website that allows you to create Bitcoin wallets, and is no way an official Bitcoin operation. Which grossly overstated the event in the eyes of the general public.

I personally recommend cointelegraph.com and coindesk.com for keeping tabs on happenings within the cryptocurrency space.

Finally, never invest more than you can afford to lose, and never borrow money to invest in cryptocurrency.

Conclusion

Well there we have it, a summary of the cryptocurrency market and its direction as we head into 2018. As well as, a list of high potential coins that could have massive growth in the next 12 months and beyond. There has never been a better time to be involved in the world's fastest growing financial market, and if you haven't already invested, I hope this book gives you the confidence to do so.

Remember to only invest what you can afford to lose, and cryptocurrency investments should only make up a small percentage of your overall portfolio. I encourage you to do additional research before you invest your money, and remember to watch out for any nefarious elements like pump and dump schemes.

I wish you the best of luck in the cryptocurrency market, and I hope you make a lot of money.

Finally, if this book has proved useful to you, I'd appreciate it if you took 2 minutes to leave it a review on Amazon.

Thanks,

Stephen

Made in the USA
Las Vegas, NV
22 April 2021